Learning Python

Learn to code like a professional with Python – an open source, versatile, and powerful programming language

Fabrizio Romano

BIRMINGHAM - MUMBAI

Learning Python

First published: December 2015

Production reference: 1171215

Published by Packt Publishing Ltd.
Livery Place
35 Livery Street
Birmingham B3 2PB, UK.

ISBN 978-1-78355-171-2

www.packtpub.com

Credits

Author
Fabrizio Romano

Reviewers
Simone Burol

Julio Vicente Trigo Guijarro

Veit Heller

Commissioning Editor
Akram Hussain

Acquisition Editor
Indrajit Das

Content Development Editors
Samantha Gonsalves

Adrian Raposo

Technical Editor
Siddhi Rane

Copy Editors
Janbal Dharmaraj

Kevin McGowan

Project Coordinator
Kinjal Bari

Proofreader
Safis Editing

Indexer
Priya Sane

Graphics
Kirk D'Penha

Abhinash Sahu

Production Coordinator
Melwyn D'sa

Cover Work
Melwyn D'sa

About the Author

Fabrizio Romano was born in Italy in 1975. He holds a master's degree in computer science engineering from the University of Padova. He is also a certified Scrum master.

Before Python, he has worked with several other languages, such as C/C++, Java, PHP, and C#.

In 2011, he moved to London and started working as a Python developer for Glasses Direct, one of Europe's leading online prescription glasses retailers.

He then worked as a senior Python developer for TBG (now Sprinklr), one of the world's leading companies in social media advertising. At TBG, he and his team collaborated with Facebook and Twitter. They were the first in the world to get access to the Twitter advertising API. He wrote the code that published the first geo-narrowcasted promoted tweet in the world using the API.

He currently works as a senior platform developer at Student.com, a company that is revolutionizing the way international students find their perfect home all around the world.

He has delivered talks on *Teaching Python* and *TDD with Python* at the last two editions of EuroPython and at Skillsmatter in London.

Acknowledgements

I would like to thank Adrian Raposo and Indrajit Das from Packt Publishing for their help and support and giving me the opportunity to live this adventure. I would also like to thank everyone at Packt Publishing who have contributed to the realization of this book. Special thanks go to Siddhi Rane, my technical editor. Thank you for your kindness, for working very hard, and for going the extra mile just to make me happy.

I would like to express my deepest gratitude to Simone Burol and Julio Trigo, who have gifted me with some of their precious free time. They have reviewed the book and provided me with invaluable feedback.

A big thank you to my teammates, Matt Bennett and Jakub Kuba Borys, for their interest in this book and for their support and feedback that makes me a better coder every day.

A heartfelt thank you to Marco "Tex" Beri, who introduced me to Python with an enthusiasm second to none.

A special thanks to Dr. Naomi Ceder, from whom I learned so much over the last year. She has given me precious suggestions and has encouraged me to embrace this opportunity.

Finally, I would like to thank all my friends who have supported me in any way.

About the Reviewers

Simone Burol is an Italian software developer who was born in Treviso (Italy) in 1978. He obtained a master's degree in computer science engineering from the University of Padua (Italy), and since then worked in banking for 5 years in Venice (Italy). In 2010, he moved to London (United Kingdom), where he worked in warehouse automation for Ocado Technology and then in banking for Algomi.

Julio Vicente Trigo Guijarro is a computer scientist and software engineer with almost a decade of experience in software development. He is also a certified Scrum master, who enjoys the benefits of using agile software development (Scrum and XP).

He completed his studies in computer science and software engineering from the University of Alicante, Spain, in 2007. Since then, he has worked with several technologies and languages, including Microsoft Dynamics NAV, Java, JavaScript, and Python.

Some of the applications covered by Julio during his career include RESTful APIs, ERPs, billing platforms, payment gateways, and e-commerce websites.

He has been using Python on both personal and professional projects since 2012, and he is passionate about software design, software quality, and coding standards.

> I would like to thank my parents for their love, good advice, and continuous support.
>
> I would also like to thank all my friends that I met along the way, who enriched my life, for motivating me and helping me progress.

Veit Heller is a full stack developer, mostly working on the backend side of web projects. He currently resides in Berlin and works for a prototypical Pythonista company named Bright. In his free time, he writes interpreters for various programming languages.

I would like to thank the people at Bright for being a welcoming company that supports me in all my endeavors, my friends and my family for coping with my strangeness, and manufacturers of caffeinated drinks worldwide.

www.PacktPub.com

Support files, eBooks, discount offers, and more

For support files and downloads related to your book, please visit www.PacktPub.com.

Did you know that Packt offers eBook versions of every book published, with PDF and ePub files available? You can upgrade to the eBook version at www.PacktPub.com and as a print book customer, you are entitled to a discount on the eBook copy. Get in touch with us at service@packtpub.com for more details.

At www.PacktPub.com, you can also read a collection of free technical articles, sign up for a range of free newsletters and receive exclusive discounts and offers on Packt books and eBooks.

https://www2.packtpub.com/books/subscription/packtlib

Do you need instant solutions to your IT questions? PacktLib is Packt's online digital book library. Here, you can search, access, and read Packt's entire library of books.

Why subscribe?

- Fully searchable across every book published by Packt
- Copy and paste, print, and bookmark content
- On demand and accessible via a web browser

Free access for Packt account holders

If you have an account with Packt at www.PacktPub.com, you can use this to access PacktLib today and view 9 entirely free books. Simply use your login credentials for immediate access.

To Alan Turing, the father of Computer Science.
To Guido Van Rossum, the father of Python.
To Adriano Romano, my father, my biggest fan.

Table of Contents

Preface

Shortly after I started writing, a friend asked me if there really was a need of another *Learning Python* book.

An excellent question that we could also express in another form: What has this book to offer? What makes this book different from the average introductory book on Python?

I think there are two main differences and many good reasons why you would want to read it.

Firstly, we start with introducing some important programming concepts. We build a solid foundation by covering the critical aspects of this wonderful language.

The pace gradually increases, along with the difficulty of the subjects presented. By the end of *Chapter 7, Testing, Profiling, and Dealing with Exceptions*, we will cover all the fundamentals.

From *Chapter 8, The Edges – GUIs and Scripts*, onward, the book takes a steep turn, which brings us to difference number two.

To consolidate the knowledge acquired, there is nothing like working on a small project. So, in the second part of the book, each chapter delivers a project on a different subject. We explore scripting, graphical interfaces, data science, and web programming.

Each project is small enough to fit within a chapter and yet big enough to be relevant. Each chapter is interesting, conveys a message, and teaches something valuable.

After a short section on debugging, the book ends with a complete example that wraps things up. I tried to craft it so that you will be able to expand it in several ways.

So, this is definitely not the usual *Learning Python* book. Its approach is much more "hands-on" and practical.

I wanted to empower you to help you become a true Python ninja. But I also did my best to entertain you and foster your logical thinking and creativity along the way.

Now, have I answered the question?

What this book covers

Chapter 1, Introduction and First Steps – Take a Deep Breath, introduces you to fundamental programming concepts. It guides you to getting Python up and running on your computer and introduces you to some of its constructs.

Chapter 2, Built-in Data Types, introduces you to Python built-in data types. Python has a very rich set of native data types and this chapter will give you a description and a short example for each of them.

Chapter 3, Iterating and Making Decisions, teaches you how to control the flow of your code by inspecting conditions, applying logic, and performing loops.

Chapter 4, Functions, the Building Blocks of Code, teaches you how to write functions. Functions are the keys to reusing code, to reducing debugging time, and in general, to writing better code.

Chapter 5, Saving Time and Memory, introduces you to the functional aspects of Python programming. This chapter teaches you how to write comprehensions and generators, which are powerful tools that you can use to speed up your code and save memory.

Chapter 6, Advanced Concepts – OOP, Decorators, and Iterators, teaches you the basics of object-oriented programming with Python. It shows you the key concepts and all the potentials of this paradigm. It also shows you one of the most beloved characteristics of Python: decorators. Finally, it also covers the concept of iterators.

Chapter 7, Testing, Profiling, and Dealing with Exceptions, teaches you how to make your code more robust, fast, and stable using techniques such as testing and profiling. It also formally defines the concept of exceptions.

Chapter 8, The Edges – GUIs and Scripts, guides you through an example from two different points of view. They are at the extremities of a spectrum: one implementation is a script and the other one a proper graphical user interface application.

Chapter 9, Data Science, introduces a few key concepts and a very special tool, the Jupyter Notebook.

Chapter 10, Web Development Done Right, introduces the fundamentals of web development and delivers a project using the Django web framework. The example will be based on regular expressions.

Chapter 11, Debugging and Troubleshooting, shows you the main methods to debug your code and some examples on how to apply them.

Chapter 12, Summing Up – A Complete Example, presents a Django website that acts as an interface to an underlying slim API written with the Falcon web framework. This chapter takes all the concepts covered in the book to the next level and suggests where to go to dig deeper and take the next steps.

What you need for this book

You are encouraged to follow the examples in this book. In order to do so, you will need a computer, an Internet connection, and a browser. The book is written in Python 3.4, but it should also work with any Python 3.* version. I have written instructions on how to install Python on the three main operating systems used today: Windows, Mac, and Linux. I have also explained how to install all the extra libraries used in the various examples and provided suggestions if the reader finds any issues during the installation of any of them. No particular editor is required to type the code; however, I suggest that those who are interested in following the examples should consider adopting a proper coding environment. I have given suggestions on this matter in the first chapter.

Who this book is for

Python is the most popular introductory teaching language in the top computer science universities in the US, so if you are new to software development or if you have little experience and would like to start off on the right foot, then this language and this book are what you need. Its amazing design and portability will help you become productive regardless of the environment you choose to work with.

If you have already worked with Python or any other language, this book can still be useful to you both as a reference to Python's fundamentals and to provide a wide range of considerations and suggestions collected over two decades of experience.

Conventions

In this book, you will find a number of text styles that distinguish between different kinds of information. Here are some examples of these styles and an explanation of their meaning.

Code words in text, database table names, folder names, filenames, file extensions, pathnames, dummy URLs, user input, and Twitter handles are shown as follows: "Open up a Python console, and type import this."

A block of code is set as follows:

```
# we define a function, called local
def local():
    m = 7
    print(m)


m = 5
print(m)
```

When we wish to draw your attention to a particular part of a code block, the relevant lines or items are set in bold:

```
# we define a function, called local
def local():
    m = 7
    print(m)        .


m = 5
print(m)
```

Any command-line input or output is written as follows:

```
>>> from math import factorial
>>> factorial(5)
120
```

New terms and **important words** are shown in bold. Words that you see on the screen, for example, in menus or dialog boxes, appear in the text like this: "To open the console on Windows, go to the **Start** menu, choose **Run**, and type cmd."

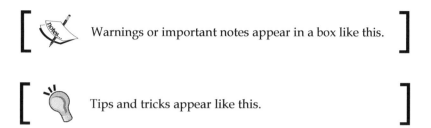

> Warnings or important notes appear in a box like this.

> Tips and tricks appear like this.

Reader feedback

Feedback from our readers is always welcome. Let us know what you think about this book—what you liked or disliked. Reader feedback is important for us as it helps us develop titles that you will really get the most out of.

To send us general feedback, simply e-mail feedback@packtpub.com, and mention the book's title in the subject of your message.

If there is a topic that you have expertise in and you are interested in either writing or contributing to a book, see our author guide at www.packtpub.com/authors.

Customer support

Now that you are the proud owner of a Packt book, we have a number of things to help you to get the most from your purchase.

Downloading the example code

You can download the example code files from your account at http://www.packtpub.com for all the Packt Publishing books you have purchased. If you purchased this book elsewhere, you can visit http://www.packtpub.com/support and register to have the files e-mailed directly to you.

Errata

Although we have taken every care to ensure the accuracy of our content, mistakes do happen. If you find a mistake in one of our books—maybe a mistake in the text or the code—we would be grateful if you could report this to us. By doing so, you can save other readers from frustration and help us improve subsequent versions of this book. If you find any errata, please report them by visiting http://www.packtpub.com/submit-errata, selecting your book, clicking on the **Errata Submission Form** link, and entering the details of your errata. Once your errata are verified, your submission will be accepted and the errata will be uploaded to our website or added to any list of existing errata under the Errata section of that title.

To view the previously submitted errata, go to https://www.packtpub.com/books/content/support and enter the name of the book in the search field. The required information will appear under the **Errata** section.

Piracy

Piracy of copyrighted material on the Internet is an ongoing problem across all media. At Packt, we take the protection of our copyright and licenses very seriously. If you come across any illegal copies of our works in any form on the Internet, please provide us with the location address or website name immediately so that we can pursue a remedy.

Please contact us at copyright@packtpub.com with a link to the suspected pirated material.

We appreciate your help in protecting our authors and our ability to bring you valuable content.

Questions

If you have a problem with any aspect of this book, you can contact us at questions@packtpub.com, and we will do our best to address the problem.

1
Introduction and First Steps – Take a Deep Breath

"Give a man a fish and you feed him for a day. Teach a man to fish and you feed him for a lifetime."

– Chinese proverb

According to Wikipedia, **computer programming** is:

"...a process that leads from an original formulation of a computing problem to executable computer programs. Programming involves activities such as analysis, developing understanding, generating algorithms, verification of requirements of algorithms including their correctness and resources consumption, and implementation (commonly referred to as coding) of algorithms in a target programming language".

In a nutshell, coding is telling a computer to do something using a language it understands.

Computers are very powerful tools, but unfortunately, they can't think for themselves. So they need to be told everything. They need to be told how to perform a task, how to evaluate a condition to decide which path to follow, how to handle data that comes from a device such as the network or a disk, and how to react when something unforeseen happens, say, something is broken or missing.

You can code in many different styles and languages. Is it hard? I would say "yes" and "no". It's a bit like writing. Everybody can learn how to write, and you can too. But what if you wanted to become a poet? Then writing alone is not enough. You have to acquire a whole other set of skills and this will take a longer and greater effort.

In the end, it all comes down to how far you want to go down the road. Coding is not just putting together some instructions that work. It is so much more!

Good code is short, fast, elegant, easy to read and understand, simple, easy to modify and extend, easy to scale and refactor, and easy to test. It takes time to be able to write code that has all these qualities at the same time, but the good news is that you're taking the first step towards it at this very moment by reading this book. And I have no doubt you can do it. Anyone can, in fact, we all program all the time, only we aren't aware of it.

Would you like an example?

Say you want to make instant coffee. You have to get a mug, the instant coffee jar, a teaspoon, water, and the kettle. Even if you're not aware of it, you're evaluating a lot of data. You're making sure that there is water in the kettle as well as the kettle is plugged-in, that the mug is clean, and that there is enough coffee in the jar. Then, you boil the water and maybe in the meantime you put some coffee in the mug. When the water is ready, you pour it into the cup, and stir.

So, how is this programming?

Well, we gathered resources (the kettle, coffee, water, teaspoon, and mug) and we verified some conditions on them (kettle is plugged-in, mug is clean, there is enough coffee). Then we started two actions (boiling the water and putting coffee in the mug), and when both of them were completed, we finally ended the procedure by pouring water in the mug and stirring.

Can you see it? I have just described the high-level functionality of a coffee program. It wasn't that hard because this is what the brain does all day long: evaluate conditions, decide to take actions, carry out tasks, repeat some of them, and stop at some point. Clean objects, put them back, and so on.

All you need now is to learn how to deconstruct all those actions you do automatically in real life so that a computer can actually make some sense of them. And you need to learn a language as well, to instruct it.

So this is what this book is for. I'll tell you how to do it and I'll try to do that by means of many simple but focused examples (my favorite kind).

A proper introduction

I love to make references to the real world when I teach coding; I believe they help people retain the concepts better. However, now is the time to be a bit more rigorous and see what coding is from a more technical perspective.

When we write code, we're instructing a computer on what are the things it has to do. Where does the action happen? In many places: the computer memory, hard drives, network cables, CPU, and so on. It's a whole "world", which most of the time is the representation of a subset of the real world.

If you write a piece of software that allows people to buy clothes online, you will have to represent real people, real clothes, real brands, sizes, and so on and so forth, within the boundaries of a program.

In order to do so, you will need to create and handle objects in the program you're writing. A person can be an object. A car is an object. A pair of socks is an object. Luckily, Python understands objects very well.

The two main features any object has are properties and methods. Let's take a person object as an example. Typically in a computer program, you'll represent people as customers or employees. The properties that you store against them are things like the name, the SSN, the age, if they have a driving license, their e-mail, gender, and so on. In a computer program, you store all the data you need in order to use an object for the purpose you're serving. If you are coding a website to sell clothes, you probably want to store the height and weight as well as other measures of your customers so that you can suggest the appropriate clothes for them. So, properties are characteristics of an object. We use them all the time: "Could you pass me that pen?" – "Which one?" – "The black one." Here, we used the "black" property of a pen to identify it (most likely amongst a blue and a red one).

Methods are things that an object can do. As a person, I have methods such as *speak, walk, sleep, wake-up, eat, dream, write, read,* and so on. All the things that I can do could be seen as methods of the objects that represents me.

So, now that you know what objects are and that they expose methods that you can run and properties that you can inspect, you're ready to start coding. Coding in fact is simply about managing those objects that live in the subset of the world that we're reproducing in our software. You can create, use, reuse, and delete objects as you please.

According to the *Data Model* chapter on the official Python documentation:

> *"Objects are Python's abstraction for data. All data in a Python program is represented by objects or by relations between objects."*

We'll take a closer look at Python objects in *Chapter 6, Advanced Concepts – OOP, Decorators, and Iterators*. For now, all we need to know is that every object in Python has an ID (or identity), a type, and a value.

Once created, the identity of an object is never changed. It's a unique identifier for it, and it's used behind the scenes by Python to retrieve the object when we want to use it.

The type as well, never changes. The type tells what operations are supported by the object and the possible values that can be assigned to it.

We'll see Python's most important data types in *Chapter 2, Built-in Data Types*.

The value can either change or not. If it can, the object is said to be **mutable**, while when it cannot, the object is said to be **immutable**.

How do we use an object? We give it a name of course! When you give an object a name, then you can use the name to retrieve the object and use it.

In a more generic sense, objects such as numbers, strings (text), collections, and so on are associated with a name. Usually, we say that this name is the name of a variable. You can see the variable as being like a box, which you can use to hold data.

So, you have all the objects you need: what now? Well, we need to use them, right? We may want to send them over a network connection or store them in a database. Maybe display them on a web page or write them into a file. In order to do so, we need to react to a user filling in a form, or pressing a button, or opening a web page and performing a search. We react by running our code, evaluating conditions to choose which parts to execute, how many times, and under which circumstances.

And to do all this, basically we need a language. That's what Python is for. Python is the language we'll use together throughout this book to instruct the computer to do something for us.

Now, enough of this theoretical stuff, let's get started.

Enter the Python

Python is the marvelous creature of Guido Van Rossum, a Dutch computer scientist and mathematician who decided to gift the world with a project he was playing around with over Christmas 1989. The language appeared to the public somewhere around 1991, and since then has evolved to be one of the leading programming languages used worldwide today.

I started programming when I was 7 years old, on a Commodore VIC 20, which was later replaced by its bigger brother, the Commodore 64. The language was BASIC. Later on, I landed on Pascal, Assembly, C, C++, Java, JavaScript, Visual Basic, PHP, ASP, ASP .NET, C#, and other minor languages I cannot even remember, but only when I landed on Python, I finally had that feeling that you have when you find the right couch in the shop. When all of your body parts are yelling, "Buy this one! This one is perfect for us!"

It took me about a day to get used to it. Its syntax is a bit different from what I was used to, and in general, I very rarely worked with a language that defines scoping with indentation. But after getting past that initial feeling of discomfort (like having new shoes), I just fell in love with it. Deeply. Let's see why.

About Python

Before we get into the gory details, let's get a sense of why someone would want to use Python (I would recommend you to read the Python page on Wikipedia to get a more detailed introduction).

To my mind, Python exposes the following qualities.

Portability

Python runs everywhere, and porting a program from Linux to Windows or Mac is usually just a matter of fixing paths and settings. Python is designed for portability and it takes care of **operating system** (**OS**) specific quirks behind interfaces that shield you from the pain of having to write code tailored to a specific platform.

Coherence

Python is extremely logical and coherent. You can see it was designed by a brilliant computer scientist. Most of the time you can just guess how a method is called, if you don't know it.

You may not realize how important this is right now, especially if you are at the beginning, but this is a major feature. It means less cluttering in your head, less skimming through the documentation, and less need for mapping in your brain when you code.

Developer productivity

According to Mark Lutz (*Learning Python, 5th Edition, O'Reilly Media*), a Python program is typically one-fifth to one-third the size of equivalent Java or C++ code. This means the job gets done faster. And faster is good. Faster means a faster response on the market. Less code not only means less code to write, but also less code to read (and professional coders read much more than they write), less code to maintain, to debug, and to refactor.

Another important aspect is that Python runs without the need of lengthy and time consuming compilation and linkage steps, so you don't have to wait to see the results of your work.

An extensive library

Python has an incredibly wide standard library (it's said to come with "batteries included"). If that wasn't enough, the Python community all over the world maintains a body of third party libraries, tailored to specific needs, which you can access freely at the **Python Package Index** (**PyPI**). When you code Python and you realize that you need a certain feature, in most cases, there is at least one library where that feature has already been implemented for you.

Software quality

Python is heavily focused on readability, coherence, and quality. The language uniformity allows for high readability and this is crucial nowadays where code is more of a collective effort than a solo experience. Another important aspect of Python is its intrinsic multi-paradigm nature. You can use it as scripting language, but you also can exploit object-oriented, imperative, and functional programming styles. It is versatile.

Software integration

Another important aspect is that Python can be extended and integrated with many other languages, which means that even when a company is using a different language as their mainstream tool, Python can come in and act as a glue agent between complex applications that need to talk to each other in some way. This is kind of an advanced topic, but in the real world, this feature is very important.

Satisfaction and enjoyment

Last but not least, the fun of it! Working with Python is fun. I can code for 8 hours and leave the office happy and satisfied, alien to the struggle other coders have to endure because they use languages that don't provide them with the same amount of well-designed data structures and constructs. Python makes coding fun, no doubt about it. And fun promotes motivation and productivity.

These are the major aspects why I would recommend Python to everyone for. Of course, there are many other technical and advanced features that I could have talked about, but they don't really pertain to an introductory section like this one. They will come up naturally, chapter after chapter, in this book.

What are the drawbacks?

Probably, the only drawback that one could find in Python, which is not due to personal preferences, is the *execution speed*. Typically, Python is slower than its compiled brothers. The standard implementation of Python produces, when you run an application, a compiled version of the source code called byte code (with the extension .pyc), which is then run by the Python interpreter. The advantage of this approach is portability, which we pay for with a slowdown due to the fact that Python is not compiled down to machine level as are other languages.

However, Python speed is rarely a problem today, hence its wide use regardless of this suboptimal feature. What happens is that in real life, hardware cost is no longer a problem, and usually it's easy enough to gain speed by parallelizing tasks. When it comes to number crunching though, one can switch to faster Python implementations, such as PyPy, which provides an average 7-fold speedup by implementing advanced compilation techniques (check http://pypy.org/ for reference).

When doing data science, you'll most likely find that the libraries that you use with Python, such as Pandas and Numpy, achieve native speed due to the way they are implemented.

If that wasn't a good enough argument, you can always consider that Python is driving the backend of services such as Spotify and Instagram, where performance is a concern. Nonetheless, Python does its job perfectly adequately.

Who is using Python today?

Not yet convinced? Let's take a very brief look at the companies that are using Python today: Google, YouTube, Dropbox, Yahoo, Zope Corporation, Industrial Light & Magic, Walt Disney Feature Animation, Pixar, NASA, NSA, Red Hat, Nokia, IBM, Netflix, Yelp, Intel, Cisco, HP, Qualcomm, and JPMorgan Chase, just to name a few.

Even games such as *Battlefield 2*, *Civilization 4*, and *QuArK* are implemented using Python.

Python is used in many different contexts, such as system programming, web programming, GUI applications, gaming and robotics, rapid prototyping, system integration, data science, database applications, and much more.

Setting up the environment

Before we talk about installing Python on your system, let me tell you about which Python version I'll be using in this book.

Python 2 versus Python 3 – the great debate

Python comes in two main versions—Python 2, which is the past—and Python 3, which is the present. The two versions, though very similar, are incompatible on some aspects.

In the real world, Python 2 is actually quite far from being the past. In short, even though Python 3 has been out since 2008, the transition phase is still far from being over. This is mostly due to the fact that Python 2 is widely used in the industry, and of course, companies aren't so keen on updating their systems just for the sake of updating, following the *if it ain't broke, don't fix it* philosophy. You can read all about the transition between the two versions on the Web.

Another issue that was hindering the transition is the availability of third-party libraries. Usually, a Python project relies on tens of external libraries, and of course, when you start a new project, you need to be sure that there is already a version 3 compatible library for any business requirement that may come up. If that's not the case, starting a brand new project in Python 3 means introducing a potential risk, which many companies are not happy to take.

At the time of writing, the majority of the most widely used libraries have been ported to Python 3, and it's quite safe to start a project in Python 3 for most cases. Many of the libraries have been rewritten so that they are compatible with both versions, mostly harnessing the power of the six (2 x 3) library, which helps introspecting and adapting the behavior according to the version used.

On my Linux box (Ubuntu 14.04), I have the following Python version:

```
>>> import sys
>>> print(sys.version)
3.4.0 (default, Apr 11 2014, 13:05:11)
[GCC 4.8.2]
```

So you can see that my Python version is 3.4.0. The preceding text is a little bit of Python code that I typed into my console. We'll talk about it in a moment.

All the examples in this book will be run using this Python version. Most of them will run also in Python 2 (I have version 2.7.6 installed as well), and those that won't will just require some minor adjustments to cater for the small incompatibilities between the two versions. Another reason behind this choice is that I think it's better to learn Python 3, and then, if you need to, learn the differences it has with Python 2, rather than going the other way around.

Don't worry about this version thing though: it's not that big an issue in practice.

Installing Python

I never really got the point of having a *setup* section in a book, regardless of what it is that you have to set up. Most of the time, between the time the author writes the instruction and the time you actually try them out, months have passed. That is, if you're lucky. One version change and things may not work the way it is described in the book. Luckily, we have the Web now, so in order to help you get up and running, I'll just give you pointers and objectives.

 If any of the URLs or resources I'll point you to are no longer there by the time you read this book, just remember: Google is your friend.

Setting up the Python interpreter

First of all, let's talk about your OS. Python is fully integrated and most likely already installed in basically almost every Linux distribution. If you have a Mac, it's likely that Python is already there as well (however, possibly only Python 2.7), whereas if you're using Windows, you probably need to install it.

Getting Python and the libraries you need up and running requires a bit of handiwork. Linux happens to be the most user friendly OS for Python programmers, Windows on the other hand is the one that requires the biggest effort, Mac being somewhere in between. For this reason, if you can choose, I suggest you to use Linux. If you can't, and you have a Mac, then go for it anyway. If you use Windows, you'll be fine for the examples in this book, but in general working with Python will require you a bit more tweaking.

My OS is Ubuntu 14.04, and this is what I will use throughout the book, along with Python 3.4.0.

The place you want to start is the official Python website: `https://www.python.org`. This website hosts the official Python documentation and many other resources that you will find very useful. Take the time to explore it.

 Another excellent, resourceful website on Python and its ecosystem is `http://docs.python-guide.org`.

Find the download section and choose the installer for your OS. If you are on Windows, make sure that when you run the installer, you check the option `install pip` (actually, I would suggest to make a complete installation, just to be safe, of all the components the installer holds). We'll talk about pip later.

Now that Python is installed in your system, the objective is to be able to open a console and run the Python interactive shell by typing `python`.

 Please note that I usually refer to the *Python interactive shell* simply as *Python console*.

To open the console in Windows, go to the **Start** menu, choose **Run**, and type `cmd`. If you encounter anything that looks like a permission problem while working on the examples of this book, please make sure you are running the console with administrator rights.

On the Mac OS X, you can start a terminal by going to **Applications | Utilities | Terminal**.

If you are on Linux, you know all that there is to know about the console.

 I will use the term *console* interchangeably to indicate the Linux **console**, the Windows **command prompt**, and the Mac **terminal**. I will also indicate the command-line prompt with the Linux default format, like this:

```
$ sudo apt-get update
```

Whatever console you open, type python at the prompt, and make sure the Python interactive shell shows up. Type exit() to quit. Keep in mind that you may have to specify python3 if your OS comes with Python 2.* preinstalled.

This is how it should look on Windows 7:

```
Administrator: C:\Windows\system32\cmd.exe - python

Microsoft Windows [Version 6.1.7601]
Copyright (c) 2009 Microsoft Corporation.  All rights reserved.

C:\Users\fab>python
Python 3.4.3 (v3.4.3:9b73f1c3e601, Feb 24 2015, 22:44:40) [MSC v.1600 64 bit (AM
D64)] on win32
Type "help", "copyright", "credits" or "license" for more information.
>>>
```

And this is how it should look on Linux:

Now that Python is set up and you can run it, it's time to make sure you have the other tool that will be indispensable to follow the examples in the book: virtualenv.

About virtualenv

As you probably have guessed by its name, **virtualenv** is all about virtual environments. Let me explain what they are and why we need them and let me do it by means of a simple example.

You install Python on your system and you start working on a website for client X. You create a project folder and start coding. Along the way you also install some libraries, for example the Django framework, which we'll see in depth in *Chapter 10, Web Development Done Right*. Let's say the Django version you install for project X is 1.7.1.

Now, your website is so good that you get another client, Y. He wants you to build another website, so you start project Y and, along the way, you need to install Django again. The only issue is that now the Django version is 1.8 and you cannot install it on your system because this would replace the version you installed for project X. You don't want to risk introducing incompatibility issues, so you have two choices: either you stick with the version you have currently on your machine, or you upgrade it and make sure the first project is still fully working correctly with the new version.

Let's be honest, neither of these options is very appealing, right? Definitely not. So, here's the solution: virtualenv!

virtualenv is a tool that allows you to create a virtual environment. In other words, it is a tool to create isolated Python environments, each of which is a folder that contains all the necessary executables to use the packages that a Python project would need (think of packages as libraries for the time being).

So you create a virtual environment for project X, install all the dependencies, and then you create a virtual environment for project Y, installing all its dependencies without the slightest worry because every library you install ends up within the boundaries of the appropriate virtual environment. In our example, project X will hold Django 1.7.1, while project Y will hold Django 1.8.

 It is of vital importance that you never install libraries directly at the system level. Linux for example relies on Python for many different tasks and operations, and if you fiddle with the system installation of Python, you risk compromising the integrity of the whole system (guess to whom this happened…). So take this as a rule, such as brushing your teeth before going to bed: *always, always create a virtual environment when you start a new project*.

To install virtualenv on your system, there are a few different ways. On a Debian-based distribution of Linux for example, you can install it with the following command:

```
$ sudo apt-get install python-virtualenv
```

Probably, the easiest way is to use `pip` though, with the following command:

```
$ sudo pip install virtualenv # sudo may by optional
```

`pip` is a package management system used to install and manage software packages written in Python.

Python 3 has built-in support for virtual environments, but in practice, the external libraries are still the default on production systems. If you have trouble getting virtualenv up and running, please refer to the virtualenv official website: `https://virtualenv.pypa.io`.

Your first virtual environment

It is very easy to create a virtual environment, but according to how your system is configured and which Python version you want the virtual environment to run, you need to run the command properly. Another thing you will need to do with a virtualenv, when you want to work with it, is to activate it. Activating a virtualenv basically produces some path juggling behind the scenes so that when you call the Python interpreter, you're actually calling the active virtual environment one, instead of the mere system one.

I'll show you a full example on both Linux and Windows. We will:

1. Create a folder named `learning.python` under your project root (which in my case is a folder called `srv`, in my home folder). Please adapt the paths according to the setup you fancy on your box.

2. Within the `learning.python` folder, we will create a virtual environment called `.lpvenv`.

> Some developers prefer to call all virtual environments using the same name (for example, `.venv`). This way they can run scripts against any virtualenv by just knowing the name of the project they dwell in. This is a very common technique that I use as well. The dot in `.venv` is because in Linux/Mac prepending a name with a dot makes that file or folder invisible.

3. After creating the virtual environment, we will activate it (this is slightly different between Linux, Mac, and Windows).

4. Then, we'll make sure that we are running the desired Python version (3.4.*) by running the Python interactive shell.

5. Finally, we will deactivate the virtual environment using the deactivate command.

These five simple steps will show you all you have to do to start and use a project.

Here's an example of how those steps might look like on Linux (commands that start with a # are comments):

```
fab@xps: ~/srv/learning.python
                    fab@xps: ~/srv/learning.python 80x28
fab@xps:srv$ # step 1 - create folder
fab@xps:srv$ mkdir learning.python
fab@xps:srv$ cd learning.python
fab@xps:learning.python$ : step 2 - create virtual environment
fab@xps:learning.python$ which python3.4
/usr/bin/python3.4
fab@xps:learning.python$ virtualenv -p /usr/bin/python3.4 .lpvenv
Running virtualenv with interpreter /usr/bin/python3.4
Using base prefix '/usr'
New python executable in .lpvenv/bin/python3.4
Also creating executable in .lpvenv/bin/python
Installing setuptools, pip...done.
fab@xps:learning.python$ # step 3 - activate virtual environment
fab@xps:learning.python$ source .lpvenv/bin/activate
(.lpvenv)fab@xps:learning.python$ # step 4 - verify which python
(.lpvenv)fab@xps:learning.python$ which python
/home/fab/srv/learning.python/.lpvenv/bin/python
(.lpvenv)fab@xps:learning.python$ python
Python 3.4.0 (default, Apr 11 2014, 13:05:11)
[GCC 4.8.2] on linux
Type "help", "copyright", "credits" or "license" for more information.
>>> exit()
(.lpvenv)fab@xps:learning.python$ # step 5 - deactivate virtual environment
(.lpvenv)fab@xps:learning.python$ deactivate
fab@xps:learning.python$ 
```

Notice that I had to explicitly tell virtualenv to use the Python 3.4 interpreter because on my box Python 2.7 is the default one. Had I not done that, I would have had a virtual environment with Python 2.7 instead of Python 3.4.

You can combine the two instructions for *step 2* in one single command like this:

```
$ virtualenv -p $( which python3.4 ) .lpvenv
```

I preferred to be explicitly verbose in this instance, to help you understand each bit of the procedure.

Another thing to notice is that in order to activate a virtual environment, we need to run the /bin/activate script, which needs to be sourced (when a script is "sourced", it means that its effects stick around when it's done running). This is very important. Also notice how the prompt changes after we activate the virtual environment, showing its name on the left (and how it disappears when we deactivate). In Mac OS, the steps are the same so I won't repeat them here.

Now let's have a look at how we can achieve the same result in Windows. You will probably have to play around a bit, especially if you have a different Windows or Python version than I'm using here. This is all good experience though, so try and think positively at the initial struggle that every coder has to go through in order to get things going.

Here's how it should look on Windows (commands that start with `::` are comments):

```
Administrator: C:\Windows\system32\cmd.exe

C:\Users\fab\srv>:: step 1 - create folder
C:\Users\fab\srv>mkdir learning.python

C:\Users\fab\srv>cd learning.python

C:\Users\fab\srv\learning.python>:: step 2 - create virtual environment
C:\Users\fab\srv\learning.python>virtualenv -p \Python34\python.exe .lpvenv
Already using interpreter C:\Python34\python.exe
Using base prefix 'C:\\Python34'
New python executable in .lpvenv\Scripts\python.exe
Installing setuptools, pip...done.

C:\Users\fab\srv\learning.python>:: step 3 - activate virtual environment
C:\Users\fab\srv\learning.python>.lpvenv\Scripts\activate
(.lpvenv) C:\Users\fab\srv\learning.python>:: step 4 - verify which python
(.lpvenv) C:\Users\fab\srv\learning.python>where python
C:\Users\fab\srv\learning.python\.lpvenv\Scripts\python.exe
C:\Python34\python.exe

(.lpvenv) C:\Users\fab\srv\learning.python>python
Python 3.4.3 (v3.4.3:9b73f1c3e601, Feb 24 2015, 22:44:40) [MSC v.1600 64 bit (AM
D64)] on win32
Type "help", "copyright", "credits" or "license" for more information.
>>> exit()

(.lpvenv) C:\Users\fab\srv\learning.python>:: step 5 - deactivate virtual env
(.lpvenv) C:\Users\fab\srv\learning.python>deactivate
C:\Users\fab\srv\learning.python>
```

Notice there are a few small differences from the Linux version. Apart from the commands to create and navigate the folders, one important difference is how you activate your virtualenv. Also, in Windows there is no `which` command, so we used the `where` command.

At this point, you should be able to create and activate a virtual environment. Please try and create another one without me guiding you, get acquainted to this procedure because it's something that you will always be doing: *we never work system-wide with Python*, remember? It's extremely important.

So, with the scaffolding out of the way, we're ready to talk a bit more about Python and how you can use it. Before we do it though, allow me to spend a few words about the console.

Your friend, the console

In this era of GUIs and touchscreen devices, it seems a little ridiculous to have to resort to a tool such as the console, when everything is just about one click away.

But the truth is every time you remove your right hand from the keyboard (or the left one, if you're a lefty) to grab your mouse and move the cursor over to the spot you want to click, you're losing time. Getting things done with the console, counter-intuitively as it may be, results in higher productivity and speed. I know, you have to trust me on this.

Speed and productivity are important and personally, I have nothing against the mouse, but there is another very good reason for which you may want to get well acquainted with the console: when you develop code that ends up on some server, the console might be the only available tool. If you make friends with it, I promise you, you will never get lost when it's of utmost importance that you don't (typically, when the website is down and you have to investigate very quickly what's going on).

So it's really up to you. If you're in doubt, please grant me the benefit of the doubt and give it a try. It's easier than you think, and you'll never regret it. There is nothing more pitiful than a good developer who gets lost within an SSH connection to a server because they are used to their own custom set of tools, and only to that.

Now, let's get back to Python.

How you can run a Python program

There are a few different ways in which you can run a Python program.

Running Python scripts

Python can be used as a scripting language. In fact, it always proves itself very useful. Scripts are files (usually of small dimensions) that you normally execute to do something like a task. Many developers end up having their own arsenal of tools that they fire when they need to perform a task. For example, you can have scripts to parse data in a format and render it into another different format. Or you can use a script to work with files and folders. You can create or modify configuration files, and much more. Technically, there is not much that cannot be done in a script.

It's quite common to have scripts running at a precise time on a server. For example, if your website database needs cleaning every 24 hours (for example, the table that stores the user sessions, which expire pretty quickly but aren't cleaned automatically), you could set up a cron job that fires your script at 3:00 A.M. every day.

 According to Wikipedia, the software utility Cron is a time-based job scheduler in Unix-like computer operating systems. People who set up and maintain software environments use cron to schedule jobs (commands or shell scripts) to run periodically at fixed times, dates, or intervals.

I have Python scripts to do all the menial tasks that would take me minutes or more to do manually, and at some point, I decided to automate. For example, I have a laptop that doesn't have a *Fn* key to toggle the touchpad on and off. I find this very annoying, and I don't want to go clicking about through several menus when I need to do it, so I wrote a small script that is smart enough to tell my system to toggle the touchpad active state, and now I can do it with one simple click from my launcher. Priceless.

We'll devote half of *Chapter 8, The Edges – GUIs and Scripts* on scripting with Python.

Running the Python interactive shell

Another way of running Python is by calling the interactive shell. This is something we already saw when we typed `python` on the command line of our console.

So open a console, activate your virtual environment (which by now should be second nature to you, right?), and type `python`. You will be presented with a couple of lines that should look like this (if you are on Linux):

```
Python 3.4.0 (default, Apr 11 2014, 13:05:11)
[GCC 4.8.2] on linux
Type "help", "copyright", "credits" or "license" for more information.
```

Those >>> are the prompt of the shell. They tell you that Python is waiting for you to type something. If you type a simple instruction, something that fits in one line, that's all you'll see. However, if you type something that requires more than one line of code, the shell will change the prompt to . . ., giving you a visual clue that you're typing a multiline statement (or anything that would require more than one line of code).

Go on, try it out, let's do some basic maths:

```
>>> 2 + 4
6
>>> 10 / 4
2.5
>>> 2 ** 1024
179769313486231590772930519078902473361797697894230657273430081157732675
805500963132708477322407536021120113879871393357658789768814416622492847430
639474124377767893424865485276302219601246094119453082952085005768838150
682342462881473913110540827237163350510684586298239947245938479716304835356
329624224137216
```

The last operation is showing you something incredible. We raise 2 to the power of 1024, and Python is handling this task with no trouble at all. Try to do it in Java, C++, or C#. It won't work, unless you use special libraries to handle such big numbers.

I use the interactive shell every day. It's extremely useful to debug very quickly, for example, to check if a data structure supports an operation. Or maybe to inspect or run a piece of code.

When you use Django (a web framework), the interactive shell is coupled with it and allows you to work your way through the framework tools, to inspect the data in the database, and many more things. You will find that the interactive shell will soon become one of your dearest friends on the journey you are embarking on.

Another solution, which comes in a much nicer graphic layout, is to use **IDLE (Integrated DeveLopment Environment)**. It's quite a simple IDE, which is intended mostly for beginners. It has a slightly larger set of capabilities than the naked interactive shell you get in the console, so you may want to explore it. It comes for free in the Windows Python installer and you can easily install it in any other system. You can find information about it on the Python website.

Guido Van Rossum named Python after the British comedy group Monty Python, so it's rumored that the name IDLE has been chosen in honor of Erik Idle, one of Monty Python's founding members.

Running Python as a service

Apart from being run as a script, and within the boundaries of a shell, Python can be coded and run as proper software. We'll see many examples throughout the book about this mode. And we'll understand more about it in a moment, when we'll talk about how Python code is organized and run.

Running Python as a GUI application

Python can also be run as a **GUI (Graphical User Interface)**. There are several frameworks available, some of which are cross-platform and some others are platform-specific. In *Chapter 8, The Edges – GUIs and Scripts*, we'll see an example of a GUI application created using *Tkinter*, which is an object-oriented layer that lives on top of **Tk** (Tkinter means Tk Interface).

> Tk is a graphical user interface toolkit that takes desktop application development to a higher level than the conventional approach. It is the standard GUI for **Tcl (Tool Command Language)**, but also for many other dynamic languages and can produce rich native applications that run seamlessly under Windows, Linux, Mac OS X, and more.

Tkinter comes bundled with Python, therefore it gives the programmer easy access to the GUI world, and for these reasons, I have chosen it to be the framework for the GUI examples that I'll present in this book.

Among the other GUI frameworks, we find that the following are the most widely used:

- PyQt
- wxPython
- PyGtk

Describing them in detail is outside the scope of this book, but you can find all the information you need on the Python website in the *GUI Programming* section. If GUIs are what you're looking for, remember to choose the one you want according to some principles. Make sure they:

- Offer all the features you may need to develop your project
- Run on all the platforms you may need to support
- Rely on a community that is as wide and active as possible
- Wrap graphic drivers/tools that you can easily install/access

How is Python code organized

Let's talk a little bit about how Python code is organized. In this paragraph, we'll start going down the rabbit hole a little bit more and introduce a bit more technical names and concepts.

Starting with the basics, how is Python code organized? Of course, you write your code into files. When you save a file with the extension .py, that file is said to be a Python module.

> If you're on Windows or Mac, which typically hide file extensions to the user, please make sure you change the configuration so that you can see the complete name of the files. This is not strictly a requirement, but a hearty suggestion.

It would be impractical to save all the code that it is required for software to work within one single file. That solution works for *scripts*, which are usually not longer than a few hundred lines (and often they are quite shorter than that).

A complete Python application can be made of hundreds of thousands of lines of code, so you will have to scatter it through different modules. Better, but not nearly good enough. It turns out that even like this it would still be impractical to work with the code. So Python gives you another structure, called **package**, which allows you to group modules together. A package is nothing more than a folder, which must contain a special file, __init__.py that doesn't need to hold any code but whose presence is required to tell Python that the folder is not just some folder, but it's actually a package (note that as of Python 3.3 __init__.py is not strictly required any more).

As always, an example will make all of this much clearer. I have created an example structure in my book project, and when I type in my Linux console:

```
$ tree -v example
```

I get a tree representation of the contents of the ch1/example folder, which holds the code for the examples of this chapter. Here's how a structure of a real simple application could look like:

```
example/
├── core.py
├── run.py
└── util
    ├── __init__.py
    ├── db.py
    ├── math.py
    └── network.py
```

You can see that within the root of this example, we have two modules, `core.py` and `run.py`, and one package: `util`. Within `core.py`, there may be the core logic of our application. On the other hand, within the `run.py` module, we can probably find the logic to start the application. Within the `util` package, I expect to find various utility tools, and in fact, we can guess that the modules there are called by the type of tools they hold: `db.py` would hold tools to work with databases, `math.py` would of course hold mathematical tools (maybe our application deals with financial data), and `network.py` would probably hold tools to send/receive data on networks.

As explained before, the `__init__.py` file is there just to tell Python that `util` is a package and not just a mere folder.

Had this software been organized within modules only, it would have been much harder to infer its structure. I put a *module only* example under the `ch1/files_only` folder, see it for yourself:

```
$ tree -v files_only
```

This shows us a completely different picture:

```
files_only/
├── core.py
├── db.py
├── math.py
├── network.py
└── run.py
```

It is a little harder to guess what each module does, right? Now, consider that this is just a simple example, so you can guess how much harder it would be to understand a real application if we couldn't organize the code in packages and modules.

How do we use modules and packages

When a developer is writing an application, it is very likely that they will need to apply the same piece of logic in different parts of it. For example, when writing a parser for the data that comes from a form that a user can fill in a web page, the application will have to validate whether a certain field is holding a number or not. Regardless of how the logic for this kind of validation is written, it's very likely that it will be needed in more than one place. For example in a poll application, where the user is asked many question, it's likely that several of them will require a numeric answer. For example:

- What is your age
- How many pets do you own
- How many children do you have
- How many times have you been married

It would be very bad practice to copy paste (or, more properly said: duplicate) the validation logic in every place where we expect a numeric answer. This would violate the **DRY (Don't Repeat Yourself)** principle, which states that you should never repeat the same piece of code more than once in your application. I feel the need to stress the importance of this principle: *you should never repeat the same piece of code more than once in your application* (got the irony?).

There are several reasons why repeating the same piece of logic can be very bad, the most important ones being:

- There could be a bug in the logic, and therefore, you would have to correct it in every place that logic is applied.

- You may want to amend the way you carry out the validation, and again you would have to change it in every place it is applied.

- You may forget to fix/amend a piece of logic because you missed it when searching for all its occurrences. This would leave wrong/inconsistent behavior in your application.

- Your code would be longer than needed, for no good reason.

Python is a wonderful language and provides you with all the tools you need to apply all the coding best practices. For this particular example, we need to be able to reuse a piece of code. To be able to reuse a piece of code, we need to have a construct that will hold the code for us so that we can call that construct every time we need to repeat the logic inside it. That construct exists, and it's called **function**.

I'm not going too deep into the specifics here, so please just remember that a function is a block of organized, reusable code which is used to perform a task. Functions can assume many forms and names, according to what kind of environment they belong to, but for now this is not important. We'll see the details when we are able to appreciate them, later on, in the book. Functions are the building blocks of modularity in your application, and they are almost indispensable (unless you're writing a super simple script, you'll use functions all the time). We'll explore functions in *Chapter 4, Functions, the Building Blocks of Code*.

Python comes with a very extensive library, as I already said a few pages ago. Now, maybe it's a good time to define what a library is: a **library** is a collection of functions and objects that provide functionalities that enrich the abilities of a language.

For example, within Python's `math` library we can find a plethora of functions, one of which is the `factorial` function, which of course calculates the factorial of a number.

> In mathematics, the **factorial** of a non-negative integer number *N*, denoted as *N!*, is defined as the product of all positive integers less than or equal to N. For example, the factorial of 5 is calculated as:
>
> `5! = 5 * 4 * 3 * 2 * 1 = 120`
>
> The factorial of `0` is `0! = 1`, to respect the convention for an empty product.

So, if you wanted to use this function in your code, all you would have to do is to import it and call it with the right input values. Don't worry too much if input values and the concept of calling is not very clear for now, please just concentrate on the import part.

> We use a library by importing what we need from it, and then we use it.

In Python, to calculate the factorial of number 5, we just need the following code:

```
>>> from math import factorial
>>> factorial(5)
120
```

> Whatever we type in the shell, if it has a printable representation, will be printed on the console for us (in this case, the result of the function call: 120).

So, let's go back to our example, the one with `core.py`, `run.py`, `util`, and so on.

In our example, the package `util` is our utility library. Our custom utility belt that holds all those reusable tools (that is, functions), which we need in our application. Some of them will deal with databases (`db.py`), some with the network (`network.py`), and some will perform mathematical calculations (`math.py`) that are outside the scope of Python's standard `math` library and therefore, we had to code them for ourselves.

We will see in detail how to import functions and use them in their dedicated chapter. Let's now talk about another very important concept: Python's execution model.

Python's execution model

In this paragraph, I would like to introduce you to a few very important concepts, such as scope, names, and namespaces. You can read all about Python's execution model in the official Language reference, of course, but I would argue that it is quite technical and abstract, so let me give you a less formal explanation first.

Names and namespaces

Say you are looking for a book, so you go to the library and ask someone for the book you want to fetch. They tell you something like "second floor, section X, row three". So you go up the stairs, look for section X, and so on.

It would be very different to enter a library where all the books are piled together in random order in one big room. No floors, no sections, no rows, no order. Fetching a book would be extremely hard.

When we write code we have the same issue: we have to try and organize it so that it will be easy for someone who has no prior knowledge about it to find what they're looking for. When software is structured correctly, it also promotes code reuse. On the other hand, disorganized software is more likely to expose scattered pieces of duplicated logic.

First of all, let's start with the book. We refer to a book by its title and in Python lingo, that would be a name. Python names are the closest abstraction to what other languages call variables. Names basically refer to objects and are introduced by name binding operations. Let's make a quick example (notice that anything that follows a # is a comment):

```
>>> n = 3  # integer number
>>> address = "221b Baker Street, NW1 6XE, London"  # S. Holmes
>>> employee = {
...     'age': 45,
...     'role': 'CTO',
...     'SSN': 'AB1234567',
... }
>>> # let's print them
>>> n
3
>>> address
'221b Baker Street, NW1 6XE, London'
>>> employee
```

```
{'role': 'CTO', 'SSN': 'AB1234567', 'age': 45}
>>> # what if I try to print a name I didn't define?
>>> other_name
Traceback (most recent call last):
  File "<stdin>", line 1, in <module>
NameError: name 'other_name' is not defined
```

We defined three objects in the preceding code (do you remember what are the three features every Python object has?):

- An integer number n (type: int, value: 3)

- A string address (type: str, value: Sherlock Holmes' address)

- A dictionary employee (type: dict, value: a dictionary which holds three key/value pairs)

Don't worry, I know you're not supposed to know what a dictionary is. We'll see in the next chapter that it's the king of Python data structures.

 Have you noticed that the prompt changed from >>> to ... when I typed in the definition of employee? That's because the definition spans over multiple lines.

So, what are n, address and employee? They are **names**. Names that we can use to retrieve data within our code. They need to be kept somewhere so that whenever we need to retrieve those objects, we can use their names to fetch them. We need some space to hold them, hence: namespaces!

A **namespace** is therefore a mapping from names to objects. Examples are the set of built-in names (containing functions that are always accessible for free in any Python program), the global names in a module, and the local names in a function. Even the set of attributes of an object can be considered a namespace.

The beauty of namespaces is that they allow you to define and organize your names with clarity, without overlapping or interference. For example, the namespace associated with that book we were looking for in the library can be used to import the book itself, like this:

```
from library.second_floor.section_x.row_three import book
```

We start from the library namespace, and by means of the dot (.) operator, we walk into that namespace. Within this namespace, we look for second_floor, and again we walk into it with the . operator. We then walk into section_x, and finally within the last namespace, row_tree, we find the name we were looking for: book.

Walking through a namespace will be clearer when we'll be dealing with real code examples. For now, just keep in mind that namespaces are places where names are associated to objects.

There is another concept, which is closely related to that of a namespace, which I'd like to briefly talk about: the **scope**.

Scopes

According to Python's documentation, *a scope is a textual region of a Python program, where a namespace is directly accessible*. Directly accessible means that when you're looking for an unqualified reference to a name, Python tries to find it in the namespace.

Scopes are determined statically, but actually during runtime they are used dynamically. This means that by inspecting the source code you can tell what the scope of an object is, but this doesn't prevent the software to alter that during runtime. There are four different scopes that Python makes accessible (not necessarily all of them present at the same time, of course):

- The **local** scope, which is the innermost one and contains the local names.
- The **enclosing** scope, that is, the scope of any enclosing function. It contains non-local names and also non-global names.
- The **global** scope contains the global names.
- The **built-in** scope contains the built-in names. Python comes with a set of functions that you can use in a off-the-shelf fashion, such as `print`, `all`, `abs`, and so on. They live in the built-in scope.

The rule is the following: when we refer to a name, Python starts looking for it in the current namespace. If the name is not found, Python continues the search to the enclosing scope and this continue until the built-in scope is searched. If a name hasn't been found after searching the built-in scope, then Python raises a `NameError` **exception**, which basically means that the name hasn't been defined (you saw this in the preceding example).

The order in which the namespaces are scanned when looking for a name is therefore: **local, enclosing, global, built-in** (LEGB).

This is all very theoretical, so let's see an example. In order to show you Local and Enclosing namespaces, I will have to define a few functions. Don't worry if you are not familiar with their syntax for the moment, we'll study functions in *Chapter 4, Functions, the Building Blocks of Code*. Just remember that in the following code, when you see def, it means I'm defining a function.

```
scopes1.py
    # Local versus Global

    # we define a function, called local
    def local():
        m = 7
        print(m)

    m = 5
    print(m)

    # we call, or `execute` the function local
    local()
```

In the preceding example, we define the same name m, both in the global scope and in the local one (the one defined by the function local). When we execute this program with the following command (have you activated your virtualenv?):

```
$ python scopes1.py
```

We see two numbers printed on the console: 5 and 7.

What happens is that the Python interpreter parses the file, top to bottom. First, it finds a couple of comment lines, which are skipped, then it parses the definition of the function local. When called, this function does two things: it sets up a name to an object representing number 7 and prints it. The Python interpreter keeps going and it finds another name binding. This time the binding happens in the global scope and the value is 5. The next line is a call to the print function, which is executed (and so we get the first value printed on the console: 5).

After this, there is a call to the function local. At this point, Python executes the function, so at this time, the binding m = 7 happens and it's printed.

One very important thing to notice is that the part of the code that belongs to the definition of the function local is indented by four spaces on the right. Python in fact defines scopes by indenting the code. You walk into a scope by indenting and walk out of it by unindenting. Some coders use two spaces, others three, but the suggested number of spaces to use is four. It's a good measure to maximize readability. We'll talk more about all the conventions you should embrace when writing Python code later.

What would happen if we removed that m = 7 line? Remember the LEGB rule. Python would start looking for m in the local scope (function `local`), and, not finding it, it would go to the next enclosing scope. The next one in this case is the global one because there is no enclosing function wrapped around `local`. Therefore, we would see two number 5 printed on the console. Let's actually see how the code would look like:

scopes2.py
```
    # Local versus Global

    def local():
        # m doesn't belong to the scope defined by the local function
        # so Python will keep looking into the next enclosing scope.
        # m is finally found in the global scope
        print(m, 'printing from the local scope')

    m = 5
    print(m, 'printing from the global scope')

    local()
```

Running scopes2.py will print this:

```
(.lpvenv) fab@xps:ch1$ python scopes2.py
5 printing from the global scope
5 printing from the local scope
```

As expected, Python prints m the first time, then when the function `local` is called, m isn't found in its scope, so Python looks for it following the LEGB chain until m is found in the global scope.

Let's see an example with an extra layer, the enclosing scope:

scopes3.py
```
    # Local, Enclosing and Global

    def enclosing_func():
        m = 13
        def local():
            # m doesn't belong to the scope defined by the local
            # function so Python will keep looking into the next
            # enclosing scope. This time m is found in the enclosing
            # scope
            print(m, 'printing from the local scope')

        # calling the function local
        local()
```

```
m = 5
print(m, 'printing from the global scope')

enclosing_func()
```

Running `scopes3.py` will print on the console:

```
(.lpvenv) fab@xps:ch1$ python scopes3.py
5 printing from the global scope
13 printing from the local scope
```

As you can see, the `print` instruction from the function `local` is referring to `m` as before. `m` is still not defined within the function itself, so Python starts walking scopes following the LEGB order. This time `m` is found in the enclosing scope.

Don't worry if this is still not perfectly clear for now. It will come to you as we go through the examples in the book. The *Classes* section of the Python tutorial (official documentation) has an interesting paragraph about scopes and namespaces. Make sure you read it at some point if you wish for a deeper understanding of the subject.

Before we finish off this chapter, I would like to talk a bit more about objects. After all, basically everything in Python is an object, so I think they deserve a bit more attention.

> **Downloading the example code**
>
> You can download the example code files from your account at `http://www.packtpub.com` for all the Packt Publishing books you have purchased. If you purchased this book elsewhere, you can visit `http://www.packtpub.com/support` and register to have the files e-mailed directly to you.

Object and classes

When I introduced objects in the *A proper introduction* section, I said that we use them to represent real-life objects. For example, we sell goods of any kind on the Web nowadays and we need to be able to handle, store, and represent them properly. But objects are actually so much more than that. Most of what you will ever do, in Python, has to do with manipulating objects.

So, without going too much into detail (we'll do that in *Chapter 6, Advanced Concepts – OOP, Decorators, and Iterators*), I want to give you the *in a nutshell* kind of explanation about classes and objects.

We've already seen that objects are Python's abstraction for data. In fact, everything in Python is an object. Numbers, strings (data structures that hold text), containers, collections, even functions. You can think of them as if they were boxes with at least three features: an ID (unique), a type, and a value.

But how do they come to life? How do we create them? How to we write our own custom objects? The answer lies in one simple word: classes.

Objects are, in fact, instances of classes. The beauty of Python is that classes are objects themselves, but let's not go down this road. It leads to one of the most advanced concepts of this language: **metaclasses**. We'll talk very briefly about them in *Chapter 6*, *Advanced Concepts – OOP, Decorators, and Iterators*. For now, the best way for you to get the difference between classes and objects, is by means of an example.

Say a friend tells you "I bought a new bike!" You immediately understand what she's talking about. Have you seen the bike? No. Do you know what color it is? Nope. The brand? Nope. Do you know anything about it? Nope. But at the same time, you know everything you need in order to understand what your friend meant when she told you she bought a new bike. You know that a bike has two wheels attached to a frame, a saddle, pedals, handlebars, brakes, and so on. In other words, even if you haven't seen the bike itself, you know the concept of bike. An abstract set of features and characteristics that together form something called bike.

In computer programming, that is called a **class**. It's that simple. Classes are used to create objects. In fact, objects are said to be **instances of classes**.

In other words, we all know what a bike is, we know the class. But then I have my own bike, which is an instance of the class bike. And my bike is an object with its own characteristics and methods. You have your own bike. Same class, but different instance. Every bike ever created in the world is an instance of the bike class.

Let's see an example. We will write a class that defines a bike and then we'll create two bikes, one red and one blue. I'll keep the code very simple, but don't fret if you don't understand everything about it; all you need to care about at this moment is to understand the difference between class and object (or instance of a class):

```
bike.py
    # let's define the class Bike
    class Bike:
        def __init__(self, colour, frame_material):
            self.colour = colour
            self.frame_material = frame_material

        def brake(self):
            print("Braking!")
```

```
# let's create a couple of instances
red_bike = Bike('Red', 'Carbon fiber')
blue_bike = Bike('Blue', 'Steel')

# let's inspect the objects we have, instances of the Bike class.
print(red_bike.colour)  # prints: Red
print(red_bike.frame_material)  # prints: Carbon fiber
print(blue_bike.colour)  # prints: Blue
print(blue_bike.frame_material)  #  prints: Steel

# let's brake!
red_bike.brake()  # prints: Braking!
```

 I hope by now I don't need to tell you to run the file every time,
right? The filename is indicated in the first line of the code block.
Just run $ `python filename`, and you'll be fine.

So many interesting things to notice here. First things first; the definition of a class happens with the `class` statement (highlighted in the code). Whatever code comes after the `class` statement, and is indented, is called the body of the class. In our case, the last line that belongs to the class definition is the `print("Braking!")` one.

After having defined the class we're ready to create instances. You can see that the class body hosts the definition of two methods. A method is basically (and simplistically) a function that belongs to a class.

The first method, __init__ is an **initializer**. It uses some Python magic to set up the objects with the values we pass when we create it.

 Every method that has leading and trailing double underscore, in
Python, is called **magic method**. Magic methods are used by Python
for a multitude of different purposes, hence it's never a good idea to
name a custom method using two leading and trailing underscores.
This naming convention is best left to Python.

The other method we defined, `brake`, is just an example of an additional method that we could call if we wanted to brake the bike. It contains just a `print` statement, of course, it's an example.

We created two bikes then. One has red color and a carbon fiber frame, and the other one has blue color and steel frame. We pass those values upon creation. After creation, we print out the color property and frame type of the red bike, and the frame type of the blue one just as an example. We also call the `brake` method of the `red_bike`.

One last thing to notice. You remember I told you that the set of attributes of an object is considered to be a namespace? I hope it's clearer now, what I meant. You see that by getting to the `frame_type` property through different namespaces (`red_bike`, `blue_bike`) we obtain different values. No overlapping, no confusion.

The dot (`.`) operator is of course the means we use to walk into a namespace, in the case of objects as well.

Guidelines on how to write good code

Writing good code is not as easy as it seems. As I already said before, good code exposes a long list of qualities that is quite hard to put together. Writing good code is, to some extent, an art. Regardless of where on the path you will be happy to settle, there is something that you can embrace which will make your code instantly better: **PEP8**.

According to Wikipedia:

> *"Python's development is conducted largely through the Python Enhancement Proposal (PEP) process. The PEP process is the primary mechanism for proposing major new features, for collecting community input on an issue, and for documenting the design decisions that have gone into Python."*

Among all the PEPs, probably the most famous one is PEP8. It lays out a simple but effective set of guidelines to define Python aesthetic so that we write beautiful Python code. If you take one suggestion out of this chapter, please let it be this: use it. Embrace it. You will thank me later.

Coding today is no longer a check-in/check-out business. Rather, it's more of a social effort. Several developers collaborate to a piece of code through tools like git and mercurial, and the result is code that is fathered by many different hands.

 Git and Mercurial are probably the most used distributed revision control systems today. They are essential tools designed to help teams of developers collaborate on the same software.

These days, more than ever, we need to have a consistent way of writing code, so that readability is maximized. When all developers of a company abide with PEP8, it's not uncommon for any of them landing on a piece of code to think they wrote it themselves. It actually happens to me all the time (I always forget the code I write).

This has a tremendous advantage: when you read code that you could have written yourself, you read it easily. Without a convention, every coder would structure the code the way they like most, or simply the way they were taught or are used to, and this would mean having to interpret every line according to someone else's style. It would mean having to lose much more time just trying to understand it. Thanks to PEP8, we can avoid this. I'm such a fan of it that I won't sign off a code review if the code doesn't respect it. So please take the time to study it, it's very important.

In the examples of this book, I will try to respect it as much as I can. Unfortunately, I don't have the luxury of 79 characters (which is the maximum line length suggested by PEP*), and I will have to cut down on blank lines and other things, but I promise you I'll try to layout my code so that it's as readable as possible.

The Python culture

Python has been adopted widely in all coding industries. It's used by many different companies for many different purposes, and it's also used in education (it's an excellent language for that purpose, because of its many qualities and the fact that it's easy to learn).

One of the reasons Python is so popular today is that the community around it is vast, vibrant, and full of brilliant people. Many events are organized all over the world, mostly either around Python or its main web framework, Django.

Python is open, and very often so are the minds of those who embrace it. Check out the community page on the Python website for more information and get involved!

There is another aspect to Python which revolves around the notion of being **Pythonic**. It has to do with the fact that Python allows you to use some idioms that aren't found elsewhere, at least not in the same form or easiness of use (I feel quite claustrophobic when I have to code in a language which is not Python now).

Anyway, over the years, this concept of being Pythonic has emerged and, the way I understand it, is something along the lines of *doing things the way they are supposed to be done in Python.*

To help you understand a little bit more about Python's culture and about being Pythonic, I will show you the *Zen of Python*. A lovely Easter egg that is very popular. Open up a Python console and type `import this`. What follows is the result of this line:

```
>>> import this
The Zen of Python, by Tim Peters
```

```
Beautiful is better than ugly.

Explicit is better than implicit.

Simple is better than complex.

Complex is better than complicated.

Flat is better than nested.

Sparse is better than dense.

Readability counts.

Special cases aren't special enough to break the rules.

Although practicality beats purity.

Errors should never pass silently.

Unless explicitly silenced.

In the face of ambiguity, refuse the temptation to guess.

There should be one-- and preferably only one --obvious way to do it.

Although that way may not be obvious at first unless you're Dutch.

Now is better than never.

Although never is often better than *right* now.

If the implementation is hard to explain, it's a bad idea.

If the implementation is easy to explain, it may be a good idea.

Namespaces are one honking great idea -- let's do more of those!
```

There are two levels of reading here. One is to consider it as a set of guidelines that have been put down in a fun way. The other one is to keep it in mind, and maybe read it once in a while, trying to understand how it refers to something deeper. Some Python characteristics that you will have to understand deeply in order to write Python the way it's supposed to be written. Start with the fun level, and then dig deeper. Always dig deeper.

A note on the IDEs

Just a few words about **Integrated Development Environments** (IDEs). To follow the examples in this book you don't need one, any text editor will do fine. If you want to have more advanced features such as syntax coloring and auto completion, you will have to fetch yourself an IDE. You can find a comprehensive list of open source IDEs (just Google "python ides") on the Python website. I personally use Sublime Text editor. It's free to try out and it costs just a few dollars. I have tried many IDEs in my life, but this is the one that makes me most productive.

Two extremely important pieces of advice:

- Whatever IDE you will chose to use, try to learn it well so that you can exploit its strengths, but *don't depend on it*. Exercise yourself to work with VIM (or any other text editor) once in a while, learn to be able to do some work on any platform, with any set of tools.

- Whatever text editor/IDE you will use, when it comes to writing Python, *indentation is four spaces*. Don't use tabs, don't mix them with spaces. Use four spaces, not two, not three, not five. Just use four. The whole world works like that, and you don't want to become an outcast because you were fond of the three-space layout.

Summary

In this chapter, we started to explore the world of programming and that of Python. We've barely scratched the surface, just a little, touching concepts that will be discussed later on in the book in greater detail.

We talked about Python's main features, who is using it and for what, and what are the different ways in which we can write a Python program.

In the last part of the chapter, we flew over the fundamental notions of namespace, scope, class, and object. We also saw how Python code can be organized using modules and packages.

On a practical level, we learned how to install Python on our system, how to make sure we have the tools we need, pip and virtualenv, and we also created and activated our first virtual environment. This will allow us to work in a self-contained environment without the risk of compromising the Python system installation.

Now you're ready to start this journey with me. All you need is enthusiasm, an activated virtual environment, this book, your fingers, and some coffee.

Try to follow the examples, I'll keep them simple and short. If you put them under your fingertips, you will retain them much better than if you just read them.

In the next chapter, we will explore Python's rich set of built-in data types. There's much to cover and much to learn!

2

Built-in Data Types

"Data! Data! Data!" he cried impatiently. "I can't make bricks without clay."

- Sherlock Holmes - The Adventure of the Copper Beeches

Everything you do with a computer is managing data. Data comes in many different shapes and flavors. It's the music you listen, the movie you stream, the PDFs you open. Even the chapter you're reading at this very moment is just a file, which is data.

Data can be simple, an integer number to represent an age, or complex, like an order placed on a website. It can be about a single object or about a collection of them.

Data can even be about data, that is, metadata. Data that describes the design of other data structures or data that describes application data or its context.

In Python, *objects are abstraction for data*, and Python has an amazing variety of data structures that you can use to represent data, or combine them to create your own custom data. Before we delve into the specifics, I want you to be very clear about objects in Python, so let's talk a little bit more about them.

Everything is an object

As we already said, everything in Python is an object. But what really happens when you type an instruction like age = 42 in a Python module?

> If you go to http://pythontutor.com/, you can type that instruction into a text box and get its visual representation. Keep this website in mind, it's very useful to consolidate your understanding of what goes on behind the scenes.

So, what happens is that an object is created. It gets an `id`, the `type` is set to `int` (integer number), and the `value` to 42. A name `age` is placed in the global namespace, pointing to that object. Therefore, whenever we are in the global namespace, after the execution of that line, we can retrieve that object by simply accessing it through its name: `age`.

If you were to move house, you would put all the knives, forks, and spoons in a box and label it cutlery. Can you see it's exactly the same concept? Here's a screenshot of how it may look like (you may have to tweak the settings to get to the same view):

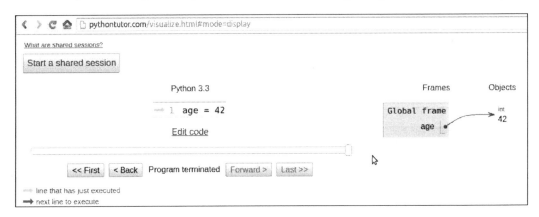

So, for the rest of this chapter, whenever you read something such as `name = some_value`, think of a name placed in the namespace that is tied to the scope in which the instruction was written, with a nice arrow pointing to an object that has an `id`, a `type`, and a `value`. There is a little bit more to say about this mechanism, but it's much easier to talk about it over an example, so we'll get back to this later.

Mutable or immutable? That is the question

A first fundamental distinction that Python makes on data is about whether or not the value of an object changes. If the value can change, the object is called **mutable**, while if the value cannot change, the object is called **immutable**.

It is very important that you understand the distinction between mutable and immutable because it affects the code you write, so here's a question:

```
>>> age = 42
>>> age
42
```

```
>>> age = 43    #A
>>> age
43
```

In the preceding code, on the line #A, have I changed the value of age? Well, no. But now it's 43 (I hear you say...). Yes, it's 43, but 42 was an integer number, of the type int, which is immutable. So, what happened is really that on the first line, age is a name that is set to point to an int object, whose value is 42. When we type age = 43, what happens is that another object is created, of the type int and value 43 (also, the id will be different), and the name age is set to point to it. So, we didn't change that 42 to 43. We actually just pointed age to a different location: the new int object whose value is 43. Let's see the same code also printing the IDs:

```
>>> age = 42
>>> id(age)
10456352
>>> age = 43
>>> id(age)
10456384
```

Notice that we print the IDs by calling the built-in id function. As you can see, they are different, as expected. Bear in mind that age points to one object at a time: 42 first, then 43. Never together.

Now, let's see the same example using a mutable object. For this example, let's just use a Person object, that has a property age:

```
>>> fab = Person(age=39)
>>> fab.age
39
>>> id(fab)
139632387887456
>>> fab.age = 29    # I wish!
>>> id(fab)
139632387887456    # still the same id
```

In this case, I set up an object fab whose type is Person (a custom class). On creation, the object is given the age of 39. I'm printing it, along with the object id, right afterwards. Notice that, even after I change age to be 29, the ID of fab stays the same (while the ID of age has changed, of course). Custom objects in Python are mutable (unless you code them not to be). Keep this concept in mind, it's very important. I'll remind you about it through the rest of the chapter.

Numbers

Let's start by exploring Python's built-in data types for numbers. Python was designed by a man with a master's degree in mathematics and computer science, so it's only logical that it has amazing support for numbers.

Numbers are immutable objects.

Integers

Python integers have unlimited range, subject only to the available virtual memory. This means that it doesn't really matter how big a number you want to store: as long as it can fit in your computer's memory, Python will take care of it. Integer numbers can be positive, negative, and 0 (zero). They support all the basic mathematical operations, as shown in the following example:

```
>>> a = 12
>>> b = 3
>>> a + b  # addition
15
>>> b - a  # subtraction
-9
>>> a // b  # integer division
4
>>> a / b  # true division
4.0
>>> a * b  # multiplication
36
>>> b ** a  # power operator
531441
>>> 2 ** 1024  # a very big number, Python handles it gracefully
179769313486231590772930519078902473361797697894230657273430081157
732675805500963132708477322407536021120113879871393357658789768814
416622492847430639474124377767893424865485276302219601246094119
45308295208500576883815068234246288147391311054082723716335051068
4586298239947245938479716304835356329624224137216
```

The preceding code should be easy to understand. Just notice one important thing: Python has two division operators, one performs the so-called **true division** (/), which returns the quotient of the operands, and the other one, the so-called **integer division** (//), which returns the *floored* quotient of the operands. See how that is different for positive and negative numbers:

```
>>> 7 / 4  # true division
1.75
>>> 7 // 4  # integer division, flooring returns 1
1
>>> -7 / 4  # true division again, result is opposite of previous
-1.75
>>> -7 // 4  # integer div., result not the opposite of previous
-2
```

This is an interesting example. If you were expecting a -1 on the last line, don't feel bad, it's just the way Python works. The result of an integer division in Python is always rounded towards minus infinity. If instead of flooring you want to truncate a number to an integer, you can use the built-in int function, like shown in the following example:

```
>>> int(1.75)
1
>>> int(-1.75)
-1
```

Notice that truncation is done towards 0.

There is also an operator to calculate the remainder of a division. It's called modulo operator, and it's represented by a percent (%):

```
>>> 10 % 3  # remainder of the division 10 // 3
1
>>> 10 % 4  # remainder of the division 10 // 4
2
```

Booleans

Boolean algebra is that subset of algebra in which the values of the variables are the truth values: true and false. In Python, `True` and `False` are two keywords that are used to represent truth values. Booleans are a subclass of integers, and behave respectively like 1 and 0. The equivalent of the `int` class for Booleans is the `bool` class, which returns either `True` or `False`. Every built-in Python object has a value in the Boolean context, which means they basically evaluate to either `True` or `False` when fed to the `bool` function. We'll see all about this in *Chapter 3, Iterating and Making Decisions*.

Boolean values can be combined in Boolean expressions using the logical operators and, or, and not. Again, we'll see them in full in the next chapter, so for now let's just see a simple example:

```
>>> int(True)  # True behaves like 1
1
>>> int(False)  # False behaves like 0
0
>>> bool(1)  # 1 evaluates to True in a boolean context
True
>>> bool(-42)  # and so does every non-zero number
True
>>> bool(0)  # 0 evaluates to False
False
>>> # quick peak at the operators (and, or, not)
>>> not True
False
>>> not False
True
>>> True and True
True
>>> False or True
True
```

You can see that `True` and `False` are subclasses of integers when you try to add them. Python upcasts them to integers and performs addition:

```
>>> 1 + True
2
>>> False + 42
```

42

```
>>> 7 - True
6
```

 Upcasting is a type conversion operation that goes from a subclass to its parent. In the example presented here, True and False, which belong to a class derived from the integer class, are converted back to integers when needed. This topic is about inheritance and will be explained in detail in *Chapter 6, Advanced Concepts – OOP, Decorators, and Iterators.*

Reals

Real numbers, or floating point numbers, are represented in Python according to the IEEE 754 double-precision binary floating-point format, which is stored in 64 bits of information divided into three sections: sign, exponent, and mantissa.

 Quench your thirst for knowledge about this format on Wikipedia: http://en.wikipedia.org/wiki/Double-precision_ floating-point_format

Usually programming languages give coders two different formats: single and double precision. The former taking up 32 bits of memory, and the latter 64. Python supports only the double format. Let's see a simple example:

```
>>> pi = 3.1415926536  # how many digits of PI can you remember?
>>> radius = 4.5
>>> area = pi * (radius ** 2)
>>> area
63.61725123519331
```

 In the calculation of the area, I wrapped the radius ** 2 within braces. Even though that wasn't necessary because the power operator has higher precedence than the multiplication one, I think the formula reads more easily like that.

The `sys.float_info` struct sequence holds information about how floating point numbers will behave on your system. This is what I see on my box:

```
>>> import sys
>>> sys.float_info
sys.float_info(max=1.7976931348623157e+308, max_exp=1024, max_10_exp=308,
min=2.2250738585072014e-308, min_exp=-1021, min_10_exp=-307, dig=15,
mant_dig=53, epsilon=2.220446049250313e-16, radix=2, rounds=1)
```

Let's make a few considerations here: we have 64 bits to represent float numbers. This means we can represent at most $2 ** 64 == 18,446,744,073,709,551,616$ numbers with that amount of bits. Take a look at the `max` and `epsilon` value for the float numbers, and you'll realize it's impossible to represent them all. There is just not enough space so they are approximated to the closest representable number. You probably think that only extremely big or extremely small numbers suffer from this issue. Well, think again:

```
>>> 3 * 0.1 - 0.3  # this should be 0!!!
5.551115123125783e-17
```

What does this tell you? It tells you that double precision numbers suffer from approximation issues even when it comes to simple numbers like 0.1 or 0.3. Why is this important? It can be a big problem if you're handling prices, or financial calculations, or any kind of data that needs not to be approximated. Don't worry, Python gives you the **Decimal** type, which doesn't suffer from these issues, we'll see them in a bit.

Complex numbers

Python gives you complex numbers support out of the box. If you don't know what complex numbers are, you can look them up on the Web. They are numbers that can be expressed in the form $a + ib$ where a and b are real numbers, and i (or j if you're an engineer) is the imaginary unit, that is, the square root of -1. a and b are called respectively the *real* and *imaginary* part of the number.

It's actually unlikely you'll be using them, unless you're coding something scientific. Let's see a small example:

```
>>> c = 3.14 + 2.73j
>>> c.real  # real part
3.14
>>> c.imag  # imaginary part
2.73
```

```
>>> c.conjugate()  # conjugate of A + Bj is A - Bj
(3.14-2.73j)
>>> c * 2  # multiplication is allowed
(6.28+5.46j)
>>> c ** 2  # power operation as well
(2.4067000000000007+17.1444j)
>>> d = 1 + 1j  # addition and subtraction as well
>>> c - d
(2.14+1.73j)
```

Fractions and decimals

Let's finish the tour of the number department with a look at fractions and decimals. Fractions hold a rational numerator and denominator in their lowest forms. Let's see a quick example:

```
>>> from fractions import Fraction
>>> Fraction(10, 6)  # mad hatter?
Fraction(5, 3)  # notice it's been reduced to lowest terms
>>> Fraction(1, 3) + Fraction(2, 3)  # 1/3 + 2/3 = 3/3 = 1/1
Fraction(1, 1)
>>> f = Fraction(10, 6)
>>> f.numerator
5
>>> f.denominator
3
```

Although they can be very useful at times, it's not that common to spot them in commercial software. Much easier instead, is to see decimal numbers being used in all those contexts where precision is everything, for example, scientific and financial calculations.

 It's important to remember that arbitrary precision decimal numbers come at a price in performance, of course. The amount of data to be stored for each number is far greater than it is for fractions or floats as well as the way they are handled, which requires the Python interpreter much more work behind the scenes. Another interesting thing to know is that you can get and set the precision by accessing `decimal.getcontext().prec`.

Let's see a quick example with `Decimal` numbers:

```
>>> from decimal import Decimal as D  # rename for brevity
>>> D(3.14)  # pi, from float, so approximation issues
Decimal('3.140000000000000124344978758017532527446746826171875')
>>> D('3.14')  # pi, from a string, so no approximation issues
Decimal('3.14')
>>> D(0.1) * D(3) - D(0.3)  # from float, we still have the issue
Decimal('2.775557561565156540423631668E-17')
>>> D('0.1') * D(3) - D('0.3')  # from string, all perfect
Decimal('0.0')
```

Notice that when we construct a `Decimal` number from a `float`, it takes on all the approximation issues the `float` may come from. On the other hand, when the `Decimal` has no approximation issues, for example, when we feed an `int` or a `string` representation to the constructor, then the calculation has no quirky behavior. When it comes to money, use decimals.

This concludes our introduction to built-in numeric types, let's now see sequences.

Immutable sequences

Let's start with immutable sequences: strings, tuples, and bytes.

Strings and bytes

Textual data in Python is handled with **str** objects, more commonly known as strings. They are immutable sequences of **unicode code points**. Unicode code points can represent a character, but can also have other meanings, such as formatting data for example. Python, unlike other languages, doesn't have a `char` type, so a single character is rendered simply by a string of length 1. Unicode is an excellent way to handle data, and should be used for the internals of any application. When it comes to store textual data though, or send it on the network, you may want to encode it, using an appropriate encoding for the medium you're using. String literals are written in Python using single, double or triple quotes (both single or double). If built with triple quotes, a string can span on multiple lines. An example will clarify the picture:

```
>>> # 4 ways to make a string
>>> str1 = 'This is a string. We built it with single quotes.'
>>> str2 = "This is also a string, but built with double quotes."
```

```
>>> str3 = '''This is built using triple quotes,
... so it can span multiple lines.'''
>>> str4 = """This too
... is a multiline one
... built with triple double-quotes."""
>>> str4   #A
'This too\nis a multiline one\nbuilt with triple double-quotes.'
>>> print(str4)   #B
This too
is a multiline one
built with triple double-quotes.
```

In #A and #B, we print str4, first implicitly, then explicitly using the print function. A nice exercise would be to find out why they are different. Are you up to the challenge? (hint, look up the str function)

Strings, like any sequence, have a length. You can get this by calling the len function:

```
>>> len(str1)
49
```

Encoding and decoding strings

Using the encode/decode methods, we can encode unicode strings and decode bytes objects. **Utf-8** is a variable length character encoding, capable of encoding all possible unicode code points. It is the dominant encoding for the Web (and not only). Notice also that by adding a literal b in front of a string declaration, we're creating a *bytes* object.

```
>>> s = "This is üɲícODe"  # unicode string: code points
>>> type(s)
<class 'str'>
>>> encoded_s = s.encode('utf-8')  # utf-8 encoded version of s
>>> encoded_s
b'This is \xc3\xbc\xc5\x8b\xc3\xadcODe'  # result: bytes object
>>> type(encoded_s)  # another way to verify it
<class 'bytes'>
>>> encoded_s.decode('utf-8')  # let's revert to the original
'This is üɲícODe'
>>> bytes_obj = b"A bytes object"  # a bytes object
>>> type(bytes_obj)
<class 'bytes'>
```

Indexing and slicing strings

When manipulating sequences, it's very common to have to access them at one precise position (indexing), or to get a subsequence out of them (slicing). When dealing with immutable sequences, both operations are read-only.

While indexing comes in one form, a zero-based access to any position within the sequence, slicing comes in different forms. When you get a slice of a sequence, you can specify the start and stop positions, and the step. They are separated with a colon (:) like this: my_sequence[start:stop:step]. All the arguments are optional, start is inclusive, stop is exclusive. It's much easier to show an example, rather than explain them further in words:

```
>>> s = "The trouble is you think you have time."
>>> s[0]  # indexing at position 0, which is the first char
'T'
>>> s[5]  # indexing at position 5, which is the sixth char
'r'
>>> s[:4]  # slicing, we specify only the stop position
'The '
>>> s[4:]  # slicing, we specify only the start position
'trouble is you think you have time.'
>>> s[2:14]  # slicing, both start and stop positions
'e trouble is'
>>> s[2:14:3]  # slicing, start, stop and step (every 3 chars)
'erb '
>>> s[:]  # quick way of making a copy
'The trouble is you think you have time.'
```

Of all the lines, the last one is probably the most interesting. If you don't specify a parameter, Python will fill in the default for you. In this case, start will be the start of the string, stop will be the end of the sting, and step will be the default 1. This is an easy and quick way of obtaining a copy of the string s (same value, but different object). Can you find a way to get the reversed copy of a string using slicing? (don't look it up, find it for yourself)

Tuples

The last immutable sequence type we're going to see is the tuple. A **tuple** is a sequence of arbitrary Python objects. In a tuple, items are separated by commas. They are used everywhere in Python, because they allow for patterns that are hard to reproduce in other languages. Sometimes tuples are used implicitly, for example to set up multiple variables on one line, or to allow a function to return multiple different objects (usually a function returns one object only, in many other languages), and even in the Python console, you can use tuples implicitly to print multiple elements with one single instruction. We'll see examples for all these cases:

```
>>> t = ()   # empty tuple
>>> type(t)
<class 'tuple'>
>>> one_element_tuple = (42, )   # you need the comma!
>>> three_elements_tuple = (1, 3, 5)
>>> a, b, c = 1, 2, 3   # tuple for multiple assignment
>>> a, b, c   # implicit tuple to print with one instruction
(1, 2, 3)
>>> 3 in three_elements_tuple   # membership test
True
```

Notice that the membership operator in can also be used with lists, strings, dictionaries, and in general with collection and sequence objects.

> Notice that to create a tuple with one item, we need to put that comma after the item. The reason is that without the comma that item is just itself wrapped in braces, kind of in a redundant mathematical expression. Notice also that on assignment, braces are optional so my_tuple = 1, 2, 3 is the same as my_tuple = (1, 2, 3).

One thing that tuple assignment allows us to do, is *one-line swaps*, with no need for a third temporary variable. Let's see first a more traditional way of doing it:

```
>>> a, b = 1, 2
>>> c = a   # we need three lines and a temporary var c
>>> a = b
>>> b = c
>>> a, b   # a and b have been swapped
(2, 1)
```

And now let's see how we would do it in Python:

```
>>> a, b = b, a  # this is the Pythonic way to do it
>>> a, b
(1, 2)
```

Take a look at the line that shows you the Pythonic way of swapping two values: do you remember what I wrote in *Chapter 1, Introduction and First Steps – Take a Deep Breath*. A Python program is typically one-fifth to one-third the size of equivalent Java or C++ code, and features like one-line swaps contribute to this. Python is elegant, where elegance in this context means also economy.

Because they are immutable, tuples can be used as keys for dictionaries (we'll see this shortly). The `dict` objects need keys to be immutable because if they could change, then the value they reference wouldn't be found any more (because the path to it depends on the key). If you are into data structures, you know how nice a feature this one is to have. To me, tuples are Python's built-in data that most closely represent a mathematical vector. This doesn't mean that this was the reason for which they were created though. Tuples usually contain an heterogeneous sequence of elements, while on the other hand lists are most of the times homogeneous. Moreover, tuples are normally accessed via unpacking or indexing, while lists are usually iterated over.

Mutable sequences

Mutable sequences differ from their immutable sisters in that they can be changed after creation. There are two mutable sequence types in Python: lists and byte arrays. I said before that the dictionary is the king of data structures in Python. I guess this makes the list its rightful queen.

Lists

Python lists are mutable sequences. They are very similar to tuples, but they don't have the restrictions due to immutability. Lists are commonly used to store collections of homogeneous objects, but there is nothing preventing you to store heterogeneous collections as well. Lists can be created in many different ways, let's see an example:

```
>>> []  # empty list
[]
>>> list()  # same as []
[]
>>> [1, 2, 3]  # as with tuples, items are comma separated
```

```
[1, 2, 3]
>>> [x + 5 for x in [2, 3, 4]]   # Python is magic
[7, 8, 9]
>>> list((1, 3, 5, 7, 9))   # list from a tuple
[1, 3, 5, 7, 9]
>>> list('hello')   # list from a string
['h', 'e', 'l', 'l', 'o']
```

In the previous example, I showed you how to create a list using different techniques. I would like you to take a good look at the line that says `Python is magic`, which I am not expecting you to fully understand at this point (unless you cheated and you're not a novice!). That is called a **list comprehension**, a very powerful functional feature of Python, which we'll see in detail in *Chapter 5, Saving Time and Memory*. I just wanted to make your mouth water at this point.

Creating lists is good, but the real fun comes when we use them, so let's see the main methods they gift us with:

```
>>> a = [1, 2, 1, 3]
>>> a.append(13)   # we can append anything at the end
>>> a
[1, 2, 1, 3, 13]
>>> a.count(1)   # how many `1` are there in the list?
2
>>> a.extend([5, 7])   # extend the list by another (or sequence)
>>> a
[1, 2, 1, 3, 13, 5, 7]
>>> a.index(13)   # position of `13` in the list (0-based indexing)
4
>>> a.insert(0, 17)   # insert `17` at position 0
>>> a
[17, 1, 2, 1, 3, 13, 5, 7]
>>> a.pop()   # pop (remove and return) last element
7
>>> a.pop(3)   # pop element at position 3
1
>>> a
[17, 1, 2, 3, 13, 5]
>>> a.remove(17)   # remove `17` from the list
>>> a
[1, 2, 3, 13, 5]
>>> a.reverse()   # reverse the order of the elements in the list
```

```
>>> a
[5, 13, 3, 2, 1]
>>> a.sort()  # sort the list
>>> a
[1, 2, 3, 5, 13]
>>> a.clear()  # remove all elements from the list
>>> a
[]
```

The preceding code gives you a roundup of list's main methods. I want to show you how powerful they are, using `extend` as an example. You can extend lists using any sequence type:

```
>>> a = list('hello')  # makes a list from a string
>>> a
['h', 'e', 'l', 'l', 'o']
>>> a.append(100)  # append 100, heterogeneous type
>>> a
['h', 'e', 'l', 'l', 'o', 100]
>>> a.extend((1, 2, 3))  # extend using tuple
>>> a
['h', 'e', 'l', 'l', 'o', 100, 1, 2, 3]
>>> a.extend('...')  # extend using string
>>> a
['h', 'e', 'l', 'l', 'o', 100, 1, 2, 3, '.', '.', '.']
```

Now, let's see what are the most common operations you can do with lists:

```
>>> a = [1, 3, 5, 7]
>>> min(a)  # minimum value in the list
1
>>> max(a)  # maximum value in the list
7
>>> sum(a)  # sum of all values in the list
16
>>> len(a)  # number of elements in the list
4
>>> b = [6, 7, 8]
>>> a + b  # `+` with list means concatenation
[1, 3, 5, 7, 6, 7, 8]
>>> a * 2  # `*` has also a special meaning
[1, 3, 5, 7, 1, 3, 5, 7]
```

The last two lines in the preceding code are quite interesting because they introduce us to a concept called **operator overloading**. In short, it means that operators such as +, -. *, %, and so on, may represent different operations according to the context they are used in. It doesn't make any sense to sum two lists, right? Therefore, the + sign is used to concatenate them. Hence, the * sign is used to concatenate the list to itself according to the right operand. Now, let's take a step further down the rabbit hole and see something a little more interesting. I want to show you how powerful the sort method can be and how easy it is in Python to achieve results that require a great deal of effort in other languages:

```
>>> from operator import itemgetter
>>> a = [(5, 3), (1, 3), (1, 2), (2, -1), (4, 9)]
>>> sorted(a)
[(1, 2), (1, 3), (2, -1), (4, 9), (5, 3)]
>>> sorted(a, key=itemgetter(0))
[(1, 3), (1, 2), (2, -1), (4, 9), (5, 3)]
>>> sorted(a, key=itemgetter(0, 1))
[(1, 2), (1, 3), (2, -1), (4, 9), (5, 3)]
>>> sorted(a, key=itemgetter(1))
[(2, -1), (1, 2), (5, 3), (1, 3), (4, 9)]
>>> sorted(a, key=itemgetter(1), reverse=True)
[(4, 9), (5, 3), (1, 3), (1, 2), (2, -1)]
```

The preceding code deserves a little explanation. First of all, a is a list of tuples. This means each element in a is a tuple (a *2-tuple*, to be picky). When we call sorted(some_list), we get a sorted version of some_list. In this case, the sorting on a 2-tuple works by sorting them on the first item in the tuple, and on the second when the first one is the same. You can see this behavior in the result of sorted(a), which yields [(1, 2), (1, 3), ...]. Python also gives us the ability to control on which element(s) of the tuple the sorting must be run against. Notice that when we instruct the sorted function to work on the first element of each tuple (by key=itemgetter(0)), the result is different: [(1, 3), (1, 2), ...]. The sorting is done only on the first element of each tuple (which is the one at position 0). If we want to replicate the default behavior of a simple sorted(a) call, we need to use key=itemgetter(0, 1), which tells Python to sort first on the elements at position 0 within the tuples, and then on those at position 1. Compare the results and you'll see they match.

For completeness, I included an example of sorting only on the elements at position 1, and the same but in reverse order. If you have ever seen sorting in Java, I expect you to be on your knees crying with joy at this very moment.

The Python sorting algorithm is very powerful, and it was written by Tim Peters (we've already seen this name, can you recall when?). It is aptly named **Timsort**, and it is a blend between **merge** and **insertion sort** and has better time performances than most other algorithms used for mainstream programming languages. Timsort is a stable sorting algorithm, which means that when multiple records have the same key, their original order is preserved. We've seen this in the result of sorted(a, key=itemgetter(0)) which has yielded [(1, 3), (1, 2), ...] in which the order of those two tuples has been preserved because they have the same value at position 0.

Byte arrays

To conclude our overview of mutable sequence types, let's spend a couple of minutes on the bytearray type. Basically, they represent the mutable version of bytes objects. They expose most of the usual methods of mutable sequences as well as most of the methods of the bytes type. Items are integers in the range [0, 256).

When it comes to intervals, I'm going to use the standard notation for open/closed ranges. A square bracket on one end means that the value is included, while a round brace means it's excluded. The granularity is usually inferred by the type of the edge elements so, for example, the interval [3, 7] means all integers between 3 and 7, inclusive. On the other hand, (3, 7) means all integers between 3 and 7 exclusive (hence 4, 5, and 6). Items in a bytearray type are integers between 0 and 256, 0 is included, 256 is not. One reason intervals are often expressed like this is to ease coding. If we break a range [a, b) into N consecutive ranges, we can easily represent the original one as a concatenation like this:

$$[a, k_1) + [k_1, k_2) + [k_2, k_3) + ... + [k_{N-1}, b)$$

The middle points (k_i) being excluded on one end, and included on the other end, allow for easy concatenation and splitting when intervals are handled in the code.

Let's see a quick example with the type bytearray:

```
>>> bytearray()  # empty bytearray object
bytearray(b'')
>>> bytearray(10)  # zero-filled instance with given length
bytearray(b'\x00\x00\x00\x00\x00\x00\x00\x00\x00\x00')
>>> bytearray(range(5))  # bytearray from iterable of integers
bytearray(b'\x00\x01\x02\x03\x04')
```

```
>>> name = bytearray(b'Lina')   # A - bytearray from bytes
>>> name.replace(b'L', b'l')
bytearray(b'lina')
>>> name.endswith(b'na')
True
>>> name.upper()
bytearray(b'LINA')
>>> name.count(b'L')
1
```

As you can see in the preceding code, there are a few ways to create a bytearray object. They can be useful in many situations, for example, when receiving data through a **socket**, they eliminate the need to concatenate data while polling, hence they prove very handy. On the line #A, I created the name bytearray from the string b'Lina' to show you how the bytearray object exposes methods from both sequences and strings, which is extremely handy. If you think about it, they can be considered as mutable strings.

Set types

Python also provides two set types, set and frozenset. The set type is mutable, while frozenset is immutable. They are unordered collections of immutable objects.

Hashability is a characteristic that allows an object to be used as a set member as well as a key for a dictionary, as we'll see very soon.

> An object is hashable if it has a hash value which never changes during its lifetime.

Objects that compare equally must have the same hash value. Sets are very commonly used to test for membership, so let's introduce the in operator in the following example:

```
>>> small_primes = set()   # empty set
>>> small_primes.add(2)   # adding one element at a time
>>> small_primes.add(3)
>>> small_primes.add(5)
>>> small_primes
{2, 3, 5}
```

```
>>> small_primes.add(1)   # Look what I've done, 1 is not a prime!
>>> small_primes
{1, 2, 3, 5}
>>> small_primes.remove(1)   # so let's remove it
>>> 3 in small_primes   # membership test
True
>>> 4 in small_primes
False
>>> 4 not in small_primes   # negated membership test
True
>>> small_primes.add(3)   # trying to add 3 again
>>> small_primes
{2, 3, 5}   # no change, duplication is not allowed
>>> bigger_primes = set([5, 7, 11, 13])   # faster creation
>>> small_primes | bigger_primes   # union operator `|`
{2, 3, 5, 7, 11, 13}
>>> small_primes & bigger_primes   # intersection operator `&`
{5}
>>> small_primes - bigger_primes   # difference operator `-`
{2, 3}
```

In the preceding code, you can see two different ways to create a set. One creates an empty set and then adds elements one at a time. The other creates the set using a list of numbers as argument to the constructor, which does all the work for us. Of course, you can create a set from a list or tuple (or any iterable) and then you can add and remove members from the set as you please.

Another way of creating a set is by simply using the curly braces notation, like this:

```
>>> small_primes = {2, 3, 5, 5, 3}
>>> small_primes
{2, 3, 5}
```

Notice I added some duplication to emphasize that the result set won't have any.

 We'll see iterable objects and iteration in the next chapter. For now, just know that iterable objects are objects you can iterate on in a direction.

Let's see an example about the immutable counterpart of the set type: `frozenset`.

```
>>> small_primes = frozenset([2, 3, 5, 7])
>>> bigger_primes = frozenset([5, 7, 11])
>>> small_primes.add(11)   # we cannot add to a frozenset
Traceback (most recent call last):
  File "<stdin>", line 1, in <module>
AttributeError: 'frozenset' object has no attribute 'add'
>>> small_primes.remove(2)   # neither we can remove
Traceback (most recent call last):
  File "<stdin>", line 1, in <module>
AttributeError: 'frozenset' object has no attribute 'remove'
>>> small_primes & bigger_primes   # intersect, union, etc. allowed
frozenset({5, 7})
```

As you can see, `frozenset` objects are quite limited in respect of their mutable counterpart. They still prove very effective for membership test, union, intersection and difference operations, and for performance reasons.

Mapping types – dictionaries

Of all the built-in Python data types, the dictionary is probably the most interesting one. It's the only standard mapping type, and it is the backbone of every Python object.

A dictionary maps keys to values. Keys need to be hashable objects, while values can be of any arbitrary type. Dictionaries are mutable objects.

There are quite a few different ways to create a dictionary, so let me give you a simple example of how to create a dictionary equal to {'A': 1, 'Z': -1} in five different ways:

```
>>> a = dict(A=1, Z=-1)
>>> b = {'A': 1, 'Z': -1}
>>> c = dict(zip(['A', 'Z'], [1, -1]))
>>> d = dict([('A', 1), ('Z', -1)])
>>> e = dict({'Z': -1, 'A': 1})
>>> a == b == c == d == e   # are they all the same?
True   # indeed!
```

Have you noticed those double equals? Assignment is done with one equal, while to check whether an object is the same as another one (or 5 in one go, in this case), we use double equals. There is also another way to compare objects, which involves the **is** operator, and checks whether the two objects are the same (if they have the same ID, not just the value), but unless you have a good reason to use it, you should use the double equal instead. In the preceding code, I also used one nice function: `zip`. It is named after the real-life zip, which glues together two things taking one element from each at a time. Let me show you an example:

```
>>> list(zip(['h', 'e', 'l', 'l', 'o'], [1, 2, 3, 4, 5]))
[('h', 1), ('e', 2), ('l', 3), ('l', 4), ('o', 5)]
>>> list(zip('hello', range(1, 6)))  # equivalent, more Pythonic
[('h', 1), ('e', 2), ('l', 3), ('l', 4), ('o', 5)]
```

In the preceding example, I have created the same list in two different ways, one more explicit, and the other a little bit more Pythonic. Forget for a moment that I had to wrap the `list` constructor around the `zip` call (the reason is because `zip` returns an iterator, not a `list`), and concentrate on the result. See how `zip` has coupled the first elements of its two arguments together, then the second ones, then the third ones, and so on and so forth? Take a look at your pants (or at your purse if you're a lady) and you'll see the same behavior in your actual zip. But let's go back to dictionaries and see how many wonderful methods they expose for allowing us to manipulate them as we want. Let's start with the basic operations:

```
>>> d = {}
>>> d['a'] = 1  # let's set a couple of (key, value) pairs
>>> d['b'] = 2
>>> len(d)  # how many pairs?
2
>>> d['a']  # what is the value of 'a'?
1
>>> d  # how does `d` look now?
{'a': 1, 'b': 2}
>>> del d['a']  # let's remove `a`
>>> d
{'b': 2}
>>> d['c'] = 3  # let's add 'c': 3
>>> 'c' in d  # membership is checked against the keys
True
>>> 3 in d  # not the values
```

```
False
>>> 'e' in d
False
>>> d.clear()  # let's clean everything from this dictionary
>>> d
{}
```

Notice how accessing keys of a dictionary, regardless of the type of operation we're performing, is done through square brackets. Do you remember strings, list, and tuples? We were accessing elements at some position through square brackets as well. Yet another example of Python's consistency.

Let's see now three special objects called dictionary views: keys, values, and items. These objects provide a dynamic view of the dictionary entries and they change when the dictionary changes. keys() returns all the keys in the dictionary, values() returns all the values in the dictionary, and items() returns all the *(key, value)* pairs in the dictionary.

> It's very important to know that, even if a dictionary is not intrinsically ordered, according to the Python documentation: "*Keys and values are iterated over in an arbitrary order which is non-random, varies across Python implementations, and depends on the dictionary's history of insertions and deletions. If keys, values and items views are iterated over with no intervening modifications to the dictionary, the order of items will directly correspond.*"

Enough with this chatter, let's put all this down into code:

```
>>> d = dict(zip('hello', range(5)))
>>> d
{'e': 1, 'h': 0, 'o': 4, 'l': 3}
>>> d.keys()
dict_keys(['e', 'h', 'o', 'l'])
>>> d.values()
dict_values([1, 0, 4, 3])
>>> d.items()
dict_items([('e', 1), ('h', 0), ('o', 4), ('l', 3)])
>>> 3 in d.values()
True
>>> ('o', 4) in d.items()
True
```

A few things to notice in the preceding code. First, notice how we're creating a dictionary by iterating over the zipped version of the string `'hello'` and the list `[0, 1, 2, 3, 4]`. The string `'hello'` has two `'l'` characters inside, and they are paired up with the values 2 and 3 by the zip function. Notice how in the dictionary, the second occurrence of the `'l'` key (the one with value 3), overwrites the first one (the one with value 2). Another thing to notice is that when asking for any view, the original order is lost, but is consistent within the views, as expected. Notice also that you may have different results when you try this code on your machine. Python doesn't guarantee that, it only guarantees the consistency of the order in which the views are presented.

We'll see how these views are fundamental tools when we talk about iterating over collections. Let's take a look now at some other methods exposed by Python's dictionaries, there's plenty of them and they are very useful:

```
>>> d
{'e': 1, 'h': 0, 'o': 4, 'l': 3}
>>> d.popitem()  # removes a random item
('e', 1)
>>> d
{'h': 0, 'o': 4, 'l': 3}
>>> d.pop('l')  # remove item with key `l`
3
>>> d.pop('not-a-key')  # remove a key not in dictionary: KeyError
Traceback (most recent call last):
  File "<stdin>", line 1, in <module>
KeyError: 'not-a-key'
>>> d.pop('not-a-key', 'default-value')  # with a default value?
'default-value'  # we get the default value
>>> d.update({'another': 'value'})  # we can update dict this way
>>> d.update(a=13)  # or this way (like a function call)
>>> d
{'a': 13, 'another': 'value', 'h': 0, 'o': 4}
>>> d.get('a')  # same as d['a'] but if key is missing no KeyError
13
>>> d.get('a', 177)  # default value used if key is missing
13
>>> d.get('b', 177)  # like in this case
177
>>> d.get('b')  # key is not there, so None is returned
```

All these methods are quite simple to understand, but it's worth talking about that None, for a moment. Every function in Python returns None, unless the return statement is explicitly used, but we'll see this when we explore functions. None is frequently used to represent the absence of a value, as when default arguments are not passed to a function. Some inexperienced coders sometimes write code that returns either False or None. Both False and None evaluate to False so it may seem there is not much difference between them. But actually, I would argue there is quite an important difference: False means that we have information, and the information we have is False. None means *no information*. And no information is very different from an information, which is False. In layman's terms, if you ask your mechanic "is my car ready?" there is a big difference between the answer "No, it's not" (*False*) and "I have no idea" (*None*).

One last method I really like of dictionaries is setdefault. It behaves like get, but also sets the key with the given value if it is not there. Let's see and example:

```
>>> d = {}
>>> d.setdefault('a', 1)  # 'a' is missing, we get default value
1
>>> d
{'a': 1}  # also, the key/value pair ('a', 1) has now been added
>>> d.setdefault('a', 5)  # let's try to override the value
1
>>> d
{'a': 1}  # didn't work, as expected
```

So, we're now at the end of this tour. Test your knowledge about dictionaries trying to foresee how d looks like after this line.

```
>>> d = {}
>>> d.setdefault('a', {}).setdefault('b', []).append(1)
```

It's not that complicated, but don't worry if you don't get it immediately. I just wanted to spur you to experiment with dictionaries.

This concludes our tour of built-in data types. Before I make some considerations about what we've seen in this chapter, I want to briefly take a peek at the collections module.

The collections module

When Python general purpose built-in containers (`tuple`, `list`, `set`, and `dict`) aren't enough, we can find specialized container data types in the `collections` module. They are:

Data type	Description
`namedtuple()`	A factory function for creating tuple subclasses with named fields
`deque`	A `list`-like container with fast appends and pops on either end
`ChainMap`	A `dict`-like class for creating a single view of multiple mappings
`Counter`	A `dict` subclass for counting hashable objects
`OrderedDict`	A `dict` subclass that remembers the order entries were added
`defaultdict`	A `dict` subclass that calls a factory function to supply missing values
`UserDict`	A wrapper around dictionary objects for easier dict subclassing
`UserList`	A wrapper around list objects for easier list subclassing
`UserString`	A wrapper around string objects for easier string subclassing

We don't have the room to cover all of them, but you can find plenty of examples in the official documentation, so here I'll just give a small example to show you `namedtuple`, `defaultdict`, and `ChainMap`.

Named tuples

A `namedtuple` is a `tuple`-like object that has fields accessible by attribute lookup as well as being indexable and iterable (it's actually a subclass of `tuple`). This is sort of a compromise between a full-fledged object and a tuple, and it can be useful in those cases where you don't need the full power of a custom object, but you want your code to be more readable by avoiding weird indexing. Another use case is when there is a chance that items in the tuple need to change their position after refactoring, forcing the coder to refactor also all the logic involved, which can be very tricky. As usual, an example is better than a thousand words (or was it a picture?). Say we are handling data about the left and right eye of a patient. We save one value for the left eye (position 0) and one for the right eye (position 1) in a regular tuple. Here's how that might be:

```
>>> vision = (9.5, 8.8)
>>> vision
(9.5, 8.8)
>>> vision[0]  # left eye (implicit positional reference)
```

```
9.5
>>> vision[1]   # right eye (implicit positional reference)
8.8
```

Now let's pretend we handle `vision` object all the time, and at some point the designer decides to enhance them by adding information for the combined vision, so that a `vision` object stores data in this format: *(left eye, combined, right eye)*.

Do you see the trouble we're in now? We may have a lot of code that depends on `vision[0]` being the left eye information (which still is) and `vision[1]` being the right eye information (which is no longer the case). We have to refactor our code wherever we handle these objects, changing `vision[1]` to `vision[2]`, and it can be painful. We could have probably approached this a bit better from the beginning, by using a `namedtuple`. Let me show you what I mean:

```
>>> from collections import namedtuple
>>> Vision = namedtuple('Vision', ['left', 'right'])
>>> vision = Vision(9.5, 8.8)
>>> vision[0]
9.5
>>> vision.left   # same as vision[0], but explicit
9.5
>>> vision.right   # same as vision[1], but explicit
8.8
```

If within our code we refer to left and right eye using `vision.left` and `vision.right`, all we need to do to fix the new design issue is to change our factory and the way we create instances. The rest of the code won't need to change.

```
>>> Vision = namedtuple('Vision', ['left', 'combined', 'right'])
>>> vision = Vision(9.5, 9.2, 8.8)
>>> vision.left   # still perfect
9.5
>>> vision.right   # still perfect (though now is vision[2])
8.8
>>> vision.combined   # the new vision[1]
9.2
```

You can see how convenient it is to refer to those values by name rather than by position. After all, a wise man once wrote "*Explicit is better than implicit*" (can you recall where? Think *zen* if you don't...). This example may be a little extreme, of course it's not likely that our code designer will go for a change like this, but you'd be amazed to see how frequently issues similar to this one happen in a professional environment, and how painful it is to refactor them.

Defaultdict

The `defaultdict` data type is one of my favorites. It allows you to avoid checking if a key is in a dictionary by simply inserting it for you on your first access attempt, with a default value whose type you pass on creation. In some cases, this tool can be very handy and shorten your code a little. Let's see a quick example: say we are updating the value of `age`, by adding one year. If `age` is not there, we assume it was `0` and we update it to `1`.

```
>>> d = {}
>>> d['age'] = d.get('age', 0) + 1  # age not there, we get 0 + 1
>>> d
{'age': 1}
>>> d = {'age': 39}
>>> d['age'] = d.get('age', 0) + 1  # d is there, we get 40
>>> d
{'age': 40}
```

Now let's see how it would work with a `defaultdict` data type. The second line is actually the short version of a 4-lines long `if` clause that we would have to write if dictionaries didn't have the `get` method. We'll see all about `if` clauses in *Chapter 3, Iterating and Making Decisions*.

```
>>> from collections import defaultdict
>>> dd = defaultdict(int)  # int is the default type (0 the value)
>>> dd['age'] += 1  # short for dd['age'] = dd['age'] + 1
>>> dd
defaultdict(<class 'int'>, {'age': 1})  # 1, as expected
>>> dd['age'] = 39
>>> dd['age'] += 1
>>> dd
defaultdict(<class 'int'>, {'age': 40})  # 40, as expected
```

Notice how we just need to instruct the `defaultdict` factory that we want an `int` number to be used in case the key is missing (we'll get `0`, which is the default for the `int` type). Also, notice that even though in this example there is no gain on the number of lines, there is definitely a gain in readability, which is very important. You can also use a different technique to instantiate a `defaultdict` data type, which involves creating a factory object. For digging deeper, please refer to the official documentation.

ChainMap

The `ChainMap` is an extremely nice data type which was introduced in Python 3.3. It behaves like a normal dictionary but according to the Python documentation: *is provided for quickly linking a number of mappings so they can be treated as a single unit.* This is usually much faster than creating one dictionary and running multiple update calls on it. `ChainMap` can be used to simulate nested scopes and is useful in templating. The underlying mappings are stored in a list. That list is public and can be accessed or updated using the maps attribute. Lookups search the underlying mappings successively until a key is found. In contrast, writes, updates, and deletions only operate on the first mapping.

A very common use case is providing defaults, so let's see an example:

```
>>> from collections import ChainMap
>>> default_connection = {'host': 'localhost', 'port': 4567}
>>> connection = {'port': 5678}
>>> conn = ChainMap(connection, default_connection) # map creation
>>> conn['port']  # port is found in the first dictionary
5678
>>> conn['host']  # host is fetched from the second dictionary
'localhost'
>>> conn.maps  # we can see the mapping objects
[{'port': 5678}, {'host': 'localhost', 'port': 4567}]
>>> conn['host'] = 'packtpub.com'  # let's add host
>>> conn.maps
[{'host': 'packtpub.com', 'port': 5678},
 {'host': 'localhost', 'port': 4567}]
>>> del conn['port']  # let's remove the port information
>>> conn.maps
[{'host': 'packtpub.com'},
 {'host': 'localhost', 'port': 4567}]
>>> conn['port']  # now port is fetched from the second dictionary
```

```
4567
>>> dict(conn)   # easy to merge and convert to regular dictionary
{'host': 'packtpub.com', 'port': 4567}
```

I just love how Python makes your life easy. You work on a `ChainMap` object, configure the first mapping as you want, and when you need a complete dictionary with all the defaults as well as the customized items, you just feed the `ChainMap` object to a `dict` constructor. If you have never coded in other languages, such as Java or C++, you probably won't be able to fully appreciate how precious this is, how Python makes your life so much easier. I do, I feel claustrophobic every time I have to code in some other language.

Final considerations

That's it. Now you have seen a very good portion of the data structures that you will use in Python. I encourage you to take a dive into the Python documentation and experiment further with each and every data type we've seen in this chapter. It's worth it, believe me. Everything you'll write will be about handling data, so make sure your knowledge about it is rock solid.

Before we leap into the next chapter, I'd like to make some final considerations about different aspects that to my mind are important and not to be neglected.

Small values caching

When we discussed objects at the beginning of this chapter, we saw that when we assigned a name to an object, Python creates the object, sets its value, and then points the name to it. We can assign different names to the same value and we expect different objects to be created, like this:

```
>>> a = 1000000
>>> b = 1000000
>>> id(a) == id(b)
False
```

In the preceding example, `a` and `b` are assigned to two `int` objects, which have the same value but they are not the same object, as you can see, their `id` is not the same. So let's do it again:

```
>>> a = 5
>>> b = 5
>>> id(a) == id(b)
True
```

Oh oh! Is Python broken? Why are the two objects the same now? We didn't do `a = b = 5`, we set them up separately. Well, the answer is performances. Python caches short strings and small numbers, to avoid having many copies of them clogging up the system memory. Everything is handled properly under the hood so you don't need to worry a bit, but make sure that you remember this behavior should your code ever need to fiddle with IDs.

How to choose data structures

As we've seen, Python provides you with several built-in data types and sometimes, if you're not that experienced, choosing the one that serves you best can be tricky, especially when it comes to collections. For example, say you have many dictionaries to store, each of which represents a customer. Within each customer dictionary there's an `'id': 'code'` unique identification code. In what kind of collection would you place them? Well, unless I know more about these customers, it's very hard to answer. What kind of access will I need? What sort of operations will I have to perform on each of them, and how many times? Will the collection change over time? Will I need to modify the customer dictionaries in any way? What is going to be the most frequent operation I will have to perform on the collection?

If you can answer the preceding questions, then you will know what to choose. If the collection never shrinks or grows (in other words, it won't need to add/delete any customer object after creation) or shuffles, then tuples are a possible choice. Otherwise lists are a good candidate. Every customer dictionary has a unique identifier though, so even a dictionary could work. Let me draft these options for you:

```
# example customer objects
customer1 = {'id': 'abc123', 'full_name': 'Master Yoda'}
customer2 = {'id': 'def456', 'full_name': 'Obi-Wan Kenobi'}
customer3 = {'id': 'ghi789', 'full_name': 'Anakin Skywalker'}
# collect them in a tuple
customers = (customer1, customer2, customer3)
# or collect them in a list
customers = [customer1, customer2, customer3]
# or maybe within a dictionary, they have a unique id after all
customers = {
    'abc123': customer1,
    'def456': customer2,
    'ghi789': customer3,
}
```

Some customers we have there, right? I probably wouldn't go with the tuple option, unless I wanted to highlight that the collection is not going to change. I'd say usually a list is better, it allows for more flexibility.

Another factor to keep in mind is that tuples and lists are ordered collections, while if you use a dictionary or a set you lose the ordering, so you need to know if ordering is important in your application.

What about performances? For example in a list, operations such as insertion and membership can take *O(n)*, while they are *O(1)* for a dictionary. It's not always possible to use dictionaries though, if we don't have the guarantee that we can uniquely identify each item of the collection by means of one of its properties, and that the property in question is hashable (so it can be a key in `dict`).

> If you're wondering what *O(n)* and *O(1)* mean, please Google "*big O notation*" and get a gist of it from anywhere. In this context, let's just say that if performing an operation *Op* on a data structure takes *O(f(n))*, it would mean that *Op* takes at most a time $t \leq c \cdot f(n)$ to complete, where *c* is some positive constant, *n* is the size of the input, and *f* is some function. So, think of *O(...)* as an upper bound for the running time of an operation (it can be used also to size other measurable quantities, of course).

Another way of understanding if you have chosen the right data structure is by looking at the code you have to write in order to manipulate it. If everything comes easily and flows naturally, then you probably have chosen correctly, but if you find yourself thinking your code is getting unnecessarily complicated, then you probably should try and decide whether you need to reconsider your choices. It's quite hard to give advice without a practical case though, so when you choose a data structure for your data, try to keep ease of use and performance in mind and give precedence to what matters most in the context you are.

About indexing and slicing

At the beginning of this chapter, we saw slicing applied on strings. Slicing in general applies to a sequence, so tuples, lists, strings, etc. With lists, slicing can also be used for assignment. I've almost never seen this used in professional code, but still, you know you can. Could you slice dictionaries or sets? I hear you scream "*Of course not! They are not ordered!*". Excellent, I see we're on the same page here, so let's talk about indexing.

There is one characteristic about Python indexing I haven't mentioned before. I'll show you by example. How do you address the last element of a collection? Let's see:

```
>>> a = list(range(10))  # `a` has 10 elements. Last one is 9.
>>> a
[0, 1, 2, 3, 4, 5, 6, 7, 8, 9]
>>> len(a)  # its length is 10 elements
10
>>> a[len(a) - 1]  # position of last one is len(a) - 1
9
>>> a[-1]  # but we don't need len(a)! Python rocks!
9
>>> a[-2]  # equivalent to len(a) - 2
8
>>> a[-3]  # equivalent to len(a) - 3
7
```

If the list a has 10 elements, because of the *0-index* positioning system of Python, the first one is at position 0 and the last one is at position 9. In the preceding example, the elements are conveniently placed in a position equal to their value: 0 is at position 0, 1 at position 1, and so on.

So, in order to fetch the last element, we need to know the length of the whole list (or tuple, or string, and so on) and then subtract 1. Hence: len(a) - 1. This is so common an operation that Python provides you with a way to retrieve elements using **negative indexing**. This proves very useful when you do some serious data manipulation. Here's a nice diagram about how indexing works on the string "HelloThere":

Positive Indexing									
0	1	2	3	4	5	6	7	8	9
H	e	l	l	o	T	h	e	r	e
-10	-9	-8	-7	-6	-5	-4	-3	-2	-1
Negative Indexing									

Trying to address indexes greater than 9 or smaller than -10 will raise an IndexError, as expected.

About the names

You may have noticed that, in order to keep the example as short as possible, I have called many objects using simple letters, like a, b, c, d, and so on. This is perfectly ok when you debug on the console or when you show that a + b == 7, but it's bad practice when it comes to professional coding (or any type of coding, for all that matter). I hope you will indulge me if I sometimes do it, the reason is to present the code in a more compact way.

In a real environment though, when you choose names for your data, you should choose them carefully and they should reflect what the data is about. So, if you have a collection of Customer objects, customers is a perfectly good name for it. Would customers_list, customers_tuple, or customers_collection work as well? Think about it for a second. Is it good to tie the name of the collection to the data type? I don't think so, at least in most cases. So I'd say if you have an excellent reason to do so go ahead, otherwise don't. The reason is, once that customers_tuple starts being used in different places of your code, and you realize you actually want to use a list instead of a tuple, you're up for some fun refactoring (also known as **wasted time**). Names for data should be nouns, and names for functions should be verbs. Names should be as expressive as possible. Python is actually a very good example when it comes to names. Most of the time you can just guess what a function is called if you know what it does. Crazy, huh?

Chapter 2, Meaningful Names of *Clean Code, Robert C. Martin, Prentice Hall* is entirely dedicated to names. It's an amazing book that helped me improve my coding style in many different ways, a must read if you want to take your coding to the next level.

Summary

In this chapter, we've explored the built-in data types of Python. We've seen how many they are and how much can be achieved by just using them in different combinations.

We've seen number types, sequences, sets, mappings, collections, we've seen that everything is an object, we've learned the difference between mutable and immutable, and we've also learned about slicing and indexing (and, proudly, negative indexing as well).

We've presented simple examples, but there's much more that you can learn about this subject, so stick your nose into the official documentation and explore.

Most of all, I encourage you to try out all the exercises by yourself, get your fingers using that code, build some muscle memory, and experiment, experiment, experiment. Learn what happens when you divide by zero, when you combine different number types into a single expression, when you manage strings. Play with all data types. Exercise them, break them, discover all their methods, enjoy them and learn them well, damn well.

If your foundation is not rock solid, how good can your code be? And data is the foundation for everything. Data shapes what dances around it.

The more you progress with the book, the more it's likely that you will find some discrepancies or maybe a small typo here and there in my code (or yours). You will get an error message, something will break. That's wonderful! When you code, things break all the time, you debug and fix all the time, so consider errors as useful exercises to learn something new about the language you're using, and not as failures or problems. Errors will keep coming up until your very last line of code, that's for sure, so you may as well start making your peace with them now.

The next chapter is about iterating and making decisions. We'll see how to actually put those collections in use, and take decisions based on the data we're presented with. We'll start to go a little faster now that your knowledge is building up, so make sure you're comfortable with the contents of this chapter before you move to the next one. Once more, have fun, explore, break things. It's a very good way to learn.

3
Iterating and Making Decisions

"Insanity: doing the same thing over and over again and expecting different results."

- Albert Einstein

In the previous chapter, we've seen Python built-in data types. Now that you're familiar with data in its many forms and shapes, it's time to start looking at how a program can use it.

According to Wikipedia:

In computer science, control flow (or alternatively, flow of control) refers to the specification of the order in which the individual statements, instructions or function calls of an imperative program are executed or evaluated.

In order to control the flow of a program, we have two main weapons: **conditional programming** (also known as **branching**) and **looping**. We can use them in many different combinations and variations, but in this chapter, instead of going through all possible various forms of those two constructs in a "documentation" fashion, I'd rather give you the basics and then I'll write a couple of small scripts with you. In the first one, we'll see how to create a rudimentary prime number generator, while in the second one, we'll see how to apply discounts to customers based on coupons. This way you should get a better feeling about how conditional programming and looping can be used.

Conditional programming

Conditional programming, or branching, is something you do every day, every moment. It's about evaluating conditions: *if the light is green, then I can cross, if it's raining, then I'm taking the umbrella*, and *if I'm late for work, then I'll call my manager*.

The main tool is the `if` statement, which comes in different forms and colors, but basically what it does is evaluate an expression and, based on the result, choose which part of the code to execute. As usual, let's see an example:

conditional.1.py

```
late = True
if late:
    print('I need to call my manager!')
```

This is possibly the simplest example: when fed to the `if` statement, `late` acts as a conditional expression, which is evaluated in a Boolean context (exactly like if we were calling `bool(late)`). If the result of the evaluation is `True`, then we enter the body of code immediately after the `if` statement. Notice that the `print` instruction is indented: this means it belongs to a scope defined by the `if` clause. Execution of this code yields:

```
$ python conditional.1.py
I need to call my manager!
```

Since `late` is `True`, the `print` statement was executed. Let's expand on this example:

conditional.2.py

```
late = False
if late:
    print('I need to call my manager!')  #1
else:
    print('no need to call my manager...')  #2
```

This time I set `late = False`, so when I execute the code, the result is different:

```
$ python conditional.2.py
no need to call my manager...
```

Depending on the result of evaluating the `late` expression, we can either enter block #1 or block #2, *but not both*. Block #1 is executed when `late` evaluates to `True`, while block #2 is executed when `late` evaluates to `False`. Try assigning `False`/`True` values to the `late` name, and see how the output for this code changes accordingly.

The preceding example also introduces the `else` clause, which becomes very handy when we want to provide an alternative set of instructions to be executed when an expression evaluates to `False` within an `if` clause. The else clause is optional, as it's evident by comparing the preceding two examples.

A specialized else: elif

Sometimes all you need is to do something if a condition is met (simple `if` clause). Other times you need to provide an alternative, in case the condition is `False` (`if`/`else` clause), but there are situations where you may have more than two paths to choose from, so, since calling the manager (or not calling them) is kind of a binary type of example (either you call or you don't), let's change the type of example and keep expanding. This time we decide tax percentages. If my income is less then 10k, I won't pay any taxes. If it is between 10k and 30k, I'll pay 20% taxes. If it is between 30k and 100k, I'll pay 35% taxes, and over 100k, I'll (gladly) pay 45% taxes. Let's put this all down into beautiful Python code:

taxes.py

```
income = 15000
if income < 10000:
    tax_coefficient = 0.0   #1
elif income < 30000:
    tax_coefficient = 0.2   #2
elif income < 100000:
    tax_coefficient = 0.35  #3
else:
    tax_coefficient = 0.45  #4

print('I will pay:', income * tax_coefficient, 'in taxes')
```

Executing the preceding code yields:

```
$ python taxes.py
I will pay: 3000.0 in taxes
```

Let's go through the example line by line: we start by setting up the income value. In the example, my income is 15k. We enter the `if` clause. Notice that this time we also introduced the `elif` clause, which is a contraction for `else-if`, and it's different from a bare `else` clause in that it also has its own condition. So, the `if` expression `income < 10000`, evaluates to `False`, therefore block #1 is not executed. The control passes to the next condition evaluator: `elif income < 30000`. This one evaluates to `True`, therefore block #2 is executed, and because of this, Python then resumes execution after the whole `if/elif/elif/else` clause (which we can just call `if` clause from now on). There is only one instruction after the `if` clause, the `print` call, which tells us I will pay 3k in taxes this year (*15k * 20%*). Notice that the order is mandatory: `if` comes first, then (optionally) as many `elif` as you need, and then (optionally) an `else` clause.

Interesting, right? No matter how many lines of code you may have within each block, when one of the conditions evaluates to `True`, the associated block is executed and then execution resumes after the whole clause. If none of the conditions evaluates to `True` (for example, `income = 200000`), then the body of the `else` clause would be executed (block #4). This example expands our understanding of the behavior of the `else` clause. Its block of code is executed when none of the preceding `if/elif/.../elif` expressions has evaluated to `True`.

Try to modify the value of `income` until you can comfortably execute all blocks at your will (one per execution, of course). And then try the **boundaries**. This is crucial, whenever you have conditions expressed as **equalities** or **inequalities** (`==`, `!=`, `<`, `>`, `<=`, `>=`), those numbers represent boundaries. It is essential to test boundaries thoroughly. Should I allow you to drive at 18 or 17? Am I checking your age with `age < 18`, or `age <= 18`? You can't imagine how many times I had to fix subtle bugs that stemmed from using the wrong operator, so go ahead and experiment with the preceding code. Change some `<` to `<=` and set income to be one of the boundary values (10k, 30k, 100k) as well as any value in between. See how the result changes, get a good understanding of it before proceeding.

Before we move to the next topic, let's see another example that shows us how to nest `if` clauses. Say your program encounters an error. If the alert system is the console, we print the error. If the alert system is an e-mail, we send it according to the severity of the error. If the alert system is anything other than console or e-mail, we don't know what to do, therefore we do nothing. Let's put this into code:

`errorsalert.py`

```
alert_system = 'console'  # other value can be 'email'
error_severity = 'critical'  # other values: 'medium' or 'low'
error_message = 'OMG! Something terrible happened!'
```

```
if alert_system == 'console':
    print(error_message)   #1
elif alert_system == 'email':
    if error_severity == 'critical':
        send_email('admin@example.com', error_message)   #2
    elif error_severity == 'medium':
        send_email('support.1@example.com', error_message)   #3
    else:
        send_email('support.2@example.com', error_message)   #4
```

The preceding example is quite interesting, in its silliness. It shows us two nested `if` clauses (**outer** and **inner**). It also shows us the outer `if` clause doesn't have any `else`, while the inner one does. Notice how indentation is what allows us to nest one clause within another one.

If `alert_system == 'console'`, body #1 is executed, and nothing else happens. On the other hand, if `alert_system == 'email'`, then we enter into another `if` clause, which we called inner. In the inner `if` clause, according to `error_severity`, we send an e-mail to either an admin, first-level support, or second-level support (blocks #2, #3, and #4). The `send_email` function is not defined in this example, therefore trying to run it would give you an error. In the source code of the book, which you can download from the website, I included a trick to redirect that call to a regular `print` function, just so you can experiment on the console without actually sending an e-mail. Try changing the values and see how it all works.

The ternary operator

One last thing I would like to show you before moving on to the next subject, is the **ternary operator** or, in layman's terms, the short version of an `if`/`else` clause. When the value of a name is to be assigned according to some condition, sometimes it's easier and more readable to use the ternary operator instead of a proper `if` clause. In the following example, the two code blocks do exactly the same thing:

ternary.py

```
order_total = 247   # GBP

# classic if/else form
if order_total > 100:
    discount = 25   # GBP
else:
    discount = 0   # GBP
print(order_total, discount)
```

```
# ternary operator
discount = 25 if order_total > 100 else 0
print(order_total, discount)
```

For simple cases like this, I find it very nice to be able to express that logic in one line instead of four. Remember, as a coder, you spend much more time reading code then writing it, so Python conciseness is invaluable.

Are you clear on how the ternary operator works? Basically is `name = something if condition else something-else`. So `name` is assigned `something` if `condition` evaluates to `True`, and `something-else` if `condition` evaluates to `False`.

Now that you know everything about controlling the path of the code, let's move on to the next subject: looping.

Looping

If you have any experience with looping in other programming languages, you will find Python's way of looping a bit different. First of all, what is looping? **Looping** means being able to repeat the execution of a code block more than once, according to the loop parameters we're given. There are different looping constructs, which serve different purposes, and Python has distilled all of them down to just two, which you can use to achieve everything you need. These are the **for** and **while** statements.

While it's definitely possible to do everything you need using either of them, they serve different purposes and therefore they're usually used in different contexts. We'll explore this difference thoroughly through this chapter.

The for loop

The `for` loop is used when looping over a sequence, like a list, tuple, or a collection of objects. Let's start with a simple example that is more like C++ style, and then let's gradually see how to achieve the same results in Python (you'll love Python's syntax).

simple.for.py

```
for number in [0, 1, 2, 3, 4]:
    print(number)
```

This simple snippet of code, when executed, prints all numbers from 0 to 4. The `for` loop is fed the list `[0, 1, 2, 3, 4]` and at each iteration, `number` is given a value from the sequence (which is iterated sequentially, in order), then the body of the loop is executed (the print line). `number` changes at every iteration, according to which value is coming next from the sequence. When the sequence is exhausted, the `for` loop terminates, and the execution of the code resumes normally with the code after the loop.

Iterating over a range

Sometimes we need to iterate over a range of numbers, and it would be quite unpleasant to have to do so by hardcoding the list somewhere. In such cases, the `range` function comes to the rescue. Let's see the equivalent of the previous snippet of code:

simple.for.py

```
for number in range(5):
    print(number)
```

The range function is used extensively in Python programs when it comes to creating sequences: you can call it by passing one value, which acts as `stop` (counting from 0), or you can pass two values (`start` and `stop`), or even three (`start`, `stop`, and `step`). Check out the following example:

```
>>> list(range(10))  # one value: from 0 to value (excluded)
[0, 1, 2, 3, 4, 5, 6, 7, 8, 9]
>>> list(range(3, 8))  # two values: from start to stop (excluded)
[3, 4, 5, 6, 7]
>>> list(range(-10, 10, 4))  # three values: step is added
[-10, -6, -2, 2, 6]
```

For the moment, ignore that we need to wrap `range(...)` within a `list`. The `range` object is a little bit special, but in this case we're just interested in understanding what are the values it will return to us. You see that the deal is the same with slicing: `start` is included, `stop` excluded, and optionally you can add a `step` parameter, which by default is 1.

Try modifying the parameters of the `range()` call in our `simple.for.py` code and see what it prints, get comfortable with it.

Iterating over a sequence

Now we have all the tools to iterate over a sequence, so let's build on that example:

simple.for.2.py

```
surnames = ['Rivest', 'Shamir', 'Adleman']
for position in range(len(surnames)):
    print(position, surnames[position])
```

The preceding code adds a little bit of complexity to the game. Execution will show this result:

```
$ python simple.for.2.py
0 Rivest
1 Shamir
2 Adleman
```

Let's use the **inside-out** technique to break it down, ok? We start from the innermost part of what we're trying to understand, and we expand outwards. So, len(surnames) is the length of the surnames list: 3. Therefore, range(len(surnames)) is actually transformed into range(3). This gives us the range [0, 3), which is basically a sequence (0, 1, 2). This means that the for loop will run three iterations. In the first one, position will take value 0, while in the second one, it will take value 1, and finally value 2 in the third and last iteration. What is (0, 1, 2), if not the possible indexing positions for the surnames list? At position 0 we find 'Rivest', at position 1, 'Shamir', and at position 2, 'Adleman'. If you are curious about what these three men created together, change print(position, surnames[position]) to print(surnames[position][0], end='') add a final print() outside of the loop, and run the code again.

Now, this style of looping is actually much closer to languages like Java or C++. In Python it's quite rare to see code like this. You can just iterate over any sequence or collection, so there is no need to get the list of positions and retrieve elements out of a sequence at each iteration. It's expensive, needlessly expensive. Let's change the example into a more Pythonic form:

simple.for.3.py

```
surnames = ['Rivest', 'Shamir', 'Adleman']
for surname in surnames:
    print(surname)
```

Now that's something! It's practically English. The `for` loop can iterate over the `surnames` list, and it gives back each element in order at each interaction. Running this code will print the three surnames, one at a time. It's much easier to read, right?

What if you wanted to print the position as well though? Or what if you actually needed it for any reason? Should you go back to the `range(len(...))` form? No. You can use the `enumerate` built-in function, like this:

`simple.for.4.py`

```
surnames = ['Rivest', 'Shamir', 'Adleman']
for position, surname in enumerate(surnames):
    print(position, surname)
```

This code is very interesting as well. Notice that enumerate gives back a 2-tuple `(position, surname)` at each iteration, but still, it's much more readable (and more efficient) than the `range(len(...))` example. You can call `enumerate` with a `start` parameter, like `enumerate(iterable, start)`, and it will start from `start`, rather than `0`. Just another little thing that shows you how much thought has been given in designing Python so that it makes your life easy.

Using a `for` loop it is possible to iterate over lists, tuples, and in general anything that in Python is called iterable. This is a very important concept, so let's talk about it a bit more.

Iterators and iterables

According to the Python documentation, an iterable is:

> *"An object capable of returning its members one at a time. Examples of iterables include all sequence types (such as* `list`, `str`, *and tuple) and some non-sequence types like* `dict`, `file` *objects, and objects of any classes you define with an* `__iter__()` *or* `__getitem__()` *method. Iterables can be used in a* `for` *loop and in many other places where a sequence is needed (*`zip()`, `map()`, *...). When an iterable object is passed as an argument to the built-in function* `iter()`, *it returns an iterator for the object. This iterator is good for one pass over the set of values. When using iterables, it is usually not necessary to call* `iter()` *or deal with iterator objects yourself. The* `for` *statement does that automatically for you, creating a temporary unnamed variable to hold the iterator for the duration of the loop."*

Simply put, what happens when you write `for k in sequence: ... body ...`, is that the `for` loop asks `sequence` for the next element, it gets something back, it calls that something `k`, and then executes its body. Then, once again, the `for` loop asks `sequence` again for the next element, it calls it `k` again, and executes the body again, and so on and so forth, until the sequence is exhausted. Empty sequences will result in zero executions of the body.

Some data structures, when iterated over, produce their elements in order, like lists, tuples, and strings, while some others don't, like sets and dictionaries.

Python gives us the ability to iterate over iterables, using a type of object called **iterator**. According to the official documentation, an iterator is:

> *"An object representing a stream of data. Repeated calls to the iterator's* `__next__` *() method (or passing it to the built-in function* `next()` *) return successive items in the stream. When no more data are available a* `StopIteration` *exception is raised instead. At this point, the iterator object is exhausted and any further calls to its* `__next__` *() method just raise* `StopIteration` *again. Iterators are required to have an* `__iter__` *() method that returns the iterator object itself so every iterator is also iterable and may be used in most places where other iterables are accepted. One notable exception is code which attempts multiple iteration passes. A container object (such as a* `list`*) produces a fresh new iterator each time you pass it to the* `iter()` *function or use it in a* `for` *loop. Attempting this with an iterator will just return the same exhausted iterator object used in the previous iteration pass, making it appear like an empty container."*

Don't worry if you don't fully understand all the preceding legalese, you will in due time. I put it here as a handy reference for the future.

In practice, the whole iterable/iterator mechanism is somewhat hidden behind the code. Unless you need to code your own iterable or iterator for some reason, you won't have to worry about this too much. But it's very important to understand how Python handles this key aspect of control flow because it will shape the way you will write your code.

Iterating over multiple sequences

Let's see another example of how to iterate over two sequences of the same length, in order to work on their respective elements in pairs. Say we have a list of people and a list of numbers representing the age of the people in the first list. We want to print a pair person/age on one line for all of them. Let's start with an example and let's refine it gradually.

multiple.sequences.py

```
people = ['Jonas', 'Julio', 'Mike', 'Mez']
ages = [25, 30, 31, 39]
for position in range(len(people)):
    person = people[position]
    age = ages[position]
    print(person, age)
```

By now, this code should be pretty straightforward for you to understand. We need to iterate over the list of positions (0, 1, 2, 3) because we want to retrieve elements from two different lists. Executing it we get the following:

```
$ python multiple.sequences.py
Jonas 25
Julio 30
Mike 31
Mez 39
```

This code is both inefficient and not Pythonic. Inefficient because retrieving an element given the position can be an expensive operation, and we're doing it from scratch at each iteration. The mail man doesn't go back to the beginning of the road each time he delivers a letter, right? He moves from house to house. From one to the next one. Let's try to make it better using enumerate:

multiple.sequences.enumerate.py

```
people = ['Jonas', 'Julio', 'Mike', 'Mez']
ages = [25, 30, 31, 39]
for position, person in enumerate(people):
    age = ages[position]
    print(person, age)
```

Better, but still not perfect. And still a bit ugly. We're iterating properly on `people`, but we're still fetching `age` using positional indexing, which we want to lose as well. Well, no worries, Python gives you the `zip` function, remember? Let's use it!

`multiple.sequences.zip.py`

```
people = ['Jonas', 'Julio', 'Mike', 'Mez']
ages = [25, 30, 31, 39]
for person, age in zip(people, ages):
    print(person, age)
```

Ah! So much better! Once again, compare the preceding code with the first example and admire Python's elegance. The reason I wanted to show this example is twofold. On the one hand, I wanted to give you an idea of how shorter the code in Python can be compared to other languages where the syntax doesn't allow you to iterate over sequences or collections as easily. And on the other hand, and much more importantly, notice that when the `for` loop asks `zip(sequenceA, sequenceB)` for the next element, it gets back a `tuple`, not just a single object. It gets back a `tuple` with as many elements as the number of sequences we feed to the `zip` function. Let's expand a little on the previous example in two ways: using explicit and implicit assignment:

`multiple.sequences.explicit.py`

```
people = ['Jonas', 'Julio', 'Mike', 'Mez']
ages = [25, 30, 31, 39]
nationalities = ['Belgium', 'Spain', 'England', 'Bangladesh']
for person, age, nationality in zip(people, ages, nationalities):
    print(person, age, nationality)
```

In the preceding code, we added the nationalities list. Now that we feed three sequences to the `zip` function, the for loop gets back a *3-tuple* at each iteration. Notice that the position of the elements in the tuple respects the position of the sequences in the `zip` call. Executing the code will yield the following result:

```
$ python multiple.sequences.explicit.py
Jonas 25 Belgium
Julio 30 Spain
Mike 31 England
Mez 39 Bangladesh
```

Sometimes, for reasons that may not be clear in a simple example like the preceding one, you may want to explode the tuple within the body of the `for` loop. If that is your desire, it's perfectly possible to do so.

```
multiple.sequences.implicit.py
```

```
    people = ['Jonas', 'Julio', 'Mike', 'Mez']
    ages = [25, 30, 31, 39]
    nationalities = ['Belgium', 'Spain', 'England', 'Bangladesh']
    for data in zip(people, ages, nationalities):
        person, age, nationality = data
        print(person, age, nationality)
```

It's basically doing what the `for` loop does automatically for you, but in some cases you may want to do it yourself. Here, the 3-tuple `data` that comes from `zip(...)`, is exploded within the body of the `for` loop into three variables: `person`, `age`, and `nationality`.

The while loop

In the preceding pages, we saw the `for` loop in action. It's incredibly useful when you need to loop over a sequence or a collection. The key point to keep in mind, when you need to be able to discriminate which looping construct to use, is that the `for` loop rocks when you have to iterate over a finite amount of elements. It can be a huge amount, but still, something that at some point ends.

There are other cases though, when you just need to loop until some condition is satisfied, or even loop indefinitely until the application is stopped. Cases where we don't really have something to iterate on, and therefore the `for` loop would be a poor choice. But fear not, for these cases Python provides us with the `while` loop.

The `while` loop is similar to the `for` loop, in that they both loop and at each iteration they execute a body of instructions. What is different between them is that the `while` loop doesn't loop over a sequence (it can, but you have to manually write the logic and it wouldn't make any sense, you would just want to use a `for` loop), rather, it loops as long as a certain condition is satisfied. When the condition is no longer satisfied, the loop ends.

As usual, let's see an example which will clarify everything for us. We want to print the binary representation of a positive number. In order to do so, we repeatedly divide the number by two, collecting the remainder, and then produce the inverse of the list of remainders. Let me give you a small example using number 6, which is 110 in binary.

```
    6 / 2 = 3 (remainder: 0)
    3 / 2 = 1 (remainder: 1)
    1 / 2 = 0 (remainder: 1)
    List of remainders: 0, 1, 1.
    Inverse is 1, 1, 0, which is also the binary representation of 6: 110
```

Let's write some code to calculate the binary representation for number 39: 100111_2.

`binary.py`

```python
n = 39
remainders = []
while n > 0:
    remainder = n % 2  # remainder of division by 2
    remainders.append(remainder)  # we keep track of remainders
    n //= 2  # we divide n by 2

# reassign the list to its reversed copy and print it
remainders = remainders[::-1]
print(remainders)
```

In the preceding code, I highlighted two things: `n > 0`, which is the condition to keep looping, and `remainders[::-1]` which is a nice and easy way to get the reversed version of a list (missing `start` and `end` parameters, `step = -1`, produces the same list, from `end` to `start`, in reverse order). We can make the code a little shorter (and more Pythonic), by using the `divmod` function, which is called with a number and a divisor, and returns a tuple with the result of the integer division and its remainder. For example, `divmod(13, 5)` would return `(2, 3)`, and indeed $5 * 2 + 3 = 13$.

`binary.2.py`

```python
n = 39
remainders = []
while n > 0:
    n, remainder = divmod(n, 2)
    remainders.append(remainder)

# reassign the list to its reversed copy and print it
remainders = remainders[::-1]
print(remainders)
```

In the preceding code, we have reassigned n to the result of the division by 2, and the remainder, in one single line.

Notice that the condition in a `while` loop is a condition to continue looping. If it evaluates to `True`, then the body is executed and then another evaluation follows, and so on, until the condition evaluates to `False`. When that happens, the loop is exited immediately without executing its body.

If the condition never evaluates to `False`, the loop becomes a so called **infinite loop**. Infinite loops are used for example when polling from network devices: you ask the socket if there is any data, you do something with it if there is any, then you sleep for a small amount of time, and then you ask the socket again, over and over again, without ever stopping.

Having the ability to loop over a condition, or to loop indefinitely, is the reason why the `for` loop alone is not enough, and therefore Python provides the `while` loop.

 By the way, if you need the binary representation of a number, checkout the `bin` function.

Just for fun, let's adapt one of the examples (`multiple.sequences.py`) using the while logic.

`multiple.sequences.while.py`

```
people = ['Jonas', 'Julio', 'Mike', 'Mez']
ages = [25, 30, 31, 39]
position = 0
while position < len(people):
    person = people[position]
    age = ages[position]
    print(person, age)
    position += 1
```

In the preceding code, I have highlighted the *initialization*, *condition*, and *update* of the variable `position`, which makes it possible to simulate the equivalent `for` loop code by handling the iteration variable manually. Everything that can be done with a `for` loop can also be done with a `while` loop, even though you can see there's a bit of boilerplate you have to go through in order to achieve the same result. The opposite is also true, but simulating a never ending `while` loop using a `for` loop requires some real trickery, so why would you do that? Use the right tool for the job, and 99.9% of the times you'll be fine.

So, to recap, use a `for` loop when you need to iterate over one (or a combination of) iterable, and a `while` loop when you need to loop according to a condition being satisfied or not. If you keep in mind the difference between the two purposes, you will never choose the wrong looping construct.

Let's now see how to alter the normal flow of a loop.

The break and continue statements

According to the task at hand, sometimes you will need to alter the regular flow of a loop. You can either skip a single iteration (as many times you want), or you can break out of the loop entirely. A common use case for skipping iterations is for example when you're iterating over a list of items and you need to work on each of them only if some condition is verified. On the other hand, if you're iterating over a collection of items, and you have found one of them that satisfies some need you have, you may decide not to continue the loop entirely and therefore break out of it. There are countless possible scenarios, so it's better to see a couple of examples.

Let's say you want to apply a 20% discount to all products in a basket list for those which have an expiration date of today. The way you achieve this is to use the **continue** statement, which tells the looping construct (for or while) to immediately stop execution of the body and go to the next iteration, if any. This example will take us a little deeper down the rabbit whole, so be ready to jump.

discount.py

```
from datetime import date, timedelta

today = date.today()
tomorrow = today + timedelta(days=1)  # today + 1 day is tomorrow
products = [
    {'sku': '1', 'expiration_date': today, 'price': 100.0},
    {'sku': '2', 'expiration_date': tomorrow, 'price': 50},
    {'sku': '3', 'expiration_date': today, 'price': 20},
]
for product in products:
    if product['expiration_date'] != today:
        continue
    product['price'] *= 0.8  # equivalent to applying 20% discount
    print(
        'Price for sku', product['sku'],
        'is now', product['price'])
```

You see we start by importing the date and timedelta objects, then we set up our products. Those with sku 1 and 3 have an expiration date of today, which means we want to apply 20% discount on them. We loop over each product and we inspect the expiration date. If it is not (inequality operator, !=) today, we don't want to execute the rest of the body suite, so we continue.

Notice that is not important where in the body suite you place the `continue` statement (you can even use it more than once). When you reach it, execution stops and goes back to the next iteration. If we run the `discount.py` module, this is the output:

```
$ python discount.py
Price for sku 1 is now 80.0
Price for sku 3 is now 16.0
```

Which shows you that the last two lines of the body haven't been executed for sku number 2.

Let's now see an example of breaking out of a loop. Say we want to tell if at least any of the elements in a list evaluates to `True` when fed to the `bool` function. Given that we need to know if there is at least one, when we find it we don't need to keep scanning the list any further. In Python code, this translates to using the **break** statement. Let's write this down into code:

`any.py`

```python
items = [0, None, 0.0, True, 0, 7]  # True and 7 evaluate to True
found = False  # this is called "flag"
for item in items:
    print('scanning item', item)
    if item:
        found = True  # we update the flag
        break

if found:  # we inspect the flag
    print('At least one item evaluates to True')
else:
    print('All items evaluate to False')
```

The preceding code is such a common pattern in programming, you will see it a lot. When you inspect items this way, basically what you do is to set up a `flag` variable, then start the inspection. If you find one element that matches your criteria (in this example, that evaluates to `True`), then you update the flag and stop iterating. After iteration, you inspect the flag and take action accordingly. Execution yields:

```
$ python any.py
scanning item 0
scanning item None
scanning item 0.0
scanning item True
At least one item evaluates to True
```

See how execution stopped after `True` was found?

The `break` statement acts exactly like the `continue` one, in that it stops executing the body of the loop immediately, but also, prevents any other iteration to run, effectively breaking out of the loop.

The `continue` and `break` statements can be used together with no limitation in their number, both in the `for` and `while` looping constructs.

 By the way, there is no need to write code to detect if there is at least one element in a sequence that evaluates to `True`. Just check out the `any` built-in function.

A special else clause

One of the features I've seen only in the Python language is the ability to have `else` clauses after `while` and `for` loops. It's very rarely used, but it's definitely nice to have. In short, you can have an `else` suite after a `for` or `while` loop. If the loop ends normally, because of exhaustion of the iterator (`for` loop) or because the condition is finally not met (`while` loop), then the `else` suite (if present) is executed. In case execution is interrupted by a `break` statement, the `else` clause is not executed. Let's take an example of a `for` loop that iterates over a group of items, looking for one that would match some condition. In case we don't find at least one that satisfies the condition, we want to raise an **exception**. This means we want to arrest the regular execution of the program and signal that there was an error, or exception, that we cannot deal with. Exceptions will be the subject of *Chapter 7, Testing, Profiling, and Dealing with Exceptions*, so don't worry if you don't fully understand them now. Just bear in mind that they will alter the regular flow of the code. Let me now show you two examples that do exactly the same thing, but one of them is using the special `for ... else` syntax. Say that we want to find among a collection of people one that could drive a car.

for.no.else.py

```
class DriverException(Exception):
    pass

people = [('James', 17), ('Kirk', 9), ('Lars', 13), ('Robert', 8)]
driver = None
for person, age in people:
    if age >= 18:
```

```
        driver = (person, age)
        break

if driver is None:
    raise DriverException('Driver not found.')
```

Notice the `flag` pattern again. We set driver to be `None`, then if we find one we update the `driver` flag, and then, at the end of the loop, we inspect it to see if one was found. I kind of have the feeling that those kids would drive a very metallic car, but anyway, notice that if a driver is not found, a `DriverException` is raised, signaling the program that execution cannot continue (we're lacking the driver).

The same functionality can be rewritten a bit more elegantly using the following code:

for.else.py

```
class DriverException(Exception):
    pass

people = [('James', 17), ('Kirk', 9), ('Lars', 13), ('Robert', 8)]
for person, age in people:
    if age >= 18:
        driver = (person, age)
        break
else:
    raise DriverException('Driver not found.')
```

Notice that we aren't forced to use the `flag` pattern any more. The exception is raised as part of the `for` loop logic, which makes good sense because the `for` loop is checking on some condition. All we need is to set up a `driver` object in case we find one, because the rest of the code is going to use that information somewhere. Notice the code is shorter and more elegant, because the logic is now correctly grouped together where it belongs.

Putting this all together

Now that you have seen all there is to see about conditionals and loops, it's time to spice things up a little, and see those two examples I anticipated at the beginning of this chapter. We'll mix and match here, so you can see how one can use all these concepts together. Let's start by writing some code to generate a list of prime numbers up to some limit. Please bear in mind that I'm going to write a very inefficient and rudimentary algorithm to detect primes. The important thing for you is to concentrate on those bits in the code that belong to this chapter's subject.

Example 1 – a prime generator

According to Wikipedia:

> *"A prime number (or a prime) is a natural number greater than 1 that has no positive divisors other than 1 and itself. A natural number greater than 1 that is not a prime number is called a composite number."*

Based on this definition, if we consider the first 10 natural numbers, we can see that 2, 3, 5, and 7 are primes, while 1, 4, 6, 8, 9, 10 are not. In order to have a computer tell you if a number N is prime, you can divide that number by all natural numbers in the range [2, N). If any of those divisions yields zero as a remainder, then the number is not a prime. Enough chatter, let's get down to business. I'll write two versions of this, the second of which will exploit the `for ... else` syntax.

primes.py

```
primes = []  # this will contain the primes in the end
upto = 100  # the limit, inclusive
for n in range(2, upto + 1):
    is_prime = True  # flag, new at each iteration of outer for
    for divisor in range(2, n):
        if n % divisor == 0:
            is_prime = False
            break
    if is_prime:  # check on flag
        primes.append(n)
print(primes)
```

Lots of things to notice in the preceding code. First of all we set up an empty list `primes`, which will contain the primes at the end. The limit is 100, and you can see it's inclusive in the way we call `range()` in the outer loop. If we wrote `range(2, upto)` that would be [2, upto), right? Therefore `range(2, upto + 1)` gives us *[2, upto + 1) == [2, upto]*.

So, two `for` loops. In the outer one we loop over the candidate primes, that is, all natural numbers from 2 to `upto`. Inside each iteration of this outer loop we set up a flag (which is set to `True` at each iteration), and then start dividing the current n by all numbers from 2 to $n - 1$. If we find a proper divisor for n, it means n is composite, and therefore we set the flag to `False` and break the loop. Notice that when we break the inner one, the outer one keeps on going normally. The reason why we break after having found a proper divisor for n is that we don't need any further information to be able to tell that n is not a prime.

When we check on the is_prime flag, if it is still `True`, it means we couldn't find any number in [2, *n*) that is a proper divisor for n, therefore n is a prime. We append n to the primes list, and hop! Another iteration, until *n* equals 100.

Running this code yields:

```
$ python primes.py
[2, 3, 5, 7, 11, 13, 17, 19, 23, 29, 31, 37, 41, 43, 47, 53, 59, 61, 67,
71, 73, 79, 83, 89, 97]
```

Before we proceed, one question: of all iterations of the outer loop, one of them is different than all the others. Could you tell which one, and why? Think about it for a second, go back to the code and try to figure it out for yourself, and then keep reading on.

Did you figure it out? If not, don't feel bad, it's perfectly normal. I asked you to do it as a small exercise because it's what coders do all the time. The skill to understand what the code does by simply looking at it is something you build over time. It's very important, so try to exercise it whenever you can. I'll tell you the answer now: the iteration that behaves differently from all others is the first one. The reason is because in the first iteration, n is 2. Therefore the innermost `for` loop won't even run, because it's a `for` loop which iterates over range(2, 2), and what is that if not [2, 2)? Try it out for yourself, write a simple `for` loop with that iterable, put a `print` in the body suite, and see if anything happens (it won't...).

Now, from an algorithmic point of view this code is inefficient so let's at least make it more beautiful:

primes.else.py

```
primes = []
upto = 100
for n in range(2, upto + 1):
    for divisor in range(2, n):
        if n % divisor == 0:
            break
    else:
        primes.append(n)
print(primes)
```

Much nicer, right? The is_prime flag is completely gone, and we append n to the primes list when we know the inner `for` loop hasn't encountered any break statements. See how the code looks cleaner and reads better?

Example 2 – applying discounts

In this example, I want to show you a technique I like a lot. In many programming languages, other than the `if/elif/else` constructs, in whatever form or syntax they may come, you can find another statement, usually called `switch/case`, that in Python is missing. It is the equivalent of a cascade of `if/elif/.../elif/else` clauses, with a syntax similar to this (warning! JavaScript code!):

switch.js

```javascript
switch (day_number) {
    case 1:
    case 2:
    case 3:
    case 4:
    case 5:
        day = "Weekday";
        break;
    case 6:
        day = "Saturday";
        break;
    case 0:
        day = "Sunday";
        break;
    default:
        day = "";
        alert(day_number + ' is not a valid day number.')
}
```

In the preceding code, we `switch` on a variable called `day_number`. This means we get its value and then we decide what case it fits in (if any). From 1 to 5 there is a cascade, which means no matter the number, [1, 5] all go down to the bit of logic that sets `day` as `"Weekday"`. Then we have single cases for 0 and 6 and a `default` case to prevent errors, which alerts the system that `day_number` is not a valid day number, that is, not in [0, 6]. Python is perfectly capable of realizing such logic using `if/elif/else` statements:

switch.py

```python
if 1 <= day_number <= 5:
    day = 'Weekday'
elif day_number == 6:
    day = 'Saturday'
elif day_number == 0:
    day = 'Sunday'
```

```
else:
    day = ''
    raise ValueError(
        str(day_number) + ' is not a valid day number.')
```

In the preceding code, we reproduce the same logic of the JavaScript snippet, in
Python, using `if/elif/else` statements. I raised `ValueError` exception just as
an example at the end, if `day_number` is not in [0, 6]. This is one possible way of
translating the `switch/case` logic, but there is also another one, sometimes called
dispatching, which I will show you in the last version of the next example.

 By the way, did you notice the first line of the previous snippet?
Have you noticed that Python can make double (actually, even
multiple) comparisons? It's just wonderful!

Let's start the new example by simply writing some code that assigns a discount to
customers based on their coupon value. I'll keep the logic down to a minimum here,
remember that all we really care about is conditionals and loops.

coupons.py

```
customers = [
    dict(id=1, total=200, coupon_code='F20'),   # F20: fixed, £20
    dict(id=2, total=150, coupon_code='P30'),   # P30: percent, 30%
    dict(id=3, total=100, coupon_code='P50'),   # P50: percent, 50%
    dict(id=4, total=110, coupon_code='F15'),   # F15: fixed, £15
]
for customer in customers:
    code = customer['coupon_code']
    if code == 'F20':
        customer['discount'] = 20.0
    elif code == 'F15':
        customer['discount'] = 15.0
    elif code == 'P30':
        customer['discount'] = customer['total'] * 0.3
    elif code == 'P50':
        customer['discount'] = customer['total'] * 0.5
    else:
        customer['discount'] = 0.0

for customer in customers:
    print(customer['id'], customer['total'], customer['discount'])
```

We start by setting up some customers. They have an order total, a coupon code, and an id. I made up four different types of coupon, two are fixed and two are percentage based. You can see that in the if/elif/else cascade I apply the discount accordingly, and I set it as a 'discount' key in the customer dict.

At the end I just print out part of the data to see if my code is working properly.

```
$ python coupons.py
1 200 20.0
2 150 45.0
3 100 50.0
4 110 15.0
```

This code is simple to understand, but all those clauses are kind of cluttering the logic. It's not easy to see what's going on at a first glance, and I don't like it. In cases like this, you can exploit a dictionary to your advantage, like this:

coupons.dict.py

```
customers = [
    dict(id=1, total=200, coupon_code='F20'),  # F20: fixed, £20
    dict(id=2, total=150, coupon_code='P30'),  # P30: percent, 30%
    dict(id=3, total=100, coupon_code='P50'),  # P50: percent, 50%
    dict(id=4, total=110, coupon_code='F15'),  # F15: fixed, £15
]
discounts = {
    'F20': (0.0, 20.0),  # each value is (percent, fixed)
    'P30': (0.3, 0.0),
    'P50': (0.5, 0.0),
    'F15': (0.0, 15.0),
}
for customer in customers:
    code = customer['coupon_code']
    percent, fixed = discounts.get(code, (0.0, 0.0))
    customer['discount'] = percent * customer['total'] + fixed

for customer in customers:
    print(customer['id'], customer['total'], customer['discount'])
```

Running the preceding code yields exactly the same result we had from the snippet before it. We spared two lines, but more importantly, we gained a lot in readability, as the body of the `for` loop now is just three lines long, and very easy to understand. The concept here is to use a dictionary as **dispatcher**. In other words, we try to fetch something from the dictionary based on a code (our `coupon_code`), and by using `dict.get(key, default)`, we make sure we also cater for when the `code` is not in the dictionary and we need a default value.

Notice that I had to apply some very simple linear algebra in order to calculate the discount properly. Each discount has a percentage and fixed part in the dictionary, represented by a 2-tuple. By applying `percent * total + fixed`, we get the correct discount. When `percent` is `0`, the formula just gives the fixed amount, and it gives `percent * total` when fixed is `0`. Simple but effective.

This technique is important because it is also used in other contexts, with functions, where it actually becomes much more powerful than what we've seen in the preceding snippet. If it's not completely clear to you how it works, I suggest you to take your time and experiment with it. Change values and add print statements to see what's going on while the program is running.

A quick peek at the itertools module

A chapter about iterables, iterators, conditional logic, and looping wouldn't be complete without spending a few words about the `itertools` module. If you are into iterating, this is a kind of heaven.

According to the Python official documentation, the `itertools` module is:

> *"A module which implements a number of iterator building blocks inspired by constructs from APL, Haskell, and SML. Each has been recast in a form suitable for Python. The module standardizes a core set of fast, memory efficient tools that are useful by themselves or in combination. Together, they form an "iterator algebra" making it possible to construct specialized tools succinctly and efficiently in pure Python."*

By no means do I have the room here to show you all the goodies you can find in this module, so I encourage you to go and check it out for yourself, I promise you'll enjoy it.

In a nutshell, it provides you with three broad categories of iterators. I will give you a very small example of one iterator taken from each one of them, just to make your mouth water a little.

Infinite iterators

Infinite iterators allow you to work with a `for` loop in a different fashion, like if it was a `while` loop.

infinite.py

```
from itertools import count
for n in count(5, 3):
    if n > 20:
        break
    print(n, end=', ')  # instead of newline, comma and space
```

Running the code gives this:

```
$ python infinite.py
5, 8, 11, 14, 17, 20,
```

The `count` factory class makes an iterator that just goes on and on counting. It starts from 5 and keeps adding 3 to it. We need to manually break it if we don't want to get stuck in an infinite loop.

Iterators terminating on the shortest input sequence

This category is very interesting. It allows you to create an iterator based on multiple iterators, combining their values according to some logic. The key point here is that among those iterators, in case any of them are shorter than the rest, the resulting iterator won't break, it will simply stop as soon as the shortest iterator is exhausted. This is very theoretical, I know, so let me give you an example using `compress`. This iterator gives you back the data according to a corresponding item in a selector being `True` or `False`:

`compress('ABC', (1, 0, 1))` would give back `'A'` and `'C'`, because they correspond to the `1`'s. Let's see a simple example:

compress.py

```
from itertools import compress
data = range(10)
even_selector = [1, 0] * 10
odd_selector = [0, 1] * 10

even_numbers = list(compress(data, even_selector))
odd_numbers = list(compress(data, odd_selector))
```

```
print(odd_selector)
print(list(data))
print(even_numbers)
print(odd_numbers)
```

Notice that `odd_selector` and `even_selector` are 20 elements long, while `data` is just 10 elements long. `compress` will stop as soon as `data` has yielded its last element. Running this code produces the following:

```
$ python compress.py
[0, 1, 0, 1, 0, 1, 0, 1, 0, 1, 0, 1, 0, 1, 0, 1, 0, 1, 0, 1]
[0, 1, 2, 3, 4, 5, 6, 7, 8, 9]
[0, 2, 4, 6, 8]
[1, 3, 5, 7, 9]
```

It's a very fast and nice way of selecting elements out of an iterable. The code is very simple, just notice that instead of using a `for` loop to iterate over each value that is given back by the compress calls, we used `list()`, which does the same, but instead of executing a body of instructions, puts all the values into a list and returns it.

Combinatoric generators

Last but not least, combinatoric generators. These are really fun, if you are into this kind of thing. Let's just see a simple example on permutations.

According to Wolfram Mathworld:

> *"A permutation, also called an "arrangement number" or "order", is a rearrangement of the elements of an ordered list S into a one-to-one correspondence with S itself."*

For example, the permutations of ABC are 6: ABC, ACB, BAC, BCA, CAB, and CBA.

If a set has N elements, then the number of permutations of them is $N!$ (N factorial). For the string ABC the permutations are $3! = 3 * 2 * 1 = 6$. Let's do it in Python:

`permutations.py`

```
from itertools import permutations
print(list(permutations('ABC')))
```

This very short snippet of code produces the following result:

```
$ python permutations.py
[('A', 'B', 'C'), ('A', 'C', 'B'), ('B', 'A', 'C'), ('B', 'C', 'A'),
('C', 'A', 'B'), ('C', 'B', 'A')]
```

Be very careful when you play with permutation. Their number grows at a rate that is proportional to the factorial of the number of the elements you're permuting, and that number can get really big, really fast.

Summary

In this chapter, we've taken another step forward to expand our coding vocabulary. We've seen how to drive the execution of the code by evaluating conditions, and we've seen how to loop and iterate over sequences and collections of objects. This gives us the power to control what happens when our code is run, which means we are getting an idea on how to shape it so that it does what we want and it reacts to data that changes dynamically.

We've also seen how to combine everything together in a couple of simple examples, and in the end we have taken a brief look at the itertools module, which is full of interesting iterators which can enrich our abilities with Python even more.

Now it's time to switch gears, to take another step forward and talk about functions. The next chapter is all about them because they are extremely important. Make sure you're comfortable with what has been done up to now: I want to provide you with interesting examples, so I'll have to go a little faster. Ready? Turn the page.

4
Functions, the Building Blocks of Code

"To create architecture is to put in order. Put what in order? Function and objects."

- Le Corbusier

In this chapter, we're going to explore functions. We already said that everything is an object in Python, and functions are no exception to this. But, what exactly is a function? A **function** is a sequence of instructions that perform a task, bundled as a unit. This unit can then be imported and used wherever it's needed. There are many advantages to using functions in your code, as we'll see shortly.

I believe the saying, *a picture is worth one thousand words*, is particularly true when explaining functions to someone who is new to this concept, so please take a look at the following image:

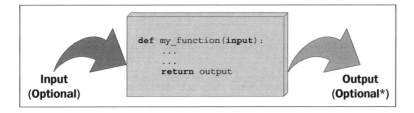

As you can see, a function is a block of instructions, packaged as a whole, like a box. Functions can accept input arguments and produce output values. Both of these are optional, as we'll see in the examples in this chapter.

A function in Python is defined by using the def keyword, after which the name of the function follows, terminated by a pair of braces (which may or may not contain input parameters) and, finally, a colon (:) signals the end of the function definition line. Immediately afterwards, indented by four spaces, we find the body of the function, which is the set of instructions that the function will execute when called.

 Note that the indentation by four spaces is not mandatory, but it is the amount of spaces suggested by **PEP8**, and, in practice, it is the most widely used spacing measure.

A function may or may not return output. If a function wants to return output, it does so by using the return keyword, followed by the desired output. If you have an eagle eye, you may have noticed the little * after **Optional** in the output section of the preceding picture. This is because a function always returns something in Python, even if you don't explicitly use the return clause. If the function has no return statement in its body, it's return value is None. The reasons behind this design choice are out of the scope of an introductory chapter, so all you need to know is that this behavior will make your life easier, as always, thank you Python.

Why use functions?

Functions are among the most important concepts and constructs of any language, so let me give you a few reasons why we need them:

- They reduce code duplication in a program. By having a specific task taken care of by a nice block of packaged code that we can import and call whenever we want, we don't need to duplicate its implementation.

- They help in splitting a complex task or procedure into smaller blocks, each of which becomes a function.

- They hide the implementation details from their users.

- They improve traceability.

- They improve readability.

Let's look at a few examples to get a better understanding of each point.

Reduce code duplication

Imagine that you are writing a piece of scientific software, and you need to calculate primes up to a limit, as we did in the previous chapter. You write several algorithms and prime numbers, being the basis of many different types of calculations, keep creeping into your code. Well, you have a nice algorithm to calculate them, so you copy and paste it to wherever you need. One day, though, your friend *Mister Smarty* gives you a better algorithm to calculate prime numbers, and this will save you a lot of time. At this point, you need to go over your whole codebase and replace the old code with the new code.

This is actually a very bad way to go about it. It's error-prone, you never know what lines you are chopping out or leaving there by mistake when you cut and paste code in other code, and you may also risk missing one of the places where prime calculation was done, leaving your software with different versions. Can you imagine if you discovered that the old way was buggy? You would have an undetected bug in your code, and bugs like this are quite hard to spot, especially in big codebases.

So, what should you do? Simple! You write a function, `get_prime_numbers(upto)`, and use it anywhere you need a list of primes. When *Mister Smarty* comes to you and gives you the new code, all you have to do is replace the body of that function with the new implementation, and you're done! The rest of the software will automatically adapt, since it's just calling the function.

Your code will be shorter, it will not suffer from inconsistencies between old and new ways of performing a task, or undetected bugs due to copy and paste failures or oversights. Use functions, and you'll only gain from it, I promise.

Splitting a complex task

Functions are very useful also to split a long or complex task into smaller pieces. The end result is that the code benefits from it in several ways, for example, readability, testability, and reuse. To give you a simple example, imagine that you're preparing a report. Your code needs to fetch data from a data source, parse it, filter it, polish it, and then a whole series of algorithms needs to be run against it, in order to produce the results which will feed the `Report` class. It's not uncommon to read procedures like this that are just one big function `do_report(data_source)`. There are tens or hundreds of lines of code which end with `return report`.

Situations like this are common in code produced by scientists. They have brilliant minds and they care about the correctness of the end result but, unfortunately, sometimes they have no training in programming theory. It is not their fault, one cannot know everything. Now, picture in your head something like a few hundred lines of code. It's very hard to follow through, to find the places where things are changing context (like finishing one task and starting the next one). Do you have the picture in your mind? Good. Don't do it! Instead, look at this code:

data.science.example.py

```
def do_report(data_source):
    # fetch and prepare data
    data = fetch_data(data_source)
    parsed_data = parse_data(data)
    filtered_data = filter_data(parsed_data)
    polished_data = polish_data(filtered_data)

    # run algorithms on data
    final_data = analyse(polished_data)

    # create and return report
    report = Report(final_data)
    return report
```

The previous example is fictitious, of course, but can you see how easy it would be to go through the code? If the end result looks wrong, it would be very easy to debug each of the single data outputs in the do_report function. Moreover, it's even easier to exclude part of the process temporarily from the whole procedure (you just need to comment out the parts you need to suspend). Code like this is easier to deal with.

Hide implementation details

Let's stay with the preceding example to talk about this point as well. You can see that, by going through the code of the do_report function, you can get a pretty good understanding without reading one single line of implementation. This is because functions hide the implementation details. This feature means that, if you don't need to delve into details, you are not forced to, in the way you would if do_report was just one big fat function. In order to understand what was going on, you would have to read the implementation details. You don't need to with functions. This reduces the time you spend reading the code and since, in a professional environment, reading code takes much more time than actually writing it, it's very important to reduce it as much as we can.

Improve readability

Coders sometimes don't see the point in writing a function with a body of one or two lines of code, so let's look at an example that shows you why you should do it.

Imagine that you need to multiply two matrices:

$$\begin{pmatrix} 1 & 2 \\ 3 & 4 \end{pmatrix} \cdot \begin{pmatrix} 5 & 1 \\ 2 & 1 \end{pmatrix} = \begin{pmatrix} 9 & 3 \\ 23 & 7 \end{pmatrix}$$

Would you prefer to have to read this code:

matrix.multiplication.nofunc.py

```
a = [[1, 2], [3, 4]]
b = [[5, 1], [2, 1]]
c = [[sum(i * j for i, j in zip(r, c)) for c in zip(*b)]
     for r in a]
```

Or would you prefer this one:

matrix.multiplication.func.py

```
# this function could also be defined in another module
def matrix_mul(a, b):
    return [[sum(i * j for i, j in zip(r, c)) for c in zip(*b)]
            for r in a]

a = [[1, 2], [3, 4]]
b = [[5, 1], [2, 1]]
c = matrix_mul(a, b)
```

It's much easier to understand that c is the result of the multiplication between a and b in the second example. It's much easier to read through the code and, if you don't need to modify that part, you don't even need to go into the implementation details.

Therefore, readability is improved here while, in the first snippet, you would have to spend time trying to understand what that complicated list comprehension was doing.

 Don't worry if you don't understand *list comprehensions*, we'll study them in the next chapter.

Improve traceability

Imagine that you have written an e-commerce website. You have displayed the product prices all over the pages. Imagine that the prices in your database are stored with no VAT, but you want to display them on the website with VAT at 20%. Here's a few ways of calculating the VAT-inclusive price from the VAT-exclusive price.

vat.py

```
price = 100  # GBP, no VAT
final_price1 = price * 1.2
final_price2 = price + price / 5.0
final_price3 = price * (100 + 20) / 100.0
final_price4 = price + price * 0.2
```

All these four different ways of calculating a VAT-inclusive price are perfectly acceptable, and I promise you I have found them all in my colleagues' code, over the years. Now, imagine that you have started selling your products in different countries and some of them have different VAT rates so you need to refactor your code (throughout the website) in order to make that VAT calculation dynamic.

How do you trace all the places in which you are performing a VAT calculation? Coding today is a collaborative task and you cannot be sure the VAT has been calculated using only one of those forms. It's going to be hell, believe me.

So, let's write a function that takes the input values, vat and price (VAT-exclusive), and returns a VAT-inclusive price.

vat.function.py

```
def calculate_price_with_vat(price, vat):
    return price * (100 + vat) / 100
```

Now you can import that function and apply it in any place of your website where you need to calculate a VAT-inclusive price and when you need to trace those calls, you can search for calculate_price_with_vat.

 Note that, in the preceding example, price is assumed to be VAT-exclusive, and vat has a percentage value (for example, 19, 20, 23, and so on).

Scopes and name resolution

Do you remember when we talked about scopes and namespaces in the first chapter? We're going to expand on that concept now. Finally, we can talk about functions and this will make everything easier to understand. Let's start with a very simple example.

scoping.level.1.py

```
def my_function():
    test = 1 # this is defined in the local scope of the function
    print('my_function:', test)

test = 0  # this is defined in the global scope
my_function()
print('global:', test)
```

I have defined the name `test` in two different places in the previous example. It is actually in two different scopes. One is the global scope (`test = 0`), and the other is the local scope of the function `my_function` (`test = 1`). If you execute the code, you'll see this:

```
$ python scoping.level.1.py
my_function: 1
global: 0
```

It's clear that `test = 1` shadows the assignment `test = 0` in `my_function`. In the global context, `test` is still `0`, as you can see from the output of the program but we define the name `test` again in the function body, and we set it to point to an integer of value `1`. Both the two `test` names therefore exist, one in the global scope, pointing to an `int` object with value 0, the other in the `my_function` scope, pointing to an `int` object with value 1. Let's comment out the line with `test = 1`. Python goes and searches for the name `test` in the next enclosing namespace (recall the *LEGB* rule: *Local, Enclosing, Global, Built-in* described in *Chapter 1, Introduction and First Steps – Take a Deep Breath*) and, in this case, we will see the value `0` printed twice. Try it in your code.

Now, let's raise the stakes here and level up:

scoping.level.2.py

```
def outer():
    test = 1  # outer scope

    def inner():
        test = 2  # inner scope
```

```
        print('inner:', test)
    inner()
    print('outer:', test)
test = 0  # global scope
outer()
print('global:', test)
```

In the preceding code, we have two levels of shadowing. One level is in the function `outer`, and the other one is in the function `inner`. It is far from rocket science, but it can be tricky. If we run the code, we get:

```
$ python scoping.level.2.py
inner: 2
outer: 1
global: 0
```

Try commenting out the line `test = 1`. What do you think the result will be? Well, when reaching the line `print('outer:', test)`, Python will have to look for `test` in the next enclosing scope, therefore it will find and print 0, instead of 1. Make sure you comment out `test = 2` as well, to see if you understand what happens, and if the LEGB rule is clear, before proceeding.

Another thing to note is that Python gives you the ability to define a function in another function. The inner function's name is defined within the namespace of the outer function, exactly as would happen with any other name.

The global and nonlocal statements

Going back to the preceding example, we can alter what happens to the shadowing of the test name by using one of these two special statements: `global` and `nonlocal`. As you can see from the previous example, when we define `test = 2` in the function `inner`, we overwrite `test` neither in the function `outer`, nor in the global scope. We can get read access to those names if we use them in a nested scope that doesn't define them, but we cannot modify them because, when we write an assignment instruction, we're actually defining a new name in the current scope.

How do we change this behavior? Well, we can use the `nonlocal` statement. According to the official documentation:

> *"The* `nonlocal` *statement causes the listed identifiers to refer to previously bound variables in the nearest enclosing scope excluding globals."*

Let's introduce it in the function `inner`, and see what happens:

scoping.level.2.nonlocal.py

```
def outer():
    test = 1  # outer scope

    def inner():
        nonlocal test
        test = 2  # nearest enclosing scope
        print('inner:', test)
    inner()
    print('outer:', test)

test = 0  # global scope
outer()
print('global:', test)
```

Notice how in the body of the function `inner` I have declared the `test` name to be `nonlocal`. Running this code produces the following result:

```
$ python scoping.level.2.nonlocal.py
inner: 2
outer: 2
global: 0
```

Wow, look at that result! It means that, by declaring `test` to be `nonlocal` in the function `inner`, we actually get to bind the name `test` to that declared in the function `outer`. If we removed the `nonlocal test` line from the function `inner` and tried the same trick in the function `outer`, we would get a `SyntaxError`, because the `nonlocal` statement works on enclosing scopes excluding the global one.

Is there a way to get to that `test = 0` in the global namespace then? Of course, we just need to use the `global` statement. Let's try it.

scoping.level.2.global.py

```
def outer():
    test = 1  # outer scope

    def inner():
        global test
        test = 2  # global scope
        print('inner:', test)
    inner()
```

```
    print('outer:', test)

test = 0  # global scope
outer()
print('global:', test)
```

Note that we have now declared the name `test` to be `global`, which will basically bind it to the one we defined in the global namespace (`test = 0`). Run the code and you should get the following:

```
$ python scoping.level.2.global.py
inner: 2
outer: 1
global: 2
```

This shows that the name affected by the assignment `test = 2` is now the `global` one. This trick would also work in the `outer` function because, in this case, we're referring to the global scope. Try it for yourself and see what changes, get comfortable with scopes and name resolution, it's very important.

Input parameters

At the beginning of this chapter, we saw that a function can take input parameters. Before we delve into all possible type of parameters, let's make sure you have a clear understanding of what passing a parameter to a function means. There are three key points to keep in mind:

- Argument passing is nothing more than assigning an object to a local variable name
- Assigning an object to an argument name inside a function doesn't affect the caller
- Changing a mutable object argument in a function affects the caller

Let's look at an example for each of these points.

Argument passing

Take a look at the following code. We declare a name x in the global scope, then we declare a function func(y) and we call it, passing x. I highlighted the call in the code.

key.points.argument.passing.py

```
x = 3
def func(y):
    print(y)
func(x)    # prints: 3
```

When func is called with x, what happens is that within its local scope, a name y is created, and it's pointed to the same object x is pointing to. This is better clarified by the following picture:

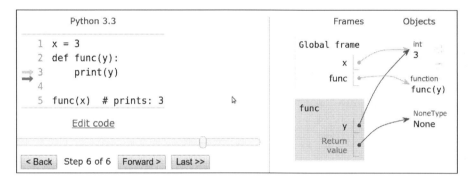

The right part of the preceding picture depicts the state of the program when execution has reached the end, after func has returned (None). Take a look at the **Frames** column, and note that we have two names, **x** and **func**, in the global namespace (**Global frame**), pointing to an **int** (with a value of three) and to a function object, respectively. Right below it, in the rectangle titled **func**, we can see the function's local namespace, in which only one name has been defined: **y**. Because we have called **func** with **x** (line 5 in the left part of the picture), **y** is pointing to the same object that **x** is pointing to. This is what happens under the hood when an argument is passed to a function. If we had used the name **x** instead of **y** in the function definition, things would have been exactly the same (only maybe a bit confusing at first), there would be a local **x** in the function, and a global **x** outside, as we saw in the *Scopes and name resolution* section.

So, in a nutshell, what really happens is that the function creates in its local scope the names defined as arguments and, when we call it, we basically tell Python which objects those names must be pointed towards.

Assignment to argument names don't affect the caller

This is something that can be tricky to understand at first, so let's look at an example.

key.points.assignment.py

```
x = 3
def func(x):
    x = 7  # defining a local x, not changing the global one

func(x)
print(x)  # prints: 3
```

In the preceding code, when the line x = 7 is executed, what happens is that within the local scope of the function func, the name x is pointed to an integer with value 7, leaving the global x unaltered.

Changing a mutable affects the caller

This is the final point, and it's very important because Python apparently behaves differently with mutables (just apparently though). Let's look at an example:

key.points.mutable.py

```
x = [1, 2, 3]
def func(x):
    x[1] = 42  # this affects the caller!

func(x)
print(x)  # prints: [1, 42, 3]
```

Wow, we actually changed the original object! If you think about it, there is nothing weird in this behavior. The name x in the function is set to point to the caller object by the function call and within the body of the function, we're not changing x, in that we're not changing its reference, or, in other words, we are not changing the object x is pointing to. What we're doing is accessing that object's element at position 1, and changing its value.

Remember point #2: "*Assigning an object to an argument name within a function doesn't affect the caller*". If that is clear to you, the following code should not be surprising.

`key.points.mutable.assignment.py`

```
x = [1, 2, 3]
def func(x):
    x[1] = 42  # this changes the caller!
    x = 'something else'  # this points x to a new string object

func(x)
print(x)  # still prints: [1, 42, 3]
```

Take a look at the two lines I have highlighted. At first, we just access the caller object again, at position 1, and change its value to number 42. Then, we reassign x to point to the string `'something else'`. This leaves the caller unaltered, according to point #2, and, in fact, the output is the same as that of the previous snippet.

Take your time to play around with this concept and experiment with prints and calls to the id function until everything is clear in your mind. This is one of the key aspects of Python and it must be very clear, otherwise you risk introducing subtle bugs into your code.

Now that we have a good understanding of input parameters and how they behave, let's see how we can specify them.

How to specify input parameters

There are five different ways of specifying input parameters. Let's look at them one by one.

Positional arguments

Positional arguments are read from left to right and they are the most common type of arguments.

`arguments.positional.py`

```
def func(a, b, c):
    print(a, b, c)
func(1, 2, 3)  # prints: 1 2 3
```

There is not much else to say. They can be as numerous as you want and they are assigned by position. In the function call, 1 comes first, 2 comes second and 3 comes third, therefore they are assigned to a, b and c respectively.

Keyword arguments and default values

Keyword arguments are assigned by keyword using the `name=value` syntax.

`arguments.keyword.py`

```
def func(a, b, c):
    print(a, b, c)
func(a=1, c=2, b=3)  # prints: 1 3 2
```

Keyword arguments act when calling the function instead of respecting the left-to-right positional assignment, k. Keyword arguments are matched by name, even when they don't respect the definition's original position (we'll see that there is a limitation to this behavior later, when we mix and match different types of arguments).

The counterpart of keyword arguments, on the definition side, is **default values**. The syntax is the same, `name=value`, and allows us to not have to provide an argument if we are happy with the given default.

`arguments.default.py`

```
def func(a, b=4, c=88):
    print(a, b, c)

func(1)              # prints: 1 4 88
func(b=5, a=7, c=9)  # prints: 7 5 9
func(42, c=9)        # prints: 42 4 9
```

The are two things to notice, which are very important. First of all, you cannot specify a default argument on the left of a positional one. Second, note how in the examples, when an argument is passed without using the `argument_name=value` syntax, it must be the first one in the list,, and it is always assigned to a. Try and scramble those arguments and see what happens. Python error messages are very good at telling you what's wrong. So, for example, if you tried something like this:

```
func(b=1, c=2, 42)  # positional argument after keyword one
```

You would get the following error:

SyntaxError: non-keyword arg after keyword arg

This informs you that you've called the function incorrectly.

Variable positional arguments

Sometimes you may want to pass a variable number of positional arguments to a function and Python provides you with the ability to do it. Let's look at a very common use case, the `minimum` function. This is a function that calculates the minimum of its input values.

arguments.variable.positional.py

```
def minimum(*n):
    # print(n)  # n is a tuple
    if n:  # explained after the code
        mn = n[0]
        for value in n[1:]:
            if value < mn:
                mn = value
        print(mn)

minimum(1, 3, -7, 9)  # n = (1, 3, -7, 9) - prints: -7
minimum()             # n = () - prints: nothing
```

As you can see, when we specify a parameter prepending a * to its name, we are telling Python that that parameter will be collecting a variable number of positional arguments, according to how the function is called. Within the function, n is a tuple. Uncomment the `print(n)` to see for yourself and play around with it for a bit.

> Have you noticed how we checked if n wasn't empty with a simple `if n:`? This is due to the fact that collection objects evaluate to `True` when non-empty, and otherwise `False` in Python. This is true for tuples, sets, lists, dictionaries, and so on.
>
> One other thing to note is that we may want to throw an error when we call the function with no arguments, instead of silently doing nothing. In this context, we're not concerned about making this function robust, but in understanding variable positional arguments.

Let's make another example to show you two things that, in my experience, are confusing to those who are new to this.

arguments.variable.positional.unpacking.py

```
def func(*args):
    print(args)

values = (1, 3, -7, 9)
func(values)    # equivalent to: func((1, 3, -7, 9))
func(*values)   # equivalent to: func(1, 3, -7, 9)
```

Take a good look at the last two lines of the preceding example. In the first one, we call `func` with one argument, a four elements tuple. In the second example, by using the `*` syntax, we're doing something called **unpacking**, which means that the four elements tuple is unpacked, and the function is called with four arguments: `1, 3, -7, 9`.

This behavior is part of the magic Python does to allow you to do amazing things when calling functions dynamically.

Variable keyword arguments

Variable keyword arguments are very similar to variable positional arguments. The only difference is the syntax (`**` instead of `*`) and that they are collected in a dictionary. Collection and unpacking work in the same way, so let's look at an example:

`arguments.variable.keyword.py`

```python
def func(**kwargs):
    print(kwargs)
# All calls equivalent. They print: {'a': 1, 'b': 42}
func(a=1, b=42)
func(**{'a': 1, 'b': 42})
func(**dict(a=1, b=42))
```

All the calls are equivalent in the preceding example. You can see that adding a `**` in front of the parameter name in the function definition tells Python to use that name to collect a variable number of keyword parameters. On the other hand, when we call the function, we can either pass `name=value` arguments explicitly, or unpack a dictionary using the same `**` syntax.

The reason why being able to pass a variable number of keyword parameters is so important may not be evident at the moment, so, how about a more realistic example? Let's define a function that connects to a database. We want to connect to a default database by simply calling this function with no parameters. We also want to connect to any other database by passing the function the appropriate arguments. Before you read on, spend a couple of minutes figuring out a solution by yourself.

`arguments.variable.db.py`

```python
def connect(**options):
    conn_params = {
        'host': options.get('host', '127.0.0.1'),
        'port': options.get('port', 5432),
        'user': options.get('user', ''),
        'pwd': options.get('pwd', ''),
```

```
        }
    print(conn_params)
    # we then connect to the db (commented out)
    # db.connect(**conn_params)

connect()
connect(host='127.0.0.42', port=5433)
connect(port=5431, user='fab', pwd='gandalf')
```

Note in the function we can prepare a dictionary of connection parameters (conn_params) in the function using default values as fallback, allowing them to be overwritten if they are provided in the function call. There are better ways to do this with fewer lines of code but we're not concerned with that now. Running the preceding code yields the following result:

```
$ python arguments.variable.db.py
{'host': '127.0.0.1', 'pwd': '', 'user': '', 'port': 5432}
{'host': '127.0.0.42', 'pwd': '', 'user': '', 'port': 5433}
{'host': '127.0.0.1', 'pwd': 'gandalf', 'user': 'fab', 'port': 5431}
```

Note the correspondence between the function calls and the output. Note how default values are either there or overridden, according to what was passed to the function.

Keyword-only arguments

Python 3 allows for a new type of parameter: the **keyword-only** parameter. We are going to study them only briefly as their use cases are not that frequent. There are two ways of specifying them, either after the variable positional arguments, or after a bare *. Let's see an example of both.

arguments.keyword.only.py

```
def kwo(*a, c):
    print(a, c)

kwo(1, 2, 3, c=7)   # prints: (1, 2, 3) 7
kwo(c=4)            # prints: () 4
# kwo(1, 2)  # breaks, invalid syntax, with the following error
# TypeError: kwo() missing 1 required keyword-only argument: 'c'

def kwo2(a, b=42, *, c):
    print(a, b, c)

kwo2(3, b=7, c=99)   # prints: 3 7 99
```

```
kwo2(3, c=13)        # prints: 3 42 13
# kwo2(3, 23)  # breaks, invalid syntax, with the following error
# TypeError: kwo2() missing 1 required keyword-only argument: 'c'
```

As anticipated, the function, kwo, takes a variable number of positional arguments (a) and a keyword-only function, c. The results of the calls are straightforward and you can uncomment the third call to see what error Python returns.

The same applies to the function, kwo2, which differs from kwo in that it takes a positional argument a, a keyword argument b, and then a keyword-only argument, c. You can uncomment the third call to see the error.

Now that you know how to specify different types of input parameters, let's see how you can combine them in function definitions.

Combining input parameters

You can combine input parameters, as long as you follow these ordering rules:

- When defining a function, normal positional arguments come first (name), then any default arguments (name=value), then the variable positional arguments (*name, or simply *), then any keyword-only arguments (either name or name=value form is good), then any variable keyword arguments (**name).

- On the other hand, when calling a function, arguments must be given in the following order: positional arguments first (value), then any combination of keyword arguments (name=value), variable positional arguments (*name), then variable keyword arguments (**name).

Since this can be a bit tricky when left hanging in the theoretical world, let's look at a couple of quick examples.

arguments.all.py

```
def func(a, b, c=7, *args, **kwargs):
    print('a, b, c:', a, b, c)
    print('args:', args)
    print('kwargs:', kwargs)

func(1, 2, 3, *(5, 7, 9), **{'A': 'a', 'B': 'b'})
func(1, 2, 3, 5, 7, 9, A='a', B='b')  # same as previous one
```

Note the order of the parameters in the function definition, and that the two calls are equivalent. In the first one, we're using the unpacking operators for iterables and dictionaries, while in the second one we're using a more explicit syntax. The execution of this yields (I printed only the result of one call):

```
$ python arguments.all.py
a, b, c: 1 2 3
args: (5, 7, 9)
kwargs: {'A': 'a', 'B': 'b'}
```

Let's now look at an example with keyword-only arguments.

arguments.all.kwonly.py

```
def func_with_kwonly(a, b=42, *args, c, d=256, **kwargs):
    print('a, b:', a, b)
    print('c, d:', c, d)
    print('args:', args)
    print('kwargs:', kwargs)

# both calls equivalent
func_with_kwonly(3, 42, c=0, d=1, *(7, 9, 11), e='E', f='F')
func_with_kwonly(3, 42, *(7, 9, 11), c=0, d=1, e='E', f='F')
```

Note that I have highlighted the keyword-only arguments in the function declaration. They come after the variable positional argument `*args`, and it would be the same if they came right after a single `*` (in which case there wouldn't be a variable positional argument). The execution of this yields (I printed only the result of one call):

```
$ python arguments.all.kwonly.py
a, b: 3 42
c, d: 0 1
args: (7, 9, 11)
kwargs: {'f': 'F', 'e': 'E'}
```

One other thing to note are the names I gave to the variable positional and keyword arguments. You're free to choose differently, but be aware that `args` and `kwargs` are the conventional names given to these parameters, at least generically. Now that you know how to define a function in all possible flavors, let me show you something tricky: mutable defaults.

Avoid the trap! Mutable defaults

One thing to be very aware of with Python is that default values are created at `def` time, therefore, subsequent calls to the same function will possibly behave differently according to the mutability of their default values. Let's look at an example:

`arguments.defaults.mutable.py`

```python
def func(a=[], b={}):
    print(a)
    print(b)
    print('#' * 12)
    a.append(len(a))  # this will affect a's default value
    b[len(a)] = len(a)  # and this will affect b's one

func()
func()
func()
```

The parameters both have mutable default values. This means that, if you affect those objects, any modification will stick around in subsequent function calls. See if you can understand the output of those calls:

```
$ python arguments.defaults.mutable.py
[]
{}
############
[0]
{1: 1}
############
[0, 1]
{1: 1, 2: 2}
############
```

It's interesting, isn't it? While this behavior may seem very weird at first, it actually makes sense, and it's very handy, for example, when using memoization techniques (Google an example of that, if you're interested).

Even more interesting is what happens when, between the calls, we introduce one that doesn't use defaults, like this:

`arguments.defaults.mutable.intermediate.call.py`

```python
func()
func(a=[1, 2, 3], b={'B': 1})
func()
```

When we run this code, this is the output:

```
$ python arguments.defaults.mutable.intermediate.call.py
[]
{}
###########
[1, 2, 3]
{'B': 1}
###########
[0]
{1: 1}
###########
```

This output shows us that the defaults are retained even if we call the function with other values. One question that comes to mind is, how do I get a fresh empty value every time? Well, the convention is the following:

arguments.defaults.mutable.no.trap.py

```
def func(a=None):
    if a is None:
        a = []
    # do whatever you want with `a` ...
```

Note that, by using the preceding technique, if a isn't passed when calling the function, you always get a brand new empty list.

Okay, enough with the input, let's look at the other side of the coin, the output.

Return values

Return values of functions are one of those things where Python is light years ahead of most other languages. Functions are usually allowed to return one object (one value) but, in Python, you can return a tuple, and this implies that you can return whatever you want. This feature allows a coder to write software that would be much harder to write in any other language, or certainly more tedious. We've already said that to return something from a function we need to use the return statement, followed by what we want to return. There can be as many return statements as needed in the body of a function.

On the other hand, if within the body of a function we don't return anything, the function will return None. This behavior is harmless and, even though I don't have the room here to go into detail explaining why Python was designed like this, let me just tell you that this feature allows for several interesting patterns, and confirms Python as a very consistent language.

I say it's harmless because you are never forced to collect the result of a function call. I'll show you what I mean with an example:

return.none.py

```
def func():
    pass
func()  # the return of this call won't be collected. It's lost.
a = func()  # the return of this one instead is collected into `a`
print(a)  # prints: None
```

Note that the whole body of the function is comprised only of the pass statement. As the official documentation tells us, pass is a null operation. When it is executed, nothing happens. It is useful as a placeholder when a statement is required syntactically, but no code needs to be executed. In other languages, we would probably just indicate that with a pair of curly braces ({}), which define an *empty scope* but in Python a scope is defined by indenting code, therefore a statement such as pass is necessary.

Notice also that the first call of the function func returns a value (None) which we don't collect. As I said before, collecting the return value of a function call is not mandatory.

Now, that's good but not very interesting so, how about we write an interesting function? Remember that in *Chapter 1, Introduction and First Steps – Take a Deep Breath*, we talked about the factorial of a function. Let's write our own here (for simplicity, I will assume the function is always called correctly with appropriate values so I won't sanity-check on the input argument):

return.single.value.py

```
def factorial(n):
    if n in (0, 1):
        return 1
    result = n
    for k in range(2, n):
        result *= k
    return result

f5 = factorial(5)  # f5 = 120
```

Note that we have two points of return. If n is either 0 or 1 (in Python it's common to use the in type of check as I did instead of the more verbose if n ==0 or n == 1:), we return 1. Otherwise, we perform the required calculation, and we return result. Can we write this function a little bit more Pythonically? Yes, but I'll let you figure out that for yourself, as an exercise.

return.single.value.2.py

```
from functools import reduce
from operator import mul

def factorial(n):
    return reduce(mul, range(1, n + 1), 1)
f5 = factorial(5)   # f5 = 120
```

I know what you're thinking, one line? Python is elegant, and concise! I think this function is readable even if you have never seen reduce or mul, but if you can't read it or understand it, set aside a few minutes and do some research on the Python documentation until its behavior is clear to you. Being able to look up functions in the documentation and understand code written by someone else is a task every developer needs to be able to perform, so think of this as a good exercise, and good luck!

 To this end, make sure you look up the help function, which comes in very handy exploring with the console.

Returning multiple values

Unlike in most other languages, in Python it's very easy to return multiple objects from a function. This feature opens up a whole world of possibilities and allows you to code in a style that is hard to reproduce with other languages. Our thinking is limited by the tools we use, therefore when Python gives you more freedom than other languages, it is actually boosting your own creativity as well. To return multiple values is very easy, you just use tuples (either explicitly or implicitly). Let's look at a simple example that mimics the divmod built-in function:

return.multiple.py

```
def moddiv(a, b):
    return a // b, a % b

print(moddiv(20, 7))   # prints (2, 6)
```

I could have wrapped the highlighted part in the preceding code in braces, making it an explicit tuple, but there's no need for that. The preceding function returns both the result and the remainder of the division, at the same time.

A few useful tips

When writing functions, it's very useful to follow guidelines so that you write them well. I'll quickly point some of them out here:

- **Functions should do one thing**: Functions that do one thing are easy to describe in one short sentence. Functions which do multiple things can be split into smaller functions which do one thing. These smaller functions are usually easier to read and understand. Remember the data science example we saw a few pages ago.

- **Functions should be small**: The smaller they are, the easier it is to test them and to write them so that they do one thing.

- **The fewer input parameters, the better**: Functions which take a lot of arguments quickly become harder to manage (among other issues).

- **Functions should be consistent in their return values**: Returning `False` or `None` is not the same thing, even if within a Boolean context they both evaluate to `False`. `False` means that we have information (`False`), while `None` means that there is no information. Try writing functions which return in a consistent way, no matter what happens in their body.

- **Functions shouldn't have side effects**: In other words, functions should not affect the values you call them with. This is probably the hardest statement to understand at this point, so I'll give you an example using lists. In the following code, note how `numbers` is not sorted by the `sorted` function, which actually returns a sorted copy of `numbers`. Conversely, the `list.sort()` method is acting on the `numbers` object itself, and that is fine because it is a method (a function that belongs to an object and therefore has the rights to modify it):

```
>>> numbers = [4, 1, 7, 5]
>>> sorted(numbers)  # won't sort the original `numbers` list
[1, 4, 5, 7]
>>> numbers  # let's verify
[4, 1, 7, 5]  # good, untouched
>>> numbers.sort()  # this will act on the list
>>> numbers
[1, 4, 5, 7]
```

Follow these guidelines and you'll write better functions, which will serve you well.

 Chapter 3, Functions in *Clean Code* by Robert C. Martin, Prentice Hall is dedicated to functions and it's probably the best set of guidelines I've ever read on the subject.

Recursive functions

When a function calls itself to produce a result, it is said to be **recursive**. Sometimes recursive functions are very useful in that they make it easier to write code. Some algorithms are very easy to write using the recursive paradigm, while others are not. There is no recursive function that cannot be rewritten in an iterative fashion, so it's usually up to the programmer to choose the best approach for the case at hand.

A recursive function usually has a set of base cases for which the return value doesn't depend on a subsequent call to the function itself and a set of recursive cases, for which the return value is calculated with one or more calls to the function itself.

As an example, we can consider the (hopefully familiar by now) `factorial` function $N!$. The base case is when N is either 0 or 1. The function returns 1 with no need for further calculation. On the other hand, in the general case, $N!$ returns the product $1 * 2 * ... * (N-1) * N$. If you think about it, $N!$ can be rewritten like this: $N! = (N-1)! * N$. As a practical example, consider $5! = 1 * 2 * 3 * 4 * 5 = (1 * 2 * 3 * 4) * 5 = 4! * 5$.

Let's write this down in code:

recursive.factorial.py

```
def factorial(n):
    if n in (0, 1):  # base case
        return 1
    return factorial(n - 1) * n  # recursive case
```

 When writing recursive functions, always consider how many nested calls you make, there is a limit. For further information on this, check out `sys.getrecursionlimit()` and `sys.setrecursionlimit()`.

Recursive functions are used a lot when writing algorithms and they can be really fun to write. As a good exercise, try to solve a couple of simple problems using both a recursive and an iterative approach.

Anonymous functions

One last type of functions that I want to talk about are **anonymous** functions. These functions, which are called **lambdas** in Python, are usually used when a fully-fledged function with its own name would be overkill, and all we want is a quick, simple one-liner that does the job.

Imagine that you want a list of all the numbers up to N which are multiples of five. Imagine that you want to filter those out using the `filter` function, which takes a function and an iterable and constructs a filter object which you can iterate on, from those elements of iterable for which the function returns `True`. Without using an anonymous function, you would do something like this:

filter.regular.py

```
def is_multiple_of_five(n):
    return not n % 5
def get_multiples_of_five(n):
    return list(filter(is_multiple_of_five, range(n)))
print(get_multiples_of_five(50))
```

I have highlighted the main logic of `get_multiples_of_five`. Note how the filter uses `is_multiple_of_five` to filter the first n natural numbers. This seems a bit excessive, the task is simple and we don't need to keep the `is_multiple_of_five` function around for anything else. Let's rewrite it using a lambda function:

filter.lambda.py

```
def get_multiples_of_five(n):
    return list(filter(lambda k: not k % 5, range(n)))
print(get_multiples_of_five(50))
```

The logic is exactly the same but the filtering function is now a lambda. Defining a lambda is very easy and follows this form: `func_name = lambda [parameter_list]: expression`. A function object is returned, which is equivalent to this: `def func_name([parameter_list]): return expression`.

Note that optional parameters are indicated following the common syntax of wrapping them in square brackets.

Let's look at another couple of examples of equivalent functions defined in the two forms:

`lambda.explained.py`

```
# example 1: adder
def adder(a, b):
    return a + b
# is equivalent to:
adder_lambda = lambda a, b: a + b

# example 2: to uppercase
def to_upper(s):
    return s.upper()
# is equivalent to:
to_upper_lambda = lambda s: s.upper()
```

The preceding examples are very simple. The first one adds two numbers, and the second one produces the uppercase version of a string. Note that I assigned what is returned by the `lambda` expressions to a name (`adder_lambda`, `to_upper_lambda`), but there is no need for that when you use lambdas in the way we did in the `filter` example before.

Function attributes

Every function is a fully-fledged object and, as such, they have many attributes. Some of them are special and can be used in an introspective way to inspect the function object at runtime. The following script is an example that shows all of them and how to display their value for an example function:

`func.attributes.py`

```
def multiplication(a, b=1):
    """Return a multiplied by b. """
    return a * b

special_attributes = [
    "__doc__", "__name__", "__qualname__", "__module__",
    "__defaults__", "__code__", "__globals__", "__dict__",
    "__closure__", "__annotations__", "__kwdefaults__",
]

for attribute in special_attributes:
    print(attribute, '->', getattr(multiplication, attribute))
```

I used the built-in `getattr` function to get the value of those attributes. `getattr(obj, attribute)` is equivalent to `obj.attribute` and comes in handy when we need to get an attribute at runtime using its string name. Running this script yields:

```
$ python func.attributes.py
__doc__ -> Return a multiplied by b.
__name__ -> multiplication
__qualname__ -> multiplication
__module__ -> __main__
__defaults__ -> (1,)
__code__ -> <code object multiplication at 0x7ff529e79300, file "ch4/
func.attributes.py", line 1>
__globals__ -> {... omitted ...}
__dict__ -> {}
__closure__ -> None
__annotations__ -> {}
__kwdefaults__ -> None
```

I have omitted the value of the `__globals__` attribute, it was too big. An explanation of the meaning of this attribute can be found in the *types* section of the *Python Data Model* documentation page.

Built-in functions

Python comes with a lot of built-in functions. They are available anywhere and you can get a list of them by inspecting the `builtin` module with `dir(__builtin__)`, or by going to the official Python documentation. Unfortunately, I don't have the room to go through all of them here. Some of them we've already seen, such as `any`, `bin`, `bool`, `divmod`, `filter`, `float`, `getattr`, `id`, `int`, `len`, `list`, `min`, `print`, `set`, `tuple`, `type`, and `zip`, but there are many more, which you should read at least once.

Get familiar with them, experiment, write a small piece of code for each of them, make sure you have them at the tip of your fingers so that you can use them when you need them.

One final example

Before we finish off this chapter, how about a final example? I was thinking we could write a function to generate a list of prime numbers up to a limit. We've already seen the code for this so let's make it a function and, to keep it interesting, let's optimize it a bit.

It turns out that you don't need to divide it by all numbers from 2 to *N*-1 to decide if a number *N* is prime. You can stop at $\sqrt{N}$. Moreover, you don't need to test the division for all numbers from 2 to $\sqrt{N}$, you can just use the primes in that range. I'll leave it to you to figure out why this works, if you're interested. Let's see how the code changes:

primes.py

```
from math import sqrt, ceil

def get_primes(n):
    """Calculate a list of primes up to n (included). """
    primelist = []
    for candidate in range(2, n + 1):
        is_prime = True
        root = int(ceil(sqrt(candidate)))  # division limit
        for prime in primelist:  # we try only the primes
            if prime > root:  # no need to check any further
                break
            if candidate % prime == 0:
                is_prime = False
                break
        if is_prime:
            primelist.append(candidate)
    return primelist
```

The code is the same as in the previous chapter. We have changed the division algorithm so that we only test divisibility using the previously calculated primes and we stopped once the testing divisor was greater than the root of the candidate. We used the result list `primelist` to get the primes for the division. We calculated the root value using a fancy formula, the integer value of the ceiling of the root of the candidate. While a simple `int(k ** 0.5) + 1` would have served our purpose as well, the formula I chose is cleaner and requires me to use a couple of imports, which I wanted to show you. Check out the functions in the `math` module, they are very interesting!

Documenting your code

I'm a big fan of code that doesn't need documentation. When you program correctly, choose the right names and take care of the details, your code should come out as self-explanatory and documentation should not be needed. Sometimes a comment is very useful though, and so is some documentation. You can find the guidelines for documenting Python in *PEP257 – Docstring conventions*, but I'll show you the basics here.

Python is documented with strings, which are aptly called **docstrings**. Any object can be documented, and you can use either one-line or multi-line docstrings. One-liners are very simple. They should not provide another signature for the function, but clearly state its purpose.

docstrings.py

```python
def square(n):
    """Return the square of a number n. """
    return n ** 2

def get_username(userid):
    """Return the username of a user given their id. """
    return db.get(user_id=userid).username
```

Using triple double-quoted strings allows you to expand easily later on. Use sentences that end in a period, and don't leave blank lines before or after.

Multi-line comments are structured in a similar way. There should be a one-liner that briefly gives you the gist of what the object is about, and then a more verbose description. As an example, I have documented a fictitious `connect` function, using the Sphinx notation, in the following example.

 Sphinx is probably the most widely used tool for creating Python documentation. In fact, the official Python documentation was written with it. It's definitely worth spending some time checking it out.

docstrings.py

```python
def connect(host, port, user, password):
    """Connect to a database.

    Connect to a PostgreSQL database directly, using the given
    parameters.
```

```
:param host: The host IP.
:param port: The desired port.
:param user: The connection username.
:param password: The connection password.
:return: The connection object.
"""
# body of the function here...
return connection
```

Importing objects

Now that you know a lot about functions, let's see how to use them. The whole point of writing functions is to be able to later reuse them, and this in Python translates to importing them into the namespace in which you need them. There are many different ways to import objects into a namespace, but the most common ones are just two: `import module_name` and `from module_name import function_name`. Of course, these are quite simplistic examples, but bear with me for the time being.

The form `import module_name` finds the module `module_name` and defines a name for it in the local namespace where the `import` statement is executed.

The form `from module_name import identifier` is a little bit more complicated than that, but basically does the same thing. It finds `module_name` and searches for an attribute (or a submodule) and stores a reference to `identifier` in the local namespace.

Both forms have the option to change the name of the imported object using the `as` clause, like this:

```
from mymodule import myfunc as better_named_func
```

Just to give you a flavor of what importing looks like, here's an example from a test module of a number theory library I wrote some years ago (it's available on Bitbucket):

`karma/test_nt.py`

```
import unittest  # imports the unittest module
from math import sqrt  # imports one function from math
from random import randint, sample  # two imports at once

from mock import patch
from nose.tools import (  # multiline import
    assert_equal,
    assert_list_equal,
```

```
        assert_not_in,
    )


    from karma import nt, utils
```

I commented some of them and I hope it's easy to follow. When you have a structure of files starting in the root of your project, you can use the dot notation to get to the object you want to import into your current namespace, be it a package, a module, a class, a function, or anything else. The `from module import` syntax also allows a catch-all clause `from module import *`, which is sometimes used to get all the names from a module into the current namespace at once, but it's frowned upon for several reasons: performances, the risk of silently shadowing other names, and so on. You can read all that there is to know about imports in the official Python documentation but, before we leave the subject, let me give you a better example.

Imagine that you have defined a couple of functions: `square(n)` and `cube(n)` in a module, `funcdef.py`, which is in the `lib` folder. You want to use them in a couple of modules which are at the same level of the `lib` folder, called `func_import.py`, and `func_from.py`. Showing the tree structure of that project produces something like this:

```
├── func_from.py
├── func_import.py
├── lib
    ├── funcdef.py
    └── __init__.py
```

Before I show you the code of each module, please remember that in order to tell Python that it is actually a package, we need to put a `__init__.py` module in it.

 There are two things to note about the `__init__.py` file. First of all, it is a fully fledged Python module so you can put code into it as you would with any other module. Second, as of Python 3.3, its presence is no longer required to make a folder be interpreted as a Python package.

The code is as follows:

`funcdef.py`

```
def square(n):
    return n ** 2
def cube(n):
    return n ** 3
```

`func_import.py`

```
import lib.funcdef
print(lib.funcdef.square(10))
print(lib.funcdef.cube(10))
```

`func_from.py`

```
from lib.funcdef import square, cube
print(square(10))
print(cube(10))
```

Both these files, when executed, print 100 and 1000. You can see how differently we then access the `square` and `cube` functions, according to how and what we imported in the current scope.

Relative imports

The imports we've seen until now are called absolute, that is to say they define the whole path of the module that we want to import, or from which we want to import an object. There is another way of importing objects into Python, which is called relative import. It's helpful in situations in which we want to rearrange the structure of large packages without having to edit sub-packages, or when we want to make a module inside a package able to import itself. Relative imports are done by adding as many leading dots in front of the module as the number of folders we need to backtrack, in order to find what we're searching for. Simply put, it is something like this:

```
from .mymodule import myfunc
```

For a complete explanation of relative imports, refer to **PEP328** (`https://www.python.org/dev/peps/pep-0328`).

In later chapters, we'll create projects using different libraries and we'll use several different types of imports, including relative ones, so make sure you take a bit of time to read up about it in the official Python documentation.

Summary

In this chapter, finally we explored the world of functions. They are extremely important and, from now on, we'll use them basically everywhere. We talked about the main reasons for using them, the most important of which are code reuse and implementation hiding.

We saw that a function object is like a box that takes optional input and produces output. We can feed input values to a function in many different ways, using positional and keyword arguments, and using variable syntax for both types.

Now you should know how to write a function, how to document it, import it into your code, and call it.

The next chapter will force me to push my foot down on the throttle even more so I suggest you take any opportunity you get to consolidate and enrich the knowledge you've gathered until now by putting your nose into the Python official documentation.

Ready for the cool stuff? Let's go!

5

Saving Time and Memory

"It's not the daily increase but daily decrease. Hack away at the unessential."

-Bruce Lee

I love this quote from Bruce Lee, he was such a wise man! Especially, the second part, *hack away at the unessential*, is to me what makes a computer program elegant. After all, if there is a better way of doing things so that we don't waste time or memory, why not?

Sometimes, there are valid reasons for not pushing our code up to the maximum limit: for example, sometimes to achieve a negligible improvement, we have to sacrifice on readability or maintainability. Does it make any sense to have a web page served in 1 second with unreadable, complicated code, when we can serve it in 1.05 seconds with readable, clean code? No, it makes no sense.

On the other hand, sometimes it's perfectly licit to try and shave off a millisecond from a function, especially when the function is meant to be called thousands of times. Every millisecond you save there means one second saved per thousand of calls, and this could be meaningful for your application.

In light of these considerations, the focus of this chapter will not be to give you the tools to push your code to the absolute limits of performance and optimization "no matter what", but rather, to give you the tools to write efficient, elegant code that reads well, runs fast, and doesn't waste resources in an obvious way.

In this chapter, I will perform several measurements and comparisons, and cautiously draw some conclusions. Please do keep in mind that on a different box with a different setup or a different operating system, results may vary. Take a look at this code:

squares.py

```
def square1(n):
    return n ** 2  # squaring through the power operator

def square2(n):
    return n * n  # squaring through multiplication
```

Both functions return the square of *n*, but which is faster? From a simple benchmark I ran on them, it looks like the second is slightly faster. If you think about it, it makes sense: calculating the power of a number involves multiplication and therefore, whatever algorithm you may use to perform the power operation, it's not likely to beat a simple multiplication like the one in square2.

Do we care about this result? In most cases no. If you're coding an e-commerce website, chances are you won't ever even need to raise a number to the second power, and if you do, you probably will have to do it a few times per page. You don't need to concern yourself on saving a few microseconds on a function you call a few times.

So, when does optimization become important? One very common case is when you have to deal with huge collections of data. If you're applying the same function on a million customer objects, then you want your function to be tuned up to its best. Gaining 1/10 of a second on a function called one million times saves you 100,000 seconds, which are about 27.7 hours. That's not the same, right? So, let's focus on collections, and let's see which tools Python gives you to handle them with efficiency and grace.

Many of the concepts we will see in this chapter are based on those of **iterator** and **iterable**. Simply put, the ability for an object to return its next element when asked, and to raise a StopIteration exception when exhausted. We'll see how to code a custom iterator and iterable objects in the next chapter.

map, zip, and filter

We'll start by reviewing map, filter, and zip, which are the main built-in functions one can employ when handling collections, and then we'll learn how to achieve the same results using two very important constructs: **comprehensions** and **generators**. Fasten your seat belt!

map

According to the official Python documentation:

> map(function, iterable, ...) *returns an iterator that applies function to every item of iterable, yielding the results. If additional iterable arguments are passed, function must take that many arguments and is applied to the items from all iterables in parallel. With multiple iterables, the iterator stops when the shortest iterable is exhausted.*

We will explain the concept of yielding later on in the chapter. For now, let's translate this into code: we'll use a *lambda* function that takes a variable number of positional arguments, and just returns them as a tuple. Also, as map returns an iterator, we'll need to wrap each call to it within a list constructor so that we exhaust the iterable by putting all of its elements into a list (you'll see an example of this in the code):

map.example.py

```
>>> map(lambda *a: a, range(3))  # without wrapping in list...
<map object at 0x7f563513b518>  # we get the iterator object
>>> list(map(lambda *a: a, range(3)))  # wrapping in list...
[(0,), (1,), (2,)]  # we get a list with its elements
>>> list(map(lambda *a: a, range(3), 'abc'))  # 2 iterables
[(0, 'a'), (1, 'b'), (2, 'c')]
>>> list(map(lambda *a: a, range(3), 'abc', range(4, 7)))  # 3
[(0, 'a', 4), (1, 'b', 5), (2, 'c', 6)]
>>> # map stops at the shortest iterator
>>> list(map(lambda *a: a, (), 'abc'))  # empty tuple is shortest
[]
>>> list(map(lambda *a: a, (1, 2), 'abc'))  # (1, 2) shortest
[(1, 'a'), (2, 'b')]
>>> list(map(lambda *a: a, (1, 2, 3, 4), 'abc'))  # 'abc' shortest
[(1, 'a'), (2, 'b'), (3, 'c')]
```

In the preceding code you can see why, in order to present you with the results, I have to wrap the calls to map within a list constructor, otherwise I get the string representation of a map object, which is not really useful in this context, is it?

You can also notice how the elements of each iterable are applied to the function: at first, the first element of each iterable, then the second one of each iterable, and so on. Notice also that map stops when the shortest of the iterables we called it with is exhausted. This is actually a very nice behavior: it doesn't force us to level off all the iterables to a common length, and it doesn't break if they aren't all the same length.

map is very useful when you have to apply the same function to one or more collections of objects. As a more interesting example, let's see the **decorate-sort-undecorate** idiom (also known as **Schwartzian transform**). It's a technique that was extremely popular when Python sorting wasn't providing *key-functions*, and therefore today is less used, but it's a cool trick that still comes at hand once in a while.

Let's see a variation of it in the next example: we want to sort in descending order by the sum of credits accumulated by students, so to have the best student at position 0. We write a function to produce a decorated object, we sort, and then we undecorate. Each student has credits in three (possibly different) subjects. To decorate an object means to transform it, either adding extra data to it, or putting it into another object, in a way that allows us to be able to sort the original objects the way we want. After the sorting, we revert the decorated objects to get the original ones from them. This is called to undecorate.

decorate.sort.undecorate.py

```
students = [
    dict(id=0, credits=dict(math=9, physics=6, history=7)),
    dict(id=1, credits=dict(math=6, physics=7, latin=10)),
    dict(id=2, credits=dict(history=8, physics=9, chemistry=10)),
    dict(id=3, credits=dict(math=5, physics=5, geography=7)),
]

def decorate(student):
    # create a 2-tuple (sum of credits, student) from student dict
    return (sum(student['credits'].values()), student)

def undecorate(decorated_student):
    # discard sum of credits, return original student dict
    return decorated_student[1]

students = sorted(map(decorate, students), reverse=True)
students = list(map(undecorate, students))
```

In the preceding code, I highlighted the tricky and important parts. Let's start by understanding what each student object is. In fact, let's print the first one:

```
{'credits': {'history': 7, 'math': 9, 'physics': 6}, 'id': 0}
```

You can see that it's a dictionary with two keys: `id` and `credit`. The value of `credit` is also a dictionary in which there are three subject/grade key/value pairs. As I'm sure you recall from our visit in the data structures world, calling `dict.values()` returns an object similar to an `iterable`, with only the values. Therefore, `sum(student['credits'].values())`, for the first student is equivalent to `sum(9, 6, 7)` (or any permutation of those numbers because dictionaries don't retain order, but luckily for us, addition is commutative).

With that out of the way, it's easy to see what is the result of calling decorate with any of the students. Let's print the result of `decorate(students[0])`:

```
(22, {'credits': {'history': 7, 'math': 9, 'physics': 6}, 'id': 0})
```

That's nice! If we decorate all the students like this, we can sort them on their total amount of credits but just sorting the list of tuples. In order to apply the decoration to each item in students, we call `map(decorate, students)`. Then we sort the result, and then we undecorate in a similar fashion. If you have gone through the previous chapters correctly, understanding this code shouldn't be too hard.

Printing students after running the whole code yields:

```
$ python decorate.sort.undecorate.py
[{'credits': {'chemistry': 10, 'history': 8, 'physics': 9}, 'id': 2},
 {'credits': {'latin': 10, 'math': 6, 'physics': 7}, 'id': 1},
 {'credits': {'history': 7, 'math': 9, 'physics': 6}, 'id': 0},
 {'credits': {'geography': 7, 'math': 5, 'physics': 5}, 'id': 3}]
```

And you can see, by the order of the student objects, that they have indeed been sorted by the sum of their credits.

For more on the *decorate-sort-undecorate* idiom, there's a very nice introduction in the sorting how-to section of the official Python documentation (`https://docs.python.org/3.4/howto/sorting.html#the-old-way-using-decorate-sort-undecorate`).

One thing to notice about the sorting part: what if two or more students share the same total sum? The sorting algorithm would then proceed sorting the tuples by comparing the `student` objects with each other. This doesn't make any sense, and in more complex cases could lead to unpredictable results, or even errors. If you want to be sure to avoid this issue, one simple solution is to create a 3-tuple instead of a 2-tuple, having the sum of credits in the first position, the position of the `student` object in the `students` list in the second one, and the `student` object itself in the third one. This way, if the sum of credits is the same, the tuples will be sorted against the position, which will always be different and therefore enough to resolve the sorting between any pair of tuples. For more considerations on this topic, please check out the sorting how-to section on the official Python documentation.

zip

We've already covered `zip` in the previous chapters, so let's just define it properly and then I want to show you how you could combine it with `map`.

According to the Python documentation:

> `zip(*iterables)` *returns an iterator of tuples, where the i-th tuple contains the i-th element from each of the argument sequences or iterables. The iterator stops when the shortest input iterable is exhausted. With a single iterable argument, it returns an iterator of 1-tuples. With no arguments, it returns an empty iterator.*

Let's see an example:

`zip.grades.py`

```
>>> grades = [18, 23, 30, 27, 15, 9, 22]
>>> avgs = [22, 21, 29, 24, 18, 18, 24]
>>> list(zip(avgs, grades))
[(22, 18), (21, 23), (29, 30), (24, 27), (18, 15), (18, 9), (24, 22)]
>>> list(map(lambda *a: a, avgs, grades))  # equivalent to zip
[(22, 18), (21, 23), (29, 30), (24, 27), (18, 15), (18, 9), (24, 22)]
```

In the preceding code, we're zipping together the average and the grade for the last exam, per each student. Notice how the code inside the two list calls produces exactly the same result, showing how easy it is to reproduce `zip` using `map`. Notice also that, as we do for `map`, we have to feed the result of the `zip` call to a `list` constructor.

A simple example on the combined use of `map` and `zip` could be a way of calculating the element-wise maximum amongst sequences, that is, the maximum of the first element of each sequence, then the maximum of the second one, and so on:

maxims.py

```
>>> a = [5, 9, 2, 4, 7]
>>> b = [3, 7, 1, 9, 2]
>>> c = [6, 8, 0, 5, 3]
>>> maxs = map(lambda n: max(*n), zip(a, b, c))
>>> list(maxs)
[6, 9, 2, 9, 7]
```

Notice how easy it is to calculate the max values of three sequences. `zip` is not strictly needed of course, we could just use `map`, but this would require us to write a much more complicated function to feed `map` with. Sometimes we may be in a situation where changing the function we feed to `map` is not even possible. In cases like these, being able to massage the data (like we're doing in this example with `zip`) is very helpful.

filter

According to the Python documentation:

> `filter(function, iterable)` *construct an iterator from those elements of iterable for which function returns True. iterable may be either a sequence, a container which supports iteration, or an iterator. If function is* None, *the identity function is assumed, that is, all elements of iterable that are false are removed.*

Let's see a very quick example:

filter.py

```
>>> test = [2, 5, 8, 0, 0, 1, 0]
>>> list(filter(None, test))
[2, 5, 8, 1]
>>> list(filter(lambda x: x, test))   # equivalent to previous one
[2, 5, 8, 1]
>>> list(filter(lambda x: x > 4, test))   # keep only items > 4
[5, 8]
```

In the preceding code, notice how the second call to filter is equivalent to the first one. If we pass a function that takes one argument and returns the argument itself, only those arguments that are `True` will make the function return `True`, therefore this behavior is exactly the same as passing `None`. It's often a very good exercise to mimic some of the built-in Python behaviors. When you succeed you can say you fully understand how Python behaves in a specific situation.

Armed with `map`, `zip`, and `filter` (and several other functions from the Python standard library) we can massage sequences very effectively. But those functions are not the only way to do it. So let's see one of the nicest features of Python: comprehensions.

Comprehensions

Python offers you different types of comprehensions: `list`, `dict`, and `set`.

We'll concentrate on the first one for now, and then it will be easy to explain the other two.

A `list` comprehension is a quick way of making a list. Usually the list is the result of some operation that may involve applying a function, filtering, or building a different data structure.

Let's start with a very simple example I want to calculate a list with the squares of the first 10 natural numbers. How would you do it? There are a couple of equivalent ways:

squares.map.py

```
# If you code like this you are not a Python guy! ;)
>>> squares = []
>>> for n in range(10):
...     squares.append(n ** 2)
...
>>> list(squares)
[0, 1, 4, 9, 16, 25, 36, 49, 64, 81]


# This is better, one line, nice and readable
>>> squares = map(lambda n: n**2, range(10))
>>> list(squares)
[0, 1, 4, 9, 16, 25, 36, 49, 64, 81]
```

The preceding example should be nothing new for you. Let's see how to achieve the same result using a list comprehension:

squares.comprehension.py

```
>>> [n ** 2 for n in range(10)]
[0, 1, 4, 9, 16, 25, 36, 49, 64, 81]
```

As simple as that. Isn't it elegant? Basically we have put a `for` loop within square brackets. Let's now filter out the odd squares. I'll show you how to do it with `map` and `filter`, and then using a `list` comprehension again.

even.squares.py

```
# using map and filter
sq1 = list(
    filter(lambda n: not n % 2, map(lambda n: n ** 2, range(10)))
)
# equivalent, but using list comprehensions
sq2 = [n ** 2 for n in range(10) if not n % 2]

print(sq1, sq1 == sq2)  # prints: [0, 4, 16, 36, 64] True
```

I think that now the difference in readability is evident. The list comprehension reads much better. It's almost English: give me all squares ($n ** 2$) for n between 0 and 9 if n is even.

According to the Python documentation:

> *A list comprehension consists of brackets containing an expression followed by a* `for` *clause, then zero or more* `for` *or* `if` *clauses. The result will be a new list resulting from evaluating the expression in the context of the* `for` *and* `if` *clauses which follow it".*

Nested comprehensions

Let's see an example of nested loops. It's very common when dealing with algorithms to have to iterate on a sequence using two placeholders. The first one runs through the whole sequence, left to right. The second one as well, but it starts from the first one, instead of 0. The concept is that of testing all pairs without duplication. Let's see the classical `for` loop equivalent.

pairs.for.loop.py

```
items = 'ABCDE'
pairs = []
for a in range(len(items)):
```

```
        for b in range(a, len(items)):
            pairs.append((items[a], items[b]))
```

If you print pairs at the end, you get:

```
[('A', 'A'), ('A', 'B'), ('A', 'C'), ('A', 'D'), ('A', 'E'), ('B', 'B'),
('B', 'C'), ('B', 'D'), ('B', 'E'), ('C', 'C'), ('C', 'D'), ('C', 'E'),
('D', 'D'), ('D', 'E'), ('E', 'E')]
```

All the tuples with the same letter are those for which b is at the same position as a. Now, let's see how we can translate this in a list comprehension:

pairs.list.comprehension.py

```
    items = 'ABCDE'
    pairs = [(items[a], items[b])
        for a in range(len(items)) for b in range(a, len(items))]
```

This version is just two lines long and achieves the same result. Notice that in this particular case, because the for loop over b has a dependency on a, it must follow the for loop over a in the comprehension. If you swap them around, you'll get a name error.

Filtering a comprehension

We can apply filtering to a comprehension. Let's first do it with filter. Let's find all Pythagorean triples whose short sides are numbers smaller than 10. We obviously don't want to test a combination twice, and therefore we'll use a trick like the one we saw in the previous example.

 A **Pythagorean triple** is a triple (a, b, c) of integer numbers satisfying the equation $a^2 + b^2 = c^2$.

pythagorean.triple.py

```
    from math import sqrt
    # this will generate all possible pairs
    mx = 10
    legs = [(a, b, sqrt(a**2 + b**2))
        for a in range(1, mx) for b in range(a, mx)]
    # this will filter out all non pythagorean triples
    legs = list(
        filter(lambda triple: triple[2].is_integer(), legs))
    print(legs)  # prints: [(3, 4, 5.0), (6, 8, 10.0)]
```

In the preceding code, we generated a list of *3-tuples*, legs. Each tuple contains two integer numbers (the legs) and the hypotenuse of the Pythagorean triangle whose legs are the first two numbers in the tuple. For example, when a = 3 and b = 4, the tuple will be (3, 4, 5.0), and when a = 5 and b = 7, the tuple will be (5, 7, 8.602325267042627).

After having all the triples done, we need to filter out all those that don't have a hypotenuse that is an integer number. In order to do this, we filter based on `float_number.is_integer()` being `True`. This means that of the two example tuples I showed you before, the one with hypotenuse 5.0 will be retained, while the one with hypotenuse 8.602325267042627 will be discarded.

This is good, but I don't like that the triple has two integer numbers and a float. They are supposed to be all integers, so let's use map to fix this:

`pythagorean.triple.int.py`

```
from math import sqrt
mx = 10
legs = [(a, b, sqrt(a**2 + b**2))
    for a in range(1, mx) for b in range(a, mx)]
legs = filter(lambda triple: triple[2].is_integer(), legs)
# this will make the third number in the tuples integer
legs = list(
    map(lambda triple: triple[:2] + (int(triple[2]), ), legs))
print(legs)  # prints: [(3, 4, 5), (6, 8, 10)]
```

Notice the step we added. We take each element in legs and we slice it, taking only the first two elements in it. Then, we concatenate the slice with a 1-tuple, in which we put the integer version of that float number that we didn't like.

Seems like a lot of work, right? Indeed it is. Let's see how to do all this with a list comprehension:

`pythagorean.triple.comprehension.py`

```
from math import sqrt
# this step is the same as before
mx = 10
legs = [(a, b, sqrt(a**2 + b**2))
    for a in range(1, mx) for b in range(a, mx)]
# here we combine filter and map in one CLEAN list comprehension
legs = [(a, b, int(c)) for a, b, c in legs if c.is_integer()]
print(legs)  # prints: [(3, 4, 5), (6, 8, 10)]
```

I know. It's much better, isn't it? It's clean, readable, shorter. In other words, elegant.

 I'm going quite fast here, as anticipated in the summary of the last chapter. Are you playing with this code? If not, I suggest you do. It's very important that you play around, break things, change things, see what happens. Make sure you have a clear understanding of what is going on. You want to become a ninja, right?

dict comprehensions

Dictionary and set comprehensions work exactly like the list ones, only there is a little difference in the syntax. The following example will suffice to explain everything you need to know:

`dictionary.comprehensions.py`

```
from string import ascii_lowercase
lettermap = dict((c, k) for k, c in enumerate(ascii_lowercase, 1))
```

If you print `lettermap`, you will see the following (I omitted the middle results, you get the gist):

```
{'a': 1,
 'b': 2,
 'c': 3,
 ... omitted results ...
 'x': 24,
 'y': 25,
 'z': 26}
```

What happens in the preceding code is that we're feeding the `dict` constructor with a comprehension (technically, a generator expression, we'll see it in a bit). We tell the `dict` constructor to make *key/value* pairs from each tuple in the comprehension. We enumerate the sequence of all lowercase ASCII letters, starting from *1*, using `enumerate`. Piece of cake. There is also another way to do the same thing, which is closer to the other dictionary syntax:

```
lettermap = {c: k for k, c in enumerate(ascii_lowercase, 1)}
```

It does exactly the same thing, with a slightly different syntax that highlights a bit more of the *key: value* part.

Dictionaries do not allow duplication in the keys, as shown in the following example:

dictionary.comprehensions.duplicates.py

```
word = 'Hello'
swaps = {c: c.swapcase() for c in word}
print(swaps)  # prints: {'o': 'O', 'l': 'L', 'e': 'E', 'H': 'h'}
```

We create a dictionary with keys, the letters in the string `'Hello'`, and values of the same letters, but with the case swapped. Notice there is only one `'l'`: `'L'` pair. The constructor doesn't complain, simply reassigns duplicates to the latest value. Let's make this clearer with another example; let's assign to each key its position in the string:

dictionary.comprehensions.positions.py

```
word = 'Hello'
positions = {c: k for k, c in enumerate(word)}
print(positions)  # prints: {'l': 3, 'o': 4, 'e': 1, 'H': 0}
```

Notice the value associated to the letter `'l'`: 3. The pair `'l'`: 2 isn't there, it has been overridden by `'l'`: 3.

set comprehensions

Set comprehensions are very similar to list and dictionary ones. Python allows both the `set()` constructor to be used, or the explicit `{}` syntax. Let's see one quick example:

set.comprehensions.py

```
word = 'Hello'
letters1 = set(c for c in word)
letters2 = {c for c in word}
print(letters1)  # prints: {'l', 'o', 'H', 'e'}
print(letters1 == letters2)  # prints: True
```

Notice how for set comprehensions, as for dictionaries, duplication is not allowed and therefore the resulting set has only four letters. Also, notice that the expressions assigned to `letters1` and `letters2` produce equivalent sets.

The syntax used to create `letters2` is very similar to the one we can use to create a dictionary comprehension. You can spot the difference only by the fact that dictionaries require keys and values, separated by columns, while sets don't.

Generators

Generators are one very powerful tool that Python gifts us with. They are based on the concepts of *iteration*, as we said before, and they allow for coding patterns that combine elegance with efficiency.

Generators are of two types:

- **Generator functions**: These are very similar to regular functions, but instead of returning results through return statements, they use yield, which allows them to suspend and resume their state between each call
- **Generator expressions**: These are very similar to the list comprehensions we've seen in this chapter, but instead of returning a list they return an object that produces results one by one

Generator functions

Generator functions come under all aspects like regular functions, with one difference: instead of collecting results and returning them at once, they can start the computation, yield one value, suspend their state saving everything they need to be able to resume and, if called again, resume and perform another step. Generator functions are automatically turned into their own iterators by Python, so you can call `next` on them.

This is all very theoretical so, let's make it clear why such a mechanism is so powerful, and then let's see an example.

Say I asked you to count out loud from 1 to a million. You start, and at some point I ask you to stop. After some time, I ask you to resume. At this point, what is the minimum information you need to be able to resume correctly? Well, you need to remember the last number you called. If I stopped you after 31415, you will just go on with 31416, and so on.

The point is, you don't need to remember all the numbers you said before 31415, nor do you need them to be written down somewhere. Well, you may not know it, but you're behaving like a generator already!

Take a good look at the following code:

`first.n.squares.py`

```
def get_squares(n):  # classic function approach
    return [x ** 2 for x in range(n)]
print(get_squares(10))
```

```
def get_squares_gen(n):  # generator approach
    for x in range(n):
        yield x ** 2  # we yield, we don't return
print(list(get_squares_gen(10)))
```

The result of the prints will be the same: [0, 1, 4, 9, 16, 25, 36, 49, 64, 81]. But there is a huge difference between the two functions. get_squares is a classic function that collects all the squares of numbers in [0, *n*) in a list, and returns it. On the other hand, get_squares_gen is a generator, and behaves very differently. Each time the interpreter reaches the yield line, its execution is suspended. The only reason those prints return the same result is because we fed get_squares_gen to the list constructor, which when called like that exhausts the generator completely by asking the next element until a StopIteration is raised. Let's see this in detail:

first.n.squares.manual.py

```
def get_squares_gen(n):
    for x in range(n):
        yield x ** 2

squares = get_squares_gen(4)  # this creates a generator object
print(squares)  # <generator object get_squares_gen at 0x7f158...>
print(next(squares))  # prints: 0
print(next(squares))  # prints: 1
print(next(squares))  # prints: 4
print(next(squares))  # prints: 9
# the following raises StopIteration, the generator is exhausted,
# any further call to next will keep raising StopIteration
print(next(squares))
```

In the preceding code, each time we call next on the generator object, we either start it (first next) or make it resume from the last suspension point (any other next).

The first time we call next on it, we get 0, which is the square of 0, then 1, then 4, then 9 and since the for loop stops after that (n is 4), then the generator naturally ends. A classic function would at that point just return None, but in order to comply with the iteration protocol, a generator will instead raise a StopIteration exception.

This explains how a for loop works for example. When you call for k in range(n), what happens under the hood is that the for loop gets an iterator out of range(n) and starts calling next on it, until StopIteration is raised, which tells the for loop that the iteration has reached its end.

Having this behavior built-in in every iteration aspect of Python makes generators even more powerful because once we write them, we'll be able to plug them in whatever iteration mechanism we want.

At this point, you're probably asking yourself why would you want to use a generator instead of a regular function. Well, the title of this chapter should suggest the answer. I'll talk about performances later, so for now let's concentrate on another aspect: sometimes generators allow you to do something that wouldn't be possible with a simple list. For example, say you want to analyze all permutations of a sequence. If the sequence has length N, then the number of its permutations is $N!$. This means that if the sequence is 10 elements long, the number of permutations is 3628800. But a sequence of 20 elements would have 2432902008176640000 permutations. They grow factorially.

Now imagine you have a classic function that is attempting to calculate all permutations, put them in a list, and return it to you. With 10 elements, it would require probably a few tens of seconds, but for 20 elements there is simply no way that it can be done.

On the other hand, a generator function will be able to start the computation and give you back the first permutation, then the second, and so on. Of course you won't have the time to parse them all, they are too many, but at least you'll be able to work with some of them.

Remember when we were talking about the `break` statement in `for` loops? When we found a number dividing a *candidate prime* we were breaking the loop, no need to go on.

Sometimes it's exactly the same, only the amount of data you have to iterate over is so huge that you cannot keep it all in memory in a list. In this case, generators are invaluable: they make possible what wouldn't be possible otherwise.

So, in order to save memory (and time), use generator functions whenever possible.

It's also worth noting that you can use the return statement in a generator function. It will produce a `StopIteration` exception to be raised, effectively ending the iteration. This is extremely important. If a `return` statement were actually to make the function return something, it would break the iteration protocol. Python consistency prevents this, and allows us great ease when coding. Let's see a quick example:

gen.yield.return.py

```
def geometric_progression(a, q):
    k = 0
    while True:
        result = a * q**k
```

```
        if result <= 100000:
            yield result
        else:
            return
        k += 1

    for n in geometric_progression(2, 5):
        print(n)
```

The preceding code yields all terms of the geometric progression a, aq, aq^2, aq^3, ... When the progression produces a term that is greater than 100,000, the generator stops (with a `return` statement). Running the code produces the following result:

```
$ python gen.yield.return.py
2
10
50
250
1250
6250
31250
```

The next term would have been 156250, which is too big.

Going beyond next

At the beginning of this chapter, I told you that generator objects are based on the iteration protocol. We'll see in the next chapter a complete example of how to write a custom iterator/iterable object. For now, I just want you to understand how `next()` works.

What happens when you call `next(generator)` is that you're calling the `generator.__next__()` method. Remember, a **method** is just a function that belongs to an object, and objects in Python can have special methods. Our friend `__next__()` is just one of these and its purpose is to return the next element of the iteration, or to raise `StopIteration` when the iteration is over and there are no more elements to return.

 In Python, an object's special methods are also called **magic methods**, or **dunder** (from "double underscore") **methods**.

When we write a generator function, Python automatically transforms it into an object that is very similar to an iterator, and when we call next(generator), that call is transformed in generator.__next__(). Let's revisit the previous example about generating squares:

first.n.squares.manual.method.py

```python
def get_squares_gen(n):
    for x in range(n):
        yield x ** 2

squares = get_squares_gen(3)
print(squares.__next__())  # prints: 0
print(squares.__next__())  # prints: 1
print(squares.__next__())  # prints: 4
# the following raises StopIteration, the generator is exhausted,
# any further call to next will keep raising StopIteration
print(squares.__next__())
```

The result is exactly as the previous example, only this time instead of using the proxy call next(squares), we're directly calling squares.__next__().

Generator objects have also three other methods that allow controlling their behavior: send, throw, and close. send allows us to communicate a value back to the generator object, while throw and close respectively allow raising an exception within the generator and closing it. Their use is quite advanced and I won't be covering them here in detail, but I want to spend a few words at least about send, with a simple example.

Take a look at the following code:

gen.send.preparation.py

```python
def counter(start=0):
    n = start
    while True:
        yield n
        n += 1

c = counter()
print(next(c))  # prints: 0
print(next(c))  # prints: 1
print(next(c))  # prints: 2
```

The preceding iterator creates a generator object that will run forever. You can keep calling it, it will never stop. Alternatively, you can put it in a `for` loop, for example, `for n in counter():` ... and it will go on forever as well.

Now, what if you wanted to stop it at some point? One solution is to use a variable to control the `while` loop. Something like this:

gen.send.preparation.stop.py

```
stop = False
def counter(start=0):
    n = start
    while not stop:
        yield n
        n += 1

c = counter()
print(next(c))    # prints: 0
print(next(c))    # prints: 1
stop = True
print(next(c))    # raises StopIteration
```

This will do it. We start with `stop = False`, and until we change it to `True`, the generator will just keep going, like before. The moment we change stop to `True` though, the `while` loop will exit, and the next call will raise a `StopIteration` exception. This trick works, but I don't like it. We depend on an external variable, and this can lead to issues: what if another function changes that `stop`? Moreover, the code is scattered. In a nutshell, this isn't good enough.

We can make it better by using `generator.send()`. When we call `generator.send()`, the value that we feed to send will be passed in to the generator, execution is resumed, and we can fetch it via the `yield` expression. This is all very complicated when explained with words, so let's see an example:

gen.send.py

```
def counter(start=0):
    n = start
    while True:
        result = yield n                # A
        print(type(result), result)     # B
        if result == 'Q':
            break
        n += 1
```

```
c = counter()
print(next(c))            # C
print(c.send('Wow!'))     # D
print(next(c))            # E
print(c.send('Q'))        # F
```

Execution of the preceding code produces the following:

```
$ python gen.send.py
0
<class 'str'> Wow!
1
<class 'NoneType'> None
2
<class 'str'> Q
Traceback (most recent call last):
  File "gen.send.py", line 14, in <module>
    print(c.send('Q'))        # F
StopIteration
```

I think it's worth going through this code line by line, like if we were executing it, and see if we can understand what's going on.

We start the generator execution with a call to next (#C). Within the generator, n is set to the same value of start. The while loop is entered, execution stops (#A) and n (0) is yielded back to the caller. 0 is printed on the console.

We then call send (#D), execution resumes and result is set to 'Wow!' (still #A), then its type and value are printed on the console (#B). result is not 'Q', therefore n is incremented by 1 and execution goes back to the while condition, which, being True, evaluates to True (that wasn't hard to guess, right?). Another loop cycle begins, execution stops again (#A), and n (1) is yielded back to the caller. 1 is printed on the console.

At this point, we call next (#E), execution is resumed again (#A), and because we are not sending anything to the generator explicitly, Python behaves exactly like functions that are not using the return statement: the yield n expression (#A) returns None. result therefore is set to None, and its type and value are yet again printed on the console (#B). Execution continues, result is not 'Q' so n is incremented by 1, and we start another loop again. Execution stops again (#A) and n (2) is yielded back to the caller. 2 is printed on the console.

And now for the grand finale: we call `send` again (#F), but this time we pass in `'Q'`, therefore when execution is resumed, `result` is set to `'Q'` (#A). Its type and value are printed on the console (#B), and then finally the `if` clause evaluates to `True` and the `while` loop is stopped by the `break` statement. The generator naturally terminates and this means a `StopIteration` exception is raised. You can see the print of its traceback on the last few lines printed on the console.

This is not at all simple to understand at first, so if it's not clear to you, don't be discouraged. You can keep reading on and then you can come back to this example after some time.

Using `send` allows for interesting patterns, and it's worth noting that `send` can only be used to resume the execution, not to start it. Only `next` starts the execution of a generator.

The yield from expression

Another interesting construct is the `yield from` expression. This expression allows you to yield values from a subiterator. Its use allows for quite advanced patterns, so let's just see a very quick example of it:

gen.yield.for.py

```
def print_squares(start, end):
    for n in range(start, end):
        yield n ** 2

for n in print_squares(2, 5):
    print(n)
```

The previous code prints the numbers 4, 9, 16 on the console (on separate lines). By now, I expect you to be able to understand it by yourself, but let's quickly recap what happens. The `for` loop outside the function gets an iterator from `print_squares(2, 5)` and calls `next` on it until iteration is over. Every time the generator is called, execution is suspended (and later resumed) on `yield n ** 2`, which returns the square of the current n.

Let's see how we can transform this code benefiting from the `yield from` expression:

gen.yield.from.py

```
def print_squares(start, end):
    yield from (n ** 2 for n in range(start, end))

for n in print_squares(2, 5):
    print(n)
```

This code produces the same result, but as you can see the `yield from` is actually running a subiterator (`n ** 2 ...`). The `yield from` expression returns to the caller each value the subiterator is producing. It's shorter and it reads better.

Generator expressions

Let's now talk about the other techniques to generate values one at a time.

The syntax is exactly the same as list comprehensions, only, instead of wrapping the comprehension with square brackets, you wrap it with round braces. That is called a **generator expression**.

In general, generator expressions behave like equivalent list comprehensions, but there is one very important thing to remember: generators allow for one iteration only, then they will be exhausted. Let's see an example:

`generator.expressions.py`

```
>>> cubes = [k**3 for k in range(10)]  # regular list
>>> cubes
[0, 1, 8, 27, 64, 125, 216, 343, 512, 729]
>>> type(cubes)
<class 'list'>
>>> cubes_gen = (k**3 for k in range(10))  # create as generator
>>> cubes_gen
<generator object <genexpr> at 0x7ff26b5db990>
>>> type(cubes_gen)
<class 'generator'>
>>> list(cubes_gen)  # this will exhaust the generator
[0, 1, 8, 27, 64, 125, 216, 343, 512, 729]
>>> list(cubes_gen)  # nothing more to give
[]
```

Look at the line in which the generator expression is created and assigned the name `cubes_gen`. You can see it's a generator object. In order to see its elements, we can use a `for` loop, a manual set of calls to `next`, or simply, feed it to a `list` constructor, which is what I did.

Notice how, once the generator has been exhausted, there is no way to recover the same elements from it again. We need to recreate it, if we want to use it from scratch again.

In the next few examples, let's see how to reproduce `map` and `filter` using generator expressions:

gen.map.py

```
def adder(*n):
    return sum(n)
s1 = sum(map(lambda n: adder(*n), zip(range(100), range(1, 101))))
s2 = sum(adder(*n) for n in zip(range(100), range(1, 101)))
```

In the previous example, `s1` and `s2` are exactly the same: they are the sum of `adder(0, 1)`, `adder(1, 2)`, `adder(2, 3)`, and so on, which translates to `sum(1, 3, 5, ...)`. The syntax is different though, I find the generator expression to be much more readable:

gen.filter.py

```
cubes = [x**3 for x in range(10)]
odd_cubes1 = filter(lambda cube: cube % 2, cubes)
odd_cubes2 = (cube for cube in cubes if cube % 2)
```

In the previous example, `odd_cubes1` and `odd_cubes2` are the same: they generate a sequence of odd cubes. Yet again, I prefer the generator syntax. This should be evident when things get a little more complicated:

gen.map.filter.py

```
N = 20
cubes1 = map(
    lambda n: (n, n**3),
    filter(lambda n: n % 3 == 0 or n % 5 == 0, range(N))
)
cubes2 = (
    (n, n**3) for n in range(N) if n % 3 == 0 or n % 5 == 0)
```

The preceding code creates to generators `cubes1` and `cubes2`. They are exactly the same, and return 2-tuples (n, n^3) when n is a multiple of 3 or 5.

If you print the list (`cubes1`), you get: `[(0, 0), (3, 27), (5, 125), (6, 216), (9, 729), (10, 1000), (12, 1728), (15, 3375), (18, 5832)]`.

See how much better the generator expression reads? It may be debatable when things are very simple, but as soon as you start nesting functions a bit, like we did in this example, the superiority of the generator syntax is evident. Shorter, simpler, more elegant.

Now, let me ask you a question: what is the difference between the following lines of code?

sum.example.py

```
s1 = sum([n**2 for n in range(10**6)])
s2 = sum((n**2 for n in range(10**6)))
s3 = sum(n**2 for n in range(10**6))
```

Strictly speaking, they all produce the same sum. The expressions to get s2 and s3 are exactly the same because the braces in s2 are redundant. They are both generator expressions inside the sum function. The expression to get s1 is different though. Inside sum, we find a list comprehension. This means that in order to calculate s1, the sum function has to call next on a list, a million times.

Do you see where we're loosing time and memory? Before sum can start calling next on that list, the list needs to have been created, which is a waste of time and space. It's much better for sum to call next on a simple generator expression. There is no need to have all the numbers from range(10**6) stored in a list.

So, *watch out for extra parentheses when you write your expressions*: sometimes it's easy to skip on these details, which makes our code much different. Don't believe me?

sum.example.2.py

```
s = sum([n**2 for n in range(10**8)])   # this is killed
# s = sum(n**2 for n in range(10**8))   # this succeeds
print(s)
```

Try running the preceding example. If I run the first line, this is what I get:

```
$ python sum.example.2.py
Killed
```

On the other hand, if I comment out the first line, and uncomment the second one, this is the result:

```
$ python sum.example.2.py
333333328333333350000000
```

Sweet generator expressions. The difference between the two lines is that in the first one, a list with the squares of the first hundred million numbers must be made before being able to sum them up. That list is huge, and we run out of memory (at least, my box did, if yours doesn't try a bigger number), therefore Python kills the process for us. Sad face.

But when we remove the square brackets, we don't make a list any more. The sum function receives 0, 1, 4, 9, and so on until the last one, and sums them up. No problems, happy face.

Some performance considerations

So, we've seen that we have many different ways to achieve the same result. We can use any combination of `map`, `zip`, `filter`, or choose to go with a comprehension, or maybe choose to use a generator, either function or expression. We may even decide to go with `for` loops: when the logic to apply to each running parameter isn't simple, they may be the best option.

Other than readability concerns though, let's talk about performances. When it comes to performances, usually there are two factors which play a major role: **space** and **time**.

Space means the size of the memory that a data structure is going to take up. The best way to choose is to ask yourself if you really need a list (or tuple) or if a simple generator function would work as well. If the answer is yes, go with the generator, it'll save a lot of space. Same goes with functions: if you don't actually need them to return a list or tuple, then you can transform them in generator functions as well.

Sometimes, you will have to use lists (or tuples), for example there are algorithms that scan sequences using multiple pointers or maybe they run over the sequence more than once. A generator function (or expression) can be iterated over only once and then it's exhausted, so in these situations, it wouldn't be the right choice.

Time is a bit harder than space because it depends on more variables and therefore it isn't possible to state that *X is faster than Y* with absolute certainty for all cases. However, based on tests run on Python today, we can say that `map` calls can be twice as fast as equivalent `for` loops, and list comprehensions can be (always generally speaking) even faster than equivalent `map` calls.

In order to fully appreciate the reason behind these statements, we need to understand how Python works, and this is a bit outside the scope of this book, for it's too technical in detail. Let's just say that `map` and `list` comprehensions run at C language speed within the interpreter, while a Python `for` loop is run as Python bytecode within the Python Virtual Machine, which is often much slower.

There are several different implementations of Python. The original one, and still the most common one, is the one written in C. C is one of the most powerful and popular programming languages still used today.

These claims I made come from books and articles that you can find on the Web, but how about we do a small exercise and try to find out for ourselves? I will write a small piece of code that collects the results of divmod(a, b) for a certain set of integer pairs (a, b). I will use the time function from the time module to calculate the elapsed time of the operations that I will perform. Let's go!

performances.py

```python
from time import time
mx = 5500  # this is the max I could reach with my computer...

t = time()  # start time for the for loop
dmloop = []
for a in range(1, mx):
    for b in range(a, mx):
        dmloop.append(divmod(a, b))
print('for loop: {:.4f} s'.format(time() - t))  # elapsed time

t = time()  # start time for the list comprehension
dmlist = [
    divmod(a, b) for a in range(1, mx) for b in range(a, mx)]
print('list comprehension: {:.4f} s'.format(time() - t))

t = time()  # start time for the generator expression
dmgen = list(
    divmod(a, b) for a in range(1, mx) for b in range(a, mx))
print('generator expression: {:.4f} s'.format(time() - t))

# verify correctness of results and number of items in each list
print(dmloop == dmlist == dmgen, len(dmloop))
```

As you can see, we're creating three lists: dmloop, dmlist, dmgen (divmod-for loop, divmod-list comprehension, divmod-generator expression). We start with the slowest option, the for loops. Then we have a list comprehension, and finally a generator expression. Let's see the output:

```
$ python performances.py
for loop: 4.3433 s
list comprehension: 2.7238 s
generator expression: 3.1380 s
True 15122250
```

The `list` comprehension runs in 63% of the time taken by the `for` loop. That's impressive. The generator expression came quite close to that, with a good 72%. The reason the generator expression is slower is that we need to feed it to the `list()` constructor and this has a little bit more overhead compared to a sheer list comprehension.

I would never go with a generator expression in a similar case though, there is no point if at the end we want a list. I would just use a list comprehension, and the result of the previous example proves me right. On the other hand, if I just had to do those `divmod` calculations without retaining the results, then a generator expression would be the way to go because in such a situation a list comprehension would unnecessarily consume a lot of space.

So, to recap: generators are very fast and allow you to save on space. List comprehensions are in general even faster, but don't save on space. Pure Python `for` loops are the slowest option. Let's see a similar example that compares a `for` loop and a `map` call:

`performances.map.py`

```
from time import time
mx = 2 * 10 ** 7

t = time()
absloop = []
for n in range(mx):
    absloop.append(abs(n))
print('for loop: {:.4f} s'.format(time() - t))

t = time()
abslist = [abs(n) for n in range(mx)]
print('list comprehension: {:.4f} s'.format(time() - t))

t = time()
absmap = list(map(abs, range(mx)))
print('map: {:.4f} s'.format(time() - t))

print(absloop == abslist == absmap)
```

This code is conceptually very similar to the previous example. The only thing that has changed is that we're applying the `abs` function instead of the `divmod` one, and we have only one loop instead of two nested ones. Execution gives the following result:

```
$ python performances.map.py
for loop: 3.1283 s
list comprehension: 1.3966 s
map: 1.2319 s
True
```

And `map` wins the race! As I told you before, giving a statement of *what is faster than what* is very tricky. In this case, the `map` call is faster than the list comprehension.

Apart from the case by case little differences though, it's quite clear that the `for` loop option is the slowest one, so let's see what are the reasons we still want to use it.

Don't overdo comprehensions and generators

We've seen how powerful list comprehensions and generator expressions can be. And they are, don't get me wrong, but the feeling that I have when I deal with them is that their complexity grows exponentially. The more you try to do within a single comprehension or a generator expression, the harder it becomes to read, understand, and therefore to maintain or change.

Open a Python console and type in `import this`, let's read the Zen of Python again, in particular, there are a few lines that I think are very important to keep in mind:

```
>>> import this
The Zen of Python, by Tim Peters

Beautiful is better than ugly.
Explicit is better than implicit.  #
Simple is better than complex.  #
Complex is better than complicated.
Flat is better than nested.
Sparse is better than dense.
Readability counts.  #
Special cases aren't special enough to break the rules.
```

```
Although practicality beats purity.
Errors should never pass silently.
Unless explicitly silenced.
In the face of ambiguity, refuse the temptation to guess.
There should be one-- and preferably only one --obvious way to do it.
Although that way may not be obvious at first unless you're Dutch.
Now is better than never.
Although never is often better than *right* now.
If the implementation is hard to explain, it's a bad idea.  #
If the implementation is easy to explain, it may be a good idea.
Namespaces are one honking great idea -- let's do more of those!
```

I have put a comment sign on the right of the main focus points here. Comprehensions and generator expressions become hard to read, more implicit than explicit, complex, and they can be hard to explain. Sometimes you have to break them apart using the inside-out technique, to understand why they produce the result they produce.

To give you an example, let's talk a bit more about Pythagorean triples. Just to remind you, a Pythagorean triple is a tuple of positive integers (a, b, c) such that $a^2 + b^2 = c^2$.

We saw earlier in this chapter how to calculate them, but we did it in a very inefficient way because we were scanning all pairs of numbers below a certain threshold, calculating the hypotenuse, and filtering out those that were not producing a triple.

A better way to get a list of Pythagorean triples is to directly generate them. There are many different formulas to do this and we'll use one of them: the **Euclidean formula**.

This formula says that any triple (a, b, c), where $a = m^2 - n^2$, $b = 2mn$, $c = m^2 + n^2$, with m and n positive integers such that $m > n$, is a Pythagorean triple. For example, when $m = 2$ and $n = 1$, we find the smallest triple: (3, 4, 5).

There is one catch though: consider the triple (6, 8, 10), that is just like (3, 4, 5) with all the numbers multiplied by 2. This triple is definitely Pythagorean, since $6^2 + 8^2 = 10^2$, but we can derive it from (3, 4, 5) simply by multiplying each of its elements by 2. Same goes for (9, 12, 15), (12, 16, 20), and in general for all the triples that we can write as (3k, 4k, 5k), with k being a positive integer greater than 1.

A triple that cannot be obtained by multiplying the elements of another one by some factor k, is called **primitive**. Another way of stating this is: if the three elements of a triple are **coprime**, then the triple is primitive. Two numbers are coprime when they don't share any prime factor amongst their divisors, that is, their **greatest common divisor (GCD)** is 1. For example, 3 and 5 are coprime, while 3 and 6 are not, because they are both divisible by 3.

So, the Euclidean formula tells us that if m and n are coprime, and $m - n$ is odd, the triple they generate is *primitive*. In the following example, we will write a generator expression to calculate all the primitive Pythagorean triples whose hypotenuse (c) is less than or equal to some integer N. This means we want all triples for which $m^2 + n^2 \leq N$. When n is *1*, the formula looks like this: $m^2 \leq N - 1$, which means we can approximate the calculation with an upper bound of $m \leq N^{1/2}$.

So, to recap: m must be greater than n, they must also be coprime, and their difference $m - n$ must be odd. Moreover, in order to avoid useless calculations we'll put the upper bound for m at *floor(sqrt(N)) + 1*.

The function `floor` for a real number x gives the maximum integer n such that $n < x$, for example, *floor(3.8) = 3*, *floor(13.1) = 13*. Taking the *floor(sqrt(N)) + 1* means taking the integer part of the square root of N and adding a minimal margin just to make sure we don't miss out any number.

Let's put all of this into code, step by step. Let's start by writing a simple `gcd` function that uses **Euclid's algorithm**:

functions.py

```
def gcd(a, b):
    """Calculate the Greatest Common Divisor of (a, b). """
    while b != 0:
        a, b = b, a % b
    return a
```

The explanation of Euclid's algorithm is available on the Web, so I won't spend any time here talking about it; we need to concentrate on the generator expression. The next step is to use the knowledge we gathered before to generate a list of primitive Pythagorean triples:

pythagorean.triple.generation.py

```
from functions import gcd
N = 50

triples = sorted(                                          # 1
```

```
    ((a, b, c) for a, b, c in (                        # 2
        ((m**2 - n**2), (2 * m * n), (m**2 + n**2))    # 3
        for m in range(1, int(N**.5) + 1)              # 4
        for n in range(1, m)                           # 5
        if (m - n) % 2 and gcd(m, n) == 1              # 6
    ) if c <= N), key=lambda *triple: sum(*triple)     # 7
)

print(triples)
```

There you go. It's not easy to read, so let's go through it line by line. At #3, we start a generator expression that is creating triples. You can see from #4 and #5 that we're looping on m in *[1, M]* with *M* being the integer part of *sqrt(N)*, plus 1. On the other hand, n loops within *[1, m)*, to respect the *m > n* rule. Worth noting how I calculated *sqrt(N)*, that is, N**.5, which is just another way to do it that I wanted to show you.

At #6, you can see the filtering conditions to make the triples primitive: (m - n) % 2 evaluates to True when (m - n) is odd, and gcd(m, n) == 1 means m and n are coprime. With these in place, we know the triples will be primitive. This takes care of the innermost generator expression. The outermost one starts at #2, and finishes at #7. We take the triples *(a, b, c)* in (...innermost generator...) such that c <= N. This is necessary because $m \le N^{1/2}$ is the lowest upper bound that we can apply, but it doesn't guarantee that *c* will actually be less than or equal to *N*.

Finally, at #1 we apply sorting, to present the list in order. At #7, after the outermost generator expression is closed, you can see that we specify the sorting key to be the sum *a + b + c*. This is just my personal preference, there is no mathematical reason behind it.

So, what do you think? Was it straightforward to read? I don't think so. And believe me, this is still a simple example; I have seen expressions way more complicated than this one.

Unfortunately some programmers think that writing code like this is cool, that it's some sort of demonstration of their superior intellectual powers, of their ability to quickly read and digest intricate code.

Within a professional environment though, I find myself having much more respect for those who write efficient, clean code, and manage to keep ego out the door. Conversely, those who don't, will produce lines at which you will stare for a long time while swearing in three languages (at least this is what I do).

Now, let's see if we can rewrite this code into something easier to read:

`pythagorean.triple.generation.for.py`

```
from functions import gcd

def gen_triples(N):
    for m in range(1, int(N**.5) + 1):            # 1
        for n in range(1, m):                     # 2
            if (m - n) % 2 and gcd(m, n) == 1:    # 3
                c = m**2 + n**2                    # 4
                if c <= N:                         # 5
                    a = m**2 - n**2                # 6
                    b = 2 * m * n                  # 7
                    yield (a, b, c)                # 8

triples = sorted(
    gen_triples(50), key=lambda *triple: sum(*triple))  # 9
print(triples)
```

I feel so much better already. Let's go through this code as well, line by line. You'll see how easier it is to understand.

We start looping at #1 and #2, in exactly the same way we were looping in the previous example. On line #3, we have the filtering for primitive triples. On line #4, we deviate a bit from what we were doing before: we calculate c, and on line #5, we filter on c being less than or equal to N. Only when c satisfies that condition, we calculate a and b, and yield the resulting tuple. It's always good to delay all calculations for as much as possible so that we don't waste time, in case eventually we have to discard those results.

On the last line, before printing the result, we apply sorting with the same key we were using in the generator expression example.

I hope you agree, this example is easier to understand. And I promise you, if you have to modify the code one day, you'll find that modifying this one is easy, while to modify the other version will take much longer (and it will be more error prone).

Both examples, when run, print the following:

```
$ python pythagorean.triple.generation.py
[(3, 4, 5), (5, 12, 13), (15, 8, 17), (7, 24, 25), (21, 20, 29), (35, 12, 37), (9, 40, 41)]
```

The moral of the story is, try and use comprehensions and generator expressions as much as you can, but if the code starts to be complicated to modify or to read, you may want to refactor into something more readable. There is nothing wrong with this.

Name localization

Now that we are familiar with all types of comprehensions and generator expression, let's talk about name localization within them. Python 3.* localizes loop variables in all four forms of comprehensions: list, dict, set, and generator expressions. This behavior is therefore different from that of the for loop. Let's see a simple example to show all the cases:

scopes.py

```
A = 100
ex1 = [A for A in range(5)]
print(A)   # prints: 100

ex2 = list(A for A in range(5))
print(A)   # prints: 100

ex3 = dict((A, 2 * A) for A in range(5))
print(A)   # prints: 100

ex4 = set(A for A in range(5))
print(A)   # prints: 100

s = 0
for A in range(5):
    s += A
print(A)   # prints: 4
```

In the preceding code, we declare a global name A = 100, and then we exercise the four comprehensions: list, generator expression, dictionary, and set. None of them alter the global name A. Conversely, you can see at the end that the for loop modifies it. The last print statement prints 4.

Let's see what happens if A wasn't there:

scopes.noglobal.py

```
ex1 = [A for A in range(5)]
print(A)   # breaks: NameError: name 'A' is not defined
```

The preceding code would work the same with any of the four types of comprehensions. After we run the first line, A is not defined in the global namespace.

Once again, the for loop behaves differently:

scopes.for.py

```
s = 0
for A in range(5):
    s += A
print(A)  # prints: 4
print(globals())
```

The preceding code shows that after a for loop, if the loop variable wasn't defined before it, we can find it in the global frame. To make sure of it, let's take a peek at it by calling the globals() built-in function:

```
$ python scopes.for.py
4
{'__spec__': None, '__name__': '__main__', 's': 10, 'A': 4, '__doc__':
None, '__cached__': None, '__package__': None, '__file__': 'scopes.
for.py', '__loader__': <_frozen_importlib.SourceFileLoader object at
0x7f05a5a183c8>, '__builtins__': <module 'builtins' (built-in)>}
```

Together with a lot of other boilerplate stuff, we can spot 'A': 4.

Generation behavior in built-ins

Amongst the built-in types, the generation behavior is now quite common. This is a major difference between Python 2 and Python 3. A lot of functions such as map, zip, and filter have been transformed so that they return objects that behave like iterables. The idea behind this change is that if you need to make a list of those results you can always wrap the call in a list() class, and you're done. On the other hand, if you just need to iterate and want to keep the impact on memory as light as possible, you can use those functions safely.

Another notable example is the range function. In Python 2 it returns a list, and there is another function called xrange that returns an object that you can iterate on, which generates the numbers on the fly. In Python 3 this function has gone, and range now behaves like it.

But this concept in general is now quite widespread. You can find it in the open() function, which is used to operate on file objects (we'll see it in one of the next chapters), but also in enumerate, in the dictionary keys, values, and items methods, and several other places.

It all makes sense: Python's aim is to try and reduce the memory footprint by avoiding wasting space wherever is possible, especially in those functions and methods that are used extensively in most situations.

Do you remember at the beginning of this chapter? I said that it makes more sense to optimize the performances of code that has to deal with a lot of objects, rather than shaving off a few milliseconds from a function that we call twice a day.

One last example

Before we part from this chapter, I'll show you a simple problem that I submitted to candidates for a Python developer role in a company I used to work for.

The problem is the following: given the sequence 0 1 1 2 3 5 8 13 21 ... write a function that would return the terms of this sequence up to some limit N.

If you haven't recognized it, that is the Fibonacci sequence, which is defined as $F(0) = 0$, $F(1) = 1$ and, for any $n > 1$, $F(n) = F(n-1) + F(n-2)$. This sequence is excellent to test knowledge about recursion, memoization techniques and other technical details, but in this case it was a good opportunity to check whether the candidate knew about generators (and too many so called Python coders didn't, when I was interviewing them).

Let's start from a rudimentary version of a function, and then improve on it:

fibonacci.first.py

```python
def fibonacci(N):
    """Return all fibonacci numbers up to N. """
    result = [0]
    next_n = 1
    while next_n <= N:
        result.append(next_n)
        next_n = sum(result[-2:])
    return result

print(fibonacci(0))   # [0]
print(fibonacci(1))   # [0, 1, 1]
print(fibonacci(50))  # [0, 1, 1, 2, 3, 5, 8, 13, 21, 34]
```

From the top: we set up the `result` list to a starting value of `[0]`. Then we start the iteration from the next element (`next_n`), which is `1`. While the next element is not greater than `N`, we keep appending it to the list and calculating the next. We calculate the next element by taking a slice of the last two elements in the `result` list and passing it to the `sum` function. Add some `print` statements here and there if this is not clear to you, but by now I would expect it not to be an issue.

When the condition of the `while` loop evaluates to `False`, we exit the loop and return `result`. You can see the result of those `print` statements in the comments next to each of them.

At this point, I would ask the candidate the following question: "What if I just wanted to iterate over those numbers?" A good candidate would then change the code like the next listing (an excellent candidate would have started with it!):

fibonacci.second.py

```
def fibonacci(N):
    """Return all fibonacci numbers up to N. """
    yield 0
    if N == 0:
        return
    a = 0
    b = 1
    while b <= N:
        yield b
        a, b = b, a + b


print(list(fibonacci(0)))   # [0]
print(list(fibonacci(1)))   # [0, 1, 1]
print(list(fibonacci(50)))  # [0, 1, 1, 2, 3, 5, 8, 13, 21, 34]
```

This is actually one of the solutions I was given. I don't know why I kept it, but I'm glad I did so I can show it to you. Now, the `fibonacci` function is a *generator function*. First we yield `0`, then if `N` is `0` we return (this will cause a `StopIteration` exception to be raised). If that's not the case, we start iterating, yielding `b` at every loop cycle, and then updating `a` and `b`. All we need in order to be able to produce the next element of the sequence is the past two: `a` and `b`, respectively.

This code is much better, has a lighter memory footprint and all we have to do to get a list of Fibonacci numbers is to wrap the call with `list()`, as usual.

But what about elegance? I cannot leave the code like that. It was decent for an interview, where the focus is more on functionality than elegance, but here I'd like to show you a nicer version:

`fibonacci.elegant.py`

```
def fibonacci(N):
    """Return all fibonacci numbers up to N. """
    a, b = 0, 1
    while a <= N:
        yield a
        a, b = b, a + b
```

Much better. The whole body of the function is four lines, five if you count the docstring. Notice how in this case using tuple assignment (`a, b = 0, 1` and `a, b = b, a + b`) helps in making the code shorter, and more readable. It's one of the features of Python I like a lot.

Summary

In this chapter, we explored the concept of iteration and generation a bit more deeply. We saw the `map`, `zip` and `filter` functions quite in detail, and how to use them as an alternative to a regular `for` loop approach.

Then we saw the concept of comprehensions, for lists, dictionaries, and sets. We saw their syntax and how to use them as an alternative to both the classic `for` loop approach and also to the use of `map`, `zip`, and `filter` functions.

Finally, we talked about the concept of generation, in two forms: generator functions and expressions. We learned how to save time and space by using generation techniques and saw how they can make possible what wouldn't normally be if we used a conventional approach based on lists.

We talked about performances, and saw that `for` loops are last in terms of speed, but they provide the best readability and flexibility to change. On the other hand, functions such as `map` and `filter` can be much faster, and comprehensions may be even better.

The complexity of the code written using these techniques grows exponentially so, in order to favor readability and ease of maintainability, we still need to use the classic `for` loop approach at times. Another difference is in the name localization, where the `for` loop behaves differently from all other types of comprehensions.

The next chapter will be all about objects and classes. Structurally similar to this one, in that we won't explore many different subjects, rather, just a few of them, but we'll try to dive a little bit more deeply.

Make sure you understand well the concepts of this chapter before jumping to the next one. We're building a wall brick by brick, and if the foundation is not solid, we won't get very far.

6

Advanced Concepts – OOP, Decorators, and Iterators

"La classe non è acqua. (Class will out)"

- Italian saying

I could probably write a small book about **object-oriented programming** (referred to as **OOP** henceforth) and classes. In this chapter, I'm facing the hard challenge of finding the balance between breadth and depth. There are simply too many things to tell, and there's plenty of them that would take more than this whole chapter if I described them alone in depth. Therefore, I will try to give you what I think is a good panoramic view of the fundamentals, plus a few things that may come in handy in the next chapters. Python's official documentation will help in filling the gaps.

We're going to explore three important concepts in this chapter: decorators, OOP, and iterators.

Decorators

In the previous chapter, I measured the execution time of various expressions. If you recall, I had to initialize a variable to the start time, and subtract it from the current time after execution in order to calculate the elapsed time. I also printed it on the console after each measurement. That was very tedious.

Every time you find yourself repeating things, an alarm bell should go off. Can you put that code in a function and avoid repetition? The answer most of the time is *yes*, so let's look at an example.

decorators/time.measure.start.py

```
from time import sleep, time

def f():
    sleep(.3)

def g():
    sleep(.5)

t = time()
f()
print('f took: ', time() - t)   # f took: 0.3003859519958496

t = time()
g()
print('g took:', time() - t)   # g took: 0.5005719661712646
```

In the preceding code, I defined two functions, f and g, which do nothing but sleep (by 0.3 and 0.5 seconds respectively). I used the sleep function to suspend the execution for the desired amount of time. I also highlighted how we calculate the time elapsed by setting t to the current time and then subtracting it when the task is done. You can see that the measure is pretty accurate.

Now, how do we avoid repeating that code and those calculations? One first potential approach could be the following:

decorators/time.measure.dry.py

```
from time import sleep, time

def f():
    sleep(.3)

def g():
    sleep(.5)

def measure(func):
    t = time()
    func()
```

```
    print(func.__name__, 'took:', time() - t)

measure(f)   # f took: 0.30041074752807617
measure(g)   # g took: 0.5006198883056641
```

Ah, much better now. The whole timing mechanism has been encapsulated into a function so we don't repeat code. We print the function name dynamically and it's easy enough to code. What if we need to pass arguments to the function we measure? This code would get just a bit more complicated, so let's see an example.

decorators/time.measure.arguments.py

```
from time import sleep, time

def f(sleep_time=0.1):
    sleep(sleep_time)

def measure(func, *args, **kwargs):
    t = time()
    func(*args, **kwargs)
    print(func.__name__, 'took:', time() - t)

measure(f, sleep_time=0.3)   # f took: 0.3004162311553955
measure(f, 0.2)   # f took: 0.20028162002563477
```

Now, f is expecting to be fed `sleep_time` (with a default value of `0.1`). I also had to change the `measure` function so that it is now accepting a function, any variable positional arguments, and any variable keyword arguments. In this way, whatever we call `measure` with, we redirect those arguments to the call to f we do inside.

This is very good, but we can push it a little bit further. Let's say we want to somehow have that timing behavior built-in in the f function, so that we could just call it and have that measure taken. Here's how we could do it:

decorators/time.measure.deco1.py

```
from time import sleep, time

def f(sleep_time=0.1):
    sleep(sleep_time)

def measure(func):
    def wrapper(*args, **kwargs):
        t = time()
        func(*args, **kwargs)
        print(func.__name__, 'took:', time() - t)
```

```
    return wrapper

f = measure(f)   # decoration point

f(0.2)   # f took: 0.2002875804901123
f(sleep_time=0.3)   # f took: 0.3003721237182617
print(f.__name__)   # wrapper   <- ouch!
```

The preceding code is probably not so straightforward. I confess that, even today, it sometimes requires me some serious concentration to understand some decorators, they can be pretty nasty. Let's see what happens here. The magic is in the **decoration point**. We basically reassign f with whatever is returned by measure when we call it with f as an argument. Within measure, we define another function, wrapper, and then we return it. So, the net effect is that after the decoration point, when we call f, we're actually calling wrapper. Since the wrapper inside is calling func, which is f, we are actually closing the loop like that. If you don't believe me, take a look at the last line.

wrapper is actually... a wrapper. It takes variable and positional arguments, and calls f with them. It also does the time measurement trick around the call.

This technique is called **decoration**, and measure is, at all effects, a **decorator**. This paradigm became so popular and widely used that at some point, Python added a special syntax for it (check **PEP 318**). Let's explore three cases: one decorator, two decorators, and one decorator that takes arguments.

decorators/syntax.py

```
def func(arg1, arg2, ...):
    pass
func = decorator(func)

# is equivalent to the following:

@decorator
def func(arg1, arg2, ...):
    pass
```

Basically, instead of manually reassigning the function to what was returned by the decorator, we prepend the definition of the function with the special syntax @decorator_name.

We can apply multiple decorators to the same function in the following way:

decorators/syntax.py

```
def func(arg1, arg2, ...):
    pass
func = deco1(deco2(func))

# is equivalent to the following:

@deco1
@deco2
def func(arg1, arg2, ...):
    pass
```

When applying multiple decorators, pay attention to the order, should it matter. In the preceding example, func is decorated with deco2 first, and the result is decorated with deco1. A good rule of thumb is: *the closer the decorator to the function, the sooner it is applied.*

Some decorators can take arguments. This technique is generally used to produce other decorators. Let's look at the syntax, and then we'll see an example of it.

decorators/syntax.py

```
def func(arg1, arg2, ...):
    pass
func = decoarg(argA, argB)(func)

# is equivalent to the following:

@decoarg(argA, argB)
def func(arg1, arg2, ...):
    pass
```

As you can see, this case is a bit different. First decoarg is called with the given arguments, and then its return value (the actual decorator) is called with func. Before I give you another example, let's fix one thing that is bothering me. I don't want to lose the original function name and docstring (and the other attributes as well, check the documentation for the details) when I decorate it. But because inside our decorator we return wrapper, the original attributes from func are lost and f ends up being assigned the attributes of wrapper. There is an easy fix for that from functools, a wonderful module from the Python standard library. I will fix the last example, and I will also rewrite its syntax to use the @ operator.

decorators/time.measure.deco2.py

```
from time import sleep, time
from functools import wraps
```

```python
def measure(func):
    @wraps(func)
    def wrapper(*args, **kwargs):
        t = time()
        func(*args, **kwargs)
        print(func.__name__, 'took:', time() - t)
    return wrapper


@measure
def f(sleep_time=0.1):
    """I'm a cat. I love to sleep! """
    sleep(sleep_time)


f(sleep_time=0.3)  # f took: 0.30039525032043457
print(f.__name__, ':', f.__doc__)
# f : I'm a cat. I love to sleep!
```

Now we're talking! As you can see, all we need to do is to tell Python that `wrapper` actually wraps `func` (by means of the `wraps` function), and you can see that the original name and docstring are now maintained.

Let's see another example. I want a decorator that prints an error message when the result of a function is greater than a threshold. I will also take this opportunity to show you how to apply two decorators at once.

decorators/two.decorators.py

```python
from time import sleep, time
from functools import wraps


def measure(func):
    @wraps(func)
    def wrapper(*args, **kwargs):
        t = time()
        result = func(*args, **kwargs)
        print(func.__name__, 'took:', time() - t)
        return result
    return wrapper


def max_result(func):
    @wraps(func)
    def wrapper(*args, **kwargs):
        result = func(*args, **kwargs)
        if result > 100:
```

```
        print('Result is too big ({0}). Max allowed is 100.'
            .format(result))
    return result
    return wrapper


@measure
@max_result
def cube(n):
    return n ** 3


print(cube(2))
print(cube(5))
```

 Take your time in studying the preceding example until you are sure you understand it well. If you do, I don't think there is any decorator you won't be able to write afterwards.

I had to enhance the `measure` decorator, so that its `wrapper` now returns the result of the call to `func`. The `max_result` decorator does that as well, but before returning, it checks that `result` is not greater than 100, which is the maximum allowed.

I decorated `cube` with both of them. First, `max_result` is applied, then `measure`. Running this code yields this result:

```
$ python two.decorators.py
cube took: 7.62939453125e-06  #
8  #
Result is too big (125). Max allowed is 100.
cube took: 1.1205673217773438e-05
125
```

For your convenience, I put a # to the right of the results of the first call: `print(cube(2))`. The result is 8, and therefore it passes the threshold check silently. The running time is measured and printed. Finally, we print the result (8).

On the second call, the result is 125, so the error message is printed, the result returned, and then it's the turn of `measure`, which prints the running time again, and finally, we print the result (125).

Had I decorated the `cube` function with the same two decorators but in a different order, the error message would follow the line that prints the running time, instead of preceding it.

A decorator factory

Let's simplify this example now, going back to a single decorator: `max_result`.
I want to make it so that I can decorate different functions with different thresholds,
and I don't want to write one decorator for each threshold. Let's amend `max_result`
so that it allows us to decorate functions specifying the threshold dynamically.

decorators/decorators.factory.py

```python
from functools import wraps

def max_result(threshold):
    def decorator(func):
        @wraps(func)
        def wrapper(*args, **kwargs):
            result = func(*args, **kwargs)
            if result > threshold:
                print(
                    'Result is too big ({0}). Max allowed is {1}.'
                    .format(result, threshold))
            return result
        return wrapper
    return decorator

@max_result(75)
def cube(n):
    return n ** 3

print(cube(5))
```

This preceding code shows you how to write a **decorator factory**. If you recall,
decorating a function with a decorator that takes arguments is the same as writing
`func = decorator(argA, argB)(func)`, so when we decorate `cube` with
`max_result(75)`, we're doing `cube = max_result(75)(cube)`.

Let's go through what happens, step by step. When we call `max_result(75)`,
we enter its body. A `decorator` function is defined inside, which takes a function
as its only argument. Inside that function, the usual decorator trick is performed.
We define a wrapper, inside of which we check the result of the original function's
call. The beauty of this approach is that from the innermost level, we can still refer
to both `func` and `threshold`, which allows us to set the threshold dynamically.

`wrapper` **returns** `result`, `decorator` **returns** `wrapper`, and `max_result` **returns** `decorator`. This means that our call `cube = max_result(75)(cube)`, actually becomes `cube = decorator(cube)`. Not just any `decorator` though, but one for which `threshold` has the value `75`. This is achieved by a mechanism called **closure**, which is outside of the scope of this chapter but nonetheless very interesting, so I mentioned it for you to do some research on it.

Running the last example produces the following result:

```
$ python decorators.factory.py
Result is too big (125). Max allowed is 75.
125
```

The preceding code allows me to use the `max_result` decorator with different thresholds at my own will, like this:

decorators/decorators.factory.py

```
@max_result(75)
def cube(n):
    return n ** 3

@max_result(100)
def square(n):
    return n ** 2

@max_result(1000)
def multiply(a, b):
    return a * b
```

Note that every decoration uses a different `threshold` value.

Decorators are very popular in Python. They are used quite often and they simplify (and beautify, I dare say) the code a lot.

Object-oriented programming

It's been quite a long and hopefully nice journey and, by now, we should be ready to explore object-oriented programming. I'll use the definition from *Kindler, E.; Krivy, I. (2011). Object-Oriented Simulation of systems with sophisticated control. International Journal of General Systems*, and adapt it to Python:

> *Object-oriented programming (OOP) is a programming paradigm based on the concept of "objects", which are data structures that contain data, in the form of attributes, and code, in the form of functions known as methods. A distinguishing feature of objects is that an object's method can access and often modify the data attributes of the object with which they are associated (objects have a notion of "self"). In OO programming, computer programs are designed by making them out of objects that interact with one another.*

Python has full support for this paradigm. Actually, as we have already said, *everything in Python is an object*, so this shows that OOP is not just supported by Python, but it's part of its very core.

The two main players in OOP are **objects** and **classes**. Classes are used to create objects (objects are instances of the classes with which they were created), so we could see them as instance factories. When objects are created by a class, they inherit the class attributes and methods. They represent concrete items in the program's domain.

The simplest Python class

I will start with the simplest class you could ever write in Python.

oop/simplest.class.py

```python
class Simplest():  # when empty, the braces are optional
    pass

print(type(Simplest))  # what type is this object?

simp = Simplest()  # we create an instance of Simplest: simp
print(type(simp))  # what type is simp?
# is simp an instance of Simplest?
print(type(simp) == Simplest)  # There's a better way for this
```

Let's run the preceding code and explain it line by line:

```
$ python oop/simplest.class.py
<class 'type'>
<class '__main__.Simplest'>
True
```

The `Simplest` class I defined only has the `pass` instruction for its body, which means it doesn't have any custom attributes or methods. I will print its type (`__main__` is the name of the scope in which top-level code executes), and I am aware that, in the comment, I wrote *object* instead of *class*. It turns out that, as you can see by the result of that `print`, *classes are actually objects*. To be precise, they are instances of `type`. Explaining this concept would lead to a talk about **metaclasses** and **metaprogramming**, advanced concepts that require a solid grasp of the fundamentals to be understood and alas this is beyond the scope of this chapter. As usual, I mentioned it to leave a pointer for you, for when you'll be ready to dig deeper.

Let's go back to the example: I used `Simplest` to create an instance, `simp`. You can see that the *syntax to create an instance is the same we use to call a function*.

Then we print what type `simp` belongs to and we verify that `simp` is in fact an instance of `Simplest`. I'll show you a better way of doing this later on in the chapter.

Up to now, it's all very simple. What happens when we write `class ClassName()`: `pass`, though? Well, what Python does is create a class object and assign it a name. This is very similar to what happens when we declare a function using `def`.

Class and object namespaces

After the class object has been created (which usually happens when the module is first imported), it basically represents a namespace. We can call that class to create its instances. Each instance inherits the class attributes and methods and is given its own namespace. We already know that, to walk a namespace, all we need to do is to use the dot (`.`) operator.

Let's look at another example:

oop/class.namespaces.py

```
class Person():
    species = 'Human'

print(Person.species)  # Human
```

```
Person.alive = True   # Added dynamically!
print(Person.alive)   # True

man = Person()
print(man.species)   # Human (inherited)
print(man.alive)   # True (inherited)

Person.alive = False
print(man.alive)   # False (inherited)

man.name = 'Darth'
man.surname = 'Vader'
print(man.name, man.surname)   # Darth Vader
```

In the preceding example, I have defined a class attribute called species. Any variable defined in the body of a class is an attribute that belongs to that class. In the code, I have also defined Person.alive, which is another class attribute. You can see that there is no restriction on accessing that attribute from the class. You can see that man, which is an instance of Person, inherits both of them, and reflects them instantly when they change.

man has also two attributes which belong to its own namespace and therefore are called **instance attributes**: name and surname.

 Class attributes are shared amongst all instances, while instance attributes are not; therefore, you should use class attributes to provide the states and behaviors to be shared by all instances, and use instance attributes for data that belongs just to one specific object.

Attribute shadowing

When you search for an attribute in an object, if it is not found, Python keeps searching in the class that was used to create that object (and keeps searching until it's either found or the end of the inheritance chain is reached). This leads to an interesting shadowing behavior. Let's look at an example:

oop/class.attribute.shadowing.py

```
class Point():
    x = 10
    y = 7

p = Point()
```

```
print(p.x)  # 10 (from class attribute)
print(p.y)  # 7 (from class attribute)

p.x = 12  # p gets its own 'x' attribute
print(p.x)  # 12 (now found on the instance)
print(Point.x)  # 10 (class attribute still the same)

del p.x  # we delete instance attribute
print(p.x)  # 10 (now search has to go again to find class attr)

p.z = 3  # let's make it a 3D point
print(p.z)  # 3

print(Point.z)
# AttributeError: type object 'Point' has no attribute 'z'
```

The preceding code is very interesting. We have defined a class called Point with two class attributes, x and y. When we create an instance, p, you can see that we can print both x and y from p's namespace (p.x and p.y). What happens when we do that is that Python doesn't find any x or y attributes on the instance, and therefore searches the class, and finds them there.

Then we give p its own x attribute by assigning p.x = 12. This behavior may appear a bit weird at first, but if you think about it, it's exactly the same as what happens in a function that declares x = 12 when there is a global x = 10 outside. We know that x = 12 won't affect the global one, and for classes and instances, it is exactly the same.

After assigning p.x = 12, when we print it, the search doesn't need to read the class attributes, because x is found on the instance, therefore we get 12 printed out.

We also print Point.x which refers to x in the class namespace.

And then, we delete x from the namespace of p, which means that, on the next line, when we print it again, Python will go again and search for it in the class, because it won't be found in the instance any more.

The last three lines show you that assigning attributes to an instance doesn't mean that they will be found in the class. Instances get whatever is in the class, but the opposite is not true.

What do you think about putting the x and y coordinates as class attributes? Do you think it was a good idea?

I, me, and myself – using the self variable

From within a class method we can refer to an instance by means of a special argument, called self by convention. self is always the first attribute of an instance method. Let's examine this behavior together with how we can share, not just attributes, but methods with all instances.

oop/class.self.py

```
class Square():
    side = 8
    def area(self):  # self is a reference to an instance
        return self.side ** 2

sq = Square()
print(sq.area())  # 64 (side is found on the class)
print(Square.area(sq))  # 64 (equivalent to sq.area())

sq.side = 10
print(sq.area())  # 100 (side is found on the instance)
```

Note how the area method is used by sq. The two calls, Square.area(sq) and sq.area(), are equivalent, and teach us how the mechanism works. Either you pass the instance to the method call (Square.area(sq)), which within the method will be called self, or you can use a more comfortable syntax: sq.area() and Python will translate that for you behind the curtains.

Let's look at a better example:

oop/class.price.py

```
class Price():
    def final_price(self, vat, discount=0):
        """Returns price after applying vat and fixed discount."""
        return (self.net_price * (100 + vat) / 100) - discount

p1 = Price()
p1.net_price = 100
print(Price.final_price(p1, 20, 10))  # 110 (100 * 1.2 - 10)
print(p1.final_price(20, 10))  # equivalent
```

The preceding code shows you that nothing prevents us from using arguments when declaring methods. We can use the exact same syntax as we used with the function, but we need to remember that the first argument will always be the instance.

Initializing an instance

Have you noticed how, before calling `p1.final_price(...)`, we had to assign `net_price` to `p1`? There is a better way to do it. In other languages, this would be called a **constructor**, but in Python, it's not. It is actually an **initializer**, since it works on an already created instance, and therefore it's called `__init__`. It's a *magic method*, which is run right after the object is created. Python objects also have a `__new__` method, which is the actual constructor. In practice, it's not so common to have to override it though, it's a practice that is mostly used when coding metaclasses, which is a fairly advanced topic that we won't explore in the book.

`oop/class.init.py`

```
class Rectangle():
    def __init__(self, sideA, sideB):
        self.sideA = sideA
        self.sideB = sideB

    def area(self):
        return self.sideA * self.sideB

r1 = Rectangle(10, 4)
print(r1.sideA, r1.sideB)  # 10 4
print(r1.area())  # 40

r2 = Rectangle(7, 3)
print(r2.area())  # 21
```

Things are finally starting to take shape. When an object is created, the `__init__` method is automatically run for us. In this case, I coded it so that when we create an object (by calling the class name like a function), we pass arguments to the creation call, like we would on any regular function call. The way we pass parameters follows the signature of the `__init__` method, and therefore, in the two creation statements, 10 and 7 will be `sideA` for `r1` and `r2` respectively, while 4 and 3 will be `sideB`. You can see that the call to `area()` from `r1` and `r2` reflects that they have different instance arguments.

Setting up objects in this way is much nicer and convenient.

OOP is about code reuse

By now it should be pretty clear: *OOP is all about code reuse*. We define a class, we create instances, and those instances use methods that are defined only in the class. They will behave differently according to how the instances have been set up by the initializer.

Inheritance and composition

But this is just half of the story, *OOP is much more powerful*. We have two main design constructs to exploit: inheritance and composition.

Inheritance means that two objects are related by means of an *Is-A* type of relationship. On the other hand, **composition** means that two objects are related by means of a *Has-A* type of relationship. It's all very easy to explain with an example:

oop/class.inheritance.py

```python
class Engine():
    def start(self):
        pass

    def stop(self):
        pass

class ElectricEngine(Engine):  # Is-A Engine
    pass

class V8Engine(Engine):  # Is-A Engine
    pass

class Car():
    engine_cls = Engine

    def __init__(self):
        self.engine = self.engine_cls()  # Has-A Engine

    def start(self):
        print(
            'Starting engine {0} for car {1}... Wroom, wroom!'
            .format(
                self.engine.__class__.__name__,
                self.__class__.__name__)
        )
        self.engine.start()

    def stop(self):
        self.engine.stop()

class RaceCar(Car):  # Is-A Car
    engine_cls = V8Engine
```

```
class CityCar(Car):   # Is-A Car
    engine_cls = ElectricEngine

class F1Car(RaceCar):   # Is-A RaceCar and also Is-A Car
    engine_cls = V8Engine

car = Car()
racecar = RaceCar()
citycar = CityCar()
f1car = F1Car()
cars = [car, racecar, citycar, f1car]

for car in cars:
    car.start()

""" Prints:
Starting engine Engine for car Car... Wroom, wroom!
Starting engine V8Engine for car RaceCar... Wroom, wroom!
Starting engine ElectricEngine for car CityCar... Wroom, wroom!
Starting engine V8Engine for car F1Car... Wroom, wroom!
"""
```

The preceding example shows you both the *Is-A* and *Has-A* types of relationships between objects. First of all, let's consider Engine. It's a simple class that has two methods, start and stop. We then define ElectricEngine and V8Engine, which both inherit from Engine. You can see that by the fact that when we define them, we put Engine within the braces after the class name.

This means that both ElectricEngine and V8Engine inherit attributes and methods from the Engine class, which is said to be their **base class**.

The same happens with cars. Car is a base class for both RaceCar and CityCar. RaceCar is also the base class for F1Car. Another way of saying this is that F1Car inherits from RaceCar, which inherits from Car. Therefore, F1Car *Is-A* RaceCar and RaceCar *Is-A* Car. Because of the transitive property, we can say that F1Car *Is-A* Car as well. CityCar too, *Is-A* Car.

When we define class A(B): pass, we say A is the *child* of B, and B is the *parent* of A. *parent* and *base* are synonyms, as well as *child* and *derived*. Also, we say that a class inherits from another class, or that it extends it.

This is the inheritance mechanism.

On the other hand, let's go back to the code. Each class has a class attribute, engine_cls, which is a reference to the engine class we want to assign to each type of car. Car has a generic Engine, while the two race cars have a powerful V8 engine, and the city car has an electric one.

When a car is created in the initializer method __init__, we create an instance of whatever engine class is assigned to the car, and set it as engine instance attribute.

It makes sense to have engine_cls shared amongst all class instances because it's quite likely that the same instances of a car will have the same kind of engine. On the other hand, it wouldn't be good to have one single engine (an instance of any Engine class) as a class attribute, because we would be sharing one engine amongst all instances, which is incorrect.

The type of relationship between a car and its engine is a *Has-A* type. A car *Has-A* engine. This is called **composition**, and reflects the fact that objects can be made of many other objects. A car *Has-A* engine, gears, wheels, a frame, doors, seats, and so on.

When designing OOP code, it is of vital importance to describe objects in this way so that we can use inheritance and composition correctly to structure our code in the best way.

Before we leave this paragraph, let's check if I told you the truth with another example:

oop/class.issubclass.isinstance.py

```
car = Car()
racecar = RaceCar()
f1car = F1Car()
cars = [(car, 'car'), (racecar, 'racecar'), (f1car, 'f1car')]
car_classes = [Car, RaceCar, F1Car]

for car, car_name in cars:
    for class_ in car_classes:
        belongs = isinstance(car, class_)
        msg = 'is a' if belongs else 'is not a'
        print(car_name, msg, class_.__name__)

""" Prints:
car is a Car
car is not a RaceCar
```

```
car is not a F1Car
racecar is a Car
racecar is a RaceCar
racecar is not a F1Car
f1car is a Car
f1car is a RaceCar
f1car is a F1Car
"""
```

As you can see, `car` is just an instance of `Car`, while `racecar` is an instance of `RaceCar` (and of `Car` by extension) and `f1car` is an instance of `F1Car` (and of both `RaceCar` and `Car`, by extension). A *banana* is an instance of *Banana*. But, also, it is a *Fruit*. Also, it is *Food*, right? This is the same concept.

To check if an object is an instance of a class, use the `isinstance` method. It is recommended over sheer type comparison (`type(object) == Class`).

Let's also check inheritance, same setup, with different `for` loops:

oop/class.issubclass.isinstance.py

```
for class1 in car_classes:
    for class2 in car_classes:
        is_subclass = issubclass(class1, class2)
        msg = '{0} a subclass of'.format(
            'is' if is_subclass else 'is not')
        print(class1.__name__, msg, class2.__name__)

""" Prints:
Car is a subclass of Car
Car is not a subclass of RaceCar
Car is not a subclass of F1Car
RaceCar is a subclass of Car
RaceCar is a subclass of RaceCar
RaceCar is not a subclass of F1Car
F1Car is a subclass of Car
F1Car is a subclass of RaceCar
F1Car is a subclass of F1Car
"""
```

Interestingly, we learn that *a class is a subclass of itself*. Check the output of the preceding example to see that it matches the explanation I provided.

 One thing to notice about conventions is that class names are always written using *CapWords*, which means *ThisWayIsCorrect*, as opposed to functions and methods, which are written *this_way_is_correct*. Also, when in the code you want to use a name which is a Python-reserved keyword or built-in function or class, the convention is to add a trailing underscore to the name. In the first `for` loop example, I'm looping through the class names using `for class_ in ...`, because `class` is a reserved word. But you already knew all this because you have thoroughly studied PEP8, right?

To help you picture the difference between *Is-A* and *Has-A*, take a look at the following diagram:

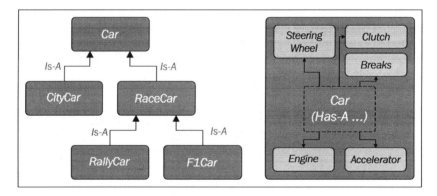

Accessing a base class

We've already seen class declarations like `class ClassA: pass` and `class ClassB(BaseClassName): pass`. When we don't specify a base class explicitly, Python will set the special **object** class as the base class for the one we're defining. Ultimately, all classes derive from `object`. Note that, if you don't specify a base class, braces are optional.

Therefore, writing `class A: pass` or `class A(): pass` or `class A(object): pass` is exactly the same thing. *object* is a special class in that it has the methods that are common to all Python classes, and it doesn't allow you to set any attributes on it.

Let's see how we can access a base class from within a class.

oop/super.duplication.py

```
class Book:
    def __init__(self, title, publisher, pages):
        self.title = title
        self.publisher = publisher
        self.pages = pages


class Ebook(Book):
    def __init__(self, title, publisher, pages, format_):
        self.title = title
        self.publisher = publisher
        self.pages = pages
        self.format_ = format_
```

Take a look at the preceding code. I highlighted the part of Ebook initialization that is duplicated from its base class Book. This is quite bad practice because we now have two sets of instructions that are doing the same thing. Moreover, any change in the signature of Book.__init__ will not reflect in Ebook. We know that Ebook *Is-A* Book, and therefore we would probably want changes to be reflected in the children classes.

Let's see one way to fix this issue:

oop/super.explicit.py

```
class Book:
    def __init__(self, title, publisher, pages):
        self.title = title
        self.publisher = publisher
        self.pages = pages


class Ebook(Book):
    def __init__(self, title, publisher, pages, format_):
        Book.__init__(self, title, publisher, pages)
        self.format_ = format_

ebook = Ebook('Learning Python', 'Packt Publishing', 360, 'PDF')
print(ebook.title)  # Learning Python
print(ebook.publisher)  # Packt Publishing
print(ebook.pages)  # 360
print(ebook.format_)  # PDF
```

Now, that's better. We have removed that nasty duplication. Basically, we tell Python to call the __init__ method of the Book class, and we feed self to the call, making sure that we bind that call to the present instance.

If we modify the logic within the __init__ method of Book, we don't need to touch Ebook, it will auto adapt to the change.

This approach is good, but we can still do a bit better. Say that we change Book's name to Liber, because we've fallen in love with Latin. We have to change the __init__ method of Ebook to reflect the change. This can be avoided by using super.

oop/super.implicit.py

```python
class Book:
    def __init__(self, title, publisher, pages):
        self.title = title
        self.publisher = publisher
        self.pages = pages

class Ebook(Book):
    def __init__(self, title, publisher, pages, format_):
        super().__init__(title, publisher, pages)
        # Another way to do the same thing is:
        # super(Ebook, self).__init__(title, publisher, pages)
        self.format_ = format_

ebook = Ebook('Learning Python', 'Packt Publishing', 360, 'PDF')
print(ebook.title)  # Learning Python
print(ebook.publisher)  # Packt Publishing
print(ebook.pages)  # 360
print(ebook.format_)  # PDF
```

super is a function that returns a proxy object that delegates method calls to a parent or sibling class. In this case, it will delegate that call to __init__ to the Book class, and the beauty of this method is that now we're even free to change Book to Liber without having to touch the logic in the __init__ method of Ebook.

Now that we know how to access a base class from a child, let's explore Python's multiple inheritance.

Multiple inheritance

Apart from composing a class using more than one base class, what is of interest here is how an attribute search is performed. Take a look at the following diagram:

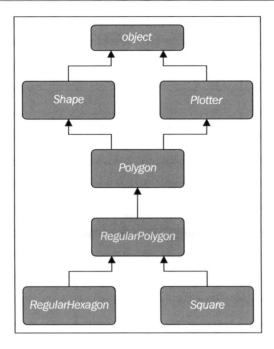

As you can see, `Shape` and `Plotter` act as base classes for all the others. `Polygon` inherits directly from them, `RegularPolygon` inherits from `Polygon`, and both `RegularHexagon` and `Square` inherit from `RegulaPolygon`. Note also that `Shape` and `Plotter` implicitly inherit from `object`, therefore we have what is called a **diamond** or, in simpler terms, more than one path to reach a base class. We'll see why this matters in a few moments. Let's translate it into some simple code:

`oop/multiple.inheritance.py`

```python
class Shape:
    geometric_type = 'Generic Shape'

    def area(self):  # This acts as placeholder for the interface
        raise NotImplementedError

    def get_geometric_type(self):
        return self.geometric_type

class Plotter:

    def plot(self, ratio, topleft):
        # Imagine some nice plotting logic here...
```

```
        print('Plotting at {}, ratio {}.'.format(
            topleft, ratio))

class Polygon(Shape, Plotter):  # base class for polygons
    geometric_type = 'Polygon'

class RegularPolygon(Polygon):  # Is-A Polygon
    geometric_type = 'Regular Polygon'

    def __init__(self, side):
        self.side = side

class RegularHexagon(RegularPolygon): # Is-A RegularPolygon
    geometric_type = 'RegularHexagon'

    def area(self):
        return 1.5 * (3 ** .5 * self.side ** 2)

class Square(RegularPolygon):  # Is-A RegularPolygon
    geometric_type = 'Square'

    def area(self):
        return self.side * self.side

hexagon = RegularHexagon(10)
print(hexagon.area())  # 259.8076211353316
print(hexagon.get_geometric_type())  # RegularHexagon
hexagon.plot(0.8, (75, 77)) # Plotting at (75, 77), ratio 0.8.

square = Square(12)
print(square.area())  # 144
print(square.get_geometric_type())  # Square
square.plot(0.93, (74, 75)) # Plotting at (74, 75), ratio 0.93.
```

Take a look at the preceding code: the class `Shape` has one attribute, `geometric_type`, and two methods: `area` and `get_geometric_type`. It's quite common to use base classes (like `Shape`, in our example) to define an *interface*: methods for which children must provide an implementation. There are different and better ways to do this, but I want to keep this example as simple as possible.

We also have the `Plotter` class, which adds the `plot` method, thereby providing plotting capabilities for any class that inherits from it. Of course, the `plot` implementation is just a dummy `print` in this example. The first interesting class is `Polygon`, which inherits from both `Shape` and `Plotter`.

There are many types of polygons, one of which is the regular one, which is both equiangular (all angles are equal) and equilateral (all sides are equal), so we create the RegularPolygon class that inherits from Polygon. Because for a regular polygon, all sides are equal, we can implement a simple __init__ method on RegularPolygon, which takes the length of the side. Finally, we create the RegularHexagon and Square classes, which both inherit from RegularPolygon.

This structure is quite long, but hopefully gives you an idea of how to specialize the classification of your objects when you design the code.

Now, please take a look at the last eight lines. Note that when I call the area method on hexagon and square, I get the correct area for both. This is because they both provide the correct implementation logic for it. Also, I can call get_geometric_type on both of them, even though it is not defined on their classes, and Python has to go all the way up to Shape to find an implementation for it. Note that, even though the implementation is provided in the Shape class, the self.geometric_type used for the return value is correctly taken from the caller instance.

The plot method calls are also interesting, and show you how you can enrich your objects with capabilities they wouldn't otherwise have. This technique is very popular in web frameworks such as Django (which we'll explore in two later chapters), which provides special classes called **mixins**, whose capabilities you can just use out of the box. All you have to do is to define the desired mixin as one the base classes for your own, and that's it.

Multiple inheritance is powerful, but can also get really messy, so we need to make sure we understand what happens when we use it.

Method resolution order

By now, we know that when you ask for someobject.attribute, and attribute is not found on that object, Python starts searching in the class someobject was created from. If it's not there either, Python searches up the inheritance chain until either attribute is found or the object class is reached. This is quite simple to understand if the inheritance chain is only comprised of single inheritance steps, which means that classes have only one parent. However, when multiple inheritance is involved, there are cases when it's not straightforward to predict what will be the next class that will be searched for if an attribute is not found.

Python provides a way to always know what is the order in which classes are searched on attribute lookup: the method resolution order.

> The **method resolution order (MRO)** is the order in which base classes are searched for a member during lookup. From version 2.3 Python uses an algorithm called **C3**, which guarantees monotonicity.
>
> In Python 2.2, **new-style classes** were introduced. The way you write a new-style class in Python 2.* is to define it with an explicit `object` base class. Classic classes were not explicitly inheriting from `object` and have been removed in Python 3.
>
> One of the differences between classic and new style-classes in Python 2.* is that new-style classes are searched with the new MRO.

With regards to the previous example, let's see what is the MRO for the `Square` class:

oop/multiple.inheritance.py

```
print(square.__class__.__mro__)
# prints:
# (<class '__main__.Square'>, <class '__main__.RegularPolygon'>,
#   <class '__main__.Polygon'>, <class '__main__.Shape'>,
#   <class '__main__.Plotter'>, <class 'object'>)
```

To get to the MRO of a class, we can go from the instance to its `__class__` attribute and from that to its `__mro__` attribute. Alternatively, we could have called `Square.__mro__`, or `Square.mro()` directly, but if you have to do it dynamically, it's more likely you will have an object in your hands rather than a class.

Note that the only point of doubt is the bisection after `Polygon`, where the inheritance chain breaks into two ways, one leads to `Shape` and the other to `Plotter`. We know by scanning the MRO for the `Square` class that `Shape` is searched before `Plotter`.

Why is this important? Well, imagine the following code:

oop/mro.simple.py

```
class A:
    label = 'a'

class B(A):
    label = 'b'

class C(A):
```

```
        label = 'c'

class D(B, C):
    pass

d = D()
print(d.label)  # Hypothetically this could be either 'b' or 'c'
```

Both B and C inherit from A, and D inherits from both B and C. This means that the lookup for the `label` attribute can reach the top (A) through both B or C. According to which is reached first, we get a different result.

So, in the preceding example we get `'b'`, which is what we were expecting, since B is the leftmost one amongst base classes of D. But what happens if I remove the `label` attribute from B? This would be the confusing situation: Will the algorithm go all the way up to A or will it get to C first? Let's find out!

oop/mro.py

```
class A:
    label = 'a'

class B(A):
    pass  # was: label = 'b'

class C(A):
    label = 'c'

class D(B, C):
    pass

d = D()
print(d.label)   # 'c'
print(d.__class__.mro())  # notice another way to get the MRO
# prints:
# [<class '__main__.D'>, <class '__main__.B'>,
#  <class '__main__.C'>, <class '__main__.A'>, <class 'object'>]
```

So, we learn that the MRO is D-B-C-A-(object), which means when we ask for d.label, we get `'c'`, which is correct.

In day to day programming, it is not quite common to have to deal with the MRO, but the first time you fight against some mixin from a framework, I promise you'll be glad I spent a paragraph explaining it.

Static and class methods

Until now, we have coded classes with attributes in the form of data and instance methods, but there are two other types of methods that we can place inside a class: **static methods** and **class methods**.

Static methods

As you may recall, when you create a class object, Python assigns a name to it. That name acts as a namespace, and sometimes it makes sense to group functionalities under it. Static methods are perfect for this use case since unlike instance methods, they are not passed any special argument. Let's look at an example of an imaginary String class.

oop/static.methods.py

```python
class String:

    @staticmethod
    def is_palindrome(s, case_insensitive=True):
        # we allow only letters and numbers
        s = ''.join(c for c in s if c.isalnum())  # Study this!
        # For case insensitive comparison, we lower-case s
        if case_insensitive:
            s = s.lower()
        for c in range(len(s) // 2):
            if s[c] != s[-c -1]:
                return False
        return True

    @staticmethod
    def get_unique_words(sentence):
        return set(sentence.split())

print(String.is_palindrome(
    'Radar', case_insensitive=False))  # False: Case Sensitive
print(String.is_palindrome('A nut for a jar of tuna'))  # True
print(String.is_palindrome('Never Odd, Or Even!'))  # True
print(String.is_palindrome(
    'In Girum Imus Nocte Et Consumimur Igni')  # Latin! Show-off!
)  # True

print(String.get_unique_words(
    'I love palindromes. I really really love them!'))
# {'them!', 'really', 'palindromes.', 'I', 'love'}
```

The preceding code is quite interesting. First of all, we learn that static methods are created by simply applying the `staticmethod` decorator to them. You can see that they aren't passed any special argument so, apart from the decoration, they really just look like functions.

We have a class, `String`, which acts as a container for functions. Another approach would be to have a separate module with functions inside. It's really a matter of preference most of the time.

The logic inside `is_palindrome` should be straightforward for you to understand by now, but, just in case, let's go through it. First we remove all characters from `s` that are not either letters or numbers. In order to do this, we use the `join` method of a string object (an empty string object, in this case). By calling `join` on an empty string, the result is that all elements in the iterable you pass to `join` will be concatenated together. We feed `join` a generator expression that says, *take any character from s if the character is either alphanumeric or a number*. I hope you have been able to find that out by yourself, maybe using the inside-out technique I showed you in one of the preceding chapters.

We then lowercase `s` if `case_insensitive` is `True`, and then we proceed to check if it is a palindrome. In order to do this, we compare the first and last characters, then the second and the second to last, and so on. If at any point we find a difference, it means the string isn't a palindrome and therefore we can return `False`. On the other hand, if we exit the `for` loop normally, it means no differences were found, and we can therefore say the string is a palindrome.

Notice that this code works correctly regardless of the length of the string, that is, if the length is odd or even. `len(s) // 2` reaches half of `s`, and if `s` is an odd amount of characters long, the middle one won't be checked (like in *RaDaR*, *D* is not checked), but we don't care; it would be compared with itself so it's always passing that check.

`get_unique_words` is much simpler, it just returns a set to which we feed a list with the words from a sentence. The `set` class removes any duplication for us, therefore we don't need to do anything else.

The `String` class provides us a nice container namespace for methods that are meant to work on strings. I could have coded a similar example with a `Math` class, and some static methods to work on numbers, but I wanted to show you something different.

Class methods

Class methods are slightly different from instance methods in that they also take a special first argument, but in this case, it is the class object itself. Two very common use cases for coding class methods are to provide factory capability to a class and to allow breaking up static methods (which you have to then call using the class name) without having to hardcode the class name in your logic. Let's look at an example of both of them.

oop/class.methods.factory.py

```python
class Point:
    def __init__(self, x, y):
        self.x = x
        self.y = y

    @classmethod
    def from_tuple(cls, coords):  # cls is Point
        return cls(*coords)

    @classmethod
    def from_point(cls, point):  # cls is Point
        return cls(point.x, point.y)

p = Point.from_tuple((3, 7))
print(p.x, p.y)  # 3 7
q = Point.from_point(p)
print(q.x, q.y)  # 3 7
```

In the preceding code, I showed you how to use a class method to create a factory for the class. In this case, we want to create a `Point` instance by passing both coordinates (regular creation `p = Point(3, 7)`), but we also want to be able to create an instance by passing a tuple (`Point.from_tuple`) or another instance (`Point.from_point`).

Within the two class methods, the `cls` argument refers to the `Point` class. As with instance method, which take `self` as the first argument, class method take a `cls` argument. Both `self` and `cls` are named after a convention that you are not forced to follow but are strongly encouraged to respect. This is something that no Python coder would change because it is so strong a convention that parsers, linters, and any tool that automatically does something with your code would expect, so it's much better to stick to it.

Let's look at an example of the other use case: splitting a static method.

oop/class.methods.split.py

```python
class String:

    @classmethod
    def is_palindrome(cls, s, case_insensitive=True):
        s = cls._strip_string(s)
        # For case insensitive comparison, we lower-case s
        if case_insensitive:
            s = s.lower()
        return cls._is_palindrome(s)

    @staticmethod
    def _strip_string(s):
        return ''.join(c for c in s if c.isalnum())

    @staticmethod
    def _is_palindrome(s):
        for c in range(len(s) // 2):
            if s[c] != s[-c -1]:
                return False
        return True

    @staticmethod
    def get_unique_words(sentence):
        return set(sentence.split())

print(String.is_palindrome('A nut for a jar of tuna'))   # True
print(String.is_palindrome('A nut for a jar of beans'))  # False
```

Compare this code with the previous version. First of all note that even though is_palindrome is now a class method, we call it in the same way we were calling it when it was a static one. The reason why we changed it to a class method is that after factoring out a couple of pieces of logic (_strip_string and _is_palindrome), we need to get a reference to them and if we have no cls in our method, the only option would be to call them like this: String._strip_string(...) and String._is_palindrome(...), which is not good practice, because we would hardcode the class name in the is_palindrome method, thereby putting ourselves in the condition of having to modify it whenever we would change the class name. Using cls will act as the class name, which means our code won't need any amendments.

Note also that, by naming the *factored-out* methods with a leading underscore, I am hinting that those methods are not supposed to be called from outside the class, but this will be the subject of the next paragraph.

Private methods and name mangling

If you have any background with languages like Java, C#, C++, or similar, then you know they allow the programmer to assign a privacy status to attributes (both data and methods). Each language has its own slightly different flavor for this, but the gist is that public attributes are accessible from any point in the code, while private ones are accessible only within the scope they are defined in.

In Python, there is no such thing. Everything is public; therefore, we rely on conventions and on a mechanism called **name mangling**.

The convention is as follows: if an attribute's name has no leading underscores it is considered public. This means you can access it and modify it freely. When the name has one leading underscore, the attribute is considered private, which means it's probably meant to be used internally and you should not use it or modify it from the outside. A very common use case for private attributes are helper methods that are supposed to be used by public ones (possibly in call chains in conjunction with other methods), and internal data, like scaling factors, or any other data that ideally we would put in a constant (a variable that cannot change, but, surprise, surprise, Python doesn't have those either).

This characteristic usually scares people from other backgrounds off; they feel threatened by the lack of privacy. To be honest, in my whole professional experience with Python, I've never heard anyone screaming *Oh my God, we have a terrible bug because Python lacks private attributes!* Not once, I swear.

That said, the call for privacy actually makes sense because without it, you risk introducing bugs into your code for real. Let's look at a simple example:

oop/private.attrs.py

```
class A:
    def __init__(self, factor):
        self._factor = factor

    def op1(self):
        print('Op1 with factor {}...'.format(self._factor))

class B(A):
    def op2(self, factor):
```

```
        self._factor = factor
        print('Op2 with factor {}...'.format(self._factor))


    obj = B(100)
    obj.op1()    # Op1 with factor 100...
    obj.op2(42)  # Op2 with factor 42...
    obj.op1()    # Op1 with factor 42...  <- This is BAD
```

In the preceding code, we have an attribute called _factor, and let's pretend it's very important that it isn't modified at runtime after the instance is created, because op1 depends on it to function correctly. We've named it with a leading underscore, but the issue here is that when we call obj.op2(42), we modify it, and this reflects in subsequent calls to op1.

Let's fix this undesired behavior by adding another leading underscore:

oop/private.attrs.fixed.py

```
    class A:
        def __init__(self, factor):
            self.__factor = factor

        def op1(self):
            print('Op1 with factor {}...'.format(self.__factor))

    class B(A):
        def op2(self, factor):
            self.__factor = factor
            print('Op2 with factor {}...'.format(self.__factor))


    obj = B(100)
    obj.op1()    # Op1 with factor 100...
    obj.op2(42)  # Op2 with factor 42...
    obj.op1()    # Op1 with factor 100...  <- Wohoo! Now it's GOOD!
```

Wow, look at that! Now it's working as desired. Python is kind of magic and in this case, what is happening is that the name mangling mechanism has kicked in.

Name mangling means that any attribute name that has at least two leading underscores and at most one trailing underscore, like __my_attr, is replaced with a name that includes an underscore and the class name before the actual name, like _ClassName__my_attr.

This means that when you inherit from a class, the mangling mechanism gives your private attribute two different names in the base and child classes so that name collision is avoided. Every class and instance object stores references to their attributes in a special attribute called `__dict__`, so let's inspect `obj.__dict__` to see name mangling in action:

oop/private.attrs.py

```
print(obj.__dict__.keys())
# dict_keys(['_factor'])
```

This is the `_factor` attribute that we find in the problematic version of this example. But look at the one that is using `__factor`:

oop/private.attrs.fixed.py

```
print(obj.__dict__.keys())
# dict_keys(['_A__factor', '_B__factor'])
```

See? `obj` has two attributes now, `_A__factor` (mangled within the A class), and `_B__factor` (mangled within the B class). This is the mechanism that makes possible that when you do `obj.__factor = 42`, `__factor` in A isn't changed, because you're actually touching `_B__factor`, which leaves `_A__factor` safe and sound.

If you're designing a library with classes that are meant to be used and extended by other developers, you will need to keep this in mind in order to avoid unintentional overriding of your attributes. Bugs like these can be pretty subtle and hard to spot.

The property decorator

Another thing that would be a crime not to mention is the `property` decorator. Imagine that you have an `age` attribute in a `Person` class and at some point you want to make sure that when you change its value, you're also checking that `age` is within a proper range, like [18, 99]. You can write accessor methods, like `get_age()` and `set_age()` (also called **getters** and **setters**) and put the logic there. `get_age()` will most likely just return `age`, while `set_age()` will also do the range check. The problem is that you may already have a lot of code accessing the `age` attribute directly, which means you're now up to some good (and potentially dangerous and tedious) refactoring. Languages like Java overcome this problem by using the accessor pattern basically by default. Many Java **Integrated Development Environments (IDEs)** autocomplete an attribute declaration by writing getter and setter accessor methods stubs for you on the fly.

Python is smarter, and does this with the `property` decorator. When you decorate a method with `property`, you can use the name of the method as if it was a data attribute. Because of this, it's always best to refrain from putting logic that would take a while to complete in such methods because, by accessing them as attributes, we are not expecting to wait.

Let's look at an example:

oop/property.py

```python
class Person:
    def __init__(self, age):
        self.age = age   # anyone can modify this freely


class PersonWithAccessors:
    def __init__(self, age):
        self._age = age

    def get_age(self):
        return self._age

    def set_age(self):
        if 18 <= age <= 99:
            self._age = age
        else:
            raise ValueError('Age must be within [18, 99]')


class PersonPythonic:
    def __init__(self, age):
        self._age = age

    @property
    def age(self):
        return self._age

    @age.setter
    def age(self, age):
        if 18 <= age <= 99:
            self._age = age
        else:
            raise ValueError('Age must be within [18, 99]')


person = PersonPythonic(39)
```

```
print(person.age)   # 39 - Notice we access as data attribute
person.age = 42  # Notice we access as data attribute
print(person.age)   # 42
person.age = 100  # ValueError: Age must be within [18, 99]
```

The `Person` class may be the first version we write. Then we realize we need to put the range logic in place so, with another language, we would have to rewrite `Person` as the `PersonWithAccessors` class, and refactor all the code that was using `Person.age`. In Python, we rewrite `Person` as `PersonPythonic` (you normally wouldn't change the name, of course) so that the age is stored in a private `_age` variable, and we define property getters and setters using that decoration, which allow us to keep using the `person` instances as we were before. A **getter** is a method that is called when we access an attribute for reading. On the other hand, a **setter** is a method that is called when we access an attribute to write it. In other languages, like Java for example, it's customary to define them as `get_age()` and `set_age(int value)`, but I find the Python syntax much neater. It allows you to start writing simple code and refactor later on, only when you need it, there is no need to pollute your code with accessors only because they may be helpful in the future.

The `property` decorator also allows for read-only data (no setter) and for special actions when the attribute is deleted. Please refer to the official documentation to dig deeper.

Operator overloading

I find Python's approach to **operator overloading** to be brilliant. To overload an operator means to give it a meaning according to the context in which it is used. For example, the + operator means addition when we deal with numbers, but concatenation when we deal with sequences.

In Python, when you use operators, you're most likely calling the special methods of some objects behind the scenes. For example, the call `a[k]` roughly translates to `type(a).__getitem__(a, k)`.

As an example, let's create a class that stores a string and evaluates to `True` if `'42'` is part of that string, and `False` otherwise. Also, let's give the class a length property which corresponds to that of the stored string.

`oop/operator.overloading.py`

```
class Weird:
    def __init__(self, s):
        self._s = s

    def __len__(self):
```

```
        return len(self._s)

    def __bool__(self):
        return '42' in self._s


weird = Weird('Hello! I am 9 years old!')
print(len(weird))   # 24
print(bool(weird))   # False

weird2 = Weird('Hello! I am 42 years old!')
print(len(weird2))   # 25
print(bool(weird2))   # True
```

That was fun, wasn't it? For the complete list of magic methods that you can override in order to provide your custom implementation of operators for your classes, please refer to the Python data model in the official documentation.

Polymorphism – a brief overview

The word **polymorphism** comes from the Greek *polys* (many, much) and *morphē* (form, shape), and its meaning is the provision of a single interface for entities of different types.

In our car example, we call `engine.start()`, regardless of what kind of engine it is. As long as it exposes the start method, we can call it. That's polymorphism in action.

In other languages, like Java, in order to give a function the ability to accept different types and call a method on them, those types need to be coded in such a way that they share an interface. In this way, the compiler knows that the method will be available regardless of the type of the object the function is fed (as long as it extends the proper interface, of course).

In Python, things are different. Polymorphism is implicit, nothing prevents you to call a method on an object, therefore, technically, there is no need to implement interfaces or other patterns.

There is a special kind of polymorphism called **ad hoc polymorphism**, which is what we saw in the last paragraph: operator overloading. The ability of an operator to change shape, according to the type of data it is fed.

I cannot spend too much time on polymorphism, but I encourage you to check it out by yourself, it will expand your understanding of OOP. Good luck!

Writing a custom iterator

Now we have all the tools to appreciate how we can write our own custom iterator. Let's first define what is an iterable and an iterator:

- **Iterable**: An object is said to be iterable if it's capable of returning its members one at a time. Lists, tuples, strings, dicts, are all iterables. Custom objects that define either of __iter__ or __getitem__ methods are also iterables.

- **Iterator**: An object is said to be an iterator if it represents a stream of data. A custom iterator is required to provide an implementation for __iter__ that returns the object itself, and an implementation for __next__, which returns the next item of the data stream until the stream is exhausted, at which point all successive calls to __next__ simply raise the StopIteration exception. Built-in functions such as iter and next are mapped to call __iter__ and __next__ on an object, behind the scenes.

Let's write an iterator that returns all the odd characters from a string first, and then the even ones.

iterators/iterator.py

```
class OddEven:

    def __init__(self, data):
        self._data = data
        self.indexes = (list(range(0, len(data), 2)) +
            list(range(1, len(data), 2)))

    def __iter__(self):
        return self

    def __next__(self):
        if self.indexes:
            return self._data[self.indexes.pop(0)]
        raise StopIteration

oddeven = OddEven('ThIsIsCoOl!')
print(''.join(c for c in oddeven))  # TIICO!hssol

oddeven = OddEven('HoLa')  # or manually...
it = iter(oddeven)  # this calls oddeven.__iter__ internally
```

```
print(next(it))    # H
print(next(it))    # L
print(next(it))    # o
print(next(it))    # a
```

So, we needed to provide an implementation for `__iter__` which returned the object itself, and then one for `__next__`. Let's go through it. What needs to happen is that we return `_data[0]`, `_data[2]`, `_data[4]`, ..., `_data[1]`, `_data[3]`, `_data[5]`, ... until we have returned every item in the data. In order to do this, we prepare a list, indexes, like [0, 2, 4, 6, ..., 1, 3, 5, ...], and while there is at least an element in it, we pop the first one and return the element from the data that is at that position, thereby achieving our goal. When `indexes` is empty, we raise `StopIteration`, as required by the iterator protocol.

There are other ways to achieve the same result, so go ahead and try to code a different one yourself. Make sure the end result works for all edge cases, empty sequences, sequences of length 1, 2, and so on.

Summary

In this chapter, we saw decorators, discovered the reasons for having them, and a few examples using one or more at the same time. We also saw decorators that take arguments, which are usually used as decorator factories.

We scratched the surface of object-oriented programming in Python. We covered all the basics in a way that you should now be able to understand fairly easily the code that will come in future chapters. We talked about all kinds of methods and attributes that one can write in a class, we explored inheritance versus composition, method overriding, properties, operator overloading, and polymorphism.

At the end, we very briefly touched base on iterators, so now you have all the knowledge to also understand generators more deeply.

In the next chapter, we take a steep turn. It will start the second half of the book, which is much more project-oriented so, from now on, it will be less theory and more code, I hope you will enjoy following the examples and getting your hands dirty, very dirty.

They say that a smooth sea never made a skillful sailor, so keep exploring, break things, read the error messages as well as the documentation, and let's see if we can get to see that white rabbit.

7
Testing, Profiling, and Dealing with Exceptions

"Code without tests is broken by design."

- Jacob Kaplan-Moss

Jacob Kaplan-Moss is one of the core developers of the Django web framework. We're going to explore it in the next chapters. I strongly agree with this quote of his. I believe code without tests shouldn't be deployed to production.

Why are tests so important? Well, for one, they give you predictability. Or, at least, they help you achieve high predictability. Unfortunately, there is always some bug that sneaks into our code. But we definitely want our code to be as predictable as possible. What we don't want is to have a surprise, our code behaving in an unpredictable way. Would you be happy to know that the software that checks on the sensors of the plane that is taking you on holidays sometimes goes crazy? No, probably not.

Therefore we need to test our code, we need to check that its behavior is correct, that it works as expected when it deals with edge cases, that it doesn't hang when the components it's talking to are down, that the performances are well within the acceptable range, and so on.

This chapter is all about this topic, making sure that your code is prepared to face the scary outside world, that is fast enough and that it can deal with unexpected or exceptional conditions.

We're going to explore testing, including a brief introduction to **test-driven development** (TDD), which is one of my favorite working methodologies. Then, we're going to explore the world of exceptions, and finally we're going to talk a little bit about performances and profiling. Deep breath, and here we go...

Testing your application

There are many different kinds of tests, so many in fact that companies often have a dedicated department, called **quality assurance** (QA), made up of individuals that spend their day testing the software the company developers produce.

To start making an initial classification, we can divide tests into two broad categories: white-box and black-box tests.

White-box tests are those which exercise the internals of the code, they inspect it down to a very fine level of granularity. On the other hand, **black-box tests** are those which consider the software under testing as if being within a box, the internals of which are ignored. Even the technology, or the language used inside the box is not important for black-box tests. What they do is to plug input to one end of the box and verify the output at the other end, and that's it.

> There is also an in-between category, called **gray-box** testing, that involves testing a system in the same way we do with the black-box approach, but having some knowledge about the algorithms and data structures used to write the software and only partial access to its source code.

There are many different kinds of tests in these categories, each of which serves a different purpose. Just to give you an idea, here's a few:

- **Front-end tests** make sure that the client side of your application is exposing the information that it should, all the links, the buttons, the advertising, everything that needs to be shown to the client. It may also verify that it is possible to walk a certain path through the user interface.

- **Scenario tests** make use of stories (or scenarios) that help the tester work through a complex problem or test a part of the system.

- **Integration tests** verify the behavior of the various components of your application when they are working together sending messages through interfaces.

- **Smoke tests** are particularly useful when you deploy a new update on your application. They check whether the most essential, vital parts of your application are still working as they should and that they are not *on fire*. This term comes from when engineers tested circuits by making sure nothing was smoking.

- **Acceptance tests**, or **user acceptance testing (UAT)** is what a developer does with a product owner (for example, in a SCRUM environment) to determine if the work that was commissioned was carried out correctly.

- **Functional tests** verify the features or functionalities of your software.

- **Destructive tests** take down parts of your system, simulating a failure, in order to establish how well the remaining parts of the system perform. These kinds of tests are performed extensively by companies that need to provide an extremely reliable service, such as Amazon, for example.

- **Performance tests** aim to verify how well the system performs under a specific load of data or traffic so that, for example, engineers can get a better understanding of which are the bottlenecks in the system that could bring it down to its knees in a heavy load situation, or those which prevent scalability.

- **Usability tests**, and the closely related **user experience (UX)** tests, aim to check if the user interface is simple and easy to understand and use. They aim to provide input to the designers so that the user experience is improved.

- **Security and penetration tests** aim to verify how well the system is protected against attacks and intrusions.

- **Unit tests** help the developer to write the code in a robust and consistent way, providing the first line of feedback and defense against coding mistakes, refactoring mistakes, and so on.

- **Regression tests** provide the developer with useful information about a feature being compromised in the system after an update. Some of the causes for a system being said to have a regression are an old bug coming back to life, an existing feature being compromised, or a new issue being introduced.

Many books and articles have been written about testing, and I have to point you to those resources if you're interested in finding out more about all the different kinds of tests. In this chapter, we will concentrate on unit tests, since they are the backbone of software crafting and form the vast majority of tests that are written by a developer.

Testing is an *art*, an art that you don't learn from books, I'm afraid. You can learn all the definitions (and you should), and try and collect as much knowledge about testing as you can but I promise you, you will be able to test your software properly only when you have done it for long enough in the field.

When you are having trouble refactoring a bit of code, because every little thing you touch makes a test blow up, you learn how to write less rigid and limiting tests, which still verify the correctness of your code but, at the same time, allow you the freedom and joy to play with it, to shape it as you want.

When you are being called too often to fix unexpected bugs in your code, you learn how to write tests more thoroughly, how to come up with a more comprehensive list of edge cases, and strategies to cope with them before they turn into bugs.

When you are spending too much time reading tests and trying to refactor them in order to change a small feature in the code, you learn to write simpler, shorter, and better focused tests.

I could go on with this *when you... you learn...*, but I guess you get the picture. You need to get your hands dirty and build experience. My suggestion? Study the theory as much as you can, and then experiment using different approaches. Also, try to learn from experienced coders; it's very effective.

The anatomy of a test

Before we concentrate on unit tests, let's see what a test is, and what its purpose is.

A **test** is a piece of code whose purpose is to verify something in our system. It may be that we're calling a function passing two integers, that an object has a property called donald_duck, or that when you place an order on some API, after a minute you can see it dissected into its basic elements, in the database.

A test is typically comprised of three sections:

- **Preparation**: This is where you set up the scene. You prepare all the data, the objects, the services you need in the places you need them so that they are ready to be used.

- **Execution**: This is where you execute the bit of logic that you're checking against. You perform an action using the data and the interfaces you have set up in the preparation phase.

- **Verification**: This is where you verify the results and make sure they are according to your expectations. You check the returned value of a function, or that some data is in the database, some is not, some has changed, a request has been made, something has happened, a method has been called, and so on.

Testing guidelines

Like software, tests can be good or bad, with the whole range of shades in the middle. In order to write good tests, here are some guidelines:

- **Keep them as simple as possible**: It's okay to violate some good coding rules, such as hardcoding values or duplicating code. Tests need first and foremost to be as readable as possible and easy to understand. When tests are hard to read or understand, you can never be sure if they are actually making sure your code is performing correctly.

- **Tests should verify one thing and one thing only**: It's very important that you keep them short and contained. It's perfectly fine to write multiple tests to exercise a single object or function. Just make sure that each test has one and only one purpose.

- **Tests should not make any unnecessary assumption when verifying data**: This is tricky to understand at first, but say you are testing the return value of a function and it is an unordered list of numbers (like [2, 3, 1]). If the order in that list is random, in the test you may be tempted to sort it and compare it with [1, 2, 3]. If you do, you will introduce an extra assumption on the ordering of the result of your function call, and *this is bad practice*. You should always find a way to verify things without introducing any assumptions or any feature that doesn't belong in the use case you're describing with your test.

- **Tests should exercise the what, rather than the how**: Tests should focus on checking *what* a function is supposed to do, rather than *how* it is doing it. For example, focus on the fact that it's calculating the square root of a number (the *what*), instead of on the fact that it is calling math.sqrt to do it (the *how*). Unless you're writing performance tests or you have a particular need to verify how a certain action is performed, try to avoid this type of testing and focus on the *what*. Testing the *how* leads to restrictive tests and makes refactoring hard. Moreover, the type of test you have to write when you concentrate on the *how* is more likely to degrade the quality of your testing code base when you amend your software frequently (more on this later).

- **Tests should assume the least possible in the preparation phase**: Say you have 10 tests that are checking how a data structure is manipulated by a function. And let's say this data structure is a dict with five key/value pairs. If you put the complete dict in each test, the moment you have to change something in that dict, you also have to amend all ten tests. On the other hand, if you strip down the test data as much as you can, you will find that, most of the time, it's possible to have the majority of tests checking only a partial version of the data, and only a few running with a full version of it. This means that when you need to change your data, you will have to amend only those tests that are actually exercising it.

- **Test should run as fast as possible**: A good test codebase could end up being much longer than the code being tested itself. It varies according to the situation and the developer but whatever the length, you'll end up having hundreds, if not thousands, of tests to run, which means the faster they run, the faster you can get back to writing code. When using TDD, for example, you run tests very often, so speed is essential.

- **Tests should use up the least possible amount of resources**: The reason for this is that every developer who checks out your code should be able to run your tests, no matter how powerful their box is. It could be a skinny virtual machine or a neglected Jenkins box, your tests should run without chewing up too many resources.

 A **Jenkins** box is a machine that runs Jenkins, software that is capable of, amongst many other things, running your tests automatically. Jenkins is frequently used in companies where developers use practices like continuous integration, extreme programming, and so on.

Unit testing

Now that you have an idea about what testing is and why we need it, let's finally introduce the developer's best friend: the **unit test**.

Before we proceed with the examples, allow me to spend some words of caution: I'll try to give you the fundamentals about unit testing, but I don't follow any particular school of thought or methodology to the letter. Over the years, I have tried many different testing approaches, eventually coming up with my own way of doing things, which is constantly evolving. To put it as Bruce Lee would have:

"Absorb what is useful, discard what is useless and add what is specifically your own".

Writing a unit test

In order to explain how to write a unit test, let's help ourselves with a simple snippet:

data.py

```
def get_clean_data(source):
    data = load_data(source)
    cleaned_data = clean_data(data)
    return cleaned_data
```

The function `get_clean_data` is responsible for getting data from `source`, cleaning it, and returning it to the caller. How do we test this function?

One way of doing this is to call it and then make sure that `load_data` was called once with `source` as its only argument. Then we have to verify that `clean_data` was called once, with the return value of `load_data`. And, finally, we would need to make sure that the return value of `clean_data` is what is returned by the `get_clean_data` function as well.

In order to do this, we need to set up the source and run this code, and this may be a problem. One of the golden rules of unit testing is that *anything that crosses the boundaries of your application needs to be simulated*. We don't want to talk to a real data source, and we don't want to actually run real functions if they are communicating with anything that is not contained in our application. A few examples would be a database, a search service, an external API, a file in the filesystem, and so on.

We need these restrictions to act as a shield, so that we can always run our tests safely without the fear of destroying something in a real data source.

Another reason is that it may be quite difficult for a single developer to reproduce the whole architecture on their box. It may require the setting up of databases, APIs, services, files and folders, and so on and so forth, and this can be difficult, time consuming, or sometimes not even possible.

> Very simply put, an **application programming interface** (API) is a set of tools for building software applications. An API expresses a software component in terms of its operations, inputs and outputs, and underlying types. For example, if you create a software that needs to interface with a data provider service, it's very likely that you will have to go through their API in order to gain access to the data.

Therefore, in our unit tests, we need to simulate all those things in some way. Unit tests need to be run by any developer without the need for the whole system to be set up on their box.

A different approach, which I always favor when it's possible to do so, is to simulate entities without using fake objects, but using special purpose test objects instead. For example, if your code talks to a database, instead of faking all the functions and methods that talk to the database and programming the fake objects so that they return what the real ones would, I'd much rather prefer to spawn a test database, set up the tables and data I need, and then patch the connection settings so that my tests are running real code, against the test database, thereby doing no harm at all. In-memory databases are excellent options for these cases.

One of the applications that allow you to spawn a database for testing, is Django. Within the `django.test` package you can find several tools that help you write your tests so that you won't have to simulate the dialog with a database. By writing tests this way, you will also be able to check on transactions, encodings, and all other database related aspects of programming. Another advantage of this approach consists in the ability of checking against things that can change from one database to another.

Sometimes, though, it's still not possible, and we need to use fakes, therefore let's talk about them.

Mock objects and patching

First of all, in Python, these fake objects are called **mocks**. Up to version 3.3, the `mock` library was a third-party library that basically every project would install via `pip` but, from version 3.3, it has been included in the standard library under the `unittest` module, and rightfully so, given its importance and how widespread it is.

The act of replacing a real object or function (or in general, any piece of data structure) with a mock, is called **patching**. The `mock` library provides the `patch` tool, which can act as a function or class decorator, and even as a context manager (more on this in *Chapter 8, The Edges – GUIs and Scripts*), that you can use to mock things out. Once you have replaced everything you need not to run, with suitable mocks, you can pass to the second phase of the test and run the code you are exercising. After the execution, you will be able to check those mocks to verify that your code has worked correctly.

Assertions

The verification phase is done through the use of assertions. An **assertion** is a function (or method) that you can use to verify equality between objects, as well as other conditions. When a condition is not met, the assertion will raise an exception that will make your test fail. You can find a list of assertions in the `unittest` module documentation, and their corresponding Pythonic version in the nose third-party library, which provides a few advantages over the sheer `unittest` module, starting from an improved test discovery strategy (which is the way a test runner detects and discovers the tests in your application).

A classic unit test example

Mocks, patches, and assertions are the basic tools we'll be using to write tests. So, finally, let's see an example. I'm going to write a function that takes a list of integers and filters out all those which aren't positive.

`filter_funcs.py`

```python
def filter_ints(v):
    return [num for num in v if is_positive(num)]

def is_positive(n):
    return n > 0
```

In the preceding example, we define the `filter_ints` function, which basically uses a list comprehension to retain all the numbers in v that are positive, discarding zeros and negative ones. I hope, by now, any further explanation of the code would be insulting.

What is interesting, though, is to start thinking about how we can test it. Well, how about we call `filter_ints` with a list of numbers and we make sure that `is_positive` is called for each of them? Of course, we would have to test `is_positive` as well, but I will show you later on how to do that. Let's write a simple test for `filter_ints` now.

> Just to be sure we're on the same page, I am putting the code for this chapter in a folder called `ch7`, which lies within the root of our project. At the same level of `ch7`, I have created a folder called `tests`, in which I have placed a folder called `test_ch7`. In this folder I have one test file, called `test_filter_func.py`.
>
> Basically, within the `tests` folder, I will recreate the tree structure of the code I'm testing, prepending everything with `test_`. This way, finding tests is really easy, as well as is keeping them tidy.

tests/test_ch7/test_filter_funcs.py

```python
from unittest import TestCase   # 1
from unittest.mock import patch, call   # 2
from nose.tools import assert_equal   # 3
from ch7.filter_funcs import filter_ints   # 4


class FilterIntsTestCase(TestCase):   # 5

    @patch('ch7.filter_funcs.is_positive')   # 6
    def test_filter_ints(self, is_positive_mock):   # 7
        # preparation
        v = [3, -4, 0, 5, 8]

        # execution
        filter_ints(v)   # 8

        # verification
        assert_equal(
            [call(3), call(-4), call(0), call(5), call(8)],
            is_positive_mock.call_args_list
        )   # 9
```

My, oh my, so little code, and yet so much to say. First of all: #1. The `TestCase` class is the base class that we use to have a contained entity in which to run our tests. It's not just a bare container; it provides you with methods to write tests more easily.

On #2, we import `patch` and `call` from the `unittest.mock` module. `patch` is responsible for substituting an object with a `Mock` instance, thereby giving us the ability to check on it after the execution phase has been completed. `call` provides us with a nice way of expressing a (for example, function) call.

On #3, you can see that I prefer to use assertions from `nose`, rather than the ones that come with the `unittest` module. To give you an example, `assert_equal(...)` would become `self.assertEqual(...)` if I didn't use `nose`. I don't enjoy typing `self.` for any assertion, if there is a way to avoid it, and I don't particularly enjoy **camel case**, therefore I always prefer to use `nose` to make my assertions.

`assert_equal` is a function that takes two parameters (and an optional third one that acts as a message) and verifies that they are the same. If they are equal, nothing happens, but if they differ, then an `AssertionError` exception is raised, telling us something is wrong. When I write my tests, I always put the expected value as the first argument, and the real one as the second. This convention saves me time when I'm reading tests.

On #4, we import the function we want to test, and then (#5) we proceed to create the class where our tests will live. Each method of this class starting with `test_`, will be interpreted as a test. As you can see, we need to decorate `test_filter_ints` with `patch` (#6). Understanding this part is crucial, we need to patch the object where it is actually used. In this case, the path is very simple: `ch7.filter_func.is_positive`.

 Patching can be very tricky, so I urge you to read the *Where to patch* section in the mock documentation: `https://docs.python.org/3/library/unittest.mock.html#where-to-patch`.

When we decorate a function using `patch`, like in our example, we get an extra argument in the test signature (#7), which I like to call as the patched function name, plus a `_mock` suffix, just to make it clear that the object has been patched (or mocked out).).

Finally, we get to the body of the test, and we have a very simple preparation phase in which we set up a list with at least one representative of all the integer number categories (negative, zero, and positive).

Then, in #8, we perform the execution phase, which runs the `filter_ints` function, without collecting its results. If all has gone as expected, the fake `is_positive` function must have been called with each of the integers in v.

We can verify this by comparing a list of call objects to the `call_args_list` attribute on the mock (#9). This attribute is the list of all the calls performed on the object since its creation.

Let's run this test. First of all, make sure that you install `nose` ($ `pip freeze` will tell you if you have it already):

```
$ pip install nose
```

Then, change into the root of the project (mine is called `learning.python`), and run the tests like this:

```
$ nosetests tests/test_ch7/
.
----------------------------------------------------------
Ran 1 test in 0.006s
OK
```

The output shows one dot (each dot is a test), a separation line, and the time taken to run the whole test suite. It also says OK at the end, which means that our tests were all successful.

Making a test fail

Good, so just for fun let's make one fail. In the test file, change the last call from `call(8)` to `call(9)`, and run the tests again:

```
$ nosetests tests/test_ch7/

F

==============================================================
FAIL: test_filter_ints (test_filter_funcs.FilterIntsTestCase)
--------------------------------------------------------------
Traceback (most recent call last):
  File "/usr/lib/python3.4/unittest/mock.py", line 1125, in patched
    return func(*args, **keywargs)
  File "/home/fab/srv/learning.python/tests/test_ch7/test_filter_funcs.
py", line 21, in test_filter_ints
    is_positive_mock.call_args_list
AssertionError: [call(3), call(-4), call(0), call(5), call(9)] !=
[call(3), call(-4), call(0), call(5), call(8)]

--------------------------------------------------------------
Ran 1 test in 0.008s

FAILED (failures=1)
```

Wow, we made the beast angry! So much wonderful information, though. This tells you that the test `test_filter_ints` (with the path to it), was run and that it failed (the big `F` at the top, where the dot was before). It gives you a `Traceback`, that tells you that in the `test_filter_funcs.py` module, at line 21, when asserting on `is_positive_mock.call_args_list`, we have a discrepancy. The test expects the list of calls to end with a `call(9)` instance, but the real list ends with a `call(8)`. This is nothing less than wonderful.

If you have a test like this, can you imagine what would happen if you refactored and introduced a bug into your function by mistake? Well, your tests will break! They will tell you that *you have screwed something up, and here's the details*. So, you go and check out what you broke.

Interface testing

Let's add another test that checks on the returned value. It's another method in the class, so I won't reproduce the whole code again:

tests/test_ch7/test_filter_funcs.py

```
def test_filter_ints_return_value(self):
    v = [3, -4, 0, -2, 5, 0, 8, -1]

    result = filter_ints(v)

    assert_list_equal([3, 5, 8], result)
```

This test is a bit different from the previous one. Firstly, we cannot mock the is_positive function, otherwise we wouldn't be able to check on the result. Secondly, we don't check on calls, but only on the result of the function when input is given.

I like this test much more than the previous one. This type of test is called an **interface test** because it checks on the interface (the set of inputs and outputs) of the function we're testing. It doesn't use any mocks, which is why I use this technique much more than the previous one. Let's run the new test suite and then let's see why I like interface testing more than those with mocks.

```
$ nosetests tests/test_ch7/

..
-------------------------------------------------------------
Ran 2 tests in 0.006s
OK
```

Two tests ran, all good (I changed that 9 back to an 8 in the first test, of course).

Comparing tests with and without mocks

Now, let's see why I don't really like mocks and use them only when I have no choice. Let's refactor the code in this way:

filter_funcs_refactored.py

```
def filter_ints(v):
    v = [num for num in v if num != 0]   # 1
    return [num for num in v if is_positive(num)]
```

The code for `is_positive` is the same as before. But the logic in `filter_ints` has now changed in a way that `is_positive` will never be called with a `0`, since they are all filtered out in #1. This leads to an interesting result, so let's run the tests again:

```
$ nosetests tests/test_ch7/test_filter_funcs_refactored.py
F.
================================================================
FAIL: test_filter_ints (test_filter_funcs_refactored.FilterIntsTestCase)
----------------------------------------------------------------
... omit ...
AssertionError: [call(3), call(-4), call(0), call(5), call(8)] !=
[call(3), call(-4), call(5), call(8)]
----------------------------------------------------------------
Ran 2 tests in 0.002s
FAILED (failures=1)
```

One test succeeded but the other one, the one with the mocked `is_positive` function, failed. The `AssertionError` message shows us that we now need to amend the list of expected calls, removing `call(0)`, because it is no longer performed.

This is not good. We have changed neither the interface of the function nor its behavior. The function is still keeping to its *original contract*. What we've done by testing it with a mocked object is limit ourselves. In fact, we now have to amend the test in order to use the new logic.

This is just a simple example but it shows one important flaw in the whole mock mechanism. *You must keep your mocks up-to-date and in sync with the code they are replacing*, otherwise you risk having issues like the preceding one, or even worse. Your tests may not fail because they are using mocked objects that perform fine, but because the real ones, now not in sync any more, are actually failing.

So *use mocks only when necessary*, only when there is no other way of testing your functions. When you cross the boundaries of your application in a test, try to use a replacement, like a test database, or a fake API, and only when it's not possible, resort to mocks. They are very powerful, but also very dangerous when not handled properly.

So, let's remove that first test and keep only the second one, so that I can show you another issue you could run into when writing tests. The whole test module now looks like this:

tests/test_ch7/test_filter_funcs_final.py

```
from unittest import TestCase
from nose.tools import assert_list_equal
from ch7.filter_funcs import filter_ints

class FilterIntsTestCase(TestCase):
    def test_filter_ints_return_value(self):
        v = [3, -4, 0, -2, 5, 0, 8, -1]
        result = filter_ints(v)
        assert_list_equal([3, 5, 8], result)
```

If we run it, it will pass.

A brief chat about triangulation. Now let me ask you: what happens if I change my filter_ints function to this?

filter_funcs_triangulation.py

```
def filter_ints(v):
    return [3, 5, 8]
```

If you run the test suite, the test we have will still pass! You may think I'm crazy but I'm showing you this because I want to talk about a concept called **triangulation**, which is very important when doing interface testing with TDD.

The whole idea is to remove cheating code, or badly performing code, by pinpointing it from different angles (like going to one vertex of a triangle from the other two) in a way that makes it impossible for our code to cheat, and the bug is exposed. We can simply modify the test like this:

tests/test_ch7/test_filter_funcs_final_triangulation.py

```
def test_filter_ints_return_value(self):
    v1 = [3, -4, 0, -2, 5, 0, 8, -1]
    v2 = [7, -3, 0, 0, 9, 1]

    assert_list_equal([3, 5, 8], filter_ints(v1))
    assert_list_equal([7, 9, 1], filter_ints(v2))
```

I have moved the execution section in the assertions directly, and you can see that we're now pinpointing our function from two different angles, thereby requiring that the real code be in it. It's no longer possible for our function to cheat.

Triangulation is a very powerful technique that teaches us to always try to exercise our code from many different angles, to cover all possible edge cases to expose any problems.

Boundaries and granularity

Let's now add a test for the is_positive function. I know it's a one-liner, but it presents us with opportunity to discuss two very important concepts: **boundaries** and **granularity**.

That 0 in the body of the function is a **boundary**, the > in the inequality is how we behave with regards to this boundary. Typically, when you set a boundary, you divide the space into three areas: what lies before the boundary, after the boundary, and on the boundary itself. In the example, before the boundary we find the negative numbers, the boundary is the element 0 and, after the boundary, we find the positive numbers. We need to test each of these areas to be sure we're testing the function correctly. So, let's see one possible solution (I will add the test to the class, but I won't show the repeated code):

tests/test_ch7/test_filter_funcs_is_positive_loose.py

```
    def test_is_positive(self):
        assert_equal(False, is_positive(-2))  # before boundary
        assert_equal(False, is_positive(0))   # on the boundary
        assert_equal(True, is_positive(2))   # after the boundary
```

You can see that we are exercising one number for each different area around the boundary. Do you think this test is good? Think about it for a minute before reading on.

The answer is no, this test is not good. Not good enough, anyway. If I change the body of the is_positive function to read return n > 1, I would expect my test to fail, but it won't. -2 is still False, as well as 0, and 2 is still True. Why does that happen? It is because we haven't taken granularity properly into account. We're dealing with integers, so what is the minimum granularity when we move from one integer to the next one? It's 1. Therefore, when we surround the boundary, taking all three areas into account is not enough. We need to do it with the minimum possible granularity. Let's change the test:

```
tests/test_ch7/test_filter_funcs_is_positive_correct.py
```

```python
    def test_is_positive(self):
        assert_equal(False, is_positive(-1))
        assert_equal(False, is_positive(0))
        assert_equal(True, is_positive(1))
```

Ah, now it's better. Now if we change the body of `is_positive` to read `return n > 1`, the third assertion will fail, which is what we want. Can you think of a better test?

```
tests/test_ch7/test_filter_funcs_is_positive_better.py
```

```python
    def test_is_positive(self):
        assert_equal(False, is_positive(0))
        for n in range(1, 10 ** 4):
            assert_equal(False, is_positive(-n))
            assert_equal(True, is_positive(n))
```

This test is even better. We test the first ten thousand integers (both positive and negative) and 0. It basically provides us with a better coverage than just the one across the boundary. So, keep this in mind. Zoom closely around each boundary with minimal granularity, but try to expand as well, finding a good compromise between optimal coverage and execution speed. We would love to check the first billion integers, but we can't wait days for our tests to run.

A more interesting example

Okay, this was as gentle an introduction as I could give you, so let's move on to something more interesting. Let's write and test a function that flattens a nested dictionary structure. For a couple of years, I have worked very closely with Twitter and Facebook APIs. Handling such humongous data structures is not easy, especially since they're often deeply nested. It turns out that it's much easier to flatten them in a way that you can work on them without losing the original structural information, and then recreate the nested structure from the flat one. To give you an example, we want something like this:

```
data_flatten.py
```

```python
nested = {
    'fullname': 'Alessandra',
    'age': 41,
    'phone-numbers': ['+447421234567', '+447423456789'],
    'residence': {
        'address': {
            'first-line': 'Alexandra Rd',
            'second-line': '',
```

```
        },
        'zip': 'N8 0PP',
        'city': 'London',
        'country': 'UK',
    },
}

flat = {
    'fullname': 'Alessandra',
    'age': 41,
    'phone-numbers': ['+447421234567', '+447423456789'],
    'residence.address.first-line': 'Alexandra Rd',
    'residence.address.second-line': '',
    'residence.zip': 'N8 0PP',
    'residence.city': 'London',
    'residence.country': 'UK',
}
```

A structure like `flat` is much simpler to manipulate. Before writing the flattener, let's make some assumptions: the keys are strings, we leave every data structure as it is unless it's a dictionary, in which case we flatten it, we use the dot as separator, but we want to be able to pass a different one to our function. Here's the code:

data_flatten.py

```python
def flatten(data, prefix='', separator='.'):
    """Flattens a nested dict structure. """
    if not isinstance(data, dict):
        return {prefix: data} if prefix else data

    result = {}
    for (key, value) in data.items():
        result.update(
            flatten(
                value,
                _get_new_prefix(prefix, key, separator),
                separator=separator))
    return result

def _get_new_prefix(prefix, key, separator):
    return (separator.join((prefix, str(key)))
            if prefix else str(key))
```

The preceding example is not difficult, but also not trivial so let's go through it. At first, we check if `data` is a dictionary. If it's not a dictionary, then it's data that doesn't need to be flattened; therefore, we simply return either `data` or, if `prefix` is not an empty string, a dictionary with one key/value pair: `prefix`/`data`.

If instead `data` is a dict, we prepare an empty `result` dict to return, then we parse the list of `data`'s items, which, at I'm sure you will remember, are 2-tuples *(key, value)*. For each *(key, value)* pair, we recursively call `flatten` on them, and we update the `result` dict with what's returned by that call. Recursion is excellent when running through nested structures.

At a glance, can you understand what the `_get_new_prefix` function does? Let's use the inside-out technique once again. I see a ternary operator that returns the stringified `key` when `prefix` is an empty string. On the other hand, when `prefix` is a non-empty string, we use the `separator` to `join` the `prefix` with the stringified version of `key`. Notice that the braces inside the call to `join` aren't redundant, we need them. Can you figure out why?

Let's write a couple of tests for this function:

`tests/test_ch7/test_data_flatten.py`

```python
# ... imports omitted ...
class FlattenTestCase(TestCase):

    def test_flatten(self):
        test_cases = [
            ({'A': {'B': 'C', 'D': [1, 2, 3], 'E': {'F': 'G'}},
             'H': 3.14,
             'J': ['K', 'L'],
             'M': 'N'},
             {'A.B': 'C',
              'A.D': [1, 2, 3],
              'A.E.F': 'G',
              'H': 3.14,
              'J': ['K', 'L'],
              'M': 'N'}),
            (0, 0),
            ('Hello', 'Hello'),
            ({'A': None}, {'A': None}),
        ]
        for (nested, flat) in test_cases:
            assert_equal(flat, flatten(nested))

    def test_flatten_custom_separator(self):
```

```
nested = {'A': {'B': {'C': 'D'}}}
assert_equal(
    {'A#B#C': 'D'}, flatten(nested, separator='#'))
```

Let's start from `test_flatten`. I defined a list of 2-tuples (`nested`, `flat`), each of which represents a test case (I highlighted `nested` to ease reading). I have one big dict with three levels of nesting, and then some smaller data structures that won't change when passed to the `flatten` function. These test cases are probably not enough to cover all edge cases, but they should give you a good idea of how you could structure a test like this. With a simple `for` loop, I cycle through each test case and assert that the result of `flatten(nested)` is equal to `flat`.

> One thing to say about this example is that, when you run it, it will show you that two tests have been run. This is actually not correct because even if technically there were only two tests running, in one of them we have multiple test cases. It would be nicer to have them run in a way that they were recognized as separate. This is possible through the use of libraries such as `nose-parameterized`, which I encourage you to check out. It's on `https://pypi.python.org/pypi/nose-parameterized`.

I also provided a second test to make sure the custom separator feature worked. As you can see, I used only one data structure, which is much smaller. We don't need to go big again, nor to test other edge cases. Remember, tests should make sure of one thing and one thing only, and `test_flatten_custom_separator` just takes care of verifying whether or not we can feed the `flatten` function a different `separator`.

I could keep blathering on about tests for about another book if only I had the space, but unfortunately, we need to stop here. I haven't told you about **doctests** (tests written in the documentation using a Python interactive shell style), and about another half a million things that could be said about this subject. You'll have to discover that for yourself.

Take a look at the documentation for the `unittest` module, the `nose` and `nose-parameterized` libraries, and `pytest` (`http://pytest.org/`), and you will be fine. In my experience, mocking and patching seem to be quite hard to get a good grasp of for developers who are new to them, so allow yourself a little time to digest these techniques. Try and learn them gradually.

Test-driven development

Let's talk briefly about **test-driven development** or **TDD**. It is a methodology that was rediscovered by Kent Beck, who wrote *Test Driven Development by Example, Addison Wesley – 2002*, which I encourage you to check out if you want to learn about the fundamentals of this subject, which I'm quite obsessed with.

> *TDD is a software development methodology that is based on the continuous repetition of a very short development cycle.*

At first, the developer writes a test, and makes it run. The test is supposed to check a feature that is not yet part of the code. Maybe is a new feature to be added, or something to be removed or amended. Running the test will make it fail and, because of this, this phase is called **Red**.

When the test has failed, the developer writes the minimal amount of code to make it pass. When running the test succeeds, we have the so-called **Green** phase. In this phase, it is okay to write code that cheats, just to make the test pass (that's why you would then use triangulation). This technique is called, *fake it 'til you make it*.

The last piece of this cycle is where the developer takes care of both the code and the tests (in separate times) and refactors them until they are in the desired state. This last phase is called **Refactor**.

The **TDD mantra** therefore recites, **Red-Green-Refactor**.

At first, it feels really weird to write tests before the code, and I must confess it took me a while to get used to it. If you stick to it, though, and force yourself to learn this slightly counter-intuitive way of working, at some point something almost magical happens, and you will see the quality of your code increase in a way that wouldn't be possible otherwise.

When you write your code before the tests, you have to take care of *what* the code has to do and *how* it has to do it, both at the same time. On the other hand, when you write tests before the code, you can concentrate on the *what* part alone, while you write them. When you write the code afterwards, you will mostly have to take care of *how* the code has to implement *what* is required by the tests. This shift in focus allows your mind to concentrate on the *what* and *how* parts in separate moments, yielding a brain power boost that will surprise you.

There are several other benefits that come from the adoption of this technique:

- **You will refactor with much more confidence**: Because when you touch your code you know that if you screw things up, you will break at least one test. Moreover, you will be able to take care of the architectural design in the refactor phase, where having tests that act as guardians will allow you to enjoy massaging the code until it reaches a state that satisfies you.

- **The code will be more readable**: This is crucial in our time, when coding is a social activity and every professional developer spends much more time reading code than writing it.

- **The code will be more loose-coupled and easier to test and maintain**: This is simply because writing the tests first forces you to think more deeply about its structure.

- **Writing tests first requires you to have a better understanding of the business requirements**: This is fundamental in delivering what was actually asked for. If your understanding of the requirements is lacking information, you'll find writing a test extremely challenging and this situation acts as a sentinel for you.

- **Having everything unit tested means the code will be easier to debug**: Moreover, small tests are perfect for providing alternative documentation. English can be misleading, but five lines of Python in a simple test are very hard to be misunderstood.

- **Higher speed**: It's faster to write tests and code than it is to write the code first and then lose time debugging it. If you don't write tests, you will probably deliver the code sooner, but then you will have to track the bugs down and solve them (and, rest assured, there will be bugs). The combined time taken to write the code and then debug it is usually longer than the time taken to develop the code with TDD, where having tests running before the code is written, ensuring that the amount of bugs in it will be much lower than in the other case.

On the other hand, the main shortcomings of this technique are:

- **The whole company needs to believe in it**: Otherwise you will have to constantly argue with your boss, who will not understand why it takes you so long to deliver. The truth is, it may take you a bit longer to deliver in the short term, but in the long term you gain a lot with TDD. However, it is quite hard to see the long term because it's not under our noses like the short term is. I have fought battles with stubborn bosses in my career, to be able to code using TDD. Sometimes it has been painful, but always well worth it, and I have never regretted it because, in the end, the quality of the result has always been appreciated.

- **If you fail to understand the business requirements, this will reflect in the tests you write, and therefore it will reflect in the code too**: This kind of problem is quite hard to spot until you do UAT, but one thing that you can do to reduce the likelihood of it happening is to pair with another developer. Pairing will inevitably require discussions about the business requirements, and this will help having a better idea about them before the tests are written.

- **Badly written tests are hard to maintain**: This is a fact. Tests with too many mocks or with extra assumptions or badly structured data will soon become a burden. Don't let this discourage you; just keep experimenting and change the way you write them until you find a way that doesn't require you a huge amount of work every time you touch your code.

I'm so passionate about TDD that when I interview for a job, I always ask if the company I'm about to join adopts it. If the answer is no, it's kind of a deal-breaker for me. I encourage you to check it out and use it. Use it until you feel something clicking in your mind. You won't regret it, I promise.

Exceptions

Even though I haven't formally introduced them to you, by now I expect you to at least have a vague idea of what an **exception** is. In the previous chapters, we've seen that when an iterator is exhausted, calling `next` on it raises a `StopIteration` exception. We've met `IndexError` when we tried accessing a list at a position that was outside the valid range. We've also met `AttributeError` when we tried accessing an attribute on an object that didn't have it, and `KeyError` when we did the same with a key and a dictionary. We've also just met `AssertionError` when running tests.

Now, the time has come for us to talk about exceptions.

Sometimes, even though an operation or a piece of code is correct, there are conditions in which something may go wrong. For example, if we're converting user input from `string` to `int`, the user could accidentally type a letter in place of a digit, making it impossible for us to convert that value into a number. When dividing numbers, we may not know in advance if we're attempting a division by zero. When opening a file, it could be missing or corrupted.

When an error is detected during execution, it is called an **exception**. Exceptions are not necessarily lethal; in fact, we've seen that `StopIteration` is deeply integrated in Python generator and iterator mechanisms. Normally, though, if you don't take the necessary precautions, an exception will cause your application to break. Sometimes, this is the desired behavior but in other cases, we want to prevent and control problems such as these. For example, we may alert the user that the file they're trying to open is corrupted or that it is missing so that they can either fix it or provide another file, without the need for the application to die because of this issue. Let's see an example of a few exceptions:

exceptions/first.example.py

```
>>> gen = (n for n in range(2))
>>> next(gen)
0
>>> next(gen)
1
>>> next(gen)
Traceback (most recent call last):
  File "<stdin>", line 1, in <module>
StopIteration
>>> print(undefined_var)
Traceback (most recent call last):
  File "<stdin>", line 1, in <module>
NameError: name 'undefined_var' is not defined
>>> mylist = [1, 2, 3]
>>> mylist[5]
Traceback (most recent call last):
  File "<stdin>", line 1, in <module>
IndexError: list index out of range
>>> mydict = {'a': 'A', 'b': 'B'}
>>> mydict['c']
Traceback (most recent call last):
  File "<stdin>", line 1, in <module>
KeyError: 'c'
>>> 1 / 0
Traceback (most recent call last):
  File "<stdin>", line 1, in <module>
ZeroDivisionError: division by zero
```

As you can see, the Python shell is quite forgiving. We can see the `Traceback`, so that we have information about the error, but the program doesn't die. This is a special behavior, a regular program or a script would normally die if nothing were done to handle exceptions.

To handle an exception, Python gives you the `try` statement. What happens when you enter the `try` clause is that Python will watch out for one or more different types of exceptions (according to how you instruct it), and if they are raised, it will allow you to react. The `try` statement is comprised of the `try` clause, which opens the statement; one or more `except` clauses (all optional) that define what to do when an exception is caught; an `else` clause (optional), which is executed when the `try` clause is exited without any exception raised; and a `finally` clause (optional), whose code is executed regardless of whatever happened in the other clauses. The `finally` clause is typically used to clean up resources. Mind the order, it's important. Also, `try` must be followed by at least one `except` clause or a `finally` clause. Let's see an example:

exceptions/try.syntax.py

```python
def try_syntax(numerator, denominator):
    try:
        print('In the try block: {}/{}'
              .format(numerator, denominator))
        result = numerator / denominator
    except ZeroDivisionError as zde:
        print(zde)
    else:
        print('The result is:', result)
        return result
    finally:
        print('Exiting')

print(try_syntax(12, 4))
print(try_syntax(11, 0))
```

The preceding example defines a simple `try_syntax` function. We perform the division of two numbers. We are prepared to catch a `ZeroDivisionError` exception if we call the function with `denominator = 0`. Initially, the code enters the `try` block. If `denominator` is not `0`, `result` is calculated and the execution, after leaving the `try` block, resumes in the `else` block. We print `result` and return it. Take a look at the output and you'll notice that just before returning `result`, which is the exit point of the function, Python executes the `finally` clause.

When `denominator` is `0`, things change. We enter the `except` block and print `zde`. The `else` block isn't executed because an exception was raised in the `try` block. Before (implicitly) returning `None`, we still execute the `finally` block. Take a look at the output and see if it makes sense to you:

```
$ python exceptions/try.syntax.py
In the try block: 12/4
The result is: 3.0
Exiting
3.0
In the try block: 11/0
division by zero
Exiting
None
```

When you execute a `try` block, you may want to catch more than one exception. For example, when trying to decode a JSON object, you may incur into `ValueError` for malformed JSON, or `TypeError` if the type of the data you're feeding to `json.loads()` is not a string. In this case, you may structure your code like this:

exceptions/json.example.py

```python
import json
json_data = '{}'
try:
    data = json.loads(json_data)
except (ValueError, TypeError) as e:
    print(type(e), e)
```

This code will catch both `ValueError` and `TypeError`. Try changing `json_data = '{}'` to `json_data = 2` or `json_data = '{{'`, and you'll see the different output.

> **JSON** stands for **JavaScript Object Notation** and it's an open standard format that uses human-readable text to transmit data objects consisting of key/value pairs. It's an exchange format widely used when moving data across applications, especially when data needs to be treated in a language or platform-agnostic way.

If you want to handle multiple exceptions differently, you can just add more except clauses, like this:

`exceptions/multiple.except.py`

```
try:
    # some code
except Exception1:
    # react to Exception1
except (Exception2, Exception3):
    # react to Exception2 and Exception3
except Exception3:
    # react to Exception3
...
```

Keep in mind that an exception is handled in the first block that defines that exception class or any of its bases. Therefore, when you stack multiple except clauses like we've just done, make sure that you put specific exceptions at the top and generic ones at the bottom. In OOP terms, children on top, grandparents at the bottom. Moreover, remember that only one except handler is executed when an exception is raised.

You can also write **custom exceptions**. In order to do that, you just have to inherit from any other exception class. Python built-in exceptions are too many to be listed here, so I have to point you towards the official documentation. One important thing to know is that every Python exception derives from BaseException, but your custom exceptions should never inherit directly from that one. The reason for it is that handling such an exception will trap also **system-exiting exceptions** such as SystemExit and KeyboardInterrupt, which derive from BaseException, and this could lead to severe issues. In case of disaster, you want to be able to *Ctrl + C* your way out of an application.

You can easily solve the problem by inheriting from Exception, which inherits from BaseException, but doesn't include any system-exiting exception in its children because they are siblings in the built-in exceptions hierarchy (see https://docs.python.org/3/library/exceptions.html#exception-hierarchy).

Programming with exceptions can be very tricky. You could inadvertently silence out errors, or trap exceptions that aren't meant to be handled. Play it safe by keeping in mind a few guidelines: always put in the try clause only the code that may cause the exception(s) that you want to handle. When you write except clauses, be as specific as you can, don't just resort to except Exception because it's easy. Use tests to make sure your code handles edge cases in a way that requires the least possible amount of exception handling. Writing an except statement without specifying any exception would catch any exception, therefore exposing your code to the same risks you incur when you derive your custom exceptions from BaseException.

You will find information about exceptions almost everywhere on the web. Some coders use them abundantly, others sparingly (I belong to the latter category). Find your own way of dealing with them by taking examples from other people's source code. There's plenty of interesting projects whose sources are open, and you can find them on either GitHub (https://github.com) or Bitbucket (https://bitbucket.org/).

Before we talk about **profiling**, let me show you an unconventional use of exceptions, just to give you something to help you expand your views on them. They are not just simply errors.

exceptions/for.loop.py

```
n = 100
found = False
for a in range(n):
    if found: break
    for b in range(n):
        if found: break
        for c in range(n):
            if 42 * a + 17 * b + c == 5096:
                found = True
                print(a, b, c)   # 79 99 95
```

The preceding code is quite a common idiom if you deal with numbers. You have to iterate over a few nested ranges and look for a particular combination of a, b, and c that satisfies a condition. In the example, condition is a trivial linear equation, but imagine something much cooler than that. What bugs me is having to check if the solution has been found at the beginning of each loop, in order to break out of them as fast as we can when it is. The break out logic interferes with the rest of the code and I don't like it, so I came up with a different solution for this. Take a look at it, and see if you can adapt it to other cases too.

exceptions/for.loop.py

```python
class ExitLoopException(Exception):
    pass

try:
    n = 100
    for a in range(n):
        for b in range(n):
            for c in range(n):
                if 42 * a + 17 * b + c == 5096:
                    raise ExitLoopException(a, b, c)
except ExitLoopException as ele:
    print(ele)  # (79, 99, 95)
```

Can you see how much more elegant it is? Now the breakout logic is entirely handled with a simple exception whose name even hints at its purpose. As soon as the result is found, we raise it, and immediately the control is given to the except clause which handles it. This is food for thought. This example indirectly shows you how to raise your own exceptions. Read up on the official documentation to dive into the beautiful details of this subject.

Profiling Python

There are a few different ways to profile a Python application. Profiling means having the application run while keeping track of several different parameters, like the number of times a function is called, the amount of time spent inside it, and so on. Profiling can help us find the bottlenecks in our application, so that we can improve only what is really slowing us down.

If you take a look at the profiling section in the standard library official documentation, you will see that there are a couple of different implementations of the same profiling interface: profile and cProfile.

- cProfile is recommended for most users, it's a C extension with reasonable overhead that makes it suitable for profiling long-running programs

- profile is a pure Python module whose interface is imitated by cProfile, but which adds significant overhead to profiled programs

This interface does **determinist profiling**, which means that all function calls, function returns and exception events are monitored, and precise timings are made for the intervals between these events. Another approach, called **statistical profiling**, randomly samples the effective instruction pointer, and deduces where time is being spent.

The latter usually involves less overhead, but provides only approximate results. Moreover, because of the way the Python interpreter runs the code, deterministic profiling doesn't add that as much overhead as one would think, so I'll show you a simple example using cProfile from the command line.

We're going to calculate Pythagorean triples (I know, you've missed them...) using the following code:

profiling/triples.py

```python
def calc_triples(mx):
    triples = []
    for a in range(1, mx + 1):
        for b in range(a, mx + 1):
            hypotenuse = calc_hypotenuse(a, b)
            if is_int(hypotenuse):
                triples.append((a, b, int(hypotenuse)))
    return triples

def calc_hypotenuse(a, b):
    return (a**2 + b**2) ** .5

def is_int(n):  # n is expected to be a float
    return n.is_integer()

triples = calc_triples(1000)
```

The script is extremely simple; we iterate over the interval [1, *mx*] with a and b (avoiding repetition of pairs by setting b >= a) and we check if they belong to a right triangle. We use calc_hypotenuse to get hypotenuse for a and b, and then, with is_int, we check if it is an integer, which means (*a*, *b*, *c*) is a Pythagorean triple. When we profile this script, we get information in tabular form. The columns are ncalls, tottime, percall, cumtime, percall, and filename:lineno(function). They represent the amount of calls we made to a function, how much time we spent in it, and so on. I'll trim a couple of columns to save space, so if you run the profiling yourself, don't worry if you get a different result.

```
$ python -m cProfile profiling/triples.py
1502538 function calls in 0.750 seconds
Ordered by: standard name
ncalls   tottime   percall filename:lineno(function)
500500    0.469     0.000 triples.py:14(calc_hypotenuse)
500500    0.087     0.000 triples.py:18(is_int)
```

1	0.000	0.000	triples.py:4(<module>)
1	0.163	0.163	triples.py:4(calc_triples)
1	0.000	0.000	{built-in method exec}
1034	0.000	0.000	{method 'append' of 'list' objects}
1	0.000	0.000	{method 'disable' of '_lsprof.Profil...
500500	0.032	0.000	{method 'is_integer' of 'float' objects}

Even with this limited amount of data, we can still infer some useful information about this code. Firstly, we can see that the time complexity of the algorithm we have chosen grows with the square of the input size. The amount of times we get inside the inner loop body is exactly *mx (mx + 1) / 2*. We run the script with mx = 1000, which means we get 500500 times inside the inner for loop. Three main things happen inside that loop, we call calc_hypotenuse, we call is_int and, if the condition is met, we append to the triples list.

Taking a look at the profiling report, we notice that the algorithm has spent 0.469 seconds inside calc_hypotenuse, which is way more than the 0.087 seconds spent inside is_int, given that they were called the same number of times, so let's see if we can boost calc_hypotenuse a little.

As it turns out, we can. As I mentioned earlier on in the book, the power operator ** is quite expensive, and in calc_hypotenuse, we're using it three times. Fortunately, we can easily transform two of those into simple multiplications, like this:

profiling/triples.py

```python
def calc_hypotenuse(a, b):
    return (a*a + b*b) ** .5
```

This simple change should improve things. If we run the profiling again, we see that now the 0.469 is now down to 0.177. Not bad! This means now we're spending only about 37% of the time inside calc_hypotenuse as we were before.

Let's see if we can improve is_int as well, by changing it like this:

profiling/triples.py

```python
def is_int(n):
    return n == int(n)
```

This implementation is different and the advantage is that it also works when n is an integer. Alas, when we run the profiling against it, we see that the time taken inside the is_int function has gone up to 0.141 seconds. This means that it has roughly doubled, compared to what it was before. In this case, we need to revert to the previous implementation.

This example was trivial, of course, but enough to show you how one could profile an application. Having the amount of calls that are performed against a function helps us understand better the time complexity of our algorithms. For example, you wouldn't believe how many coders fail to see that those two `for` loops run proportionally to the square of the input size.

One thing to mention: depending on what system you're using, results may be different. Therefore, it's quite important to be able to profile software on a system that is as close as possible to the one the software is deployed on, if not actually on that one.

When to profile?

Profiling is super cool, but we need to know when it is appropriate to do it, and in what measure we need to address the results we get from it.

Donald Knuth once said that *premature optimization is the root of all evil* and, although I wouldn't have put it down so drastically, I do agree with him. After all, who am I to disagree with the man that gave us *The Art of Computer Programming*, *TeX*, and some of the coolest algorithms I have ever studied when I was a university student?

So, first and foremost: *correctness*. You want you code to deliver the result correctly, therefore write tests, find edge cases, and stress your code in every way you think makes sense. Don't be protective, don't put things in the back of your brain for later because you think they're not likely to happen. Be thorough.

Secondly, take care of coding *best practices*. Remember readability, extensibility, loose coupling, modularity, and design. Apply OOP principles: encapsulation, abstraction, single responsibility, open/closed, and so on. Read up on these concepts. They will open horizons for you, and they will expand the way you think about code.

Thirdly, *refactor like a beast!* The Boy Scouts Rule says to *Always leave the campground cleaner than you found it*. Apply this rule to your code.

And, finally, when all of the above has been taken care of, then and only then, you take care of profiling.

Run your profiler and identify bottlenecks. When you have an idea of the bottlenecks you need to address, start with the worst one first. Sometimes, fixing a bottleneck causes a ripple effect that will expand and change the way the rest of the code works. Sometimes this is only a little, sometimes a bit more, according to how your code was designed and implemented. Therefore, start with the biggest issue first.

One of the reasons Python is so popular is that it is possible to implement it in many different ways. So, if you find yourself having troubles boosting up some part of your code using sheer Python, nothing prevents you from rolling up your sleeves, buying a couple of hundred liters of coffee, and rewriting the slow piece of code in C. Guaranteed to be fun!

Summary

In this chapter, we explored the world of testing, exceptions, and profiling.

I tried to give you a fairly comprehensive overview of testing, especially unit testing, which is the kind of testing that a developer mostly does. I hope I have succeeded in channeling the message that testing is not something that is perfectly defined and that you can learn from a book. You need to experiment with it a lot before you get comfortable. Of all the efforts a coder must make in terms of study and experimentation, I'd say testing is one of those that are most worth it.

We've briefly seen how we can prevent our program from dying because of errors, called exceptions, that happen at runtime. And, to steer away from the usual ground, I have given you an example of a somewhat unconventional use of exceptions to break out of nested `for` loops. That's not the only case, and I'm sure you'll discover others as you grow as a coder.

In the end, we very briefly touched base on profiling, with a simple example and a few guidelines. I wanted to talk about profiling for the sake of completeness, so at least you can play around with it.

We're now about to enter *Chapter 8, The Edges – GUIs and Scripts*, where we're going to get our hands dirty with scripts and GUIs and, hopefully, come up with something interesting.

I am aware that I gave you a lot of pointers in this chapter, with no links or directions. I'm afraid this is by choice. As a coder, there won't be a single day at work when you won't have to look something up in a documentation page, in a manual, on a website, and so on. I think it's vital for a coder to be able to search effectively for the information they need, so I hope you'll forgive me for this extra training. After all, it's all for your benefit.

8

The Edges – GUIs
and Scripts

"A user interface is like a joke. If you have to explain it, it's not that good."

- Martin LeBlanc

In this chapter, we're going to work on a project together. We're going to prepare a very simple HTML page with a few images, and then we're going to scrape it, in order to save those images.

We're going to write a script to do this, which will allow us to talk about a few concepts that I'd like to run by you. We're also going to add a few options to save images based on their format, and to choose the way we save them. And, when we're done with the script, we're going to write a GUI application that does basically the same thing, thus killing two birds with one stone. Having only one project to explain will allow me to show a wider range of topics in this chapter.

A **graphical user interface** (GUI) is a type of interface that allows the user to interact with an electronic device through graphical icons, buttons and widgets, as opposed to text-based or command-line interfaces, which require commands or text to be typed on the keyboard. In a nutshell, any browser, any office suite such as LibreOffice, and, in general, anything that pops up when you click on an icon, is a GUI application.

So, if you haven't already done so, this would be the perfect time to start a console and position yourself in a folder called ch8 in the root of your project for this book. Within that folder, we'll create two Python modules (scrape.py and guiscrape.py) and one standard folder (simple_server). Within simple_server, we'll write our HTML page (index.html) in simple_server. Images will be stored in ch8/simple_server/img. The structure in ch8 should look like this:

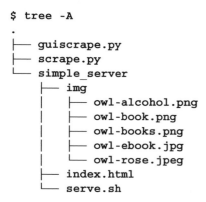

```
$ tree -A
.
├── guiscrape.py
├── scrape.py
└── simple_server
    ├── img
    │   ├── owl-alcohol.png
    │   ├── owl-book.png
    │   ├── owl-books.png
    │   ├── owl-ebook.jpg
    │   └── owl-rose.jpeg
    ├── index.html
    └── serve.sh
```

If you're using either Linux or Mac, you can do what I do and put the code to start the HTTP server in a serve.sh file. On Windows, you'll probably want to use a batch file.

The HTML page we're going to scrape has the following structure:

simple_server/index.html

```html
<!DOCTYPE html>
<html lang="en">
  <head><title>Cool Owls!</title></head>
  <body>
    <h1>Welcome to my owl gallery</h1>
    <div>
      <img src="img/owl-alcohol.png" height="128" />
      <img src="img/owl-book.png" height="128" />
      <img src="img/owl-books.png" height="128" />
      <img src="img/owl-ebook.jpg" height="128" />
      <img src="img/owl-rose.jpeg" height="128" />
```

```
      </div>
      <p>Do you like my owls?</p>
    </body>
  </html>
```

It's an extremely simple page, so let's just note that we have five images, three of which are PNGs and two are JPGs (note that even though they are both JPGs, one ends with `.jpg` and the other with `.jpeg`, which are both valid extensions for this format).

So, Python gives you a very simple HTTP server for free that you can start with the following command (in the `simple_server` folder):

```
$ python -m http.server 8000
Serving HTTP on 0.0.0.0 port 8000 ...
127.0.0.1 - - [31/Aug/2015 16:11:10] "GET / HTTP/1.1" 200 -
```

The last line is the log you get when you access `http://localhost:8000`, where our beautiful page will be served. Alternatively, you can put that command in a file called `serve.sh`, and just run that with this command (make sure it's executable):

```
$ ./serve.sh
```

It will have the same effect. If you have the code for this book, your page should look something like this:

Feel free to use any other set of images, as long as you use at least one PNG and one JPG, and that in the `src` tag you use relative paths, not absolute. I got those lovely owls from `https://openclipart.org/`.

First approach – scripting

Now, let's start writing the script. I'll go through the source in three steps: imports first, then the argument parsing logic, and finally the business logic.

The imports

scrape.py (Imports)

```
import argparse
import base64
import json
import os
from bs4 import BeautifulSoup
import requests
```

Going through them from the top, you can see that we'll need to parse the arguments. which we'll feed to the script itself (argparse). We will need the base64 library to save the images within a JSON file (base64 and json), and we'll need to open files for writing (os). Finally, we'll need BeautifulSoup for scraping the web page easily, and requests to fetch its content. requests is an extremely popular library for performing HTTP requests, built to avoid the difficulties and quirks of using the standard library urllib module. It's based on the fast urllib3 third-party library.

> We will explore the HTTP protocol and requests mechanism in *Chapter 10, Web Development Done Right* so, for now, let's just (simplistically) say that we perform an HTTP request to fetch the content of a web page. We can do it programmatically using a library such as requests, and it's more or less the equivalent of typing a URL in your browser and pressing *Enter* (the browser then fetches the content of a web page and also displays it to you).

Of all these imports, only the last two don't belong to the Python standard library, but they are so widely used throughout the world that I dare not exclude them in this book. Make sure you have them installed:

```
$ pip freeze | egrep -i "soup|requests"
beautifulsoup4==4.4.0
requests==2.7.0
```

Of course, the version numbers might be different for you. If they're not installed, use this command to do so:

```
$ pip install beautifulsoup4 requests
```

At this point, the only thing that I reckon might confuse you is the base64/json couple, so allow me to spend a few words on that.

As we saw in the previous chapter, JSON is one of the most popular formats for data exchange between applications. It's also widely used for other purposes too, for example, to save data in a file. In our script, we're going to offer the user the ability to save images as image files, or as a JSON single file. Within the JSON, we'll put a dictionary with keys as the images names and values as their content. The only issue is that saving images in the binary format is tricky, and this is where the base64 library comes to the rescue. **Base64** is a very popular binary-to-text encoding scheme that represents binary data in an ASCII string format by translating it into a radix-64 representation.

> The **radix-64** representation uses the letters *A-Z*, *a-z*, and the digits *0-9*, plus the two symbols + and / for a grand total of 64 symbols altogether. Therefore, not surprisingly, the Base64 alphabet is made up of these 64 symbols.

If you think you have never used it, think again. Every time you send an email with an image attached to it, the image gets encoded with Base64 before the email is sent. On the recipient side, images are automatically decoded into their original binary format so that the email client can display them.

Parsing arguments

Now that the technicalities are out of the way, let's see the second section of our script (it should be at the end of the scrape.py module).

scrape.py (Argument parsing and scraper triggering)

```python
if __name__ == "__main__":
    parser = argparse.ArgumentParser(
        description='Scrape a webpage.')
    parser.add_argument(
        '-t',
        '--type',
        choices=['all', 'png', 'jpg'],
        default='all',
        help='The image type we want to scrape.')
    parser.add_argument(
        '-f',
        '--format',
        choices=['img', 'json'],
```

```
        default='img',
        help='The format images are saved to.')
    parser.add_argument(
        'url',
        help='The URL we want to scrape for images.')
    args = parser.parse_args()
    scrape(args.url, args.format, args.type)
```

Look at that first line; it is a very common idiom when it comes to scripting. According to the official Python documentation, the string '__main__' is the name of the scope in which top-level code executes. A module's __name__ is set equal to '__main__' when read from standard input, a script, or from an interactive prompt.

Therefore, if you put the execution logic under that if, the result is that you will be able to use the module as a library should you need to import any of the functions or objects defined in it, because when importing it from another module, __name__ won't be '__main__'. On the other hand, when you run the script directly, like we're going to, __name__ will be '__main__', so the execution logic will run.

The first thing we do then is define our parser. I would recommend using the standard library module, argparse, which is simple enough and quite powerful. There are other options out there, but in this case, argparse will provide us with all we need.

We want to feed our script three different data: the type of images we want to save, the format in which we want to save them, and the URL for the page to be scraped.

The type can be PNG, JPG or both (default), while the format can be either image or JSON, image being the default. URL is the only mandatory argument.

So, we add the -t option, allowing also the long version --type. The choices are 'all', 'png', and 'jpg'. We set the default to 'all' and we add a help message.

We do a similar procedure for the format argument allowing both the short and long syntax (-f and --format), and finally we add the url argument, which is the only one that is specified differently so that it won't be treated as an option, but rather as a positional argument.

In order to parse all the arguments, all we need is parser.parse_args(). Very simple, isn't it?

The last line is where we trigger the actual logic, by calling the scrape function, passing all the arguments we just parsed. We will see its definition shortly.

The nice thing about `argparse` is that if you call the script by passing `-h`, it will print a nice **usage text** for you automatically. Let's try it out:

```
$ python scrape.py -h
usage: scrape.py [-h] [-t {all,png,jpg}] [-f {img,json}] url


Scrape a webpage.


positional arguments:
  url                     The URL we want to scrape for images.


optional arguments:
  -h, --help              show this help message and exit
  -t {all,png,jpg}, --type {all,png,jpg}
                          The image type we want to scrape.
  -f {img,json}, --format {img,json}
                          The format images are saved to.
```

If you think about it, the one true advantage of this is that we just need to specify the arguments and we don't have to worry about the usage text, which means we won't have to keep it in sync with the arguments' definition every time we change something. This is precious.

Here's a few different ways to call our `scrape.py` script, which demonstrate that `type` and `format` are optional, and how you can use the short and long syntax to use them:

```
$ python scrape.py http://localhost:8000
$ python scrape.py -t png http://localhost:8000
$ python scrape.py --type=jpg -f json http://localhost:8000
```

The first one is using default values for `type` and `format`. The second one will save only PNG images, and the third one will save only JPGs, but in JSON format.

The business logic

Now that we've seen the scaffolding, let's dive deep into the actual logic (if it looks intimidating don't worry; we'll go through it together). Within the script, this logic lies after the imports and before the parsing (before the `if __name__` clause):

`scrape.py` (Business logic)

```python
def scrape(url, format_, type_):
    try:
        page = requests.get(url)
    except requests.RequestException as rex:
        print(str(rex))
    else:
        soup = BeautifulSoup(page.content, 'html.parser')
        images = _fetch_images(soup, url)
        images = _filter_images(images, type_)
        _save(images, format_)


def _fetch_images(soup, base_url):
    images = []
    for img in soup.findAll('img'):
        src = img.get('src')
        img_url = (
            '{base_url}/{src}'.format(
                base_url=base_url, src=src))
        name = img_url.split('/')[-1]
        images.append(dict(name=name, url=img_url))
    return images


def _filter_images(images, type_):
    if type_ == 'all':
        return images
    ext_map = {
        'png': ['.png'],
        'jpg': ['.jpg', '.jpeg'],
    }
    return [
        img for img in images
        if _matches_extension(img['name'], ext_map[type_])
    ]


def _matches_extension(filename, extension_list):
    name, extension = os.path.splitext(filename.lower())
    return extension in extension_list


def _save(images, format_):
    if images:
        if format_ == 'img':
            _save_images(images)
        else:
```

```
            _save_json(images)
        print('Done')
    else:
        print('No images to save.')

def _save_images(images):
    for img in images:
        img_data = requests.get(img['url']).content
        with open(img['name'], 'wb') as f:
            f.write(img_data)

def _save_json(images):
    data = {}
    for img in images:
        img_data = requests.get(img['url']).content
        b64_img_data = base64.b64encode(img_data)
        str_img_data = b64_img_data.decode('utf-8')
        data[img['name']] = str_img_data

    with open('images.json', 'w') as ijson:
        ijson.write(json.dumps(data))
```

Let's start with the `scrape` function. The first thing it does is fetch the page at the given `url` argument. Whatever error may happen while doing this, we trap it in the `RequestException rex` and we print it. The `RequestException` is the base exception class for all the exceptions in the `requests` library.

However, if things go well, and we have a page back from the GET request, then we can proceed (`else` branch) and feed its content to the `BeautifulSoup` parser. The `BeautifulSoup` library allows us to parse a web page in no time, without having to write all the logic that would be needed to find all the images in a page, which we really don't want to do. It's not as easy as it seems, and reinventing the wheel is never good. To fetch images, we use the `_fetch_images` function and we filter them with `_filter_images`. Finally, we call `_save` with the result.

Splitting the code into different functions with meaningful names allows us to read it more easily. Even if you haven't seen the logic of the `_fetch_images`, `_filter_images`, and `_save` functions, it's not hard to predict what they do, right?

`_fetch_images` takes a `BeautifulSoup` object and a base URL. All it does is looping through all of the images found on the page and filling in the `'name'` and `'url'` information about them in a dictionary (one per image). All dictionaries are added to the `images` list, which is returned at the end.

There is some trickery going on when we get the name of an image. What we do is split the `img_url` (`http://localhost:8000/img/my_image_name.png`) string using `'/'` as a separator, and we take the last item as the image name. There is a more robust way of doing this, but for this example it would be overkill. If you want to see the details of each step, try to break this logic down into smaller steps, and print the result of each of them to help yourself understand.

Towards the end of the book, I'll show you another technique to debug in a much more efficient way.

Anyway, by just adding `print(images)` at the end of the `_fetch_images` function, we get this:

```
[{'url': 'http://localhost:8000/img/owl-alcohol.png', 'name': 'owl-
alcohol.png'}, {'url': 'http://localhost:8000/img/owl-book.png', 'name':
'owl-book.png'}, ...]
```

I truncated the result for brevity. You can see each dictionary has a `'url'` and `'name'` key/value pair, which we can use to fetch, identify and save our images as we like. At this point, I hear you asking what would happen if the images on the page were specified with an absolute path instead of a relative one, right? Good question!

The answer is that the script will fail to download them because this logic expects relative paths. I was about to add a bit of logic to solve this issue when I thought that, at this stage, it would be a nice exercise for you to do it, so I'll leave it up to you to fix it.

 Hint: inspect the start of that `src` variable. If it starts with `'http'`, then it's probably an absolute path.

I hope the body of the `_filter_images` function is interesting to you. I wanted to show you how to check on multiple extensions by using a mapping technique.

In this function, if `type_` is `'all'`, then no filtering is required, so we just return all the images. On the other hand, when `type_` is not `'all'`, we get the allowed extensions from the `ext_map` dictionary, and use it to filter the images in the list comprehension that ends the function body. You can see that by using another helper function, `_matches_extension`, I have made the list comprehension simpler and more readable.

All `_matches_extension` does is split the name of the image getting its extension and checking whether it is within the list of allowed ones. Can you find one micro improvement (speed-wise) that could be done to this function?

I'm sure that you're wondering why I have collected all the images in the list and then removed them, instead of checking whether I wanted to save them before adding them to the list. The first reason is that I needed `_fetch_images` in the GUI app as it is now. A second reason is that combining, fetching, and filtering would produce a longer and a bit more complicated function, and I'm trying to keep the complexity level down. A third reason is that this could be a nice exercise for you to do. Feels like we're pairing here...

Let's keep going through the code and inspect the `_save` function. You can see that, when `images` isn't empty, this basically acts as a dispatcher. We either call `_save_images` or `_save_json`, depending on which information is stored in the `format_` variable.

We are almost done. Let's jump to `_save_images`. We loop on the `images` list and for each dictionary we find there we perform a GET request on the image URL and save its content in a file, which we name as the image itself. The one important thing to note here is how we save that file.

We use a **context manager**, represented by the keyword `with`, to do that. Python's `with` statement supports the concept of a runtime context defined by a context manager. This is implemented using a pair of methods (`contextmanager.__enter__()` and `contextmanager.__exit__(exc_type, exc_val, exc_tb)`) that allow user-defined classes to define a runtime context that is entered before the statement body is executed and exited when the statement ends.

In our case, using a context manager, in conjunction with the open function, gives us the guarantee that if anything bad were to happen while writing that file, the resources involved in the process will be cleaned up and released properly regardless of the error. Have you ever tried to delete a file on Windows, only to be presented with an alert that tells you that you cannot delete the file because there is another process that is holding on to it? We're avoiding that sort of very annoying thing.

When we open a file, we get a handler for it and, no matter what happens, we want to be sure we release it when we're done with the file. A context manager is the tool we need to make sure of that.

Finally, let's now step into the `_save_json` function. It's very similar to the previous one. We basically fill in the `data` dictionary. The image name is the *key*, and the Base64 representation of its binary content is the *value*. When we're done populating our dictionary, we use the `json` library to dump it in the `images.json` file. I'll give you a small preview of that:

`images.json (truncated)`

```
{
```

```
    "owl-ebook.jpg": "/9j/4AAQSkZJRgABAQEAMQAxAAD/2wBDAAEBAQ...
    "owl-book.png": "iVBORw0KGgoAAAANSUhEUgAAASwAAAEbCAYAAAB...
    "owl-books.png": "iVBORw0KGgoAAAANSUhEUgAAASwAAAElCAYAAA...
    "owl-alcohol.png": "iVBORw0KGgoAAAANSUhEUgAAASwAAAEICAYA...
    "owl-rose.jpeg": "/9j/4AAQSkZJRgABAQEANAA0AAD/2wBDAAEBAQ...
}
```

And that's it! Now, before proceeding to the next section, make sure you play with this script and understand well how it works. Try and modify something, print out intermediate results, add a new argument or functionality, or scramble the logic. We're going to migrate it into a GUI application now, which will add a layer of complexity simply because we'll have to build the GUI interface, so it's important that you're well acquainted with the business logic: it will allow you to concentrate on the rest of the code.

Second approach – a GUI application

There are several libraries to write GUI applications in Python. The most famous ones are **tkinter**, **wxPython**, **PyGTK**, and **PyQt**. They all offer a wide range of tools and widgets that you can use to compose a GUI application.

The one I'm going to use for the rest of this chapter is tkinter. **tkinter** stands for **Tk interface** and it is the standard Python interface to the Tk GUI toolkit. Both Tk and tkinter are available on most Unix platforms, Mac OS X, as well as on Windows systems.

Let's make sure that tkinter is installed properly on your system by running this command:

```
$ python -m tkinter
```

It should open a dialog window demonstrating a simple Tk interface. If you can see that, then we're good to go. However, if it doesn't work, please search for tkinter in the Python official documentation. You will find several links to resources that will help you get up and running with it.

We're going to make a very simple GUI application that basically mimics the behavior of the script we saw in the first part of this chapter. We won't add the ability to save JPGs or PNGs singularly, but after you've gone through this chapter, you should be able to play with the code and put that feature back in by yourself.

So, this is what we're aiming for:

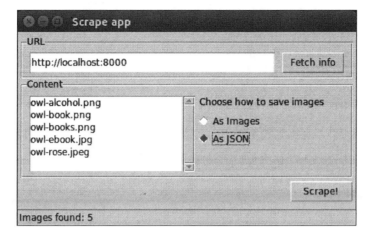

Gorgeous, isn't it? As you can see, it's a very simple interface (this is how it should look on Ubuntu). There is a frame (that is, a container) for the **URL** field and the **Fetch info** button, another frame for the **Listbox** to hold the image names and the radio button to control the way we save them, and finally there is a **Scrape!** button at the bottom. We also have a status bar, which shows us some information.

In order to get this layout, we could just place all the widgets on a root window, but that would make the layout logic quite messy and unnecessarily complicated. So, instead, we will divide the space using frames and place the widgets in those frames. This way we will achieve a much nicer result. So, this is the draft for the layout:

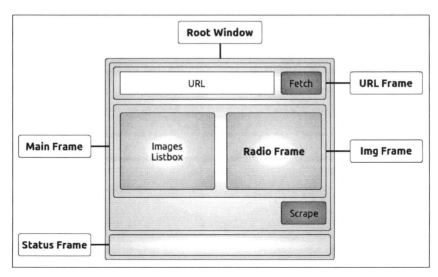

We have a **Root Window**, which is the main window of the application. We divide it into two rows, the first one in which we place the **Main Frame**, and the second one in which we place the **Status Frame** (which will hold the status bar). The **Main Frame** is subsequently divided into three rows itself. In the first one we place the **URL Frame**, which holds the URL widgets. In the second one we place the **Img Frame**, which will hold the **Listbox** and the **Radio Frame**, which will host a label and the radio button widgets. And finally a third one, which will just hold the **Scrape** button.

In order to lay out frames and widgets, we will use a layout manager called *grid*, that simply divides up the space into rows and columns, as in a matrix.

Now, all the code I'm going to write comes from the `guiscrape.py` module, so I won't repeat its name for each snippet, to save space. The module is logically divided into three sections, not unlike the script version: imports, layout logic, and business logic. We're going to analyze them line by line, in three chunks.

The imports

```
from tkinter import *
from tkinter import ttk, filedialog, messagebox
import base64
import json
import os
from bs4 import BeautifulSoup
import requests
```

We're already familiar with most of these. The interesting bit here is those first two lines. The first one is quite common practice, although it is bad practice in Python to import using the *star syntax*. You can incur in name collisions and, if the module is too big, importing everything would be expensive.

After that, we import `ttk`, `filedialog`, and `messagebox` explicitly, following the conventional approach used with this library. `ttk` is the new set of styled widgets. They behave basically like the old ones, but are capable of drawing themselves correctly according to the style your OS is set on, which is nice.

The rest of the imports is what we need in order to carry out the task you know well by now. Note that there is nothing we need to install with `pip` in this second part, we already have everything we need.

The layout logic

I'm going to paste it chunk by chunk so that I can explain it easily to you. You'll see how all those pieces we talked about in the layout draft are arranged and glued together. What I'm about to paste, as we did in the script before, is the final part of the `guiscrape.py` module. We'll leave the middle part, the business logic, for last.

```python
if __name__ == "__main__":
    _root = Tk()
    _root.title('Scrape app')
```

As you know by now, we only want to execute the logic when the module is run directly, so that first line shouldn't surprise you.

In the last two lines. we set up the main window, which is an instance of the `Tk` class. We instantiate it and give it a title. Note that I use the prepending underscore technique for all the names of the `tkinter` objects, in order to avoid potential collisions with names in the business logic. I just find it cleaner like this, but you're allowed to disagree.

```python
    _mainframe = ttk.Frame(_root, padding='5 5 5 5')
    _mainframe.grid(row=0, column=0, sticky=(E, W, N, S))
```

Here, we set up the **Main Frame**. It's a `ttk.Frame` instance. We set `_root` as its parent, and give it some padding. The `padding` is a measure in pixels of how much space should be inserted between the inner content and the borders in order to let our layout breathe a little, otherwise we have the *sardine effect*, where widgets are packed too tightly.

The second line is much more interesting. We place this `_mainframe` on the first row (`0`) and first column (`0`) of the parent object (`_root`). We also say that this frame needs to extend itself in each direction by using the `sticky` argument with all four cardinal directions. If you're wondering where they came from, it's the `from tkinter import *` magic that brought them to us.

```python
    _url_frame = ttk.LabelFrame(
        _mainframe, text='URL', padding='5 5 5 5')
    _url_frame.grid(row=0, column=0, sticky=(E, W))
    _url_frame.columnconfigure(0, weight=1)
    _url_frame.rowconfigure(0, weight=1)
```

Next, we start by placing the **URL Frame** down. This time, the parent object is _mainframe, as you will recall from our draft. This is not just a simple Frame, but it's actually a LabelFrame, which means we can set the text argument and expect a rectangle to be drawn around it, with the content of the text argument written in the top-left part of it (check out the previous picture if it helps). We position this frame at (0, 0), and say that it should expand to the left and to the right. We don't need the other two directions.

Finally, we use rowconfigure and columnconfigure to make sure it behaves correctly, should it need to resize. This is just a formality in our present layout.

```
_url = StringVar()
_url.set('http://localhost:8000')
_url_entry = ttk.Entry(
    _url_frame, width=40, textvariable=_url)
_url_entry.grid(row=0, column=0, sticky=(E, W, S, N), padx=5)
_fetch_btn = ttk.Button(
    _url_frame, text='Fetch info', command=fetch_url)
_fetch_btn.grid(row=0, column=1, sticky=W, padx=5)
```

Here, we have the code to lay out the URL textbox and the _fetch button. A textbox in this environment is called Entry. We instantiate it as usual, setting _url_frame as its parent and giving it a width. Also, and this is the most interesting part, we set the textvariable argument to be _url. _url is a StringVar, which is an object that is now connected to Entry and will be used to manipulate its content. Therefore, we don't modify the text in the _url_entry instance directly, but by accessing _url. In this case, we call the set method on it to set the initial value to the URL of our local web page.

We position _url_entry at (0, 0), setting all four cardinal directions for it to stick to, and we also set a bit of extra padding on the left and right edges by using padx, which adds padding on the x-axis (horizontal). On the other hand, pady takes care of the vertical direction.

By now, you should get that every time you call the .grid method on an object, we're basically telling the grid layout manager to place that object somewhere, according to rules that we specify as arguments in the grid() call.

Similarly, we set up and place the _fetch button. The only interesting parameter is command=fetch_url. This means that when we click this button, we actually call the fetch_url function. This technique is called **callback**.

```
_img_frame = ttk.LabelFrame(
    _mainframe, text='Content', padding='9 0 0 0')
_img_frame.grid(row=1, column=0, sticky=(N, S, E, W))
```

This is what we called **Img Frame** in the layout draft. It is placed on the second row of its parent _mainframe. It will hold the Listbox and the **Radio Frame**.

```
_images = StringVar()
_img_listbox = Listbox(
    _img_frame, listvariable=_images, height=6, width=25)
_img_listbox.grid(row=0, column=0, sticky=(E, W), pady=5)
_scrollbar = ttk.Scrollbar(
    _img_frame, orient=VERTICAL, command=_img_listbox.yview)
_scrollbar.grid(row=0, column=1, sticky=(S, N), pady=6)
_img_listbox.configure(yscrollcommand=_scrollbar.set)
```

This is probably the most interesting bit of the whole layout logic. As we did with the _url_entry, we need to drive the contents of Listbox by tying it to a variable _images. We set up Listbox so that _img_frame is its parent, and _images is the variable it's tied to. We also pass some dimensions.

The interesting bit comes from the _scrollbar instance. Note that, when we instantiate it, we set its command to _img_listbox.yview. This is the first half of the contract between a Listbox and a Scrollbar. The other half is provided by the _img_listbox.configure method, which sets the yscrollcommand=_scrollbar.set.

By providing this reciprocal bond, when we scroll on Listbox, the Scrollbar will move accordingly and vice-versa, when we operate the Scrollbar, the Listbox will scroll accordingly.

```
_radio_frame = ttk.Frame(_img_frame)
_radio_frame.grid(row=0, column=2, sticky=(N, S, W, E))
```

We place the **Radio Frame**, ready to be populated. Note that the Listbox is occupying $(0, 0)$ on _img_frame, the Scrollbar $(0, 1)$ and therefore _radio_frame will go in $(0, 2)$.

```
_choice_lbl = ttk.Label(
    _radio_frame, text="Choose how to save images")
_choice_lbl.grid(row=0, column=0, padx=5, pady=5)
_save_method = StringVar()
_save_method.set('img')
_img_only_radio = ttk.Radiobutton(
    _radio_frame, text='As Images', variable=_save_method,
    value='img')
_img_only_radio.grid(
    row=1, column=0, padx=5, pady=2, sticky=W)
_img_only_radio.configure(state='normal')
```

```
_json_radio = ttk.Radiobutton(
    _radio_frame, text='As JSON', variable=_save_method,
    value='json')
_json_radio.grid(row=2, column=0, padx=5, pady=2, sticky=W)
```

Firstly, we place the label, and we give it some padding. Note that the label and radio buttons are children of _radio_frame.

As for the Entry and Listbox objects, the Radiobutton is also driven by a bond to an external variable, which I called _save_method. Each Radiobutton instance sets a value argument, and by checking the value on _save_method, we know which button is selected.

```
_scrape_btn = ttk.Button(
    _mainframe, text='Scrape!', command=save)
_scrape_btn.grid(row=2, column=0, sticky=E, pady=5)
```

On the third row of _mainframe we place the **Scrape** button. Its command is save, which saves the images to be listed in Listbox, after we have successfully parsed a web page.

```
_status_frame = ttk.Frame(
    _root, relief='sunken', padding='2 2 2 2')
_status_frame.grid(row=1, column=0, sticky=(E, W, S))
_status_msg = StringVar()
_status_msg.set('Type a URL to start scraping...')
_status = ttk.Label(
    _status_frame, textvariable=_status_msg, anchor=W)
_status.grid(row=0, column=0, sticky=(E, W))
```

We end the layout section by placing down the status frame, which is a simple ttk.Frame. To give it a little status bar effect, we set its relief property to 'sunken' and give it a uniform padding of 2 pixels. It needs to stick to the _root window left, right and bottom parts, so we set its sticky attribute to (E, W, S).

We then place a label in it and, this time, we tie it to a StringVar object, because we will have to modify it every time we want to update the status bar text. You should be acquainted to this technique by now.

Finally, on the last line, we run the application by calling the mainloop method on the Tk instance.

```
_root.mainloop()
```

Please remember that all these instructions are placed under the if __name__ == "__main__": clause in the original script.

As you can see, the code to design our GUI application is not hard. Granted, at the beginning you have to play around a little bit. Not everything will work out perfectly at the first attempt, but I promise you it's very easy and you can find plenty of tutorials on the web. Let's now get to the interesting bit, the business logic.

The business logic

We'll analyze the business logic of the GUI application in three chunks. There is the fetching logic, the saving logic, and the alerting logic.

Fetching the web page

```python
config = {}

def fetch_url():
    url = _url.get()
    config['images'] = []
    _images.set(())    # initialized as an empty tuple
    try:
        page = requests.get(url)
    except requests.RequestException as rex:
        _sb(str(rex))
    else:
        soup = BeautifulSoup(page.content, 'html.parser')
        images = fetch_images(soup, url)
        if images:
            _images.set(tuple(img['name'] for img in images))
            _sb('Images found: {}'.format(len(images)))
        else:
            _sb('No images found')
        config['images'] = images

def fetch_images(soup, base_url):
    images = []
    for img in soup.findAll('img'):
        src = img.get('src')
        img_url = (
            '{base_url}/{src}'.format(base_url=base_url, src=src))
        name = img_url.split('/')[-1]
        images.append(dict(name=name, url=img_url))
    return images
```

First of all, let me explain that `config` dictionary. We need some way of passing data between the GUI application and the business logic. Now, instead of polluting the global namespace with many different variables, my personal preference is to have a single dictionary that holds all the objects we need to pass back and forth, so that the global namespace isn't be clogged up with all those names, and we have one single, clean, easy way of knowing where all the objects that are needed by our application are.

In this simple example, we'll just populate the `config` dictionary with the images we fetch from the page, but I wanted to show you the technique so that you have at least an example. This technique comes from my experience with JavaScript. When you code a web page, you very often import several different libraries. If each of these cluttered the global namespace with all sorts of variables, there would be severe issues in making everything work, because of name clashes and variable overriding. They make the coder's life a living hell.

So, it's much better to try and leave the global namespace as clean as we can. In this case, I find that using one `config` variable is more than acceptable.

The `fetch_url` function is quite similar to what we did in the script. Firstly, we get the `url` value by calling `_url.get()`. Remember that the `_url` object is a `StringVar` instance that is tied to the `_url_entry` object, which is an `Entry`. The text field you see on the GUI is the `Entry`, but the text behind the scenes is the value of the `StringVar` object.

By calling `get()` on `_url`, we get the value of the text which is displayed in `_url_entry`.

The next step is to prepare `config['images']` to be an empty list, and to empty the `_images` variable, which is tied to `_img_listbox`. This, of course, has the effect of cleaning up all the items in `_img_listbox`.

After this preparation step, we can try to fetch the page, using the same `try/except` logic we adopted in the script at the beginning of the chapter.

The one difference is in the action we take if things go wrong. We call `_sb(str(rex))`. `_sb` is a helper function whose code we'll see shortly. Basically, it sets the text in the status bar for us. Not a good name, right? I had to explain its behavior to you: food for thought.

If we can fetch the page, then we create the `soup` instance, and fetch the images from it. The logic of `fetch_images` is exactly the same as the one explained before, so I won't repeat myself here.

If we have images, using a quick tuple comprehension (which is actually a generator expression fed to a tuple constructor) we feed the _images StringVar and this has the effect of populating our _img_listbox with all the image names. Finally, we update the status bar.

If there were no images, we still update the status bar, and at the end of the function, regardless of how many images were found, we update config['images'] to hold the images list. In this way, we'll be able to access the images from other functions by inspecting config['images'] without having to pass that list around.

Saving the images

The logic to save the images is pretty straightforward. Here it is:

```
def save():
    if not config.get('images'):
        _alert('No images to save')
        return

    if _save_method.get() == 'img':
        dirname = filedialog.askdirectory(mustexist=True)
        _save_images(dirname)
    else:
        filename = filedialog.asksaveasfilename(
            initialfile='images.json',
            filetypes=[('JSON', '.json')])
        _save_json(filename)


def _save_images(dirname):
    if dirname and config.get('images'):
        for img in config['images']:
            img_data = requests.get(img['url']).content
            filename = os.path.join(dirname, img['name'])
            with open(filename, 'wb') as f:
                f.write(img_data)
        _alert('Done')


def _save_json(filename):
    if filename and config.get('images'):
        data = {}
        for img in config['images']:
            img_data = requests.get(img['url']).content
            b64_img_data = base64.b64encode(img_data)
```

```
                    str_img_data = b64_img_data.decode('utf-8')
                    data[img['name']] = str_img_data

            with open(filename, 'w') as ijson:
                ijson.write(json.dumps(data))
        _alert('Done')
```

When the user clicks the **Scrape** button, the `save` function is called using the callback mechanism.

The first thing that this function does is check whether there are actually any images to be saved. If not, it alerts the user about it, using another helper function, `_alert`, whose code we'll see shortly. No further action is performed if there are no images.

On the other hand, if the `config['images']` list is not empty, `save` acts as a dispatcher, and it calls `_save_images` or `_save_json`, according to which value is held by `_same_method`. Remember, this variable is tied to the radio buttons, therefore we expect its value to be either `'img'` or `'json'`.

This dispatcher is a bit different from the one in the script. According to which method we have selected, a different action must be taken.

If we want to save the images as images, we need to ask the user to choose a directory. We do this by calling `filedialog.askdirectory` and assigning the result of the call to the variable `dirname`. This opens up a nice dialog window that asks us to choose a directory. The directory we choose must exist, as specified by the way we call the method. This is done so that we don't have to write code to deal with a potentially missing directory when saving the files.

Here's how this dialog should look on Ubuntu:

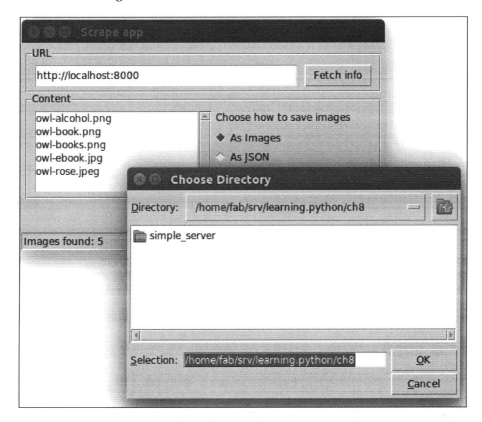

If we cancel the operation, `dirname` will be set to `None`.

Before finishing analyzing the logic in `save`, let's quickly go through `_save_images`.

It's very similar to the version we had in the script so just note that, at the beginning, in order to be sure that we actually have something to do, we check on both `dirname` and the presence of at least one image in `config['images']`.

If that's the case, it means we have at least one image to save and the path for it, so we can proceed. The logic to save the images has already been explained. The one thing we do differently this time is to join the directory (which means the complete path) to the image name, by means of `os.path.join`. In the `os.path` module there's plenty of useful methods to work with paths and filenames.

At the end of `_save_images`, if we saved at least one image, we alert the user that we're done.

Let's go back now to the other branch in `save`. This branch is executed when the user selects the **As JSON** radio button before pressing the **Scrape** button. In this case, we want to save a file; therefore, we cannot just ask for a directory. We want to give the user the ability to choose a filename as well. Hence, we fire up a different dialog: `filedialog.asksaveasfilename`.

We pass an initial filename, which is proposed to the user with the ability to change it if they don't like it. Moreover, because we're saving a JSON file, we're forcing the user to use the correct extension by passing the `filetypes` argument. It is a list with any number of 2-tuples *(description, extension)* that runs the logic of the dialog.

Here's how this dialog should look on Ubuntu:

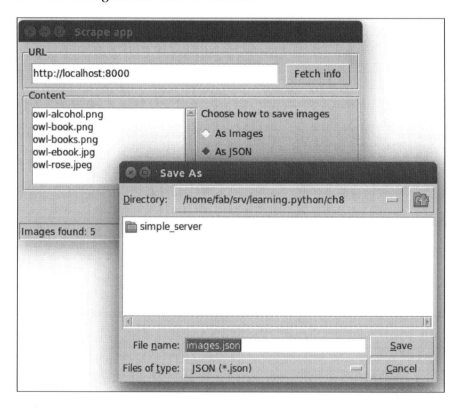

Once we have chosen a place and a filename, we can proceed with the saving logic, which is the same as it was in the previous script. We create a JSON object from a Python dictionary (`data`) that we populate with key/value pairs made by the `images` name and Base64 encoded content.

In _save_json as well, we have a little check at the beginning that makes sure that we don't proceed unless we have a file name and at least one image to save.

This ensures that if the user presses the **Cancel** button, nothing bad happens.

Alerting the user

Finally, let's see the alerting logic. It's extremely simple.

```
def _sb(msg):
    _status_msg.set(msg)

def _alert(msg):
    messagebox.showinfo(message=msg)
```

That's it! To change the status bar message all we need to do is to access _status_ msg StringVar, as it's tied to the _status label.

On the other hand, if we want to show the user a more visible message, we can fire up a message box. Here's how it should look on Ubuntu:

The messagebox object can also be used to warn the user (messagebox.showwarning) or to signal an error (messagebox.showerror). But it can also be used to provide dialogs that ask us if we're sure that we want to proceed or if we really want to delete that file, and so on.

If you inspect messagebox by simply printing out what dir(messagebox) returns, you'll find methods like askokcancel, askquestion, askretrycancel, askyesno, and askyesnocancel, as well as a set of constants to verify the response of the user, such as CANCEL, NO, OK, OKCANCEL, YES, YESNOCANCEL, and so on. You can compare these to the user's choice so that you know what the next action to execute when the dialog closes.

How to improve the application?

Now that you're accustomed to the fundamentals of designing a GUI application, I'd like to give you some suggestions on how to make ours better.

We can start from the code quality. Do you think this code is good enough, or would you improve it? If so, how? I would test it, and make sure it's robust and caters for all the various scenarios that a user might create by clicking around on the application. I would also make sure the behavior is what I would expect when the website we're scraping is down for any reason.

Another thing that we could improve is the naming. I have prudently named all the components with a leading underscore, both to highlight their somewhat "private" nature, and to avoid having name clashes with the underlying objects they are linked to. But in retrospect, many of those components could use a better name, so it's really up to you to refactor until you find the form that suits you best. You could start by giving a better name to the _sb function!

For what concerns the user interface, you could try and resize the main application. See what happens? The whole content stays exactly where it is. Empty space is added if you expand, or the whole widgets set disappears gradually if you shrink. This behavior isn't exactly nice, therefore one quick solution could be to make the root window fixed (that is, unable to resize).

Another thing that you could do to improve the application is to add the same functionality we had in the script, to save only PNGs or JPGs. In order to do this, you could place a combo box somewhere, with three values: All, PNGs, JPGs, or something similar. The user should be able to select one of those options before saving the files.

Even better, you could change the declaration of Listbox so that it's possible to select multiple images at the same time, and only the selected ones will be saved. If you manage to do this (it's not as hard as it seems, believe me), then you should consider presenting the Listbox a bit better, maybe providing alternating background colors for the rows.

Another nice thing you could add is a button that opens up a dialog to select a file. The file must be one of the JSON files the application can produce. Once selected, you could run some logic to reconstruct the images from their Base64-encoded version. The logic to do this is very simple, so here's an example:

```
with open('images.json', 'r') as f:
    data = json.loads(f.read())

for (name, b64val) in data.items():
    with open(name, 'wb') as f:
        f.write(base64.b64decode(b64val))
```

As you can see, we need to open `images.json` in read mode, and grab the `data` dictionary. Once we have it, we can loop through its items, and save each image with the Base64 decoded content. I'll leave it up to you to tie this logic to a button in the application.

Another cool feature that you could add is the ability to open up a preview pane that shows any image you select from the `Listbox`, so that the user can take a peek at the images before deciding to save them.

Finally, one last suggestion for this application is to add a menu. Maybe even a simple menu with **File** and **?** to provide the usual **Help** or **About**. Just for fun. Adding menus is not that complicated; you can add text, keyboard shortcuts, images, and so on.

Where do we go from here?

If you are interested in digging deeper into the world of GUIs, then I'd like to offer you the following suggestions.

The tkinter.tix module

Exploring `tkinter` and its themed widget set, `tkinter.ttk`, will take you some time. There's much to learn and play with. Another interesting module to explore, when you'll be familiar with this technology, is `tkinter.tix`.

The `tkinter.tix` (**Tk Interface Extension**) module provides an additional very rich set of widgets. The need for them stems from the fact that the widgets in the standard `Tk` library are far from complete.

The `tkinter.tix` library allows us to solve this problem by providing widgets like HList, ComboBox, Control (or SpinBox), and various scrollable widgets. Altogether, there are more than 40 widgets. They allow you to introduce different interaction techniques and paradigms into your applications, thus improving their quality and usability.

The turtle module

The `turtle` module is an extended reimplementation of the eponymous module from the Python standard distribution up to version Python 2.5. It's a very popular way to introduce children to programming.

It's based on the idea of an imaginary turtle starting at (0, 0) in the Cartesian plane. You can programmatically command the turtle to move forward and backwards, rotate, and so on. and by combining together all the possible moves, all sorts of intricate shapes and images can be drawn.

It's definitely worth checking out, if only to see something different.

wxPython, PyQt, and PyGTK

After you have explored the vastness of the `tkinter` realm, I'd suggest you to explore other GUI libraries: **wxPython**, **PyQt**, and **PyGTK**. You may find out one of these works better for you, or it makes easier for you to code the application you need.

I believe that coders can realize their ideas only when they are conscious about what tools they have available. If your toolset is too narrow, your ideas may seem impossible or extremely hard to realize, and they risk remaining exactly what they are, just ideas.

Of course, the technological spectrum today is humongous, so knowing everything is not possible; therefore, when you are about to learn a new technology or a new subject, my suggestion is to grow your knowledge by exploring breadth first.

Investigate several things not too deeply, and then go deep with the one or the few that looked most promising. This way you'll be able to be productive with at least one tool, and when the tool no longer fits your needs, you'll know where to dig deeper, thanks to your previous exploration.

The principle of least astonishment

When designing an interface, there are many different things to bear in mind. One of them, which for me is the most important, is the law or **principle of least astonishment**. It basically states that if in your design a necessary feature has a high astonishing factor, it may be necessary to redesign your application. To give you one example, when you're used to working with Windows, where the buttons to minimize, maximize and close a window are on the top-right corner, it's quite hard to work on Linux, where they are at the top-left corner. You'll find yourself constantly going to the top-right corner only to discover once more that the buttons are on the other side.

If a certain button has become so important in applications that it's now placed in a precise location by designers, please don't innovate. Just follow the convention. Users will only become frustrated when they have to waste time looking for a button that is not where it's supposed to be.

The disregard for this rule is the reason why I cannot work with products like Jira. It takes me minutes to do simple things that should require seconds.

Threading considerations

This topic is beyond the scope of an introductory book like this, but I do want to mention it. In a nutshell, a **thread** of execution is the smallest sequence of programmed instructions that can be managed independently by a **scheduler**. The reason we have the perception that modern computers can do many things at the same time is not only due to the fact that they have multiple processors. They also subdivide the work in different threads, which are then worked on in sequence. If their lifecycle is sufficiently short, threads can be worked on in one single go, but typically, what happens is that the OS works on a thread for a little time, then switches to another one, then to another one, then back to the first one, and so on. The order in which they are worked on depends on different factors. The end result is that, because computers are extremely fast in doing this switching, we perceive many things happening at the same time.

If you are coding a GUI application that needs to perform a long running operation when a button is clicked, you will see that your application will probably freeze until the operation has been carried out. In order to avoid this, and maintain the application's responsiveness, you may need to run that time-expensive operation in a different thread so that the OS will be able to dedicate a little bit of time to the GUI every now and then, to keep it responsive.

Threads are an advanced topic, especially in Python. Gain a good grasp of the fundamentals first, and then have fun exploring them!

Summary

In this chapter, we worked on a project together. We have written a script that scrapes a very simple web page and accepts optional commands that alter its behavior in doing so. We also coded a GUI application to do the same thing by clicking buttons instead of typing on a console. I hope you enjoyed reading it and following along as much as I enjoyed writing it.

We saw many different concepts like context managers, working with files, performing HTTP requests, and we've talked about guidelines for usability and design.

I have only been able to scratch the surface, but hopefully, you have a good starting point from which to expand your exploration.

Throughout the chapter, I have pointed you in several different ways on how to improve the application, and I have challenged you with a few exercises and questions. I hope you have taken the time to play with those ideas. One can learn a lot just by playing around with fun applications like the one we've coded together.

In the next chapter, we're going to talk about data science, or at least about the tools that a Python programmer has when it comes to facing this subject.

9
Data Science

"If we have data, let's look at data. If all we have are opinions, let's go with mine."

– Jim Barksdale, former Netscape CEO

Data science is a very broad term, and can assume several different meanings according to context, understanding, tools, and so on. There are countless books about this subject, which is not suitable for the faint-hearted.

In order to do proper data science, you need to know mathematics and statistics at the very least. Then, you may want to dig into other subjects such as pattern recognition and machine learning and, of course, there is a plethora of languages and tools you can choose from.

Unless I transform into *The Amazing Fabrizio* in the next few minutes, I won't be able to talk about everything; I won't even get close to it. Therefore, in order to render this chapter meaningful, we're going to work on a cool project together.

About 3 years ago, I was working for a top-tier social media company in London. I stayed there for 2 years, and I was privileged to work with several people whose brilliance I can only start to describe. We were the first in the world to have access to the Twitter Ads API, and we were partners with Facebook as well. That means a lot of data.

Our analysts were dealing with a huge number of campaigns and they were struggling with the amount of work they had to do, so the development team I was a part of tried to help by introducing them to Python and to the tools Python gives you to deal with data. It was a very interesting journey that led me to mentor several people in the company and eventually to Manila where, for 2 weeks, I gave intensive training in Python and data science to our analysts there.

The project we're going to do together in this chapter is a lightweight version of the final example I presented to my Manila students. I have rewritten it to a size that will fit this chapter, and made a few adjustments here and there for teaching purposes, but all the main concepts are there, so it should be fun and instructional for you to code along.

On our journey, we're going to meet a few of the tools you can find in the Python ecosystem when it comes to dealing with data, so let's start by talking about Roman gods.

IPython and Jupyter notebook

In 2001, Fernando Perez was a graduate student in physics at CU Boulder, and was trying to improve the Python shell so that he could have some niceties like those he was used to when he was working with tools such as Mathematica and Maple. The result of that effort took the name **IPython**.

In a nutshell, that small script began as an enhanced version of the Python shell and, through the effort of other coders and eventually proper funding from several different companies, it became the wonderful and successful project it is today. Some 10 years after its birth, a notebook environment was created, powered by technologies like WebSockets, the Tornado web server, jQuery, CodeMirror, and MathJax. The ZeroMQ library was also used to handle the messages between the notebook interface and the Python core that lies behind it.

The IPython notebook has become so popular and widely used that eventually, all sorts of goodies have been added to it. It can handle widgets, parallel computing, all sorts of media formats, and much, much more. Moreover, at some point, it became possible to code in languages other than Python from within the notebook.

This has led to a huge project that only recently has been split into two: IPython has been stripped down to focus more on the kernel part and the shell, while the notebook has become a brand new project called **Jupyter**. Jupyter allows interactive scientific computations to be done in more than 40 languages.

This chapter's project will all be coded and run in a Jupyter notebook, so let me explain in a few words what a notebook is.

A notebook environment is a web page that exposes a simple menu and the cells in which you can run Python code. Even though the cells are separate entities that you can run individually, they all share the same Python kernel. This means that all the names that you define in a cell (the variables, functions, and so on) will be available in any other cell.

Simply put, a Python kernel is a process in which Python is running. The notebook web page is therefore an interface exposed to the user for driving this kernel. The web page communicates to it using a very fast messaging system.

Apart from all the graphical advantages, the beauty to have such an environment consists in the ability of running a Python script in chunks, and this can be a tremendous advantage. Take a script that is connecting to a database to fetch data and then manipulate that data. If you do it in the conventional way, with a Python script, you have to fetch the data every time you want to experiment with it. Within a notebook environment, you can fetch the data in a cell and then manipulate and experiment with it in other cells, so fetching it every time is not necessary.

The notebook environment is also extremely helpful for data science because it allows for step-by-step introspection. You do one chunk of work and then verify it. You then do another chunk and verify again, and so on.

It's also invaluable for prototyping because the results are there, right in front of your eyes, immediately available.

If you want to know more about these tools, please check out `http://ipython.org/` and `http://jupyter.org/`.

I have created a very simple example notebook with a `fibonacci` function that gives you the list of all Fibonacci numbers smaller than a given N. In my browser, it looks like this:

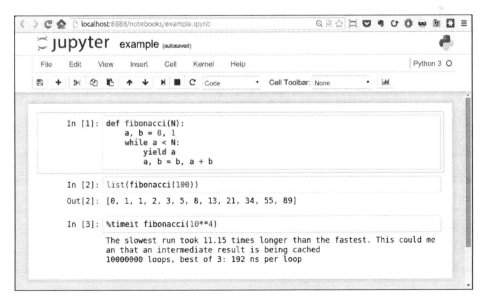

Every cell has an **In []** label. If there's nothing between the braces, it means that cell has never been executed. If there is a number, it means that the cell has been executed, and the number represents the order in which the cell was executed. Finally, a * means that the cell is currently being executed.

You can see in the picture that in the first cell I have defined the `fibonacci` function, and I have executed it. This has the effect of placing the `fibonacci` name in the global frame associated with the notebook, therefore the `fibonacci` function is now available to the other cells as well. In fact, in the second cell, I can run `fibonacci(100)` and see the results in **Out [2]**. In the third cell, I have shown you one of the several magic functions you can find in a notebook in the second cell. **%timeit** runs the code several times and provides you with a nice benchmark for it. All the measurements for the list comprehensions and generators I did in *Chapter 5, Saving Time and Memory* were carried out with this nice feature.

You can execute a cell as many times as you want, and change the order in which you run them. Cells are very malleable, you can also put in markdown text or render them as headers.

 Markdown is a lightweight markup language with plain text formatting syntax designed so that it can be converted to HTML and many other formats.

Also, whatever you place in the last row of a cell will be automatically printed for you. This is very handy because you're not forced to write `print(...)` explicitly.

Feel free to explore the notebook environment; once you're friends with it, it's a long-lasting relationship, I promise.

In order to run the notebook, you have to install a handful of libraries, each of which collaborates with the others to make the whole thing work. Alternatively, you can just install Jupyter and it will take care of everything for you. For this chapter, there are a few other dependencies that we need to install, so please run the following command:

```
$ pip install jupyter pandas matplotlib fake-factory delorean xlwt
```

Don't worry, I'll introduce you to each of these gradually. Now, when you're done installing these libraries (it may take a few minutes), you can start the notebook:

```
$ jupyter notebook
```

This will open a page in your browser at this address: `http://localhost:8888/`.

Go to that page and create a new notebook using the menu. When you have it and you're comfortable with it, we're ready to go.

If you experience any issues setting up the notebook environment, please don't get discouraged. If you get an error, it's usually just a matter of searching a little bit on the web and you'll end up on a page where someone else has had the same issue, and they have explained how to fix it. Try your best to have the notebook environment up and running before continuing with the chapter.

Our project will take place in a notebook, therefore I will tag each code snippet with the cell number it belongs to, so that you can easily reproduce the code and follow along.

 If you familiarize yourself with the keyboard shortcuts (look in the notebook's help section), you will be able to move between cells and handle their content without having to reach for the mouse. This will make you more proficient and way faster when you work in a notebook.

Dealing with data

Typically, when you deal with data, this is the path you go through: you fetch it, you clean and manipulate it, then you inspect it and present results as values, spreadsheets, graphs, and so on. I want you to be in charge of all three steps of the process without having any external dependency on a data provider, so we're going to do the following:

1. We're going to create the data, simulating the fact that it comes in a format which is not perfect or ready to be worked on.
2. We're going to clean it and feed it to the main tool we'll use in the project: **DataFrame** of `pandas`.
3. We're going to manipulate the data in the DataFrame.
4. We're going to save the DataFrame to a file in different formats.
5. Finally, we're going to inspect the data and get some results out of it.

Setting up the notebook

First things first, we need to set up the notebook. This means imports and a bit of configuration.

#1

```
import json
import calendar
import random
from datetime import date, timedelta

import faker
import numpy as np
from pandas import DataFrame
from delorean import parse
import pandas as pd

# make the graphs nicer
pd.set_option('display.mpl_style', 'default')
```

Cell #1 takes care of the imports. There are quite a few new things here: the `calendar`, `random` and `datetime` modules are part of the standard library. Their names are self-explanatory, so let's look at `faker`. The `fake-factory` library gives you this module, which you can use to prepare fake data. It's very useful in tests, when you prepare your fixtures, to get all sorts of things such as names, e-mail addresses, phone numbers, credit card details, and much more. It is all fake, of course.

`numpy` is the NumPy library, the fundamental package for scientific computing with Python. I'll spend a few words on it later on in the chapter.

`pandas` is the very core upon which the whole project is based. It stands for **Python Data Analysis Library**. Among many others, it provides the **DataFrame**, a matrix-like data structure with advanced processing capabilities. It's customary to import the `DataFrame` separately and then do `import pandas as pd`.

`delorean` is a nice third-party library that speeds up dealing with dates dramatically. Technically, we could do it with the standard library, but I see no reason not to expand a bit the range of the example and show you something different.

Finally, we have an instruction on the last line that will make our graphs at the end a little bit nicer, which doesn't hurt.

Preparing the data

We want to achieve the following data structure: we're going to have a list of user objects. Each user object will be linked to a number of campaign objects.

In Python, everything is an object, so I'm using this term in a generic way. The user object may be a string, a dict, or something else.

A **campaign** in the social media world is a promotional campaign that a media agency runs on social media networks on behalf of a client.

Remember that we're going to prepare this data so that it's not in perfect shape (but it won't be so bad either...).

#2

```
fake = faker.Faker()
```

Firstly, we instantiate the `Faker` that we'll use to create the data.

#3

```
usernames = set()
usernames_no = 1000
# populate the set with 1000 unique usernames
while len(usernames) < usernames_no:
    usernames.add(fake.user_name())
```

Then we need usernames. I want 1,000 unique usernames, so I loop over the length of the `usernames` set until it has 1,000 elements. A set doesn't allow duplicated elements, therefore uniqueness is guaranteed.

#4

```
def get_random_name_and_gender():
    skew = .6  # 60% of users will be female
    male = random.random() > skew
    if male:
        return fake.name_male(), 'M'
    else:
        return fake.name_female(), 'F'

def get_users(usernames):
    users = []
    for username in usernames:
```

```
        name, gender = get_random_name_and_gender()
        user = {
            'username': username,
            'name': name,
            'gender': gender,
            'email': fake.email(),
            'age': fake.random_int(min=18, max=90),
            'address': fake.address(),
        }
        users.append(json.dumps(user))
    return users

users = get_users(usernames)
users[:3]
```

Here, we create a list of users. Each `username` has now been augmented to a full-blown `user` dict, with other details such as name, gender, e-mail, and so on. Each `user` dict is then dumped to JSON and added to the list. This data structure is not optimal, of course, but we're simulating a scenario where users come to us like that.

Note the skewed use of `random.random()` to make 60% of users female. The rest of the logic should be very easy for you to understand.

Note also the last line. Each cell automatically prints what's on the last line; therefore, the output of this is a list with the first three users:

Out #4

```
['{"gender": "F", "age": 48, "email": "jovani.dickinson@gmail.
com", "address": "2006 Sawayn Trail Apt. 207\\nHyattview, MO 27278",
"username": "darcy00", "name": "Virgia Hilpert"}',
 '{"gender": "F", "age": 58, "email": "veum.javen@hotmail.com",
"address": "5176 Andres Plains Apt. 040\\nLakinside, GA 92446",
"username": "renner.virgie", "name": "Miss Clarabelle Kertzmann MD"}',
 '{"gender": "M", "age": 33, "email": "turner.felton@rippin.com",
"address": "1218 Jacobson Fort\\nNorth Doctor, OK 04469", "username":
"hettinger.alphonsus", "name": "Ludwig Prosacco"}']
```

I hope you're following along with your own notebook. If you do, please note that all data is generated using random functions and values; therefore, you will see different results. They will change every time you execute the notebook.

#5

```python
# campaign name format:
# InternalType_StartDate_EndDate_TargetAge_TargetGender_Currency
def get_type():
    # just some gibberish internal codes
    types = ['AKX', 'BYU', 'GRZ', 'KTR']
    return random.choice(types)

def get_start_end_dates():
    duration = random.randint(1, 2 * 365)
    offset = random.randint(-365, 365)
    start = date.today() - timedelta(days=offset)
    end = start + timedelta(days=duration)

    def _format_date(date_):
        return date_.strftime("%Y%m%d")

    return _format_date(start), _format_date(end)

def get_age():
    age = random.randint(20, 45)
    age -= age % 5
    diff = random.randint(5, 25)
    diff -= diff % 5
    return '{}-{}'.format(age, age + diff)

def get_gender():
    return random.choice(('M', 'F', 'B'))

def get_currency():
    return random.choice(('GBP', 'EUR', 'USD'))

def get_campaign_name():
    separator = '_'
    type_ = get_type()
    start_end = separator.join(get_start_end_dates())
    age = get_age()
    gender = get_gender()
    currency = get_currency()
    return separator.join(
        (type_, start_end, age, gender, currency))
```

In #5, we define the logic to generate a campaign name. Analysts use spreadsheets all the time and they come up with all sorts of coding techniques to compress as much information as possible into the campaign names. The format I chose is a simple example of that technique: there is a code that tells the campaign type, then start and end dates, then the target age and gender, and finally the currency. All values are separated by an underscore.

In the `get_type` function, I use `random.choice()` to get one value randomly out of a collection. Probably more interesting is `get_start_end_dates`. First, I get the duration for the campaign, which goes from 1 day to 2 years (randomly), then I get a random offset in time which I subtract from today's date in order to get the start date. Given that the offset is a random number between -365 and 365, would anything be different if I added it to today's date instead of subtracting it?

When I have both the start and end dates, I return a stringified version of them, joined by an underscore.

Then, we have a bit of modular trickery going on with the age calculation. I hope you remember the modulo operator (%) from *Chapter 2, Built-in Data Types*.

What happens here is that I want a date range that has multiples of 5 as extremes. So, there are many ways to do it, but what I do is to get a random number between 20 and 45 for the left extreme, and remove the remainder of the division by 5. So, if, for example, I get 28, I will remove *28 % 5 = 3* to it, getting 25. I could have just used `random.randrange()`, but it's hard to resist modular division.

The rest of the functions are just some other applications of `random.choice()` and the last one, `get_campaign_name`, is nothing more than a collector for all these puzzle pieces that returns the final campaign name.

#6

```
def get_campaign_data():
    name = get_campaign_name()
    budget = random.randint(10**3, 10**6)
    spent = random.randint(10**2, budget)
    clicks = int(random.triangular(10**2, 10**5, 0.2 * 10**5))
    impressions = int(random.gauss(0.5 * 10**6, 2))
    return {
        'cmp_name': name,
        'cmp_bgt': budget,
        'cmp_spent': spent,
        'cmp_clicks': clicks,
        'cmp_impr': impressions
    }
```

In #6, we write a function that creates a complete campaign object. I used a few different functions from the `random` module. `random.randint()` gives you an integer between two extremes. The problem with it is that it follows a uniform probability distribution, which means that any number in the interval has the same probability of coming up.

Therefore, when dealing with a lot of data, if you distribute your fixtures using a uniform distribution, the results you will get will all look similar. For this reason, I chose to use `triangular` and `gauss`, for `clicks` and `impressions`. They use different probability distributions so that we'll have something more interesting to see in the end.

Just to make sure we're on the same page with the terminology: `clicks` represents the number of clicks on a campaign advertisement, `budget` is the total amount of money allocated for the campaign, `spent` is how much of that money has already been spent, and `impressions` is the number of times the campaign has been fetched, as a resource, from its source, regardless of the amount of clicks that were performed on the campaign. Normally, the amount of impressions is greater than the amount of clicks.

Now that we have the data, it's time to put it all together:

#7

```
def get_data(users):
    data = []
    for user in users:
        campaigns = [get_campaign_data()
                     for _ in range(random.randint(2, 8))]
        data.append({'user': user, 'campaigns': campaigns})
    return data
```

As you can see, each item in `data` is a dict with a user and a list of campaigns that are associated with that user.

Cleaning the data

Let's start cleaning the data:

#8

```
rough_data = get_data(users)
rough_data[:2]  # let's take a peek
```

We simulate fetching the data from a source and then inspect it. The notebook is the perfect tool to inspect your steps. You can vary the granularity to your needs. The first item in `rough_data` looks like this:

```
[{'campaigns': [{'cmp_bgt': 130532,
    'cmp_clicks': 25576,
    'cmp_impr': 500001,
    'cmp_name': 'AKX_20150826_20170305_35-50_B_EUR',
    'cmp_spent': 57574},
    ... omit ...
  {'cmp_bgt': 884396,
    'cmp_clicks': 10955,
    'cmp_impr': 499999,
    'cmp_name': 'KTR_20151227_20151231_45-55_B_GBP',
    'cmp_spent': 318887}],
 'user': '{"age": 44, "username": "jacob43",
          "name": "Holland Strosin",
          "email": "humberto.leuschke@brakus.com",
          "address": "1038 Runolfsdottir Parks\\nElmapo...",
          "gender": "M"}'}]
```

So, we now start working with it.

```
#9
    data = []
    for datum in rough_data:
        for campaign in datum['campaigns']:
            campaign.update({'user': datum['user']})
            data.append(campaign)
    data[:2]  # let's take another peek
```

The first thing we need to do in order to be able to feed a DataFrame with this data is to denormalize it. This means transforming the data into a list whose items are campaign dicts, augmented with their relative user dict. Users will be duplicated in each campaign they belong to. The first item in `data` looks like this:

```
[{'cmp_bgt': 130532,
  'cmp_clicks': 25576,
  'cmp_impr': 500001,
  'cmp_name': 'AKX_20150826_20170305_35-50_B_EUR',
```

```
'cmp_spent': 57574,
'user': '{"age": 44, "username": "jacob43",
        "name": "Holland Strosin",
        "email": "humberto.leuschke@brakus.com",
        "address": "1038 Runolfsdottir Parks\\nElmaport...",
        "gender": "M"}'}]
```

You can see that the user object has been brought into the campaign dict which was repeated for each campaign.

Creating the DataFrame

Now it's time to create the DataFrame:

```
#10
    df = DataFrame(data)
    df.head()
```

Finally, we will create the DataFrame and inspect the first five rows using the head method. You should see something like this:

	cmp_bgt	cmp_clicks	cmp_impr	cmp_name	cmp_spent	user
0	130532	25576	500001	AKX_20150826_20170305_35-50_B_EUR	57574	{"age": 44, "username": "jacob43", "name": "Ho...
1	262852	61247	499999	AKX_20141015_20141219_40-50_F_GBP	226319	{"age": 44, "username": "jacob43", "name": "Ho...
2	12098	15582	500004	KTR_20150222_20160114_20-25_F_GBP	4354	{"age": 44, "username": "jacob43", "name": "Ho...
3	888381	35843	499998	KTR_20140918_20160416_35-50_B_EUR	472363	{"age": 44, "username": "jacob43", "name": "Ho...
4	361909	84759	499998	GRZ_20150726_20170615_25-35_M_GBP	257560	{"age": 44, "username": "jacob43", "name": "Ho...

Jupyter renders the output of the df.head() call as HTML automatically. In order to have a text-based output, simply wrap df.head() in a print call.

The DataFrame structure is very powerful. It allows us to do a great deal of manipulation on its contents. You can filter by rows, columns, aggregate on data, and many other operations. You can operate with rows or columns without suffering the time penalty you would have to pay if you were working on data with pure Python. This happens because, under the covers, pandas is harnessing the power of the NumPy library, which itself draws its incredible speed from the low-level implementation of its core. NumPy stands for **Numeric Python**, and it is one of the most widely used libraries in the data science environment.

Using a DataFrame allows us to couple the power of NumPy with spreadsheet-like capabilities so that we'll be able to work on our data in a fashion that is similar to what an analyst could do. Only, we do it with code.

But let's go back to our project. Let's see two ways to quickly get a bird's eye view of the data:

#11

```
df.count()
```

`count` yields a count of all the non-empty cells in each column. This is good to help you understand how sparse your data can be. In our case, we have no missing values, so the output is:

```
cmp_bgt        4974
cmp_clicks     4974
cmp_impr       4974
cmp_name       4974
cmp_spent      4974
user           4974
dtype: int64
```

Nice! We have 4,974 rows, and the data type is integers (`dtype: int64` means long integers because they take 64 bits each). Given that we have 1,000 users and the amount of campaigns per user is a random number between 2 and 8, we're exactly in line with what I was expecting.

#12

```
df.describe()
```

`describe` is a nice and quick way to introspect a bit further:

	cmp_bgt	cmp_clicks	cmp_impr	cmp_spent
count	4974.000000	4974.000000	4974.000000	4974.000000
mean	503272.706876	40225.764978	499999.495979	251150.604343
std	289393.747465	21910.631950	2.035355	220347.594377
min	1250.000000	609.000000	499992.000000	142.000000
25%	253647.500000	22720.750000	499998.000000	67526.750000
50%	508341.000000	36561.500000	500000.000000	187833.000000
75%	757078.250000	55962.750000	500001.000000	385803.750000
max	999631.000000	98767.000000	500006.000000	982716.000000

As you can see, it gives us several measures such as count, mean, std (standard deviation), min, max, and shows how data is distributed in the various quadrants. Thanks to this method, we could already have a rough idea of how our data is structured.

Let's see which are the three campaigns with the highest and lowest budgets:

#13

```
df.sort_index(by=['cmp_bgt'], ascending=False).head(3)
```

This gives the following output (truncated):

	cmp_bgt	cmp_clicks	cmp_impr	cmp_name
4655	999631	15343	499997	AKX_20160814_20180226_40
3708	999606	45367	499997	KTR_20150523_20150527_35
1995	999445	12580	499998	AKX_20141102_20151009_30

And (#14) a call to .tail(3), shows us the ones with the lowest budget.

Unpacking the campaign name

Now it's time to increase the complexity up a bit. First of all, we want to get rid of that horrible campaign name (cmp_name). We need to explode it into parts and put each part in one dedicated column. In order to do this, we'll use the apply method of the **Series** object.

The pandas.core.series.Series class is basically a powerful wrapper around an array (think of it as a list with augmented capabilities). We can extrapolate a Series object from a DataFrame by accessing it in the same way we do with a key in a dict, and we can call apply on that Series object, which will run a function feeding each item in the Series to it. We compose the result into a new DataFrame, and then join that DataFrame with our beloved df.

#15

```
def unpack_campaign_name(name):
    # very optimistic method, assumes data in campaign name
    # is always in good state
    type_, start, end, age, gender, currency = name.split('_')
    start = parse(start).date
    end = parse(end).date
    return type_, start, end, age, gender, currency

campaign_data = df['cmp_name'].apply(unpack_campaign_name)
campaign_cols = [
```

```
        'Type', 'Start', 'End', 'Age', 'Gender', 'Currency']
    campaign_df = DataFrame(
        campaign_data.tolist(), columns=campaign_cols, index=df.index)
    campaign_df.head(3)
```

Within `unpack_campaign_name`, we split the campaign `name` in parts. We use `delorean.parse()` to get a proper date object out of those strings (`delorean` makes it really easy to do it, doesn't it?), and then we return the objects. A quick peek at the last line reveals:

	Type	Start	End	Age	Gender	Currency
0	KTR	2016-06-16	2017-01-24	20-30	M	EUR
1	BYU	2014-10-25	2015-07-31	35-50	B	USD
2	BYU	2015-10-26	2016-03-17	35-50	M	EUR

Nice! One important thing: even if the dates appear as strings, they are just the representation of the real `date` objects that are hosted in the `DataFrame`.

Another very important thing: when joining two DataFrame instances, it's imperative that they have the same index, otherwise `pandas` won't be able to know which rows go with which. Therefore, when we create `campaign_df`, we set its index to the one from `df`. This enables us to join them. When creating this DataFrame, we also pass the columns names.

#16

```
    df = df.join(campaign_df)
```

And after the join, we take a peek, hoping to see matching data (output truncated):

#17

```
    df[['cmp_name'] + campaign_cols].head(3)
```

Gives:

	cmp_name	Type	Start	End
0	KTR_20160616_20170124_20-30_M_EUR	KTR	2016-06-16	2017-01-24
1	BYU_20141025_20150731_35-50_B_USD	BYU	2014-10-25	2015-07-31
2	BYU_20151026_20160317_35-50_M_EUR	BYU	2015-10-26	2016-03-17

As you can see, the join was successful; the campaign name and the separate columns expose the same data. Did you see what we did there? We're accessing the `DataFrame` using the square brackets syntax, and we pass a list of column names. This will produce a brand new `DataFrame`, with those columns (in the same order), on which we then call `head()`.

Unpacking the user data

We now do the exact same thing for each piece of `user` JSON data. We call `apply` on the `user` Series, running the `unpack_user_json` function, which takes a JSON `user` object and transforms it into a list of its fields, which we can then inject into a brand new DataFrame `user_df`. After that, we'll join `user_df` back with `df`, like we did with `campaign_df`.

```
#18
    def unpack_user_json(user):
        # very optimistic as well, expects user objects
        # to have all attributes
        user = json.loads(user.strip())
        return [
            user['username'],
            user['email'],
            user['name'],
            user['gender'],
            user['age'],
            user['address'],
        ]

    user_data = df['user'].apply(unpack_user_json)
    user_cols = [
        'username', 'email', 'name', 'gender', 'age', 'address']
    user_df = DataFrame(
        user_data.tolist(), columns=user_cols, index=df.index)
```

Very similar to the previous operation, isn't it? We should also note here that, when creating `user_df`, we need to instruct `DataFrame` about the column names and, very important, the index. Let's join (#19) and take a quick peek (#20):

```
    df = df.join(user_df)
    df[['user'] + user_cols].head(2)
```

The output shows us that everything went well. We're good, but we're not done yet.

If you call `df.columns` in a cell, you'll see that we still have ugly names for our columns. Let's change that:

```
#21
    better_columns = [
        'Budget', 'Clicks', 'Impressions',
        'cmp_name', 'Spent', 'user',
```

```
        'Type', 'Start', 'End',
        'Target Age', 'Target Gender', 'Currency',
        'Username', 'Email', 'Name',
        'Gender', 'Age', 'Address',
    ]
    df.columns = better_columns
```

Good! Now, with the exception of `'cmp_name'` and `'user'`, we only have nice names.

Completing the `datasetNext` step will be to add some extra columns. For each campaign, we have the amount of clicks and impressions, and we have the spent. This allows us to introduce three measurement ratios: **CTR**, **CPC**, and **CPI**. They stand for **Click Through Rate**, **Cost Per Click**, and **Cost Per Impression**, respectively.

The last two are easy to understand, but CTR is not. Suffice it to say that it is the ratio between clicks and impressions. It gives you a measure of how many clicks were performed on a campaign advertisement per impression: the higher this number, the more successful the advertisement is in attracting users to click on it.

#22

```
    def calculate_extra_columns(df):
        # Click Through Rate
        df['CTR'] = df['Clicks'] / df['Impressions']
        # Cost Per Click
        df['CPC'] = df['Spent'] / df['Clicks']
        # Cost Per Impression
        df['CPI'] = df['Spent'] / df['Impressions']
    calculate_extra_columns(df)
```

I wrote this as a function, but I could have just written the code in the cell. It's not important. What I want you to notice here is that we're adding those three columns with one line of code each, but the `DataFrame` applies the operation automatically (the division, in this case) to each pair of cells from the appropriate columns. So, even if they are masked as three divisions, these are actually *4974 * 3* divisions, because they are performed for each row. Pandas does a lot of work for us, and also does a very good job in hiding the complexity of it.

The function, `calculate_extra_columns`, takes a `DataFrame`, and works directly on it. This mode of operation is called **in-place**. Do you remember how `list.sort()` was sorting the list? It is the same deal.

We can take a look at the results by filtering on the relevant columns and calling `head`.

#23

```
df[['Spent', 'Clicks', 'Impressions',
    'CTR', 'CPC', 'CPI']].head(3)
```

This shows us that the calculations were performed correctly on each row:

	Spent	Clicks	Impressions	CTR	CPC	CPI
0	57574	25576	500001	0.051152	2.251095	0.115148
1	226319	61247	499999	0.122494	3.695185	0.452639
2	4354	15582	500004	0.031164	0.279425	0.008708

Now, I want to verify the accuracy of the results manually for the first row:

#24

```
clicks = df['Clicks'][0]
impressions = df['Impressions'][0]
spent = df['Spent'][0]
CTR = df['CTR'][0]
CPC = df['CPC'][0]
CPI = df['CPI'][0]
print('CTR:', CTR, clicks / impressions)
print('CPC:', CPC, spent / clicks)
print('CPI:', CPI, spent / impressions)
```

It yields the following output:

```
CTR: 0.0511518976962 0.0511518976962
CPC: 2.25109477635 2.25109477635
CPI: 0.115147769704 0.115147769704
```

This is exactly what we saw in the previous output. Of course, I wouldn't normally need to do this, but I wanted to show you how can you perform calculations this way. You can access a Series (a column) by passing its name to the `DataFrame`, in square brackets, and then you access each row by its position, exactly as you would with a regular list or tuple.

We're almost done with our `DataFrame`. All we are missing now is a column that tells us the duration of the campaign and a column that tells us which day of the week corresponds to the start date of each campaign. This allows me to expand on how to play with date objects.

#25

```
def get_day_of_the_week(day):
    number_to_day = dict(enumerate(calendar.day_name, 1))
    return number_to_day[day.isoweekday()]

def get_duration(row):
    return (row['End'] - row['Start']).days

df['Day of Week'] = df['Start'].apply(get_day_of_the_week)
df['Duration'] = df.apply(get_duration, axis=1)
```

We used two different techniques here but first, the code.

`get_day_of_the_week` takes a date object. If you cannot understand what it does, please take a few moments to try and understand for yourself before reading the explanation. Use the inside-out technique like we've done a few times before.

So, as I'm sure you know by now, if you put `calendar.day_name` in a `list` call, you get `['Monday', 'Tuesday', 'Wednesday', 'Thursday', 'Friday', 'Saturday', 'Sunday']`. This means that, if we enumerate `calendar.day_name` starting from 1, we get pairs such as `(1, 'Monday')`, `(2, 'Tuesday')`, and so on. If we feed these pairs to a dict, we get a mapping between the days of the week as numbers (1, 2, 3, ...) and their names. When the mapping is created, in order to get the name of a day, we just need to know its number. To get it, we call `date.isoweekday()`, which tells us which day of the week that date is (as a number). You feed that into the mapping and, boom! You have the name of the day.

`get_duration` is interesting as well. First, notice it takes an entire row, not just a single value. What happens in its body is that we perform a subtraction between a campaign end and start dates. When you subtract date objects the result is a `timedelta` object, which represents a given amount of time. We take the value of its `.days` property. It is as simple as that.

Now, we can introduce the fun part, the application of those two functions.

The first application is performed on a `Series` object, like we did before for `'user'` and `'cmp_name'`, there is nothing new here.

The second one is applied to the whole DataFrame and, in order to instruct Pandas to perform that operation on the rows, we pass `axis=1`.

We can verify the results very easily, as shown here:

```
#26
    df[['Start', 'End', 'Duration', 'Day of Week']].head(3)
```

Yields:

	Start	End	Duration	Day of Week
0	2015-08-26	2017-03-05	557	Wednesday
1	2014-10-15	2014-12-19	65	Wednesday
2	2015-02-22	2016-01-14	326	Sunday

So, we now know that between the 26th of August 2015 and the 5th of March 2017 there are 557 days, and that the 26th of August 2015 was a Wednesday.

If you're wondering what the purpose of this is, I'll provide an example. Imagine that you have a campaign that is tied to a sports event that usually takes place on a Sunday. You may want to inspect your data according to the days so that you can correlate them to the various measurements you have. We're not going to do it in this project, but it was useful to see, if only for the different way of calling `apply()` on a DataFrame.

Cleaning everything up

Now that we have everything we want, it's time to do the final cleaning: remember we still have the `'cmp_name'` and `'user'` columns. Those are useless now, so they have to go. Also, I want to reorder the columns in the DataFrame so that it is more relevant to the data it now contains. In order to do this, we just need to filter `df` on the column list we want. We'll get back a brand new DataFrame that we can reassign to `df` itself.

```
#27
    final_columns = [
        'Type', 'Start', 'End', 'Duration', 'Day of Week', 'Budget',
        'Currency', 'Clicks', 'Impressions', 'Spent', 'CTR', 'CPC',
        'CPI', 'Target Age', 'Target Gender', 'Username', 'Email',
        'Name', 'Gender', 'Age'
    ]
    df = df[final_columns]
```

I have grouped the campaign information at the beginning, then the measurements, and finally the user data at the end. Now our DataFrame is clean and ready for us to inspect.

Before we start going crazy with graphs, what about taking a snapshot of our DataFrame so that we can easily reconstruct it from a file, rather than having to redo all the steps we did to get here. Some analysts may want to have it in spreadsheet form, to do a different kind of analysis than the one we want to do, so let's see how to save a DataFrame to a file. It's easier done than said.

Saving the DataFrame to a file

We can save a DataFrame in many different ways. You can type `df.to_` and then press *Tab* to make auto-completion pop up, to see all the possible options.

We're going to save our DataFrame in three different formats, just for fun: **comma-separated values (CSV)**, JSON, and Excel spreadsheet.

#28

```
df.to_csv('df.csv')
```

#29

```
df.to_json('df.json')
```

#30

```
df.to_excel('df.xls')
```

The CSV file looks like this (output truncated):

```
Type,Start,End,Duration,Day of Week,Budget,Currency,Clicks,Impres
0,GRZ,2015-03-15,2015-11-10,240,Sunday,622551,GBP,35018,500002,787
1,AKX,2016-06-19,2016-09-19,92,Sunday,148219,EUR,45185,499997,6588
2,BYU,2014-09-25,2016-07-03,647,Thursday,537760,GBP,55771,500001,3
```

And the JSON one like this (again, output truncated):

```
{
  "Type": {
    "0": "GRZ",
    "1": "AKX",
    "2": "BYU",
```

So, it's extremely easy to save a DataFrame in many different formats, and the good news is that the opposite is also true: it's very easy to load a spreadsheet into a DataFrame. The programmers behind Pandas went a long way to ease our tasks, something to be grateful for.

Visualizing the results

Finally, the juicy bits. In this section, we're going to visualize some results. From a data science perspective, I'm not very interested in going deep into analysis, especially because the data is completely random, but nonetheless, this code will get you started with graphs and other features.

Something I learned in my life — and this may come as a surprise to you — is that *looks also counts* so it's very important that when you present your results, you do your best to *make them pretty*.

I won't try to prove to you how truthful that last statement is, but I really do believe in it. If you recall the last line of cell #1:

```
# make the graphs nicer
pd.set_option('display.mpl_style', 'default')
```

Its purpose is to make the graphs we will look at in this section a little bit prettier.

Okay, so, first of all we have to instruct the notebook that we want to use `matplotlib inline`. This means that when we ask Pandas to plot something, we will have the result rendered in the cell output frame. In order to do this, we just need one simple instruction:

#31

```
%matplotlib inline
```

You can also instruct the notebook to do this when you start it from the console by passing a parameter, but I wanted to show you this way too, since it can be annoying to have to restart the notebook just because you want to plot something. In this way, you can do it on the fly and then keep working.

Next, we're going to set some parameters on `pylab`. This is for plotting purposes and it will remove a warning that a font hasn't been found. I suggest that you do not execute this line and keep going. If you get a warning that a font is missing, come back to this cell and run it.

#32

```
import pylab
pylab.rcParams.update({'font.family' : 'serif'})
```

This basically tells Pylab to use the first available serif font. It is simple but effective, and you can experiment with other fonts too.

Now that the DataFrame is complete, let's run `df.describe()` (#33) again. The results should look something like this:

	Duration	Budget	Clicks	Impressions	Spent	CTR	CPC	CPI	Age
count	4969.000000	4969.000000	4969.000000	4969.000000	4969.000000	4969.000000	4969.000000	4969.000000	4969.000000
mean	364.414772	500490.476353	40110.432481	499999.465889	252225.839203	0.080221	9.835294	0.504452	53.854699
std	212.972833	288470.674072	21619.233699	2.047371	218765.741972	0.043239	16.326438	0.437532	21.149709
min	1.000000	1190.000000	535.000000	499992.000000	114.000000	0.001070	0.002838	0.000228	18.000000
25%	176.000000	252672.000000	22579.000000	499998.000000	69408.000000	0.045158	1.855093	0.138817	35.000000
50%	364.000000	502102.000000	37029.000000	499999.000000	192934.000000	0.074058	5.327965	0.385869	53.000000
75%	554.000000	749372.000000	55504.000000	500001.000000	384520.000000	0.111008	11.640189	0.769046	73.000000
max	730.000000	998817.000000	98739.000000	500007.000000	980234.000000	0.197479	322.773361	1.960468	90.000000

This kind of quick result is perfect to satisfy those managers who have 20 seconds to dedicate to you and just want rough numbers.

 Once again, please keep in mind that our campaigns have different currencies, so these numbers are actually meaningless. The point here is to demonstrate the DataFrame capabilities, not to get to a correct or detailed analysis of real data.

Alternatively, a graph is usually much better than a table with numbers because it's much easier to read it and it gives you immediate feedback. So, let's graph out the four pieces of information we have on each campaign: budget, spent, clicks, and impressions.

#34

```
df[['Budget', 'Spent', 'Clicks', 'Impressions']].hist(
    bins=16, figsize=(16, 6));
```

We extrapolate those four columns (this will give us another DataFrame made with only those columns) and call the histogram `hist()` method on it. We give some measurements on the bins and figure sizes, but basically everything is done automatically.

One important thing: since this instruction is the only one in this cell (which also means, it's the last one), the notebook will print its result before drawing the graph. To suppress this behavior and have only the graph drawn with no printing, just add a semicolon at the end (you thought I was reminiscing about Java, didn't you?). Here are the graphs:

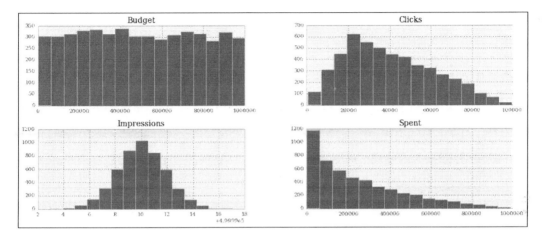

They are beautiful, aren't they? Did you notice the serif font? How about the meaning of those figures? If you go back to #6 and take a look at the way we generate the data, you will see that all these graphs make perfect sense.

Budget is simply a random integer in an interval, therefore we were expecting a *uniform distribution*, and there we have it; it's practically a constant line.

Spent is a *uniform distribution* as well, but the high end of its interval is the budget, which is moving, this means we should expect something like a quadratic hyperbole that decreases to the right. And there it is as well.

Clicks was generated with a *triangular distribution* with mean roughly 20% of the interval size, and you can see that the peak is right there, at about 20% to the left.

Finally, **Impressions** was a *Gaussian distribution*, which is the one that assumes the famous bell shape. The mean was exactly in the middle and we had standard deviation of 2. You can see that the graph matches those parameters.

Good! Let's plot out the measures we calculated:

#35

```
df[['CTR', 'CPC', 'CPI']].hist(
    bins=20, figsize=(16, 6));
```

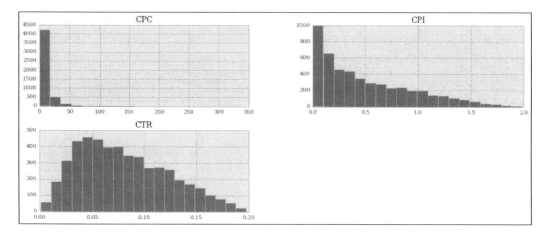

We can see that the cost per click is highly skewed to the left, meaning that most of the CPC values are very low. The cost per impression has a similar shape, but less extreme.

Now, all this is nice, but if you wanted to analyze only a particular segment of the data, how would you do it? We can apply a mask to a DataFrame, so that we get another one with only the rows that satisfy the mask condition. It's like applying a global row-wise `if` clause.

#36

```
mask = (df.Spent > 0.75 * df.Budget)
df[mask][['Budget', 'Spent', 'Clicks', 'Impressions']].hist(
    bins=15, figsize=(16, 6), color='g');
```

In this case, I prepared a mask to filter out all the rows for which the spent is less than or equal to 75% of the budget. In other words, we'll include only those campaigns for which we have spent at least three quarters of the budget. Notice that in the mask I am showing you an alternative way of asking for a DataFrame column, by using direct property access (`object.property_name`), instead of dict-like access (`object['property_name']`). If `property_name` is a valid Python name, you can use both ways interchangeably (JavaScript works like this as well).

The mask is applied in the same way that we access a dict with a key. When you apply a mask to a DataFrame, you get back another one and we select only the relevant columns on this, and call `hist()` again. This time, just for fun, we want the results to be painted green:

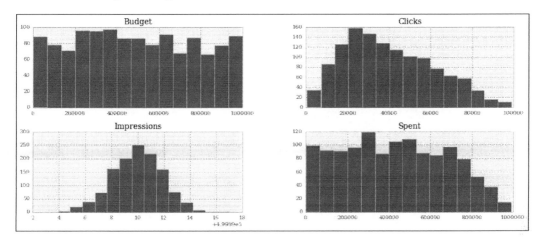

Note that the shapes of the graphs haven't changed much, apart from the spent, which is quite different. The reason for this is that we've asked only for the rows where spent is at least 75% of the budget. This means that we're including only the rows where spent is close to the budget. The budget numbers come from a uniform distribution. Therefore, it is quite obvious that the spent is now assuming that kind of shape. If you make the boundary even tighter, and ask for 85% or more, you'll see spent become more and more like budget.

Let's now ask for something different. How about the measure of spent, click, and impressions grouped by day of the week?

#37

```
df_weekday = df.groupby(['Day of Week']).sum()
df_weekday[['Impressions', 'Spent', 'Clicks']].plot(
    figsize=(16, 6), subplots=True);
```

The first line creates a new `DataFrame`, `df_weekday`, by asking for a grouping by `'Day of Week'` on `df`. The function used to aggregate the data is addition.

The second line gets a slice of df_weekday using a list of column names, something we're accustomed to by now. On the result we call plot(), which is a bit different to hist(). The option subplots=True makes plot draw three independent graphs:

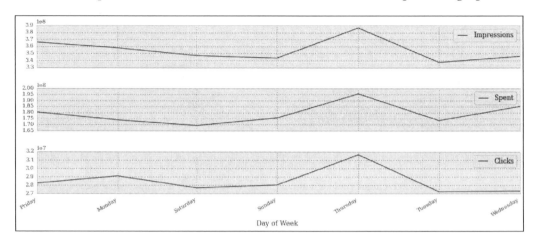

Interestingly enough, we can see that most of the action happens on Thursdays. If this were meaningful data, this would potentially be important information to give to our clients, and this is the reason I'm showing you this example.

Note that the days are sorted alphabetically, which scrambles them up a bit. Can you think of a quick solution that would fix the issue? I'll leave it to you as an exercise to come up with something.

Let's finish this presentation section with a couple more things. First, a simple aggregation. We want to aggregate on 'Target Gender' and 'Target Age', and show 'Impressions' and 'Spent'. For both, we want to see the mean and the standard deviation.

#38

```
agg_config = {
    'Impressions': {
        'Mean Impr': 'mean',
        'Std Impr': 'std',
    },
    'Spent': ['mean', 'std'],
}

df.groupby(['Target Gender', 'Target Age']).agg(agg_config)
```

It's very easy to do it. We will prepare a dictionary that we'll use as a configuration. I'm showing you two options to do it. We use a nicer format for `'Impressions'`, where we pass a nested dict with description/function as key/value pairs. On the other hand, for `'Spent'`, we just use a simpler list with just the function names.

Then, we perform a grouping on the `'Target Gender'` and `'Target Age'` columns, and we pass our configuration dict to the `agg()` method. The result is truncated and rearranged a little bit to make it fit, and shown here:

		Impressions		Spent	
Target Gender	**Target Age**	**Mean Impr**	**Std Impr**	**mean**	**std**
B	20-25	500000	2.189102	239882	209442.168488
	20-30	500000	2.245317	271285	236854.155720
	20-35	500000	1.886396	243725	174268.898935
	20-40	499999	2.100786	247740	211540.133771
	20-45	500000	1.772811	148712	118603.932051
...		...	...	...	...
M	20-25	500000	2.022023	212520	215857.323228
	20-30	500000	2.111882	292577	231663.713956
	20-35	499999	1.965177	255651	222790.960907
	20-40	499999	1.932473	282515	250023.393334
	20-45	499999	1.905746	271077	219901.462405

This is the textual representation, of course, but you can also have the HTML one. You can see that Spent has the mean and std columns whose labels are simply the function names, while Impressions features the nice titles we added to the configuration dict.

Let's do one more thing before we wrap this chapter up. I want to show you something called a **pivot table**. It's kind of a buzzword in the data environment, so an example such as this one, albeit very simple, is a must.

```
#39
    pivot = df.pivot_table(
        values=['Impressions', 'Clicks', 'Spent'],
        index=['Target Age'],
        columns=['Target Gender'],
        aggfunc=np.sum
    )
    pivot
```

We create a pivot table that shows us the correlation between the target age and impressions, clicks, and spent. These last three will be subdivided according to the target gender. The aggregation function used to calculate the results is the `numpy.sum` function (`numpy.mean` would be the default, had I not specified anything).

After creating the pivot table, we simply print it with the last line in the cell, and here's a crop of the result:

	Impressions			Clicks			Spent		
Target Gender	**B**	**F**	**M**	**B**	**F**	**M**	**B**	**F**	**M**
Target Age									
20-25	42499954	40499948	43499987	3457493	3108138	3401407	19961037	19327699	23420817
20-30	46999958	38499935	39499970	4026055	3061723	3131742	25118876	21148545	23782193
20-35	40999986	44499986	34499957	3177185	3315678	2784411	21849985	17988043	17228214
20-40	38499926	40499926	43499942	3154637	3208569	3650371	19819058	18913285	23439361
20-45	6999990	11499988	7499985	540434	952853	486264	3948282	5280748	4639397
25-30	34499979	37499967	33999950	2927039	2906621	2787992	19193461	17564978	17489240
25-35	43499973	39499982	31499977	3842891	3124853	2479525	20950036	16196097	17281155
25-40	27499973	36999941	26499972	2155983	3027652	2068474	12666195	17888093	12811784
25-45	33999981	41499988	43499964	2485752	3623777	3629015	14576611	20266282	21521781
25-50	9999985	7499983	10500012	765251	598021	815785	5715627	3564206	5091148
30-35	36499974	40999994	32999963	3030691	3672607	2965210	20269909	20762924	15639066
30-40	39999964	38999955	40499971	3186630	2904775	3518337	23996589	21778382	21769771

It's pretty clear and provides very useful information when the data is meaningful.

That's it! I'll leave you to discover more about the wonderful world of IPython, Jupyter, and data science. I strongly encourage you to get comfortable with the notebook environment. It's much better than a console, it's extremely practical and fun to use, and you can even do slides and documents with it.

Where do we go from here?

Data science is indeed a fascinating subject. As I said in the introduction, those who want to delve into its meanders need to be well trained in mathematics and statistics. Working with data that has been interpolated incorrectly renders any result about it useless. The same goes for data that has been extrapolated incorrectly or sampled with the wrong frequency. To give you an example, imagine a population of individuals that are aligned in a queue. If, for some reason, the gender of that population alternated between male and female, the queue would be something like this: F-M-F-M-F-M-F-M-F...

If you sampled it taking only the even elements, you would draw the conclusion that the population was made up only of males, while sampling the odd ones would tell you exactly the opposite.

Of course, this was just a silly example, I know, but believe me it's very easy to make mistakes in this field, especially when dealing with big data where sampling is mandatory and therefore, the quality of the introspection you make depends, first and foremost, on the quality of the sampling itself.

When it comes to data science and Python, these are the main tools you want to look at:

- **NumPy** (`http://www.numpy.org/`): This is the fundamental package for scientific computing with Python. It contains a powerful N-dimensional array object, sophisticated (broadcasting) functions, tools for integrating C/C++ and Fortran code, useful linear algebra, Fourier transform, random number capabilities, and much more.

- **Scikit-Learn** (`http://scikit-learn.org/stable/`): This is probably the most popular machine learning library in Python. It has simple and efficient tools for data mining and data analysis, accessible to everybody, and reusable in various contexts. It's built on NumPy, SciPy, and Matplotlib.

- **Pandas** (`http://pandas.pydata.org/`): This is an open source, BSD-licensed library providing high-performance, easy-to-use data structures, and data analysis tools. We've used it throughout this whole chapter.

- **IPython** (`http://ipython.org/`) / **Jupyter** (`http://jupyter.org/`): These provide a rich architecture for interactive computing.

- **Matplotlib** (`http://matplotlib.org/`): This is a Python 2D plotting library that produces publication-quality figures in a variety of hard copy formats and interactive environments across platforms. Matplotlib can be used in Python scripts, the Python and IPython shell and notebook, web application servers, and six graphical user interface toolkits.

- **Numba** (http://numba.pydata.org/): This gives you the power to speed up your applications with high performance functions written directly in Python. With a few annotations, array-oriented and math-heavy Python code can be just-in-time compiled to native machine instructions, similar in performance to C, C++, and Fortran, without having to switch languages or Python interpreters.

- **Bokeh** (http://bokeh.pydata.org/en/latest/): It's a Python-interactive visualization library that targets modern web browsers for presentation. Its goal is to provide elegant, concise construction of novel graphics in the style of D3.js, but also deliver this capability with high-performance interactivity over very large or streaming datasets.

Other than these single libraries, you can also find ecosystems such as **SciPy** (http://scipy.org/) and **Anaconda** (https://www.continuum.io/), which bundle several different packages in order to give you something that just works in an "out-of-the-box" fashion.

Installing all these tools and their several dependencies is hard on some systems, so I suggest that you try out ecosystems as well and see if you are comfortable with them. It may be worth it.

Summary

In this chapter, we talked about data science. Rather than attempting to explain anything about this extremely wide subject, we delved into a project. We familiarized ourselves with the Jupyter notebook, and with different libraries such as Pandas, Matplotlib, NumPy.

Of course, having to compress all this information into one single chapter means I could only touch briefly on the subjects I presented. I hope the project we've gone through together has been comprehensive enough to give you a good idea about what could potentially be the workflow you might follow when working in this field.

The next chapter is dedicated to web development. So, make sure you have a browser ready and let's go!

10

Web Development
Done Right

"Don't believe everything you read on the Web."

- Confucius

In this chapter, we're going to work on a website together. By working on a small project, my aim is to open a window for you to take a peek on what web development is, along with the main concepts and tools you should know if you want to be successful with it.

What is the Web?

The **World Wide Web**, or simply **Web**, is a way of accessing information through the use of a medium called the **Internet**. The Internet is a huge network of networks, a networking infrastructure. Its purpose is to connect billions of devices together, all around the globe, so that they can communicate with one another. Information travels through the Internet in a rich variety of languages called **protocols**, which allow different devices to speak the same tongue in order to share content.

The Web is an information-sharing model, built on top of the Internet, which employs the **Hypertext Transfer Protocol** (**HTTP**) as a basis for data communication. The Web, therefore, is just one of the several different ways information can be exchanged over the Internet: e-mail, instant messaging, news groups, and so on, they all rely on different protocols.

How does the Web work?

In a nutshell, HTTP is an asymmetric **request-response client-server** protocol.
An HTTP client sends a request message to an HTTP server. The server, in turn,
returns a response message. In other words, HTTP is a **pull protocol** in which the
client pulls information from the server (as opposed to a **push protocol** in which the
server pushes information down to the client). Take a look at the following image:

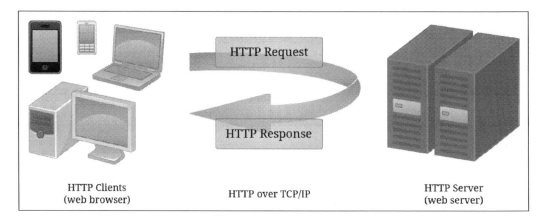

HTTP is based on **TCP/IP (Transmission Control Protocol/Internet Protocol)**,
which provides the tools for a reliable communication exchange.

An important feature of the HTTP protocol is that it's *stateless*. This means that
the current request has no knowledge about what happened in previous requests.
This is a limitation, but you can browse a website with the illusion of being logged in.
Under the covers though, what happens is that, on login, a token of user information is
saved (most often on the client side, in special files called **cookies**) so that each request
the user makes carries the means for the server to recognize the user and provide a
custom interface by showing their name, keeping their basket populated, and so on.

Even though it's very interesting, we're not going to delve into the rich details of
HTTP and how it works. However, we're going to write a small website, which
means we'll have to write the code to handle HTTP requests and return HTTP
responses. I won't keep prepending HTTP to the terms *request* and *response* from
now on, as I trust there won't be any confusion.

The Django web framework

For our project, we're going to use one of the most popular web frameworks you can find in the Python ecosystem: Django.

A **web framework** is a set of tools (libraries, functions, classes, and so on) that we can use to code a website. We need to decide what kind of requests we want to allow to be issued against our web server and how we respond to them. A web framework is the perfect tool to do that because it takes care of many things for us so that we can concentrate only on the important bits without having to reinvent the wheel.

 There are different types of frameworks. Not all of them are designed for writing code for the web. In general, a **framework** is a tool that provides functionalities to facilitate the development of software applications, products and solutions.

Django design philosophy

Django is designed according to the following principles:

- **DRY**: As in, **Don't Repeat Yourself**. Don't repeat code, and code in a way that makes the framework deduce as much as possible from as little as possible.

- **Loose coupling**: The various layers of the framework shouldn't know about each other (unless absolutely necessary for whatever reason). Loose coupling works best when paralleled with high cohesion. To quote Robert Martin: putting together things which change for the same reason, and spreading apart those which change for different reasons.

- **Less code**: Applications should use the least possible amount of code, and be written in a way that favors reuse as much as possible.

- **Consistency**: When using the Django framework, regardless of which layer you're coding against, your experience will be very consistent with the design patterns and paradigms that were chosen to lay out the project.

The framework itself is designed around the **model-template-view** (**MTV**) pattern, which is a variant of **model-view-controller** (**MVC**), which is widely employed by other frameworks. The purpose of such patterns is to separate concerns and promote code reuse and quality.

The model layer

Of the three layers, this is the one that defines the structure of the data that is handled by the application, and deals with data sources. A **model** is a class that represents a data structure. Through some Django magic, models are mapped to database tables so that you can store your data in a relational database.

 A **relational database** stores data in tables in which each column is a property of the data and each row represents a single item or entry in the collection represented by that table. Through the **primary key** of each table, which is that part of the data that allows to uniquely identify each item, it is possible to establish relationships between items belonging to different tables, that is, to put them into *relation*.

The beauty of this system is that you don't have to write database-specific code in order to handle your data. You will just have to configure your models correctly and simply use them. The work on the database is done for you by the Django **object-relational mapping (ORM)**, which takes care of translating operations done on Python objects into a language that a relational database can understand: **SQL (Structured Query Language)**.

One benefit of this approach is that you will be able to change databases without rewriting your code since all the database specific code is produced by Django on the fly, according to which database it's connected to. Relational databases speak SQL, but each of them has its own unique flavor of it; therefore, not having to hardcode any SQL in our application is a tremendous advantage.

Django allows you to modify your models at any time. When you do, you can run a command that creates a migration, which is the set of instructions needed to port the database in a state that represents the current definition of your models.

To summarize, this layer deals with defining the data structures you need to handle in your website and gives you the means to save and load them from and to the database by simply accessing the models, which are Python objects.

The view layer

The function of a view is handling a request, performing whatever action needs to be carried out, and eventually returning a response. For example, if you open your browser and request a page corresponding to a category of products in an e-commerce shop, the view will likely talk to the database, asking for all the categories that are children of the selected category (for example, to display them in a navigation sidebar) and for all the products that belong to the selected category, in order to display them on the page.

Therefore, the view is the mechanism through which we can fulfill a request. Its result, the response object, can assume several different forms: a JSON payload, text, an HTML page, and so on. When you code a website, your responses usually consist of HTML or JSON.

> The **Hypertext Markup Language**, or **HTML**, is the standard markup language used to create web pages. Web browsers run engines that are capable of interpreting HTML code and render it into what we see when we open a page of a website.

The template layer

This is the layer that provides the bridge between backend and frontend development. When a view has to return HTML, it usually does it by preparing a **context object** (a dict) with some data, and then it feeds this context to a template, which is rendered (that is to say, transformed into HTML) and returned to the caller in the form of a response (more precisely, the body of the response). This mechanism allows for maximum code reuse. If you go back to the category example, it's easy to see that, if you browse a website that sells products, it doesn't really matter which category you click on or what type of search you perform, the layout of the products page doesn't change. What does change is the data with which that page is populated.

Therefore, the layout of the page is defined by a template, which is written in a mixture of HTML and Django template language. The view that serves that page collects all the products to be displayed in the context dict, and feeds it to the template which will be rendered into an HTML page by the Django template engine.

The Django URL dispatcher

The way Django associates a **Uniform Resource Locator** (**URL**) with a view is through matching the requested URL with the patterns that are registered in a special file. A URL represents a page in a website so, for example, `http://mysite.com/categories?id=123` would probably point to the page for the category with ID `123` on my website, while `https://mysite.com/login` would probably be the user login page.

> The difference between HTTP and HTTPS is that the latter adds encryption to the protocol so that the data that you exchange with the website is secured. When you put your credit card details on a website, or log in anywhere, or do anything around sensitive data, you want to make sure that you're using HTTPS.

Regular expressions

The way Django matches URLs to patterns is through a regular expression. A **regular expression** is a sequence of characters that defines a search pattern with which we can carry out operations such as pattern and string matching, find/replace, and so on.

Regular expressions have a special syntax to indicate things like digits, letters, spaces, and so on, as well as how many times we expect a character to appear, and much more. A complete explanation of this topic is beyond of the scope of the book. However, it is a very important topic, so the project we're going to work on together will evolve around it, in the hope that you will be stimulated to find the time to explore it a bit more on your own.

To give you a quick example, imagine that you wanted to specify a pattern to match a date such as `"26-12-1947"`. This string consists of two digits, one dash, two digits, one dash, and finally four digits. Therefore, we could write it like this: `r'[0-9]{2}-[0-9]{2}-[0-9]{4}'`. We created a class by using square brackets, and we defined a range of digits inside, from 0 to 9, hence all the possible digits. Then, between curly braces, we say that we expect two of them. Then a dash, then we repeat this pattern once as it is, and once more, by changing how many digits we expect, and without the final dash. Having a class like `[0-9]` is such a common pattern that a special notation has been created as a shortcut: `'\d'`. Therefore, we can rewrite the pattern like this: `r'\d{2}-\d{2}-\d{4}'` and it will work exactly the same. That `r` in front of the string stands for *raw*, and its purpose is to alter the way every backslash `'\'` is interpreted by the regular expression engine.

A regex website

So, here we are. We'll code a website that stores regular expressions so that we'll be able to play with them a little bit.

Before we proceed creating the project, I'd like to spend a word about CSS. **CSS (Cascading Style Sheets)** are files in which we specify how the various elements on an HTML page look. You can set all sorts of properties such as shape, size, color, margins, borders, fonts, and so on. In this project, I have tried my best to achieve a decent result on the pages, but I'm neither a frontend developer nor a designer, so please don't pay too much attention to how things look. Try and focus on how they work.

Setting up Django

On the Django website (`https://www.djangoproject.com/`), you can follow the tutorial, which gives you a pretty good idea of Django's capabilities. If you want, you can follow that tutorial first and then come back to this example. So, first things first; let's install Django in your virtual environment:

```
$ pip install django
```

When this command is done, you can test it within a console (try doing it with bpython, it gives you a shell similar to IPython but with nice introspection capabilities):

```
>>> import django
>>> django.VERSION
(1, 8, 4, 'final', 0)
```

Now that Django is installed, we're good to go. We'll have to do some scaffolding, so I'll quickly guide you through that.

Starting the project

Choose a folder in the book's environment and change into that. I'll use `ch10`. From there, we start a Django project with the following command:

```
$ django-admin startproject regex
```

This will prepare the skeleton for a Django project called `regex`. Change into the `regex` folder and run the following:

```
$ python manage.py runserver
```

You should be able to go to `http://127.0.0.1:8000/` with your browser and see the *It worked!* default Django page. This means that the project is correctly set up. When you've seen the page, kill the server with *Ctrl + C* (or whatever it says in the console). I'll paste the final structure for the project now so that you can use it as a reference:

```
$ tree -A regex  # from the ch10 folder
regex
├── db.sqlite3
├── entries
│   ├── admin.py
│   ├── forms.py
│   ├── __init__.py
│   ├── migrations
│   │   ├── 0001_initial.py
│   │   └── __init__.py
│   ├── models.py
```

```
|     ├── static
|     |   └── entries
|     |       └── css
|     |           └── main.css
|     ├── templates
|     |   └── entries
|     |       ├── base.html
|     |       ├── footer.html
|     |       ├── home.html
|     |       ├── insert.html
|     |       └── list.html
|     └── views.py
├── manage.py
└── regex
    ├── __init__.py
    ├── settings.py
    ├── urls.py
    └── wsgi.py
```

Don't worry if you're missing files, we'll get there. A Django project is typically a collection of several different applications. Each application is meant to provide a functionality in a self-contained, reusable fashion. We'll create just one, called **entries**:

```
$ python manage.py startapp entries
```

Within the entries folder that has been created, you can get rid of the tests.py module.

Now, let's fix the regex/settings.py file in the regex folder. We need to add our application to the INSTALLED_APPS tuple so that we can use it (add it at the bottom of the tuple):

```
INSTALLED_APPS = (
    ... django apps ...
    'entries',
)
```

Then, you may want to fix the language and time zone according to your personal preference. I live in London, so I set them like this:

```
LANGUAGE_CODE = 'en-gb'
TIME_ZONE = 'Europe/London'
```

There is nothing else to do in this file, so you can save and close it.

Now it's time to apply the **migrations** to the database. Django needs database support to handle users, sessions, and things like that, so we need to create a database and populate it with the necessary data. Luckily, this is very easily done with the following command:

```
$ python manage.py migrate
```

 For this project, we use a SQLite database, which is basically just a file. On a real project, you would probably use a different database engine like MySQL or PostgreSQL.

Creating users

Now that we have a database, we can create a superuser using the console.

```
$ python manage.py createsuperuser
```

After entering username and other details, we have a user with admin privileges. This is enough to access the Django admin section, so try and start the server:

```
$ python manage.py runserver
```

This will start the Django development server, which is a very useful built-in web server that you can use while working with Django. Now that the server is running, we can access the admin page at `http://localhost:8000/admin/`. I will show you a screenshot of this section later. If you log in with the credentials of the user you just created and head to the **Authentication and Authorization** section, you'll find **Users**. Open that and you will be able to see the list of users. You can edit the details of any user you want as an admin. In our case, make sure you create a different one so that there are at least two users in the system (we'll need them later). I'll call the first user *Fabrizio* (username: `fab`) and the second one *Adriano* (username: `adri`) in honor of my father.

By the way, you should see that the Django admin panel comes for free automatically. You define your models, hook them up, and that's it. This is an incredible tool that shows how advanced Django's introspection capabilities are. Moreover, it is completely customizable and extendable. It's truly an excellent piece of work.

Adding the Entry model

Now that the boilerplate is out of the way, and we have a couple of users, we're ready to code. We start by adding the `Entry` model to our application so that we can store objects in the database. Here's the code you'll need to add (remember to use the project tree for reference):

entries/models.py

```
from django.db import models
from django.contrib.auth.models import User
from django.utils import timezone

class Entry(models.Model):
    user = models.ForeignKey(User)
    pattern = models.CharField(max_length=255)
    test_string = models.CharField(max_length=255)
    date_added = models.DateTimeField(default=timezone.now)

    class Meta:
        verbose_name_plural = 'entries'
```

This is the model we'll use to store regular expressions in our system. We'll store a pattern, a test string, a reference to the user who created the entry, and the moment of creation. You can see that creating a model is actually quite easy, but nonetheless, let's go through it line by line.

First we need to import the models module from `django.db`. This will give us the base class for our `Entry` model. Django models are special classes and much is done for us behind the scenes when we inherit from `models.Model`.

We want a reference to the user who created the entry, so we need to import the `User` model from Django's authorization application and we also need to import the timezone model to get access to the `timezone.now()` function, which provides us with a timezone-aware version of `datetime.now()`. The beauty of this is that it's hooked up with the `TIME_ZONE` settings I showed you before.

As for the primary key for this class, if we don't set one explicitly, Django will add one for us. A **primary key** is a key that allows us to uniquely identify an `Entry` object in the database (in this case, Django will add an auto-incrementing integer ID).

So, we define our class, and we set up four class attributes. We have a `ForeignKey` attribute that is our reference to the *User* model. We also have two `CharField` attributes that hold the pattern and test strings for our regular expressions. We also have a `DateTimeField`, whose default value is set to `timezone.now`. Note that we don't call `timezone.now` right there, it's `now`, not `now()`. So, we're not passing a `DateTime` instance (set at the moment in time when that line is parsed) rather, we're passing a *callable*, a function that is called when we save an entry in the database. This is similar to the callback mechanism we used in *Chapter 8, The Edges – GUIs and Scripts*, when we were assigning commands to button clicks.

The last two lines are very interesting. We define a class `Meta` within the `Entry` class itself. The `Meta` class is used by Django to provide all sorts of extra information for a model. Django has a great deal of logic under the hood to adapt its behavior according to the information we put in the `Meta` class. In this case, in the admin panel, the pluralized version of `Entry` would be *Entrys*, which is wrong, therefore we need to manually set it. We specify the plural all lowercase, as Django takes care of capitalizing it for us when needed.

Now that we have a new model, we need to update the database to reflect the new state of the code. In order to do this, we need to instruct Django that it needs to create the code to update the database. This code is called **migration**. Let's create it and execute it:

```
$ python manage.py makemigrations entries
$ python manage.py migrate
```

After these two instructions, the database will be ready to store `Entry` objects.

There are two different kinds of migrations: data and schema migration. **Data migrations** port data from one state to another without altering its structure. For example, a data migration could set all products for a category as out of stock by switching a flag to `False` or `0`. A **schema migration** is a set of instructions that alter the structure of the database schema. For example, that could be adding an `age` column to a `Person` table, or increasing the maximum length of a field to account for very long addresses. When developing with Django, it's quite common to have to perform both kinds of migrations over the course of development. Data evolves continuously, especially if you code in an agile environment.

Customizing the admin panel

The next step is to hook the Entry model up with the admin panel. You can do it with one line of code, but in this case, I want to add some options to customize a bit the way the admin panel shows the entries, both in the list view of all entry items in the database and in the form view that allows us to create and modify them.

All we need to do is to add the following code:

entries/admin.py

```
from django.contrib import admin
from .models import Entry


@admin.register(Entry)
class EntryAdmin(admin.ModelAdmin):
    fieldsets = [
        ('Regular Expression',
         {'fields': ['pattern', 'test_string']}),
        ('Other Information',
         {'fields': ['user', 'date_added']}),
    ]
    list_display = ('pattern', 'test_string', 'user')
    list_filter = ['user']
    search_fields = ['test_string']
```

This is simply beautiful. My guess is that you probably already understand most of it, even if you're new to Django.

So, we start by importing the admin module and the Entry model. Because we want to foster code reuse, we import the Entry model using a relative import (there's a dot before models). This will allow us to move or rename the app without too much trouble. Then, we define the EntryAdmin class, which inherits from admin.ModelAdmin. The decoration on the class tells Django to display the Entry model in the admin panel, and what we put in the EntryAdmin class tells Django how to customize the way it handles this model.

Firstly, we specify the fieldsets for the create/edit page. This will divide the page into two sections so that we get a better visualization of the content (*pattern* and *test string*) and the other details (*user* and *timestamp*) separately.

Then, we customize the way the list page displays the results. We want to see all the fields, but not the date. We also want to be able to filter on the user so that we can have a list of all the entries by just one user, and we want to be able to search on test_string.

I will go ahead and add three entries, one for myself and two on behalf of my father. The result is shown in the next two images. After inserting them, the list page looks like this:

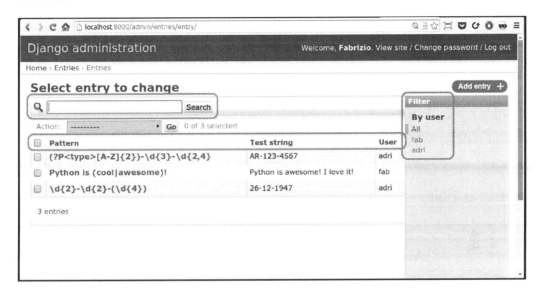

I have highlighted the three parts of this view that we customized in the `EntryAdmin` class. We can filter by user, we can search and we have all the fields displayed. If you click on a pattern, the edit view opens up.

After our customization, it looks like this:

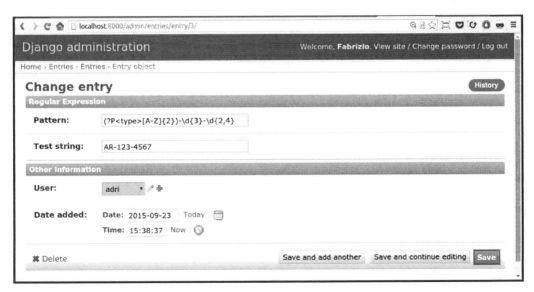

Notice how we have two sections: **Regular Expression** and **Other Information**, thanks to our custom `EntryAdmin` class. Have a go with it, add some entries to a couple of different users, get familiar with the interface. Isn't it nice to have all this for free?

Creating the form

Every time you fill in your details on a web page, you're inserting data in form fields. A **form** is a part of the **HTML Document Object Model (DOM) tree**. In HTML, you create a form by using the `form` tag. When you click on the submit button, your browser normally packs the form data together and puts it in the body of a `POST` request. As opposed to `GET` requests, which are used to ask the web server for a resource, a `POST` request normally sends data to the web server with the aim of creating or updating a resource. For this reason, handling `POST` requests usually requires more care than `GET` requests.

When the server receives data from a `POST` request, that data needs to be validated. Moreover, the server needs to employ security mechanisms to protect against various types of attacks. One attack that is very dangerous is the **cross-site request forgery (CSRF)** attack, which happens when data is sent from a domain that is not the one the user is authenticated on. Django allows you to handle this issue in a very elegant way.

So, instead of being lazy and using the Django admin to create the entries, I'm going to show you how to do it using a Django form. By using the tools the framework gives you, you get a very good degree of validation work already done (in fact, we won't need to add any custom validation ourselves).

There are two kinds of form classes in Django: `Form` and `ModelForm`. You use the former to create a form whose shape and behavior depends on how you code the class, what fields you add, and so on. On the other hand, the latter is a type of form that, albeit still customizable, infers fields and behavior from a model. Since we need a form for the `Entry` model, we'll use that one.

entries/forms.py

```
from django.forms import ModelForm
from .models import Entry


class EntryForm(ModelForm):
    class Meta:
        model = Entry
        fields = ['pattern', 'test_string']
```

Amazingly enough, this is all we have to do to have a form that we can put on a page. The only notable thing here is that we restrict the fields to only `pattern` and `test_string`. Only logged-in users will be allowed access to the insert page, and therefore we don't need to ask who the user is: we know that. As for the date, when we save an `Entry`, the `date_added` field will be set according to its default, therefore we don't need to specify that as well. We'll see in the view how to feed the user information to the form before saving. So, all the background work is done, all we need is the views and the templates. Let's start with the views.

Writing the views

We need to write three views. We need one for the home page, one to display the list of all entries for a user, and one to create a new entry. We also need views to log in and log out. But thanks to Django, we don't need to write them. I'll paste all the code, and then we'll go through it together, step by step.

`entries/views.py`

```python
import re
from django.contrib.auth.decorators import login_required
from django.contrib.messages.views import SuccessMessageMixin
from django.core.urlresolvers import reverse_lazy
from django.utils.decorators import method_decorator
from django.views.generic import FormView, TemplateView
from .forms import EntryForm
from .models import Entry


class HomeView(TemplateView):
    template_name = 'entries/home.html'

    @method_decorator(
        login_required(login_url=reverse_lazy('login')))
    def get(self, request, *args, **kwargs):
        context = self.get_context_data(**kwargs)
        return self.render_to_response(context)


class EntryListView(TemplateView):
    template_name = 'entries/list.html'

    @method_decorator(
        login_required(login_url=reverse_lazy('login')))
    def get(self, request, *args, **kwargs):
        context = self.get_context_data(**kwargs)
        entries = Entry.objects.filter(
            user=request.user).order_by('-date_added')
```

```
            matches = (self._parse_entry(entry) for entry in entries)
            context['entries'] = list(zip(entries, matches))
            return self.render_to_response(context)

        def _parse_entry(self, entry):
            match = re.search(entry.pattern, entry.test_string)
            if match is not None:
                return (
                    match.group(),
                    match.groups() or None,
                    match.groupdict() or None
                )
            return None

    class EntryFormView(SuccessMessageMixin, FormView):
        template_name = 'entries/insert.html'
        form_class = EntryForm
        success_url = reverse_lazy('insert')
        success_message = "Entry was created successfully"

        @method_decorator(
            login_required(login_url=reverse_lazy('login')))
        def get(self, request, *args, **kwargs):
            return super(EntryFormView, self).get(
                request, *args, **kwargs)

        @method_decorator(
            login_required(login_url=reverse_lazy('login')))
        def post(self, request, *args, **kwargs):
            return super(EntryFormView, self).post(
                request, *args, **kwargs)

        def form_valid(self, form):
            self._save_with_user(form)
            return super(EntryFormView, self).form_valid(form)

        def _save_with_user(self, form):
            self.object = form.save(commit=False)
            self.object.user = self.request.user
            self.object.save()
```

Let's start with the imports. We need the `re` module to handle regular expressions, then we need a few classes and functions from Django, and finally, we need the `Entry` model and the `EntryForm` form.

The home view

The first view is HomeView. It inherits from TemplateView, which means that the response will be created by rendering a template with the context we'll create in the view. All we have to do is specify the template_name class attribute to point to the correct template. Django promotes code reuse to a point that if we didn't need to make this view accessible only to logged-in users, the first two lines would have been all we needed.

However, we want this view to be accessible only to logged-in users; therefore, we need to decorate it with login_required. Now, historically views in Django used to be functions; therefore, this decorator was designed to accept a *function* not a *method* like we have in this class. We're using Django class-based views in this project so, in order to make things work, we need to transform login_required so that it accepts a method (the difference being in the first argument: self). We do this by passing login_required to method_decorator.

We also need to feed the login_required decorator with login_url information, and here comes another wonderful feature of Django. As you'll see after we're done with the views, in Django, you tie a view to a URL through a pattern, consisting of a regular expression and other information. You can give a name to each entry in the urls.py file so that when you want to refer to a URL, you don't have to hardcode its value into your code. All you have to do is get Django to reverse-engineer that URL from the name we gave to the entry in urls.py defining the URL and the view that is tied to it. This mechanism will become clearer later. For now, just think of reverse('...') as a way of getting a URL from an identifier. In this way, you only write the actual URL once, in the urls.py file, which is brilliant. In the views.py code, we need to use reverse_lazy, which works exactly like reverse with one major difference: it only finds the URL when we actually need it (in a lazy fashion). This is needed when the urls.py file hasn't been loaded yet when the reverse function is used.

The get method, which we just decorated, simply calls the get method of the parent class. Of course, the get method is the method that Django calls when a GET request is performed against the URL tied to this view.

The entry list view

This view is much more interesting than the previous one. First of all, we decorate the get method as we did before. Inside of it, we need to prepare a list of Entry objects and feed it to the template, which shows it to the user. In order to do so, we start by getting the context dict like we're supposed to do, by calling the get_context_data method of the TemplateView class. Then, we use the ORM to get a list of the entries. We do this by accessing the objects manager, and calling a filter on it. We filter the entries according to which user is logged in, and we ask for them to be sorted in a descending order (that '-' in front of the name specifies the descending order). The objects manager is the default **manager** every Django model is augmented with on creation, it allows us to interact with the database through its methods.

We parse each entry to get a list of matches (actually, I coded it so that matches is a generator expression). Finally, we add to the context an 'entries' key whose value is the coupling of entries and matches, so that each Entry instance is paired with the resulting match of its pattern and test string.

On the last line, we simply ask Django to render the template using the context we created.

Take a look at the _parse_entry method. All it does is perform a search on the entry.test_string with the entry.pattern. If the resulting match object is not None, it means that we found something. If so, we return a tuple with three elements: the overall group, the subgroups, and the group dictionary. If you're not familiar with these terms, don't worry, you'll see a screenshot soon with an example. We return None if there is no match.

The form view

Finally, let's examine EntryFormView. This is particularly interesting for a few reasons. Firstly, it shows us a nice example of Python's multiple inheritance. We want to display a message on the page, after having inserted an Entry, so we inherit from SuccessMessageMixin. But we want to handle a form as well, so we also inherit from FormView.

 Note that, when you deal with mixins and inheritance, you may have to consider the order in which you specify the base classes in the class declaration.

In order to set up this view correctly, we need to specify a few attributes at the beginning: the template to be rendered, the form class to be used to handle the data from the POST request, the URL we need to redirect the user to in the case of success, and the success message.

Another interesting feature is that this view needs to handle both GET and POST requests. When we land on the form page for the first time, the form is empty, and that is the GET request. On the other hand, when we fill in the form and want to submit the Entry, we make a POST request. You can see that the body of get is conceptually identical to HomeView. Django does everything for us.

The post method is just like get. The only reason we need to code these two methods is so that we can decorate them to require login.

Within the Django form handling process (in the FormView class), there are a few methods that we can override in order to customize the overall behavior. We need to do it with the form_valid method. This method will be called when the form validation is successful. Its purpose is to save the form so that an Entry object is created out of it, and then stored in the database.

The only problem is that our form is missing the user. We need to intercept that moment in the chain of calls and put the user information in ourselves. This is done by calling the _save_with_user method, which is very simple.

Firstly, we ask Django to save the form with the commit argument set to False. This creates an Entry instance without attempting to save it to the database. Saving it immediately would fail because the user information is not there.

The next line updates the Entry instance (self.object), adding the user information and, on the last line, we can safely save it. The reason I called it object and set it on the instance like that was to follow what the original FormView class does.

We're fiddling with the Django mechanism here, so if we want the whole thing to work, we need to pay attention to when and how we modify its behavior, and make sure we don't alter it incorrectly. For this reason, it's very important to remember to call the form_valid method of the base class (we use super for that) at the end of our own customized version, to make sure that every other action that method usually performs is carried out correctly.

Note how the request is tied to each view instance (self.request) so that we don't need to pass it through when we refactor our logic into methods. Note also that the user information has been added to the request automatically by Django. Finally, note that the reason why all the process is split into very small methods like these is so that we can only override those that we need to customize. All this removes the need to write a lot of code.

Now that we have the views covered, let's see how we couple them to the URLs.

Tying up URLs and views

In the `urls.py` module, we tie each view to a URL. There are many ways of doing this. I chose the simplest one, which works perfectly for the extent of this exercise, but you may want to explore this argument more deeply if you intend to work with Django. This is the core around which the whole website logic will revolve; therefore, you should try to get it down correctly. Note that the `urls.py` module belongs to the project folder.

regex/urls.py

```
from django.conf.urls import include, url
from django.contrib import admin
from django.contrib.auth import views as auth_views
from django.core.urlresolvers import reverse_lazy
from entries.views import HomeView, EntryListView, EntryFormView

urlpatterns = [
    url(r'^admin/', include(admin.site.urls)),
    url(r'^entries/$', EntryListView.as_view(), name='entries'),
    url(r'^entries/insert$',
        EntryFormView.as_view(),
        name='insert'),

    url(r'^login/$',
        auth_views.login,
        kwargs={'template_name': 'admin/login.html'},
        name='login'),
    url(r'^logout/$',
        auth_views.logout,
        kwargs={'next_page': reverse_lazy('home')},
        name='logout'),

    url(r'^$', HomeView.as_view(), name='home'),
]
```

As you can see, the magic comes from the `url` function. Firstly, we pass it a regular expression; then the view; and finally, a name, which is what we will use in the `reverse` and `reverse_lazy` functions to recover the URL.

Note that, when using class-based views, we have to transform them into functions, which is what `url` is expecting. To do that, we call the `as_view()` method on them.

Note also that the first `url` entry, for the admin, is special. Instead of specifying a URL and a view, it specifies a URL prefix and another `urls.py` module (from the `admin.site` package). In this way, Django will complete all the URLs for the admin section by prepending `'admin/'` to all the URLs specified in `admin.site.urls`. We could have done the same for our entries app (and we should have), but I feel it would have been a bit too much for this simple project.

In the regular expression language, the `'^'` and `'$'` symbols represent the *start* and *end* of a string. Note that if you use the inclusion technique, as for the admin, the `'$'` is missing. Of course, this is because `'admin/'` is just a prefix, which needs to be completed by all the definitions in the included `urls` module.

Something else worth noticing is that we can also include the stringified version of a path to a view, which we do for the `login` and `logout` views. We also add information about which templates to use with the `kwargs` argument. These views come straight from the `django.contrib.auth` package, by the way, so that we don't need to write a single line of code to handle authentication. This is brilliant and saves us a lot of time.

Each `url` declaration must be done within the `urlpatterns` list and on this matter, it's important to consider that, when Django is trying to find a view for a URL that has been requested, the patterns are exercised in order, from top to bottom. The first one that matches is the one that will provide the view for it so, in general, you have to put specific patterns before generic ones, otherwise they will never get a chance to be caught. For example, `'^shop/categories/$'` needs to come before `'^shop'` (note the absence of the `'$'` in the latter), otherwise it would never be called. Our example for the entries works fine because I thoroughly specified URLs using the `'$'` at the end.

So, models, forms, admin, views and URLs are all done. All that is left to do is take care of the templates. I'll have to be very brief on this part because HTML can be very verbose.

Writing the templates

All templates inherit from a base one, which provides the HTML structure for all others, in a very OOP type of fashion. It also specifies a few blocks, which are areas that can be overridden by children so that they can provide custom content for those areas. Let's start with the base template:

`entries/templates/entries/base.html`

```
{% load static from staticfiles %}
<!DOCTYPE html>
<html lang="en">
```

```
<head>
  {% block meta %}
    <meta charset="utf-8">
    <meta name="viewport"
      content="width=device-width, initial-scale=1.0">
  {% endblock meta %}

  {% block styles %}
    <link href="{% static "entries/css/main.css" %}"
      rel="stylesheet">
  {% endblock styles %}

  <title> {% block title %}Title{% endblock title %} </title>
</head>

<body>
  <div id="page-content">
    {% block page-content %}
    {% endblock page-content %}
  </div>
  <div id="footer">
    {% block footer %}
    {% endblock footer %}
  </div>
</body>
</html>
```

There is a good reason to repeat the `entries` folder from the `templates` one. When you deploy a Django website, you collect all the template files under one folder. If you don't specify the paths like I did, you may get a `base.html` template in the entries app, and a `base.html` template in another app. The last one to be collected will override any other file with the same name. For this reason, by putting them in a `templates/entries` folder and using this technique for each Django app you write, you avoid the risk of name collisions (the same goes for any other static file).

There is not much to say about this template, really, apart from the fact that it loads the `static` tag so that we can get easy access to the `static` path without hardcoding it in the template by using {% static ... %}. The code in the special {% ... %} sections is code that defines logic. The code in the special {{ ... }} represents variables that will be rendered on the page.

We define three blocks: `title`, `page-content`, and `footer`, whose purpose is to hold the title, the content of the page, and the footer. Blocks can be optionally overridden by child templates in order to provide different content within them.

Here's the footer:

entries/templates/entries/footer.html

```
<div class="footer">
  Go back <a href="{% url "home" %}">home</a>.
</div>
```

It gives us a nice link to the home page.

The home page template is the following:

entries/templates/entries/home.html

```
{% extends "entries/base.html" %}
{% block title%}Welcome to the Entry website.{% endblock title %}

{% block page-content %}
  <h1>Welcome {{ user.first_name }}!</h1>

  <div class="home-option">To see the list of your entries
    please click <a href="{% url "entries" %}">here.</a>
  </div>
  <div class="home-option">To insert a new entry please click
    <a href="{% url "insert" %}">here.</a>
  </div>
  <div class="home-option">To login as another user please click
    <a href="{% url "logout" %}">here.</a>
  </div>
    <div class="home-option">To go to the admin panel
    please click <a href="{% url "admin:index" %}">here.</a>
  </div>
{% endblock page-content %}
```

It extends the `base.html` template, and overrides `title` and `page-content`. You can see that basically all it does is provide four links to the user. These are the list of entries, the insert page, the logout page, and the admin page. All of this is done without hardcoding a single URL, through the use of the `{% url ... %}` tag, which is the template equivalent of the `reverse` function.

The template for inserting an `Entry` is as follows:

`entries/templates/entries/insert.html`

```
{% extends "entries/base.html" %}
{% block title%}Insert a new Entry{% endblock title %}

{% block page-content %}
  {% if messages %}
    {% for message in messages %}
      <p class="{{ message.tags }}">{{ message }}</p>
    {% endfor %}
  {% endif %}

  <h1>Insert a new Entry</h1>
  <form action="{% url "insert" %}" method="post">
    {% csrf_token %}{{ form.as_p }}
    <input type="submit" value="Insert">
  </form><br>
{% endblock page-content %}

{% block footer %}
  <div><a href="{% url "entries" %}">See your entries.</a></div>
  {% include "entries/footer.html" %}
{% endblock footer %}
```

There is some conditional logic at the beginning to display messages, if any, and then we define the form. Django gives us the ability to render a form by simply calling `{{ form.as_p }}` (alternatively, `form.as_ul` or `form.as_table`). This creates all the necessary fields and labels for us. The difference between the three commands is in the way the form is laid out: as a paragraph, as an unordered list or as a table. We only need to wrap it in form tags and add a submit button. This behavior was designed for our convenience; we need the freedom to shape that `<form>` tag as we want, so Django isn't intrusive on that. Also, note that `{% csrf_token %}`. It will be rendered into a token by Django and will become part of the data sent to the server on submission. This way Django will be able to verify that the request was from an allowed source, thus avoiding the aforementioned *cross-site request forgery* issue. Did you see how we handled the token when we wrote the view for the `Entry` insertion? Exactly. We didn't write a single line of code for it. Django takes care of it automatically thanks to a **middleware** class (`CsrfViewMiddleware`). Please refer to the official Django documentation to explore this subject further.

For this page, we also use the footer block to display a link to the home page. Finally, we have the list template, which is the most interesting one.

entries/templates/entries/list.html

```
{% extends "entries/base.html" %}
{% block title%} Entries list {% endblock title %}

{% block page-content %}
 {% if entries %}
  <h1>Your entries ({{ entries|length }} found)</h1>
  <div><a href="{% url "insert" %}">Insert new entry.</a></div>

  <table class="entries-table">
   <thead>
     <tr><th>Entry</th><th>Matches</th></tr>
   </thead>
   <tbody>
    {% for entry, match in entries %}
     <tr class="entries-list {% cycle 'light-gray' 'white' %}">
      <td>
        Pattern: <code class="code">
         "{{ entry.pattern }}"</code><br>
        Test String: <code class="code">
         "{{ entry.test_string }}"</code><br>
        Added: {{ entry.date_added }}
      </td>
      <td>
        {% if match %}
         Group: {{ match.0 }}<br>
         Subgroups:
          {{ match.1|default_if_none:"none" }}<br>
         Group Dict: {{ match.2|default_if_none:"none" }}
        {% else %}
         No matches found.
        {% endif %}
      </td>
     </tr>
    {% endfor %}
   </tbody>
  </table>
 {% else %}
  <h1>You have no entries</h1>
  <div><a href="{% url "insert" %}">Insert new entry.</a></div>
 {% endif %}
{% endblock page-content %}
```

```
{% block footer %}
  {% include "entries/footer.html" %}
{% endblock footer %}
```

It may take you a while to get used to the template language, but really, all there is to it is the creation of a table using a `for` loop. We start by checking if there are any entries and, if so, we create a table. There are two columns, one for the `Entry`, and the other for the match.

In the `Entry` column, we display the `Entry` object (apart from the user) and in the `Matches` column, we display that 3-tuple we created in the `EntryListView`. Note that to access the attributes of an object, we use the same dot syntax we use in Python, for example `{{ entry.pattern }}` or `{{ entry.test_string }}`, and so on.

When dealing with lists and tuples, we cannot access items using the square brackets syntax, so we use the dot one as well (`{{ match.0 }}` is equivalent to `match[0]`, and so on.). We also use a filter, through the pipe (`|`) operator to display a custom value if a match is `None`.

The Django template language (which is not properly Python) is kept simple for a precise reason. If you find yourself limited by the language, it means you're probably trying to do something in the template that should actually be done in the view, where that logic is more relevant.

Allow me to show you a couple of screenshots of the *list* and *insert* templates. This is what the list of entries looks like for my father:

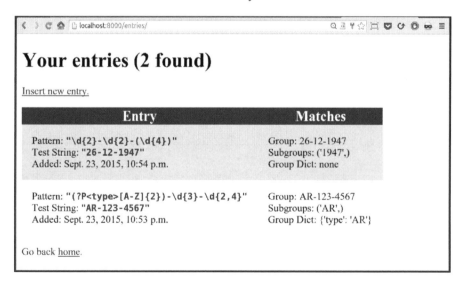

Note how the use of the cycle tag alternates the background color of the rows from white to light gray. Those classes are defined in the `main.css` file.

The `Entry` insertion page is smart enough to provide a few different scenarios. When you land on it at first, it presents you with just an empty form. If you fill it in correctly, it will display a nice message for you (see the following picture). However, if you fail to fill in both fields, it will display an error message before them, alerting you that those fields are required.

Note also the custom footer, which includes both a link to the entries list and a link to the home page:

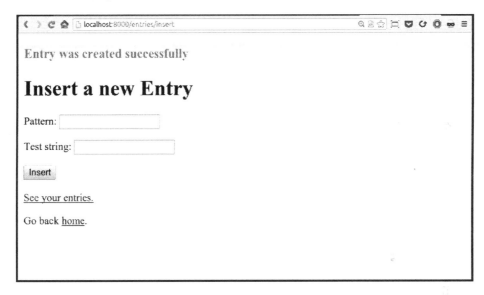

And that's it! You can play around with the CSS styles if you wish. Download the code for the book and have fun exploring and extending this project. Add something else to the model, create and apply a migration, play with the templates, there's lots to do!

Django is a very powerful framework, and offers so much more than what I've been able to show you in this chapter, so you definitely want to check it out. The beauty of it is that it's Python, so reading its source code is a very useful exercise.

The future of web development

Computer science is a very young subject, compared to other branches of science that have existed alongside humankind for centuries or more. One of its main characteristics is that it moves extremely fast. It leaps forward with such speed that, in just a few years, you can see changes that are comparable to real world changes that took a century to happen. Therefore, as a coder, you must pay attention to what happens in this world, all the time.

Something that is happening now is that because powerful computers are now quite cheap and almost everyone has access to them, the trend is to try and avoid putting too much workload on the backend, and let the frontend handle part of it. Therefore, in the last few years, JavaScript frameworks and libraries like jQuery and Backbone have become very popular and web development has shifted from a paradigm where the backend takes care of handling data, preparing it, and serving it to the frontend to display it, to a paradigm where the backend is sometimes just used as an API, a sheer data provider. The frontend fetches the data from the backend with an API call, and then it takes care of the rest. This shift facilitates the existence of paradigms like **Single-Page Application** (**SPA**), where, ideally, the whole page is loaded once and then evolves, based on the content that usually comes from the backend. E-commerce websites that load the results of a search in a page that doesn't refresh the surrounding structure, are made with similar techniques. Browsers can perform asynchronous calls (**AJAX**) that can return data which can be read, manipulated and injected back into the page with JavaScript code.

So, if you're planning to work on web development, I strongly suggest you to get acquainted with JavaScript (if you're not already), and also with APIs. In the last few pages of this chapter, I'll give you an example of how to make a simple API using two different Python microframeworks: Flask and Falcon.

Writing a Flask view

Flask (`http://flask.pocoo.org/`) is a Python microframework. It provides fewer features than Django, but it's supposedly faster and quicker to get up and running. To be honest, getting Django up and running nowadays is also very quickly done, but Flask is so popular that it's good to see an example of it, nonetheless.

In your `ch10` folder, create a `flask` folder with the following structure:

```
$ tree -A flask  # from the ch10 folder
flask
├── main.py
└── templates
    └── main.html
```

Basically, we're going to code two simple files: a Flask application and an HTML template. Flask uses Jinja2 as template engine. It's extremely popular and very fast, and just recently even Django has started to offer native support for it, which is something that Python coders have longed for, for a long time.

flask/templates/main.html

```html
<!doctype html>
<title>Hello from Flask</title>
<h1>
  {% if name %}
    Hello {{ name }}!
  {% else %}
    Hello shy person!
  {% endif %}
</h1>
```

The template is almost offensively simple; all it does is to change the greeting according to the presence of the name variable. A bit more interesting is the Flask application that renders it:

flask/main.py

```python
from flask import Flask, render_template

app = Flask(__name__)

@app.route('/')
@app.route('/<name>')
def hello(name=None):
    return render_template('main.html', name=name)

if __name__ == '__main__':
    app.run()
```

We create an app object, which is a Flask application. We only feed the fully-qualified name of the module, which is stored in __name__.

Then, we write a simple hello view, which takes an optional name argument. In the body of the view, we simply render the main.html template, passing to it the name argument, regardless of its value.

What's interesting is the routing. Differently from Django's way of tying up views and URLs (the urls.py module), in Flask you decorate your view with one or more @app.route decorators. In this case, we accept both the root URL without anything else, or with name information.

Change into the `flask` folder and type (make sure you have Flask installed with `$ pip install flask`):

```
$ python main.py
```

You can open a browser and go to `http://127.0.0.1:5000/`. This URL has no name information; therefore, you will see **Hello shy person!** It is written all nice and big. Try to add something to that URL like `http://127.0.0.1:5000/Adriano`. Hit *Enter* and the page will change to **Hello Adriano!**.

Of course, Flask offers you much more than this but we don't have the room to see a more complex example. It's definitely worth exploring, though. Several projects use it successfully and it's fun and it is nice to create websites or APIs with it. Flask's author, Armin Ronacher, is a successful and very prolific coder. He also created or collaborated on several other interesting projects like Werkzeug, Jinja2, Click, and Sphinx.

Building a JSON quote server in Falcon

Falcon (`http://falconframework.org/`) is another microframework written in Python, which was designed to be light, fast and flexible. I think this relatively young project will evolve to become something really popular due to its speed, which is impressive, so I'm happy to show you a tiny example using it.

We're going to build a view that returns a randomly chosen quote from the *Buddha*.

In your `ch10` folder, create a new one called `falcon`. We'll have two files: `quotes.py` and `main.py`. To run this example, install Falcon and Gunicorn (`$ pip install falcon gunicorn`). Falcon is the framework, and **Gunicorn (Green Unicorn)** is a Python WSGI HTTP Server for Unix (which, in layman terms, means the technology that is used to run the server). When you're all set up, start by creating the `quotes.py` file.

`falcon/quotes.py`

```
quotes = [
    "Thousands of candles can be lighted from a single candle, "
    "and the life of the candle will not be shortened. "
    "Happiness never decreases by being shared.",
    ...
    "Peace comes from within. Do not seek it without.",
]
```

You will find the complete list of quotes in the source code for this book. If you don't have it, you can also fill in your favorite quotes. Note that not every line has a comma at the end. In Python, it's possible to concatenate strings like that, as long as they are in brackets (or braces). It's called **implicit concatenation**.

The code for the main app is not long, but it is interesting:

`falcon/main.py`

```
import json
import random
import falcon
from quotes import quotes

class QuoteResource:
    def on_get(self, req, resp):
        quote = {
            'quote': random.choice(quotes),
            'author': 'The Buddha'
        }
        resp.body = json.dumps(quote)

api = falcon.API()
api.add_route('/quote', QuoteResource())
```

Let's start with the class. In Django we had a `get` method, in Flask we defined a function, and here we write an `on_get` method, a naming style that reminds me of C# event handlers. It takes a request and a response argument, both automatically fed by the framework. In its body, we define a dict with a randomly chosen quote, and the author information. Then we dump that dict to a JSON string and set the response body to its value. We don't need to return anything, Falcon will take care of it for us.

At the end of the file, we create the Falcon application, and we call `add_route` on it to tie the handler we have just written to the URL we want.

When you're all set up, change to the `falcon` folder and type:

`$ gunicorn main:api`

Then, make a request (or simply open the page with your browser) to `http://127.0.0.1:8000/quote`. When I did it, I got this JSON in response:

```
{
    quote: "The mind is everything. What you think you become.",
    author: "The Buddha"
}
```

Whatever the framework you end up using for your web development, try and keep yourself informed about other choices too. Sometimes you may be in situations where a different framework is the right way to go, and having a working knowledge of different tools will give you an advantage.

Summary

In this chapter, we caught a glimpse of web development. We talked about important concepts like the DRY philosophy and the concept of a framework as a tool that provides us with many things we need in order to write code to serve requests. We also talked about the MTV pattern, and how nicely these three layers play together to realize a request-response path.

Later on, we briefly introduced regular expressions, which is a subject of paramount importance, and it's the layer which provides the tools for URL routing.

There are many different frameworks out there, and Django is definitely one of the best and most widely used, so it's definitely worth exploring, especially its source code, which is very well written.

There are other very interesting and important frameworks too, like Flask. They provide fewer features but, in general, they are faster, both in execution time and to set up. One that is extremely fast is the relatively young Falcon project, whose benchmarks are outstanding.

It's important to get a solid understanding of how the request-response mechanism works, and how the Web in general works, so that eventually it won't matter too much which framework you have to use. You will be able to pick it up quickly because it will only be a matter of getting familiar with a way of doing something you already know a lot about.

Explore at least three frameworks and try to come up with different use cases to decide which one of them could be the ideal choice. When you are able to make that choice, you will know you have a good enough understanding of them.

The next chapter is about debugging and troubleshooting. We'll learn how to deal with errors and issues so that if you get in trouble when coding (don't worry, normally it only happens about all the time), you will be able to quickly find the solution to your problem and move on.

11
Debugging and Troubleshooting

"If debugging is the process of removing software bugs, then programming must be the process of putting them in."

- Edsger W. Dijkstra

In the life of a professional coder, debugging and troubleshooting take up a significant amount of time. Even if you work on the most beautiful codebase ever written by man, there will still be bugs in it, that is guaranteed.

We spend an awful lot of time reading other people's code and, in my opinion, a good software developer is someone who keeps their attention high, even when they're reading code that is not reported to be wrong or buggy.

Being able to debug code efficiently and quickly is a skill that any coder needs to keep improving. Some think that because they have read the manual, they're fine, but the reality is, the number of variables in the game is so big that there is no manual. There are guidelines that one can follow, but there is no magic book that will teach you everything you need to know in order to become good at this.

I feel that on this particular subject, I have learned the most from my colleagues. It amazes me to observe someone very skilled attacking a problem. I enjoy seeing the steps they take, the things they verify to exclude possible causes, and the way they consider the suspects that eventually lead them to the solution to the problem.

Every colleague we work with can teach us something, or surprise us with a fantastic guess that turns out to be the right one. When that happens, don't just remain in wonderment (or worse, in envy), but seize the moment and ask them how they got to that guess and why. The answer will allow you to see if there is something you can study in deep later on so that, maybe next time, you'll be the one who will catch the bug.

Some bugs are very easy to spot. They come out of coarse mistakes and, once you see the effects of those mistakes, it's easy to find a solution that fixes the problem.

But there are other bugs which are much more subtle, much more slippery, and require true expertise, and a great deal of creativity and out-of-the-box thinking, to be dealt with.

The worst of all, at least for me, are the nondeterministic ones. These sometimes happen, and sometimes don't. Some happen only in environment A but not in environment B, even though A and B are supposed to be exactly the same. Those bugs are the true evil ones, and they can drive you crazy.

And of course, bugs don't just happen in the sandbox, right? With your boss telling you "*don't worry! take your time to fix this, have lunch first!*". Nope. They happen on a Friday at half past five, when your brain is cooked and you just want to go home. It's in those moments, when everyone is getting upset in a split second, when your boss is breathing on your neck, that you have to be able to keep calm. And I do mean it. That's the most important skill to have if you want to be able to fight bugs effectively. If you allow your mind to get stressed, say goodbye to creative thinking, to logic deduction, and to everything you need at that moment. So take a deep breath, sit properly, and focus.

In this chapter, I will try to demonstrate some useful techniques that you can employ according to the severity of the bug, and a few suggestions that will hopefully boost your weapons against bugs and issues.

Debugging techniques

In this part, I'll present you with the most common techniques, the ones I use most often, however, please don't consider this list to be exhaustive.

Debugging with print

This is probably the easiest technique of all. It's not very effective, it cannot be used everywhere and it requires access to both the source code and a terminal that will run it (and therefore show the results of the print function calls).

However, in many situations, this is still a quick and useful way to debug. For example, if you are developing a Django website and what happens in a page is not what would you expect, you can fill the view with prints and keep an eye on the console while you reload the page. I've probably done it a million times.

When you scatter calls to `print` in your code, you normally end up in a situation where you duplicate a lot of debugging code, either because you're printing a timestamp (like we did when we were measuring how fast list comprehensions and generators were), or because you have to somehow build a string of some sort that you want to display.

Another issue is that it's extremely easy to forget calls to `print` in your code.

So, for these reasons, rather than using a bare call to `print`, I sometimes prefer to code a custom function. Let's see how.

Debugging with a custom function

Having a custom function in a snippet that you can quickly grab and paste into the code, and then use to debug, can be very useful. If you're fast, you can always code one on the fly. The important thing is to code it in a way that it won't leave stuff around when you eventually remove the calls and its definition, therefore *it's important to code it in a way that is completely self-contained*. Another good reason for this requirement is that it will avoid potential name clashes with the rest of the code.

Let's see an example of such a function.

custom.py

```python
def debug(*msg, print_separator=True):
    print(*msg)
    if print_separator:
        print('-' * 40)

debug('Data is ...')
debug('Different', 'Strings', 'Are not a problem')
debug('After while loop', print_separator=False)
```

In this case, I am using a keyword-only argument to be able to print a separator, which is a line of 40 dashes.

The function is very simple, I just redirect whatever is in `msg` to a call to `print` and, if `print_separator` is `True`, I print a line separator. Running the code will show:

```
$ python custom.py
Data is ...
----------------------------------------
Different Strings Are not a problem
----------------------------------------
After while loop
```

As you can see, there is no separator after the last line.

This is just one easy way to somehow augment a simple call to the `print` function. Let's see how we can calculate a time difference between calls, using one of Python's tricky features to our advantage.

custom_timestamp.py

```python
from time import sleep

def debug(*msg, timestamp=[None]):
    print(*msg)
    from time import time  # local import
    if timestamp[0] is None:
        timestamp[0] = time()   #1
    else:
        now = time()
        print(' Time elapsed: {:.3f}s'.format(
            now - timestamp[0]))
        timestamp[0] = now   #2

debug('Entering nasty piece of code...')
sleep(.3)
debug('First step done.')
sleep(.5)
debug('Second step done.')
```

This is a bit trickier, but still quite simple. First notice we import the `time` function from the `time` module from the `debug` function. This allows us to avoid having to add that import outside of the function, and maybe forget it there.

Take a look at how I defined `timestamp`. It's a list, of course, but what's important here is that it is a *mutable* object. This means that it will be set up when Python parses the function and it will retain its value throughout different calls. Therefore, if we put a timestamp in it after each call, we can keep track of time without having to use an external global variable. I borrowed this trick from my studies on **closures**, a technique that I encourage you to read about because it's very interesting.

Right, so, after having printed whatever message we had to print and importing time, we then inspect the content of the only item in `timestamp`. If it is None, we have no previous reference, therefore we set the value to the current time (#1).

On the other hand, if we have a previous reference, we can calculate a difference (which we nicely format to three decimal digits) and then we finally put the current time again in `timestamp` (#2). It's a nice trick, isn't it?

Running this code shows this result:

```
$ python custom_timestamp.py
Entering nasty piece of code...
First step done.
  Time elapsed: 0.300s
Second step done.
  Time elapsed: 0.501s
```

Whatever is your situation, having a self contained function like this can be very useful.

Inspecting the traceback

We briefly talked about the traceback in *Chapter 7, Testing, Profiling, and Dealing with Exceptions* when we saw several different kinds of exceptions. The traceback gives you information about what happened in your application that went wrong. You get a great help from reading it. Let's see a very small example:

traceback_simple.py

```
d = {'some': 'key'}
key = 'some-other'
print(d[key])
```

We have a dict and we have tried to access a key which isn't in it. You should remember that this will raise a `KeyError` exception. Let's run the code:

```
$ python traceback_simple.py
Traceback (most recent call last):
  File "traceback_simple.py", line 3, in <module>
    print(d[key])
KeyError: 'some-other'
```

You can see that we get all the information we need: the module name, the line that caused the error (both the number and the instruction), and the error itself. With this information, you can go back to the source code and try and understand what's going wrong.

Let's now create a more interesting example that builds on this, and exercises a feature that is only available in Python 3. Imagine that we're validating a dict, working on mandatory fields, therefore we expect them to be there. If not, we need to raise a custom `ValidationError`, that we will trap further upstream in the process that runs the validator (which is not shown here, it could be anything, really). It should be something like this:

```
traceback_validator.py

    class ValidatorError(Exception):
        """Raised when accessing a dict results in KeyError. """

    d = {'some': 'key'}
    mandatory_key = 'some-other'
    try:
        print(d[mandatory_key])
    except KeyError:
        raise ValidatorError(
            '`{}` not found in d.'.format(mandatory_key))
```

We define a custom exception that is raised when the mandatory key isn't there. Note that its body consists of its documentation string so we don't need to add any other statements.

Very simply, we define a dummy dict and try to access it using `mandatory_key`. We trap the `KeyError` and raise `ValidatorError` when that happens. The purpose of doing this is that we may also want to raise `ValidatorError` in other circumstances, not necessarily as a consequence of a mandatory key being missing. This technique allows us to run the validation in a simple `try`/`except` that only cares about `ValidatorError`.

The thing is, in Python 2, this code would just display the last exception (ValidatorError), which means we would lose the information about the KeyError that precedes it. In Python 3, this behavior has changed and exceptions are now chained so that you have a much better information report when something happens. The code produces this result:

```
$ python traceback_validator.py
Traceback (most recent call last):
  File "traceback_validator.py", line 7, in <module>
    print(d[mandatory_key])
KeyError: 'some-other'


During handling of the above exception, another exception occurred:


Traceback (most recent call last):
  File "traceback_validator.py", line 10, in <module>
    '`{}` not found in d.'.format(mandatory_key))
__main__.ValidatorError: `some-other` not found in d.
```

This is brilliant, because we can see the traceback of the exception that led us to raise ValidationError, as well as the traceback for the ValidationError itself.

I had a nice discussion with one of my reviewers about the traceback you get from the pip installer. He was having trouble setting everything up in order to review the code for *Chapter 9, Data Science*. His fresh Ubuntu installation was missing a few libraries that were needed by the pip packages in order to run correctly.

The reason he was blocked was that he was trying to fix the errors displayed in the traceback starting from the top one. I suggested that he started from the bottom one instead, and fix that. The reason was that, if the installer had gotten to that last line, I guess that before that, whatever error may have occurred, it was still possible to recover from it. Only after the last line, pip decided it wasn't possible to continue any further, and therefore I started fixing that one. Once the libraries required to fix that error had been installed, everything else went smoothly.

Reading a traceback can be tricky, and my friend was lacking the necessary experience to address this problem correctly, therefore, if you end up in the same situation, don't be discouraged, and try to shake things up a bit, don't take anything for granted.

Python has a huge and wonderful community and it's very unlikely that, when you encounter a problem, you're the first one to see it, so open a browser and search. By doing so, your searching skills will also improve because you will have to trim the error down to the minimum but essential set of details that will make your search effective.

If you want to play and understand the traceback a bit better, in the standard library there is a module called, surprise surprise, `traceback` that you can use. It provides a standard interface to extract, format, and print stack traces of Python programs, mimicking exactly the behavior of the Python interpreter when it prints a stack trace.

Using the Python debugger

Another very effective way of debugging Python is to use the Python debugger: **pdb**. If you are addicted to the IPython console, like me, you should definitely check out the **ipdb** library. *ipdb* augments the standard *pdb* interface like IPython does with the Python console.

There are several different ways of using this debugger (whichever version, it is not important), but the most common one consists of simply setting a breakpoint and running the code. When Python reaches the breakpoint, execution is suspended and you get console access to that point so that you can inspect all the names, and so on. You can also alter data on the fly to change the flow of the program.

As a toy example, let's pretend we have a parser that is raising a `KeyError` because a key is missing in a dict. The dict is from a JSON payload that we cannot control, and we just want, for the time being, to cheat and pass that control, since we're interested in what comes afterwards. Let's see how we could intercept this moment, inspect the data, fix it and get to the bottom, with *ipdb*.

ipdebugger.py

```
# d comes from a JSON payload we don't control
d = {'first': 'v1', 'second': 'v2', 'fourth': 'v4'}
# keys also comes from a JSON payload we don't control
keys = ('first', 'second', 'third', 'fourth')

def do_something_with_value(value):
    print(value)

for key in keys:
    do_something_with_value(d[key])

print('Validation done.')
```

As you can see, this code will break when `key` gets the value `'third'`, which is missing in the dict. Remember, we're pretending that both `d` and `keys` come dynamically from a JSON payload we don't control, so we need to inspect them in order to fix `d` and pass the `for` loop. If we run the code as it is, we get the following:

```
$ python ipdebugger.py
v1
v2
Traceback (most recent call last):
  File "ipdebugger.py", line 10, in <module>
    do_something_with_value(d[key])
KeyError: 'third'
```

So we see that that `key` is missing from the dict, but since every time we run this code we may get a different dict or `keys` tuple, this information doesn't really help us. Let's inject a call to *ipdb*.

ipdebugger_ipdb.py

```
    # d comes from a JSON payload we don't control
    d = {'first': 'v1', 'second': 'v2', 'fourth': 'v4'}
    # keys also comes from a JSON payload we don't control
    keys = ('first', 'second', 'third', 'fourth')

    def do_something_with_value(value):
        print(value)

    import ipdb
    ipdb.set_trace()  # we place a breakpoint here

    for key in keys:
        do_something_with_value(d[key])

    print('Validation done.')
```

If we now run this code, things get interesting (note that your output may vary a little and that all the comments in this output were added by me):

```
$ python ipdebugger_ipdb.py
> /home/fab/srv/l.p/ch11/ipdebugger_ipdb.py(12)<module>()
     11
---> 12 for key in keys:  # this is where the breakpoint comes
     13     do_something_with_value(d[key])
```

```
ipdb> keys  # let's inspect the keys tuple
('first', 'second', 'third', 'fourth')
ipdb> !d.keys()  # now the keys of d
dict_keys(['first', 'fourth', 'second'])  # we miss 'third'
ipdb> !d['third'] = 'something dark side...'  # let's put it in
ipdb> c  # ... and continue
v1
v2
something dark side...
v4
Validation done.
```

This is very interesting. First, note that, when you reach a breakpoint, you're served a console that tells you where you are (the Python module) and which line is the next one to be executed. You can, at this point, perform a bunch of exploratory actions, such as inspecting the code before and after the next line, printing a stacktrace, interacting with the objects, and so on. Please consult the official Python documentation on *pdb* to learn more about this. In our case, we first inspect the keys tuple. After that, we inspect the keys of d.

Have you noticed that exclamation mark I prepended to d? It's needed because d is a command in the *pdb* interface that moves the frame (*d*)own.

 I indicate commands within the *ipdb* shell with this notation: each command is activated by one letter, which typically is the first letter of the command name. So, *d* for *down*, *n* for *next*, and *s* for *step* become, more concisely, (*d*)own, (*n*)ext and (*s*)tep.

I guess this is a good enough reason to have better names, right? Indeed, but I needed to show you this, so I chose to use d. In order to tell *pdb* that we're not yielding a (*d*)own command, we put "!" in front of d and we're fine.

After seeing the keys of d, we see that 'third' is missing, so we put it in ourselves (could this be dangerous? think about it). Finally, now that all the keys are in, we type c, which means (*c*)ontinue.

pdb also gives you the ability to proceed with your code one line at a time using (*n*)ext, to (*s*)tep into a function for deeper analysis, or handling breaks with (*b*)reak. For a complete list of commands, please refer to the documentation or type (*h*)elp in the console.

You can see from the output that we could finally get to the end of the validation.

pdb (or *ipdb*) are invaluable tools that I use every day, I couldn't live without them. So, go and have fun, set a breakpoint somewhere and try and inspect, follow the official documentation and try the commands in your code to see their effect and learn them well.

Inspecting log files

Another way of debugging a misbehaving application is to inspect its log files. **Log files** are special files in which an application writes down all sorts of things, normally related to what's going on inside of it. If an important procedure is started, I would typically expect a line for that in the logs. It is the same when it finishes, and possibly for what happens inside of it.

Errors need to be logged so that when a problem happens we can inspect what went wrong by taking a look at the information in the log files.

There are many different ways to set up a logger in Python. Logging is very malleable and you can configure it. In a nutshell, there are normally four players in the game: loggers, handlers, filters, and formatters:

- **Loggers** expose the interface that the application code uses directly
- **Handlers** send the log records (created by loggers) to the appropriate destination
- **Filters** provide a finer grained facility for determining which log records to output
- **Formatters** specify the layout of the log records in the final output

Logging is performed by calling methods on instances of the Logger class. Each line you log has a level. The levels normally used are: DEBUG, INFO, WARNING, ERROR, and CRITICAL. You can import them from the logging module. They are in order of severity and it's very important to use them properly because they will help you filter the contents of a log file based on what you're searching for. Log files usually become extremely big so it's very important to have the information in them written properly so that you can find it quickly when it matters.

You can log to a file but you can also log to a network location, to a queue, to a console, and so on. In general, if you have an architecture that is deployed on one machine, logging to a file is acceptable, but when your architecture spans over multiple machines (such as in the case of **service-oriented architectures**), it's very useful to implement a centralized solution for logging so that all log messages coming from each service can be stored and investigated in a single place. It helps a lot, otherwise you can really go crazy trying to correlate giant files from several different sources to figure out what went wrong.

A **service-oriented architecture (SOA)** is an architectural pattern in software design in which application components provide services to other components via a communications protocol, typically over a network. The beauty of this system is that, when coded properly, each service can be written in the most appropriate language to serve its purpose. The only thing that matters is the communication with the other services, which needs to happen via a common format so that data exchange can be done.

Here, I will present you with a very simple logging example. We will log a few messages to a file:

log.py

```python
import logging

logging.basicConfig(
    filename='ch11.log',
    level=logging.DEBUG,   # minimum level capture in the file
    format='[%(asctime)s] %(levelname)s:%(message)s',
    datefmt='%m/%d/%Y %I:%M:%S %p')

mylist = [1, 2, 3]
logging.info('Starting to process `mylist`...')

for position in range(4):
    try:
        logging.debug('Value at position {} is {}'.format(
            position, mylist[position]))
    except IndexError:
        logging.exception('Faulty position: {}'.format(position))

logging.info('Done parsing `mylist`.')
```

Let's go through it line by line. First, we import the `logging` module, then we set up a basic configuration. In general, a production logging configuration is much more complicated than this, but I wanted to keep things as easy as possible. We specify a filename, the minimum logging level we want to capture in the file, and the message format. We'll log the date and time information, the level, and the message.

I will start by logging an `info` message that tells me we're about to process our list. Then, I will log (this time using the DEBUG level, by using the `debug` function) which is the value at some position. I'm using `debug` here because I want to be able to filter out these logs in the future (by setting the minimum level to `logging.INFO` or more), because I might have to handle very big lists and I don't want to log all the values.

If we get an `IndexError` (and we do, since I'm looping over `range(4)`), we call `logging.exception()`, which is the same as `logging.error()`, but it also prints the traceback.

At the end of the code, I log another `info` message saying we're done. The result is this:

```
[10/08/2015 04:17:06 PM]  INFO:Starting to process `mylist`...

[10/08/2015 04:17:06 PM]  DEBUG:Value at position 0 is 1

[10/08/2015 04:17:06 PM]  DEBUG:Value at position 1 is 2

[10/08/2015 04:17:06 PM]  DEBUG:Value at position 2 is 3

[10/08/2015 04:17:06 PM]  ERROR:Faulty position: 3

Traceback (most recent call last):

  File "log.py", line 15, in <module>

    position, mylist[position]))

IndexError: list index out of range

[10/08/2015 04:17:06 PM]  INFO:Done parsing `mylist`.
```

This is exactly what we need to be able to debug an application that is running on a box, and not on our console. We can see what went on, the traceback of any exception raised, and so on.

> The example presented here only scratches the surface of logging. For a more in-depth explanation, you can find a very nice introduction in the how to (`https://docs.python.org/3.4/howto/logging.html`) section of the official Python documentation.

Logging is an art, you need to find a good balance between logging everything and logging nothing. Ideally, you should log anything that you need to make sure your application is working correctly, and possibly all errors or exceptions.

Other techniques

In this final section, I'd like to demonstrate briefly a couple of techniques that you may find useful.

Profiling

We talked about profiling in *Chapter 7, Testing, Profiling, and Dealing with Exceptions*, and I'm only mentioning it here because profiling can sometimes explain weird errors that are due to a component being too slow. Especially when networking is involved, having an idea of the timings and latencies your application has to go through is very important in order to understand what may be going on when problems arise, therefore I suggest you get acquainted with profiling techniques also for a troubleshooting perspective.

Assertions

Assertions are a nice way to make your code ensure your assumptions are verified. If they are, all proceeds regularly but, if they are not, you get a nice exception that you can work with. Sometimes, instead of inspecting, it's quicker to drop a couple of assertions in the code just to exclude possibilities. Let's see an example:

assertions.py

```
mylist = [1, 2, 3]  # this ideally comes from some place
assert 4 == len(mylist)  # this will break
for position in range(4):
    print(mylist[position])
```

This code simulates a situation in which `mylist` isn't defined by us like that, of course, but we're assuming it has four elements. So we put an assertion there, and the result is this:

```
$ python assertions.py
Traceback (most recent call last):
  File "assertions.py", line 3, in <module>
    assert 4 == len(mylist)
AssertionError
```

This tells us exactly where the problem is.

Where to find information

In the Python official documentation, there is a section dedicated to debugging and profiling, where you can read up about the `bdb` debugger framework, and about modules such as `faulthandler`, `timeit`, `trace`, `tracemalloc`, and of course *pdb*. Just head to the standard library section in the documentation and you'll find all this information very easily.

Troubleshooting guidelines

In this short section, I'll like to give you a few tips that come from my troubleshooting experience.

Using console editors

First, get comfortable using **vim** or **nano** as an editor, and learn the basics of the console. When things break bad you don't have the luxury of your editor with all the bells and whistles there. You have to connect to a box and work from there. So it's a very good idea to be comfortable browsing your production environment with console commands, and be able to edit files using console-based editors such as vi, vim, or nano. Don't let your usual development environment spoil you, because you'll have to pay a price if you do.

Where to inspect

My second suggestion is on where to place your debugging breakpoints. It doesn't matter if you are using `print`, a custom function, or *ipdb*, you still have to choose where to place the calls that provide you with the information, right?

Well, some places are better than others, and there are ways to handle the debugging progression that are better than others.

I normally avoid placing a breakpoint in an `if` clause because, if that clause is not exercised, I lose the chance of getting the information I wanted. Sometimes it's not easy or quick to get to the breakpoint, so think carefully before placing them.

Another important thing is where to start. Imagine that you have 100 lines of code that handle your data. Data comes in at line 1, and somehow it's wrong at line 100. You don't know where the bug is, so what do you do? You can place a breakpoint at line 1 and patiently go through all the lines, checking your data. In the worst case scenario, 99 lines later (and many coffee cups) you spot the bug. So, consider using a different approach.

You start at line 50, and inspect. If the data is good, it means the bug happens later, in which case you place your next breakpoint at line 75. If the data at line 50 is already bad, you go on by placing a breakpoint at line 25. Then, you repeat. Each time, you move either backwards or forwards, by half the jump you did last time.

In our worst case scenario, your debugging would go from 1, 2, 3, ..., 99 to 50, 75, 87, 93, 96, ..., 99 which is way faster. In fact, it's logarithmic. This searching technique is called **binary search**, it's based on a divide and conquer approach and it's very effective, so try to master it.

Using tests to debug

Do you remember *Chapter 7, Testing, Profiling, and Dealing with Exceptions*, about tests? Well, if we have a bug and all tests are passing, it means something is wrong or missing in our test codebase. So, one approach is to modify the tests in such a way that they cater for the new edge case that has been spotted, and then work your way through the code. This approach can be very beneficial, because it makes sure that your bug will be covered by a test when it's fixed.

Monitoring

Monitoring is also very important. Software applications can go completely crazy and have non-deterministic hiccups when they encounter edge case situations such as the network being down, a queue being full, an external component being unresponsive, and so on. In these cases, it's important to have an idea of what was the big picture when the problem happened and be able to correlate it to something related to it in a subtle, perhaps mysterious way.

You can monitor API endpoints, processes, web pages availability and load time, and basically almost everything that you can code. In general, when starting an application from scratch, it can be very useful to design it keeping in mind how you want to monitor it.

Summary

In this short chapter, we saw different techniques and suggestions to debug and troubleshoot our code. Debugging is an activity that is always part of a software developer's work, so it's important to be good at it.

If approached with the correct attitude, it can be fun and rewarding.

We saw techniques to inspect our code base on functions, logging, debuggers, traceback information, profiling, and assertions. We saw simple examples of most of them and we also talked about a set of guidelines that will help when it comes to face the fire.

Just *remember to always stay calm and focused*, and debugging will be easier already. This too, is a skill that needs to be learned and it's the most important. An agitated and stressed mind cannot work properly, logically and creatively, therefore, if you don't strengthen it, it will be hard for you to put all of your knowledge to good use.

In the next chapter, we will end the book with another small project whose goal is to leave you more thirsty than you were when you started this journey with me.

Ready?

12

Summing Up – A Complete Example

"Do not dwell in the past, do not dream of the future, concentrate the mind on the present moment."

– The Shakyamuni Buddha

In this chapter, I will show you one last project. If you've worked well in the rest of the book, this example should be easy. I tried my best to craft it in a way that it will neither be too hard for those who have only read the book, nor too simple for those who also took the time to work on the examples, and maybe have read up on the links and topics I suggested.

The challenge

One problem that we all have these days is remembering passwords. We have passwords for everything: websites, phones, cards, bank accounts, and so on. The amount of information we have to memorize is just too much, so many people end up using the same password over and over again. This is very bad, of course, so at some point, tools were invented to alleviate this problem. One of these tools is called **KeepassX**, and basically it works like this: you start the software by setting up a special password called **master password**. Once inside, you store a record for each password you need to memorize, for example, your e-mail account, the bank website, credit card information, and so on. When you close the software, it encrypts the database used to store all that information, so that the data can only be accessed by the owner of the master password. Therefore, kind of in a *Lord of The Rings* fashion, by just owning one password, you rule them all.

Our implementation

Our goal in this chapter is to create something similar but web-based, and the way I want to implement it is by writing two applications.

One will be an API written in Falcon. Its purpose will be twofold, it will be able to both generate and validate passwords. It will provide the caller with information about the validity and a score which should indicate how strong the password is.

The second application is a Django website, which will provide the interface to handle records. Each record will retain information such as the username, e-mail, password, URL, and so on. It will show a list of all the records, and it will allow the user to create, update and delete them. Passwords will be encrypted before being stored in the database.

The purpose of the whole project is, therefore, to mimic the way KeepassX works, even though it is in a much simpler fashion. It will be up to you, if you like this idea, to develop it further in order to add other features and make it more secure. I will make sure to give you some suggestions on how to extend it, towards the end.

This chapter will therefore be quite dense, code-wise. It's the price I have to pay for giving you an interesting example in a restricted amount of space.

Before we start, please make sure you are comfortable with the projects presented in *Chapter 10, Web Development Done Right* so that you're familiar with the basics of web development. Make sure also that you have installed all the `pip` packages needed for this project: `django`, `falcon`, `cryptography`, and `nose-parameterized`. If you download the source code for the book, you'll find everything you need to install in the `requirements` folder, while the code for this chapter will be in `ch12`.

Implementing the Django interface

I hope you're comfortable with the concepts presented in *Chapter 10, Web Development Done Right* which was mostly about Django. If you haven't read it, this is probably a good time, before reading on here.

The setup

In your root folder (`ch12`, for me), which will contain the root for the interface and the root for the API, start by running this command:

```
$ django-admin startproject pwdweb
```

This will create the structure for a Django project, which we know well by now.
I'll show you the final structure of the interface project here:

```
$ tree -A pwdweb
pwdweb
├── db.sqlite3
├── manage.py
├── pwdweb
│   ├── __init__.py
│   ├── settings.py
│   ├── urls.py
│   └── wsgi.py
└── records
    ├── admin.py
    ├── forms.py
    ├── __init__.py
    ├── migrations
    │   ├── 0001_initial.py
    │   └── __init__.py
    ├── models.py
    ├── static
    │   └── records
    │       ├── css
    │       │   └── main.css
    │       └── js
    │           ├── api.js
    │           └── jquery-2.1.4.min.js
    ├── templates
    │   └── records
    │       ├── base.html
    │       ├── footer.html
    │       ├── home.html
    │       ├── list.html
    │       ├── messages.html
    │       ├── record_add_edit.html
    │       └── record_confirm_delete.html
    ├── templatetags
    │   └── record_extras.py
    ├── urls.py
    └── views.py
```

As usual, don't worry if you don't have all the files, we'll add them gradually.
Change to the pwdweb folder, and make sure Django is correctly set up: $ python
manage.py runserver (ignore the warning about unapplied migrations).

Shut down the server and create an app: $ `python manage.py startapp` `records`. That is excellent, now we can start coding. First things first, let's open `pwdweb/settings.py` and start by adding `'records',` at the end of the `INSTALLED_APP` tuple (note that the comma is included in the code). Then, go ahead and fix the `LANGUAGE_CODE` and `TIME_ZONE` settings according to your preference and finally, add the following line at the bottom:

```
ENCRYPTION_KEY = b'qMhPGx-ROWUDr4veh0ybPRL6viIUNe0vcPDmy67x6CQ='
```

This is a custom encryption key that has nothing to do with Django settings, but we will need it later on, and this is the best place for it to be. Don't worry for now, we'll get back to it.

The model layer

We need to add just one model for the records application: `Record`. This model will represent each record we want to store in the database:

`records/models.py`

```python
from cryptography.fernet import Fernet
from django.conf import settings
from django.db import models

class Record(models.Model):
    DEFAULT_ENCODING = 'utf-8'

    title = models.CharField(max_length=64, unique=True)
    username = models.CharField(max_length=64)
    email = models.EmailField(null=True, blank=True)
    url = models.URLField(max_length=255, null=True, blank=True)
    password = models.CharField(max_length=2048)
    notes = models.TextField(null=True, blank=True)
    created = models.DateTimeField(auto_now_add=True)
    last_modified = models.DateTimeField(auto_now=True)

    def encrypt_password(self):
        self.password = self.encrypt(self.password)

    def decrypt_password(self):
        self.password = self.decrypt(self.password)

    def encrypt(self, plaintext):
        return self.cypher('encrypt', plaintext)
```

```
def decrypt(self, cyphertext):
    return self.cypher('decrypt', cyphertext)

def cypher(self, cypher_func, text):
    fernet = Fernet(settings.ENCRYPTION_KEY)
    result = getattr(fernet, cypher_func)(
        self._to_bytes(text))
    return self._to_str(result)

def _to_str(self, bytes_str):
    return bytes_str.decode(self.DEFAULT_ENCODING)

def _to_bytes(self, s):
    return s.encode(self.DEFAULT_ENCODING)
```

Firstly, we set the DEFAULT_ENCODING class attribute to 'utf-8', which is the most popular type of encoding for the web (and not only the web). We set this attribute on the class to avoid hardcoding a string in more than one place.

Then, we proceed to set up all the model's fields. As you can see, Django allows you to specify very specific fields, such as EmailField and URLField. The reason why it's better to use these specific fields instead of a plain and simple CharField is we'll get e-mail and URL validation for free when we create a form for this model, which is brilliant.

All the options are quite standard, and we saw them in *Chapter 10, Web Development Done Right* but I want to point out a few things anyway. Firstly, title needs to be unique so that each Record object has a unique title and we don't want to risk having doubles. Each database treats strings a little bit differently, according to how it is set up, which engine it runs, and so on, so I haven't made the title field the primary key for this model, which would have been the natural thing to do. I prefer to avoid the pain of having to deal with weird string errors and I am happy with letting Django add a primary key to the model automatically.

Another option you should understand is the null=True, blank=True couple. The former allows the field to be NULL, which makes it non-mandatory, while the second allows it to be *blank* (that is to say, an empty string). Their use is quite peculiar in Django, so I suggest you to take a look at the official documentation to understand exactly how to use them.

Finally, the dates: created needs to have auto_add_now=True, which will set the current moment in time on the object when it's created. On the other hand, last_modified needs to be updated every time we save the model, hence we set auto_now=True.

After the field definitions, there are a few methods for encrypting and decrypting the password. It is always a very bad idea to save passwords as they are in a database, therefore you should always encrypt them before saving them.

Normally, when saving a password, you encrypt it using a **one way encryption** algorithm (also known as a **one way hash function**). This means that, once you have created the hash, there is no way for you to revert it back to the original password.

This kind of encryption is normally used for authentication: the user puts their username and password in a form and, on submission, the code fetches the hash from the user record in the database and compares it with the hash of the password the user has just put in the form. If the two hashes match, it means that they were produced by the same password, therefore authentication is granted.

In this case though, we need to be able to recover the passwords, otherwise this whole application wouldn't be very useful. Therefore, we will use a so-called **symmetric encryption** algorithm to encrypt them. The way this works is very simple: the password (called **plaintext**) is passed to an *encrypt* function, along with a *secret key*. The algorithm produces an encrypted string (called **cyphertext**) out of them, which is what you store in the database. When you want to recover the password, you will need the cyphertext and the secret key. You feed them to a *decrypt* function, and you get back your original password. This is exactly what we need.

In order to perform symmetric encryption, we need the `cryptography` package, which is why I instructed you to install it.

All the methods in the `Record` class are very simple. `encrypt_password` and `decrypt_password` are shortcuts to `encrypt` and `decrypt` the `password` field and reassign the result to itself.

The `encrypt` and `decrypt` methods are dispatchers for the `cypher` method, and `_to_str` and `_to_bytes` are just a couple of helpers. The `cryptography` library works with *bytes* objects, so we need those helpers to go back and forth between bytes and strings, using a common encoding.

The only interesting logic is in the `cypher` method. I could have coded it directly in the `encrypt` and `decrypt` ones, but that would have resulted in a bit of redundancy, and I wouldn't have had the chance to show you a different way of accessing an object's attribute, so let's analyze the body of `cypher`.

We start by creating an instance of the `Fernet` class, which provides us with the symmetric encryption functionality we need. We set the instance up by passing the secret key in the settings (`ENCRYPTION_KEY`). After creating `fernet`, we need to use it. We can use it to either encrypt or decrypt, according to what value is given to the `cypher_func` parameter. We use `getattr` to get an attribute from an object given the object itself and the name of the attribute. This technique allows us to fetch any attribute from an object dynamically.

The result of `getattr(fernet, cypher_func)`, with `cyper_func` being `'encrypt'`, for example, is the same as `fernet.encrypt`. The `getattr` function returns a method, which we then call with the bytes representation of the text argument. We then return the result, in string format.

Here's what this function is equivalent to when it's called by the encrypt dispatcher:

```
def cypher_encrypt(self, text):
        fernet = Fernet(settings.ENCRYPTION_KEY)
        result = fernet.encrypt(
            self._to_bytes(text))
        return self._to_str(result)
```

When you take the time to understand it properly, you'll see it's not as difficult as it sounds.

So, we have our model, hence it's time to migrate (I hope you remember that this will create the tables in the database for your application):

```
$ python manage.py makemigrations
$ python manage.py migrate
```

Now you should have a nice database with all the tables you need to run the interface application. Go ahead and create a superuser (`$ python manage.py createsuperuser`).

By the way, if you want to generate your own encryption key, it is as easy as this:

```
>>> from cryptography.fernet import Fernet
>>> Fernet.generate_key()
```

A simple form

We need a form for the `Record` model, so we'll use the `ModelForm` technique we saw in *Chapter 10, Web Development Done Right*.

`records/forms.py`

```python
from django.forms import ModelForm, Textarea
from .models import Record


class RecordForm(ModelForm):
    class Meta:
        model = Record
        fields = ['title', 'username', 'email', 'url',
                  'password', 'notes']
        widgets = {'notes': Textarea(
            attrs={'cols': 40, 'rows': 4})}
```

We create a `RecordForm` class that inherits from `ModelForm`, so that the form is created automatically thanks to the introspection capabilities of Django. We only specify which model to use, which fields to display (we exclude the dates, which are handled automatically) and we provide minimal styling for the dimensions of the notes field, which will be displayed using a `Textarea` (which is a multiline text field in HTML).

The view layer

There are a total of five pages in the interface application: home, record list, record creation, record update, and record delete confirmation. Hence, there are five views that we have to write. As you'll see in a moment, Django helps us a lot by giving us views we can reuse with minimum customization. All the code that follows belongs to the `records/views.py` file.

Imports and home view

Just to break the ice, here are the imports and the view for the home page:

```python
from django.contrib import messages
from django.contrib.messages.views import SuccessMessageMixin
from django.core.urlresolvers import reverse_lazy
from django.views.generic import TemplateView
from django.views.generic.edit import (
    CreateView, UpdateView, DeleteView)
from .forms import RecordForm
```

```
from .models import Record

class HomeView(TemplateView):
    template_name = 'records/home.html'
```

We import a few tools from Django. There are a couple of messaging-related objects, a URL lazy reverser, and four different types of view. We also import our `Record` model and `RecordForm`. As you can see, the `HomeView` class consists of only two lines since we only need to specify which template we want to use, the rest just reuses the code from `TemplateView`, as it is. It's so easy, it almost feels like cheating.

Listing all records

After the home view, we can write a view to list all the `Record` instances that we have in the database.

```
class RecordListView(TemplateView):
    template_name = 'records/list.html'

    def get(self, request, *args, **kwargs):
        context = self.get_context_data(**kwargs)
        records = Record.objects.all().order_by('title')   #1
        for record in records:
            record.plaintext = record.decrypt(record.password) #2
        context['records'] = records
        return self.render_to_response(context)
```

All we need to do is sub-class `TemplateView` again, and override the `get` method. We need to do a couple of things: we fetch all the records from the database and sort them by `title` (#1) and then parse all the records in order to add the attribute `plaintext` (#2) onto each of them, to show the original password on the page. Another way of doing this would be to add a read-only property to the `Record` model, to do the decryption on the fly. I'll leave it to you, as a fun exercise, to amend the code to do it.

After recovering and augmenting the records, we put them in the `context` dict and finish as usual by invoking `render_to_response`.

Creating records

Here's the code for the creation view:

```
class EncryptionMixin:
    def form_valid(self, form):
        self.encrypt_password(form)
        return super(EncryptionMixin, self).form_valid(form)
```

```
    def encrypt_password(self, form):
        self.object = form.save(commit=False)
        self.object.encrypt_password()
        self.object.save()


class RecordCreateView(
        EncryptionMixin, SuccessMessageMixin, CreateView):
    template_name = 'records/record_add_edit.html'
    form_class = RecordForm
    success_url = reverse_lazy('records:add')
    success_message = 'Record was created successfully'
```

A part of its logic has been factored out in order to be reused later on in the update view. Let's start with `EncryptionMixin`. All it does is override the `form_valid` method so that, prior to saving a new `Record` instance to the database, we make sure we call `encrypt_password` on the object that results from saving the form. In other words, when the user submits the form to create a new `Record`, if the form validates successfully, then the `form_valid` method is invoked. Within this method what usually happens is that an object is created out of the `ModelForm` instance, like this:

```
    self.object = form.save()
```

We need to interfere with this behavior because running this code as it is would save the record with the original password, which isn't encrypted. So we change this to call `save` on the `form` passing `commit=False`, which creates the `Record` instance out of the `form`, but doesn't attempt to save it in the database. Immediately afterwards, we encrypt the password on that instance and then we can finally call save on it, actually committing it to the database.

Since we need this behavior both for creating and updating records, I have factored it out in a mixin.

 Perhaps, a better solution for this password encryption logic is to create a custom `Field` (inheriting from `CharField` is the easiest way to do it) and add the necessary logic to it, so that when we handle `Record` instances from and to the database, the encryption and decryption logic is performed automatically for us. Though more elegant, this solution needs me to digress and explain a lot more about Django internals, which is too much for the extent of this example. As usual, you can try to do it yourself, if you feel like a challenge.

After creating the `EncryptionMixin` class, we can use it in the `RecordCreateView` class. We also inherit from two other classes: `SuccessMessageMixin` and `CreateView`. The message mixin provides us with the logic to quickly set up a message when creation is successful, and the `CreateView` gives us the necessary logic to create an object from a form.

You can see that all we have to code is some customization: the template name, the form class, and the success message and URL. Everything else is gracefully handled for us by Django.

Updating records

The code to update a `Record` instance is only a tiny bit more complicated. We just need to add some logic to decrypt the password before we populate the form with the record data.

```
class RecordUpdateView(
        EncryptionMixin, SuccessMessageMixin, UpdateView):
    template_name = 'records/record_add_edit.html'
    form_class = RecordForm
    model = Record
    success_message = 'Record was updated successfully'

    def get_context_data(self, **kwargs):
        kwargs['update'] = True
        return super(
            RecordUpdateView, self).get_context_data(**kwargs)

    def form_valid(self, form):
        self.success_url = reverse_lazy(
            'records:edit',
            kwargs={'pk': self.object.pk}
        )
        return super(RecordUpdateView, self).form_valid(form)

    def get_form_kwargs(self):
        kwargs = super(RecordUpdateView, self).get_form_kwargs()
        kwargs['instance'].decrypt_password()
        return kwargs
```

In this view, we still inherit from both `EncryptionMixin` and `SuccessMessageMixin`, but the view class we use is `UpdateView`.

The first four lines are customization as before, we set the template name, the form class, the `Record` model, and the success message. We cannot set the `success_url` as a class attribute because we want to redirect a successful edit to the same edit page for that record and, in order to do this, we need the ID of the instance we're editing. No worries, we'll do it another way.

First, we override `get_context_data` in order to set `'update'` to `True` in the `kwargs` argument, which means that a key `'update'` will end up in the `context` dict that is passed to the template for rendering the page. We do this because we want to use the same template for creating and updating a record, therefore we will use this variable in the context to be able to understand in which situation we are. There are other ways to do this but this one is quick and easy and I like it because it's explicit.

After overriding `get_context_data`, we need to take care of the URL redirection. We do this in the `form_valid` method since we know that, if we get there, it means the `Record` instance has been successfully updated. We reverse the `'records:edit'` view, which is exactly the view we're working on, passing the primary key of the object in question. We take that information from `self.object.pk`.

One of the reasons it's helpful to have the object saved on the view instance is that we can use it when needed without having to alter the signature of the many methods in the view in order to pass the object around. This design is very helpful and allows us to achieve a lot with very few lines of code.

The last thing we need to do is to decrypt the password on the instance before populating the form for the user. It's simple enough to do it in the `get_form_kwargs` method, where you can access the `Record` instance in the `kwargs` dict, and call `decrypt_password` on it.

This is all we need to do to update a record. If you think about it, the amount of code we had to write is really very little, thanks to Django class-based views.

A good way of understanding which is the best method to override, is to take a look at the Django official documentation or, even better in this case, check out the source code and look at the class-based views section. You'll be able to appreciate how much work has been done there by Django developers so that you only have to touch the smallest amounts of code to customize your views.

Deleting records

Of the three actions, deleting a record is definitely the easiest one. All we need is the following code:

```
class RecordDeleteView(SuccessMessageMixin, DeleteView):
    model = Record
    success_url = reverse_lazy('records:list')

    def delete(self, request, *args, **kwargs):
        messages.success(
            request, 'Record was deleted successfully')
        return super(RecordDeleteView, self).delete(
            request, *args, **kwargs)
```

We only need to inherit from `SuccessMessageMixin` and `DeleteView`, which gives us all we need. We set up the model and the success URL as class attributes, and then we override the `delete` method only to add a nice message that will be displayed in the list view (which is where we redirect to after deletion).

We don't need to specify the template name, since we'll use a name that Django infers by default: `record_confirm_delete.html`.

With this final view, we're all set to have a nice interface that we can use to handle `Record` instances.

Setting up the URLs

Before we move on to the template layer, let's set up the URLs. This time, I want to show you the inclusion technique I talked about in *Chapter 10, Web Development Done Right*.

pwdweb/urls.py

```
from django.conf.urls import include, url
from django.contrib import admin
from records import urls as records_url
from records.views import HomeView

urlpatterns = [
    url(r'^admin/', include(admin.site.urls)),
    url(r'^records/', include(records_url, namespace='records')),
    url(r'^$', HomeView.as_view(), name='home'),
]
```

These are the URLs for the main project. We have the usual admin, a home page, and then for the records section, we include another `urls.py` file, which we define in the `records` application. This technique allows for apps to be reusable and self-contained. Note that, when including another `urls.py` file, you can pass namespace information, which you can then use in functions such as `reverse`, or the `url` template tag. For example, we've seen that the path to the `RecordUpdateView` was `'records:edit'`. The first part of that string is the namespace, and the second is the name that we have given to the view, as you can see in the following code:

records/urls.py

```python
from django.conf.urls import include, url
from django.contrib import admin
from .views import (RecordCreateView, RecordUpdateView,
                    RecordDeleteView, RecordListView)

urlpatterns = [
    url(r'^add/$', RecordCreateView.as_view(), name='add'),
    url(r'^edit/(?P<pk>[0-9]+)/$', RecordUpdateView.as_view(),
        name='edit'),
    url(r'^delete/(?P<pk>[0-9]+)/$', RecordDeleteView.as_view(),
        name='delete'),
    url(r'^$', RecordListView.as_view(), name='list'),
]
```

We define four different `url` instances. There is one for adding a record, which doesn't need primary key information since the object doesn't exist yet. Then we have two `url` instances for updating and deleting a record, and for those we need to also specify primary key information to be passed to the view. Since `Record` instances have integer IDs, we can safely pass them on the URL, following good URL design practice. Finally, we define one `url` instance for the list of records.

All `url` instances have `name` information which is used in views and templates.

The template layer

Let's start with the template we'll use as the basis for the rest:

records/templates/records/base.html

```html
{% load static from staticfiles %}
<!DOCTYPE html>
<html lang="en">
  <head>
    <meta charset="utf-8">
```

```
    <meta name="viewport"
          content="width=device-width, initial-scale=1.0">
    <link href="{% static "records/css/main.css" %}"
          rel="stylesheet">
    <title>{% block title %}Title{% endblock title %}</title>
  </head>

  <body>
    <div id="page-content">
      {% block page-content %}{% endblock page-content %}
    </div>
    <div id="footer">{% block footer %}{% endblock footer %}</div>
    {% block scripts %}
      <script
        src="{% static "records/js/jquery-2.1.4.min.js" %}">
      </script>
    {% endblock scripts %}
  </body>
</html>
```

It's very similar to the one I used in *Chapter 10, Web Development Done Right* although it is a bit more compressed and with one major difference. We will import jQuery in every page.

> jQuery is the most popular JavaScript library out there. It allows
> you to write code that works on all the main browsers and it gives
> you many extra tools such as the ability to perform asynchronous
> calls (**AJAX**) from the browser itself. We'll use this library to
> perform the calls to the API, both to generate and validate our
> passwords. You can download it at https://jquery.com/, and
> put it in the pwdweb/records/static/records/js/ folder
> (you may have to amend the import in the template).

I highlighted the only interesting part of this template for you. Note that we load the JavaScript library at the end. This is common practice, as JavaScript is used to manipulate the page, so loading libraries at the end helps in avoiding situations such as JavaScript code failing because the element needed hadn't been rendered on the page yet.

Home and footer templates

The home template is very simple:

records/templates/records/home.html

```
{% extends "records/base.html" %}
{% block title %}Welcome to the Records website.{% endblock %}

{% block page-content %}
  <h1>Welcome {{ user.first_name }}!</h1>
  <div class="home-option">To create a record click
    <a href="{% url "records:add" %}">here.</a>
  </div>
  <div class="home-option">To see all records click
    <a href="{% url "records:list" %}">here.</a>
  </div>
{% endblock page-content %}
```

There is nothing new here when compared to the home.html template we saw in *Chapter 10, Web Development Done Right*. The footer template is actually exactly the same:

records/templates/records/footer.html

```
<div class="footer">
  Go back <a href="{% url "home" %}">home</a>.
</div>
```

Listing all records

This template to list all records is fairly simple:

records/templates/records/list.html

```
{% extends "records/base.html" %}
{% load record_extras %}
{% block title %}Records{% endblock title %}

{% block page-content %}
  <h1>Records</h1><span name="top"></span>
  {% include "records/messages.html" %}

  {% for record in records %}
  <div class="record {% cycle 'row-light-blue' 'row-white' %}"
      id="record-{{ record.pk }}">
    <div class="record-left">
```

```
      <div class="record-list">
        <span class="record-span">Title</span>{{ record.title }}
      </div>
      <div class="record-list">
        <span class="record-span">Username</span>
        {{ record.username }}
      </div>
      <div class="record-list">
        <span class="record-span">Email</span>{{ record.email }}
      </div>
      <div class="record-list">
        <span class="record-span">URL</span>
          <a href="{{ record.url }}" target="_blank">
            {{ record.url }}</a>
      </div>
      <div class="record-list">
        <span class="record-span">Password</span>
        {% hide_password record.plaintext %}
      </div>
    </div>
    <div class="record-right">
      <div class="record-list">
        <span class="record-span">Notes</span>
        <textarea rows="3" cols="40" class="record-notes"
                  readonly>{{ record.notes }}</textarea>
      </div>
      <div class="record-list">
        <span class="record-span">Last modified</span>
        {{ record.last_modified }}
      </div>
      <div class="record-list">
        <span class="record-span">Created</span>
        {{ record.created }}
      </div>

    </div>
    <div class="record-list-actions">
      <a href="{% url "records:edit" pk=record.pk %}">» edit</a>
      <a href="{% url "records:delete" pk=record.pk %}">» delete
      </a>
    </div>
  </div>
  {% endfor %}
{% endblock page-content %}
```

```
{% block footer %}
  <p><a href="#top">Go back to top</a></p>
  {% include "records/footer.html" %}
{% endblock footer %}
```

For this template as well, I have highlighted the parts I'd like you to focus on. Firstly, I load a custom tags module, `record_extras`, which we'll need later. I have also added an anchor at the top, so that we'll be able to put a link to it at the bottom of the page, to avoid having to scroll all the way up.

Then, I included a template to provide me with the HTML code to display Django messages. It's a very simple template which I'll show you shortly.

Then, we define a list of `div` elements. Each `Record` instance has a container `div`, in which there are two other main `div` elements: `record-left` and `record-right`. In order to display them side by side, I have set this class in the `main.css` file:

```
.record-left { float: left; width: 300px; }
```

The outermost `div` container (the one with class `record`), has an `id` attribute, which I have used as an anchor. This allows us to click on **cancel** on the record delete page, so that if we change our minds and don't want to delete the record, we can get back to the list page, and at the right position.

Each attribute of the record is then displayed in `div` elements whose class is `record-list`. Most of these classes are just there to allow me to set a bit of padding and dimensions on the HTML elements.

The next interesting bit is the `hide_password` tag, which takes the plaintext, which is the unencrypted password. The purpose of this custom tag is to display a sequence of `'*'` characters, as long as the original password, so that if someone is passing by while you're on the page, they won't see your passwords. However, hovering on that sequence of `'*'` characters will show you the original password in the tooltip. Here's the code for the `hide_password` tag:

records/templatetags/record_extras.py

```
from django import template
from django.utils.html import escape

register = template.Library()

@register.simple_tag
def hide_password(password):
    return '<span title="{0}">{1}</span>'.format(
        escape(password), '*' * len(password))
```

There is nothing fancy here. We just register this function as a simple tag and then we can use it wherever we want. It takes a `password` and puts it as a `tooltip` of a `span` element, whose main content is a sequence of `'*'` characters. Just note one thing: we need to escape the password, so that we're sure it won't break our HTML (think of what might happen if the password contained a double-quote `` ` " ` ``, for example).

As far as the `list.html` template is concerned, the next interesting bit is that we set the `readonly` attribute to the `textarea` element, so as not to give the impression to the user that they can modify notes on the fly.

Then, we set a couple of links for each `Record` instance, right at the bottom of the container `div`. There is one for the edit page, and another for the delete page. Note that we need to pass the `url` tag not only the `namespace:name` string, but also the primary key information, as required by the URL setup we made in the `urls.py` module for those views.

Finally, we import the footer and set the link to the anchor on top of the page.

Now, as promised, here is the code for the messages:

`records/templates/records/messages.html`

```
{% if messages %}
  {% for message in messages %}
    <p class="{{ message.tags }}">{{ message }}</p>
  {% endfor %}
{% endif %}
```

This code takes care of displaying messages only when there is at least one to display. We give the `p` tag `class` information to display success messages in green and error messages in red.

If you grab the `main.css` file from the source code for the book, you will now be able to visualize the list page (yours will be blank, you still need to insert data into it), and it should look something like this:

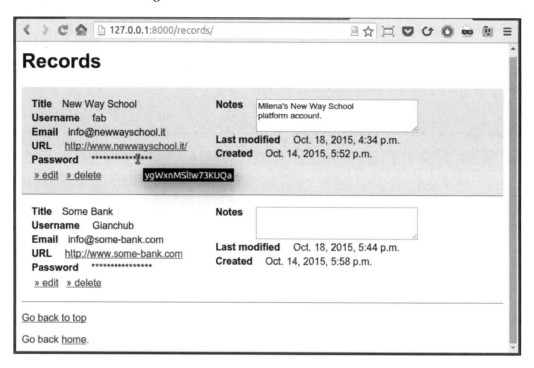

As you can see, I have two records in the database at the moment. I'm hovering on the password of the first one, which is my platform account at my sister's school, and the password is displayed in the tooltip. The division in two `div` elements, *left* and *right*, helps in making rows smaller so that the overall result is more pleasing to the eye. The important information is on the left and the ancillary information is on the right. The row color alternates between a very light shade of blue and white.

Each row has an **edit** and **delete** link, at its bottom left. We'll show the pages for those two links right after we see the code for the templates that create them.

The CSS code that holds all the information for this interface is the following:

`records/static/records/css/main.css`

```
html, body, * {
  font-family: 'Trebuchet MS', Helvetica, sans-serif; }
a { color: #333; }
.record {
  clear: both; padding: 1em; border-bottom: 1px solid #666;}
```

```
.record-left { float: left; width: 300px;}
.record-list { padding: 2px 0; }
.fieldWrapper { padding: 5px; }
.footer { margin-top: 1em; color: #333; }
.home-option { padding: .6em 0; }
.record-span { font-weight: bold; padding-right: 1em; }
.record-notes { vertical-align: top; }
.record-list-actions { padding: 4px 0; clear: both; }
.record-list-actions a { padding: 0 4px; }
#pwd-info { padding: 0 6px; font-size: 1.1em; font-weight: bold;}
#id_notes { vertical-align: top; }
/* Messages */
.success, .errorlist {font-size: 1.2em; font-weight: bold; }
.success {color: #25B725; }
.errorlist {color: #B12B2B; }
/* colors */
.row-light-blue { background-color: #E6F0FA; }
.row-white { background-color: #fff; }
.green { color: #060; }
.orange { color: #FF3300; }
.red { color: #900; }
```

Please remember, I'm not a CSS guru so just take this file as it is, a fairly naive way to provide styling to our interface.

Creating and editing records

Now for the interesting part. Creating and updating a record. We'll use the same template for both, so we expect some decisional logic to be there that will tell us in which of the two situations we are. As it turns out, it will not be that much code. The most exciting part of this template, however, is its associated JavaScript file which we'll examine right afterwards.

records/templates/records/record_add_edit.html

```
{% extends "records/base.html" %}
{% load static from staticfiles %}
{% block title %}
  {% if update %}Update{% else %}Create{% endif %} Record
{% endblock title %}

{% block page-content %}
  <h1>{% if update %}Update a{% else %}Create a new{% endif %}
    Record
  </h1>
```

```
{% include "records/messages.html" %}

<form action="." method="post">{% csrf_token %}
  {{ form.non_field_errors }}

  <div class="fieldWrapper">{{ form.title.errors }}
    {{ form.title.label_tag }} {{ form.title }}</div>

  <div class="fieldWrapper">{{ form.username.errors }}
    {{ form.username.label_tag }} {{ form.username }}</div>

  <div class="fieldWrapper">{{ form.email.errors }}
    {{ form.email.label_tag }} {{ form.email }}</div>

  <div class="fieldWrapper">{{ form.url.errors }}
    {{ form.url.label_tag }} {{ form.url }}</div>

  <div class="fieldWrapper">{{ form.password.errors }}
    {{ form.password.label_tag }} {{ form.password }}
    <span id="pwd-info"></span></div>

  <button type="button" id="validate-btn">
    Validate Password</button>
  <button type="button" id="generate-btn">
    Generate Password</button>

  <div class="fieldWrapper">{{ form.notes.errors }}
    {{ form.notes.label_tag }} {{ form.notes }}</div>

  <input type="submit"
    value="{% if update %}Update{% else %}Insert{% endif %}">
</form>
{% endblock page-content %}

{% block footer %}
  <br>{% include "records/footer.html" %}<br>
  Go to <a href="{% url "records:list" %}">the records list</a>.
{% endblock footer %}

{% block scripts %}
  {{ block.super }}
  <script src="{% static "records/js/api.js" %}"></script>
{% endblock scripts %}
```

As usual, I have highlighted the important parts, so let's go through this code together.

You can see the first bit of decision logic in the `title` block. Similar decision logic is also displayed later on, in the header of the page (the `h1` HTML tag), and in the `submit` button at the end of the form.

Apart from this logic, what I'd like you to focus on is the form and what's inside it. We set the action attribute to a dot, which means *this page*, so that we don't need to customize it according to which view is serving the page. Also, we immediately take care of the *cross-site request forgery* token, as explained in *Chapter 10, Web Development Done Right*.

Note that, this time, we cannot leave the whole form rendering up to Django since we want to add in a couple of extra things, so we go down one level of granularity and ask Django to render each individual field for us, along with any errors, along with its label. This way we still save a lot of effort, and at the same time, we can also customize the form as we like. In situations like this, it's not uncommon to write a small template to render a field, in order to avoid repeating those three lines for each field. In this case though, the form is so small I decided to avoid raising the complexity level up any further.

The `span` element, `pwd-info`, contains the information about the password that we get from the API. The two buttons after that, `validate-btn` and `generate-btn`, are hooked up with the AJAX calls to the API.

At the end of the template, in the `scripts` block, we need to load the `api.js` JavaScript file which contains the code to work with the API. We also need to use `block.super`, which will load whatever code is in the same block in the parent template (for example, jQuery). `block.super` is basically the template equivalent of a call to `super(ClassName, self)` in Python. It's important to load jQuery before our library, since the latter is based on the former.

Talking to the API

Let's now take a look at that JavaScript. I don't expect you to understand everything. Firstly, this is a Python book and secondly, you're supposed to be a beginner (though by now, *ninja trained*), so fear not. However, as JavaScript has, by now, become essential if you're dealing with a web environment, having a working knowledge of it is extremely important even for a Python developer, so try and get the most out of what I'm about to show you. We'll see the password generation first:

records/static/records/js/api.js

```
var baseURL = 'http://127.0.0.1:5555/password';

var getRandomPassword = function() {
  var apiURL = '{url}/generate'.replace('{url}', baseURL);
  $.ajax({
    type: 'GET',
    url: apiURL,
    success: function(data, status, request) {
      $('#id_password').val(data[1]);
    },
    error: function() { alert('Unexpected error'); }
  });
}

$(function() {
  $('#generate-btn').click(getRandomPassword);
});
```

Firstly, we set a variable for the base API URL: baseURL. Then, we define the getRandomPassword function, which is very simple. At the beginning, it defines the apiURL extending baseURL with a replacement technique. Even if the syntax is different from that of Python, you shouldn't have any issues understanding this line.

After defining the apiURL, the interesting bit comes up. We call $.ajax, which is the jQuery function that performs the AJAX calls. That $ is a shortcut for jQuery. As you can see in the body of the call, it's a GET request to apiURL. If it succeeds (success: ...), an anonymous function is run, which sets the value of the id_password text field to the second element of the returned data. We'll see the structure of the data when we examine the API code, so don't worry about that now. If an error occurs, we simply alert the user that there was an unexpected error.

 The reason why the password field in the HTML has id_password as the ID is due to the way Django renders forms. You can customize this behavior using a custom prefix, for example. In this case, I'm happy with the Django defaults.

After the function definition, we run a couple of lines of code to bind the click event on the generate-btn button to the getRandomPassword function. This means that, after this code has been run by the browser engine, every time we click the generate-btn button, the getRandomPassword function is called.

That wasn't so scary, was it? So let's see what we need for the validation part.

Now there is a value in the **password** field and we want to validate it. We need to call the API and inspect its response. Since passwords can have weird characters, I don't want to pass them on the URL, therefore I will use a POST request, which allows me to put the password in its body. To do this, I need the following code:

```
var validatePassword = function() {
  var apiURL = '{url}/validate'.replace('{url}', baseURL);
  $.ajax({
    type: 'POST',
    url: apiURL,
    data: JSON.stringify({'password': $('#id_password').val()}),
    contentType: "text/plain",  // Avoid CORS preflight
    success: function(data, status, request) {
      var valid = data['valid'], infoClass, grade;
      var msg = (valid?'Valid':'Invalid') + ' password.';
      if (valid) {
        var score = data['score']['total'];
        grade = (score<10?'Poor':(score<18?'Medium':'Strong'));
        infoClass = (score<10?'red':(score<18?'orange':'green'));
        msg += ' (Score: {score}, {grade})'
          .replace('{score}', score).replace('{grade}', grade);
      }
      $('#pwd-info').html(msg);
      $('#pwd-info').removeClass().addClass(infoClass);
    },
    error: function(data) { alert('Unexpected error'); }
  });
}

$(function() {
  $('#validate-btn').click(validatePassword);
});
```

The concept is the same as before, only this time it's for the `validate-btn` button. The body of the AJAX call is similar. We use a POST instead of a GET request, and we define the data as a JSON object, which is the equivalent of using `json.dumps({'password': 'some_pwd'})` in Python.

The `contentType` line is a quick hack to avoid problems with the CORS preflight behavior of the browser. **Cross-origin resource sharing (CORS)** is a mechanism that allows restricted resources on a web page to be requested from another domain outside of the domain from which the request originated. In a nutshell, since the API is located at `127.0.0.1:5555` and the interface is running at `127.0.0.1:8000`, without this hack, the browser wouldn't allow us to perform the calls. In a production environment, you may want to check the documentation for JSONP, which is a much better (albeit more complex) solution to this issue.

The body of the anonymous function which is run if the call succeeds is apparently only a bit complicated. All we need to do is understand if the password is valid (from `data['valid']`), and assign it a grade and a CSS class based on its score. Validity and score information come from the API response.

The only tricky bit in this code is the JavaScript ternary operator, so let's see a comparative example for it:

```
# Python
error = 'critical' if error_level > 50 else 'medium'
// JavaScript equivalent
error = (error_level > 50 ? 'critical' : 'medium');
```

With this example, you shouldn't have any issue reading the rest of the logic in the function. I know, I could have just used a regular `if (...)`, but JavaScript coders use the ternary operator all the time, so you should get used to it. It's good training to scratch our heads a bit harder in order to understand code.

Lastly, I'd like you to take a look at the end of that function. We set the `html` of the `pwd-info` span element to the message we assembled (`msg`), and then we style it. In one line, we remove all the CSS classes from that element (`removeClass()` with no parameters does that), and we add the `infoClass` to it. `infoClass` is either `'red'`, `'orange'`, or `'green'`. If you go back to the `main.css` file, you'll see them at the bottom.

Now that we've seen both the template code and the JavaScript to make the calls, let's see a screenshot of the page. We're going to edit the first record, the one about my sister's school.

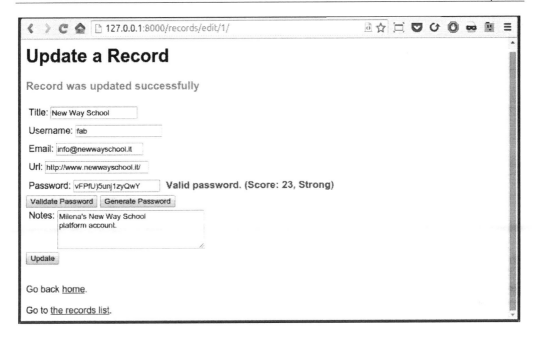

In the picture, you can see that I updated the password by clicking on the **Generate Password** button. Then, I saved the record (so you could see the nice message on top), and, finally, I clicked on the **Validate Password** button.

The result is shown in green on the right-hand side of the **Password** field. It's strong (23 is actually the maximum score we can get) so the message is displayed in a nice shade of green.

Deleting records

To delete a record, go to the list and click on the **delete** link. You'll be redirected to a page that asks you for confirmation; you can then choose to proceed and delete the poor record, or to cancel the request and go back to the list page. The template code is the following:

```
records/templates/records/record_confirm_delete.html
    {% extends "records/base.html" %}
    {% block title %}Delete record{% endblock title %}

    {% block page-content %}
      <h1>Confirm Record Deletion</h1>
      <form action="." method="post">{% csrf_token %}
        <p>Are you sure you want to delete "{{ object }}"?</p>
```

```
        <input type="submit" value="Confirm" /> 
        <a href="{% url "records:list" %}#record-{{ object.pk }}">
            » cancel</a>
    </form>
{% endblock page-content %}
```

Since this is a template for a standard Django view, we need to use the naming conventions adopted by Django. Therefore, the record in question is called **object** in the template. The {{ object }} tag displays a string representation for the object, which is not exactly beautiful at the moment, since the whole line will read: **Are you sure you want to delete "Record object"?**.

This is because we haven't added a __str__ method to our Model class yet, which means that Python has no idea of what to show us when we ask for a string representation of an instance. Let's change this by completing our model, adding the __str__ method at the bottom of the class body:

records/models.py

```
    class Record(models.Model):
        ...

        def __str__(self):
            return '{}'.format(self.title)
```

Restart the server and now the page will read: **Are you sure you want to delete "Some Bank"?** where *Some Bank* is the title of the record whose **delete** link I clicked on.

We could have just used {{ object.title }}, but I prefer to fix the root of the problem, not just the effect. Adding a __str__ method is in fact something that you ought to do for all of your models.

The interesting bit in this last template is actually the link for canceling the operation. We use the url tag to go back to the list view (records:list), but we add anchor information to it so that it will eventually read something like this (this is for pk=2):

http://127.0.0.1:8000/records/#record-2

This will go back to the list page and scroll down to the container div that has ID record 2, which is nice.

This concludes the interface. Even though this section was similar to what we saw in *Chapter 10, Web Development Done Right*, we've been able to concentrate more on the code in this chapter. We've seen how useful Django class-based views are, and we even touched on some cool JavaScript. Run $ python manage.py runserver and your interface should be up and running at http://127.0.0.1:8000.

If you are wondering, `127.0.0.1` means the `localhost` — your computer — while `8000` is the port to which the server is bound, to listen for incoming requests.

Now it's time to spice things up a bit with the second part of this project.

Implementing the Falcon API

The structure of the Falcon project we're about to code is nowhere near as extended as the interface one. We'll code five files altogether. In your ch12 folder, create a new one called `pwdapi`. This is its final structure:

```
$ tree -A pwdapi/
pwdapi/
├── core
│   ├── handlers.py
│   └── passwords.py
├── main.py
└── tests
    └── test_core
        ├── test_handlers.py
        └── test_passwords.py
```

The API was all coded using TDD, so we're also going to explore the tests. However, I think it's going to be easier for you to understand the tests if you first see the code, so we're going to start with that.

The main application

This is the code for the Falcon application:

`main.py`

```python
import falcon
from core.handlers import (
    PasswordValidatorHandler,
    PasswordGeneratorHandler,
)

validation_handler = PasswordValidatorHandler()
generator_handler = PasswordGeneratorHandler()

app = falcon.API()
app.add_route('/password/validate/', validation_handler)
app.add_route('/password/generate/', generator_handler)
```

As in the example in *Chapter 10*, *Web Development Done Right*, we start by creating one instance for each of the handlers we need, then we create a `falcon.API` object and, by calling its `add_route` method, we set up the routing to the URLs of our API. We'll get to the definitions of the handlers in a moment. Firstly, we need a couple of helpers.

Writing the helpers

In this section, we will take a look at a couple of classes that we'll use in our handlers. It's always good to factor out some logic following the **Single Responsibility Principle**.

> In OOP, the **Single Responsibility Principle (SRP)** states that every class should have responsibility for a single part of the functionality provided by the software, and that responsibility should be entirely encapsulated by the class. All of its services should be narrowly aligned with that responsibility.
>
> The Single Responsibility Principle is the *S* in **S.O.L.I.D.**, an acronym for the first five OOP and software design principles introduced by Robert Martin.
>
> I heartily suggest you to open a browser and read up on this subject, it is very important.

All the code in the helpers section belongs to the `core/passwords.py` module. Here's how it begins:

```
from math import ceil
from random import sample
from string import ascii_lowercase, ascii_uppercase, digits

punctuation = '!#$%&()*+-?@_|'
allchars = ''.join(
    (ascii_lowercase, ascii_uppercase, digits, punctuation))
```

We'll need to handle some randomized calculations but the most important part here is the allowed characters. We will allow letters, digits, and a set of punctuation characters. To ease writing the code, we will merge those parts into the `allchars` string.

Coding the password validator

The `PasswordValidator` class is my favorite bit of logic in the whole API.
It exposes an `is_valid` and a `score` method. The latter runs all defined validators
("private" methods in the same class), and collects the scores into a single dict which
is returned as a result. I'll write this class method by method so that it does not
get too complicated:

```
class PasswordValidator:
    def __init__(self, password):
        self.password = password.strip()
```

It begins by setting `password` (with no leading or trailing spaces) as an instance
attribute. This way we won't then have to pass it around from method to method.
All the methods that will follow belong to this class.

```
    def is_valid(self):
        return (len(self.password) > 0 and
                all(char in allchars for char in self.password))
```

A password is valid when its length is greater than 0 and all of its characters belong
to the `allchars` string. When you read the `is_valid` method, it's practically English
(that's how amazing Python is). `all` is a built-in function that tells you if all the
elements of the iterable you feed to it are `True`.

```
    def score(self):
        result = {
            'length': self._score_length(),
            'case': self._score_case(),
            'numbers': self._score_numbers(),
            'special': self._score_special(),
            'ratio': self._score_ratio(),
        }
        result['total'] = sum(result.values())
        return result
```

This is the other main method. It's very simple, it just prepares a dict with all the
results from the validators. The only independent bit of logic happens at the end,
when we sum the grades from each validator and assign it to a `'total'` key in the
dict, just for convenience.

As you can see, we score a password by length, by letter case, by the presence
of numbers, and special characters, and, finally, by the ratio between letters and
numbers. Letters allow a character to be between $26 * 2 = 52$ different possible
choices, while digits allow only 10. Therefore, passwords whose letters to digits
ratio is higher are more difficult to crack.

Let's see the length validator:

```
def _score_length(self):
    scores_list = ([0]*4) + ([1]*4) + ([3]*4) + ([5]*4)
    scores = dict(enumerate(scores_list))
    return scores.get(len(self.password), 7)
```

We assign 0 points to passwords whose length is less than four characters, 1 point for those whose length is less than 8, 3 for a length less than 12, 5 for a length less than 16, and 7 for a length of 16 or more.

In order to avoid a waterfall of if/elif clauses, I have adopted a functional style here. I prepared a score_list, which is basically [0, 0, 0, 0, 1, 1, 1, 1, 3, ...]. Then, by enumerating it, I got a (*length, score*) pair for each length less than 16. I put those pairs into a dict, which gives me the equivalent in dict form, so it should look like this: {0:0, 1:0, 2:0, 3:0, 4:1, 5:1, ...}. I then perform a get on this dict with the length of the password, setting a value of 7 as the default (which will be returned for lengths of 16 or more, which are not in the dict).

I have nothing against if/elif clauses, of course, but I wanted to take the opportunity to show you different coding styles in this final chapter, to help you get used to reading code which deviates from what you would normally expect. It's only beneficial.

```
def _score_case(self):
    lower = bool(set(ascii_lowercase) & set(self.password))
    upper = bool(set(ascii_uppercase) & set(self.password))
    return int(lower or upper) + 2 * (lower and upper)
```

The way we validate the case is again with a nice trick. lower is True when the intersection between the password and all lowercase characters is non-empty, otherwise it's False. upper behaves in the same way, only with uppercase characters.

To understand the evaluation that happens on the last line, let's use the inside-out technique once more: lower or upper is True when at least one of the two is True. When it's True, it will be converted to a 1 by the int class. This equates to saying, if there is at least one character, regardless of the casing, the score gets 1 point, otherwise it stays at 0.

Now for the second part: lower and upper is True when both of them are True, which means that we have at least one lowercase and one uppercase character. This means that, to crack the password, a brute-force algorithm would have to loop through 52 letters instead of just 26. Therefore, when that's True, we get an extra two points.

This validator therefore produces a result in the range (0, 1, 3), depending on what the password is.

```
def _score_numbers(self):
    return 2 if (set(self.password) & set(digits)) else 0
```

Scoring on the numbers is simpler. If we have at least one number, we get two points, otherwise we get 0. In this case, I used a ternary operator to return the result.

```
def _score_special(self):
    return 4 if (
        set(self.password) & set(punctuation)) else 0
```

The special characters validator has the same logic as the previous one but, since special characters add quite a bit of complexity when it comes to cracking a password, we have scored four points instead of just two.

The last one validates the ratio between the letters and the digits.

```
def _score_ratio(self):
    alpha_count = sum(
        1 if c.lower() in ascii_lowercase else 0
        for c in self.password)
    digits_count = sum(
        1 if c in digits else 0 for c in self.password)
    if digits_count == 0:
        return 0
    return min(ceil(alpha_count / digits_count), 7)
```

I highlighted the conditional logic in the expressions in the sum calls. In the first case, we get a 1 for each character whose lowercase version is in ascii_lowercase. This means that summing all those 1's up gives us exactly the count of all the letters. Then, we do the same for the digits, only we use the digits string for reference, and we don't need to lowercase the character. When digits_count is 0, alpha_count / digits_count would cause a ZeroDivisionError, therefore we check on digits_count and when it's 0 we return 0. If we have digits, we calculate the ceiling of the *letters:digits* ratio, and return it, capped at 7.

Of course, there are many different ways to calculate a score for a password. My aim here is not to give you the finest algorithm to do that, but to show you how you could go about implementing it.

Coding the password generator

The password generator is a much simpler class than the validator. However, I have coded it so that we won't need to create an instance to use it, just to show you yet again a different coding style.

```
class PasswordGenerator:

    @classmethod
    def generate(cls, length, bestof=10):
        candidates = sorted([
            cls._generate_candidate(length)
            for k in range(max(1, bestof))
        ])
        return candidates[-1]

    @classmethod
    def _generate_candidate(cls, length):
        password = cls._generate_password(length)
        score = PasswordValidator(password).score()
        return (score['total'], password)

    @classmethod
    def _generate_password(cls, length):
        chars = allchars * (ceil(length / len(allchars)))
        return ''.join(sample(chars, length))
```

Of the three methods, only the first one is meant to be used. Let's start our analysis with the last one: _generate_password.

This method simply takes a length, which is the desired length for the password we want, and calls the sample function to get a population of length elements out of the chars string. The return value of the sample function is a list of length elements, and we need to make it a string using join.

Before we can call sample, think about this, what if the desired length exceeds the length of allchars? The call would result in ValueError: Sample larger than the population.

Because of this, we create the chars string in a way that it is made by concatenating the allchars string to itself just enough times to cover the desired length. To give you an example, let's say we need a password of 27 characters, and let's pretend allchars is 10 characters long. length / len(allchars) gives 2.7, which, when passed to the ceil function, becomes 3. This means that we're going to assign chars to a triple concatenation of the allchars string, hence chars will be *10 * 3 = 30* characters long, which is enough to cover our requirements.

Note that, in order for these methods to be called without creating an instance of this class, we need to decorate them with the `classmethod` decorator. The convention is then to call the first argument, `cls`, instead of `self`, because Python, behind the scenes, will pass the class object to the call.

The code for `_generate_candidate` is also very simple. We just generate a password and, given the length, we calculate its score, and return a tuple (*score, password*).

We do this so that in the `generate` method we can generate 10 (by default) passwords each time the method is called and return the one that has the highest score. Since our generation logic is based on a random function, it's always a good way to employ a technique like this to avoid worst case scenarios.

This concludes the code for the helpers.

Writing the handlers

As you may have noticed, the code for the helpers isn't related to Falcon at all. It is just pure Python that we can reuse when we need it. On the other hand, the code for the handlers is of course based on Falcon. The code that follows belongs to the `core/handlers.py` module so, as we did before, let's start with the first few lines:

```python
import json
import falcon
from .passwords import PasswordValidator, PasswordGenerator

class HeaderMixin:
    def set_access_control_allow_origin(self, resp):
        resp.set_header('Access-Control-Allow-Origin', '*')
```

That was very simple. We import `json`, `falcon`, and our helpers, and then we set up a mixin which we'll need in both handlers. The need for this mixin is to allow the API to serve requests that come from somewhere else. This is the other side of the CORS coin to what we saw in the JavaScript code for the interface. In this case, we boldly go where no security expert would ever dare, and allow requests to come from any domain (`'*'`). We do this because this is an exercise and, in this context, it is fine, but don't do it in production, okay?

Coding the password validator handler

This handler will have to respond to a POST request, therefore I have coded an on_post method, which is the way you react to a POST request in Falcon.

```
class PasswordValidatorHandler(HeaderMixin):

    def on_post(self, req, resp):
        self.process_request(req, resp)
        password = req.context.get('_body', {}).get('password')
        if password is None:
            resp.status = falcon.HTTP_BAD_REQUEST
            return None

        result = self.parse_password(password)
        resp.body = json.dumps(result)

    def parse_password(self, password):
        validator = PasswordValidator(password)
        return {
            'password': password,
            'valid': validator.is_valid(),
            'score': validator.score(),
        }

    def process_request(self, req, resp):
        self.set_access_control_allow_origin(resp)

        body = req.stream.read()
        if not body:
            raise falcon.HTTPBadRequest('Empty request body',
                'A valid JSON document is required.')
        try:
            req.context['_body'] = json.loads(
                body.decode('utf-8'))
        except (ValueError, UnicodeDecodeError):
            raise falcon.HTTPError(
                falcon.HTTP_753, 'Malformed JSON',
                'JSON incorrect or not utf-8 encoded.')
```

Let's start with the on_post method. First of all, we call the process_request method, which does a sanity check on the request body. I won't go into finest detail because it's taken from the Falcon documentation, and it's a standard way of processing a request. Let's just say that, if everything goes well (the highlighted part), we get the body of the request (already decoded from JSON) in req.context['_body']. If things go badly for any reason, we return an appropriate error response.

Let's go back to `on_post`. We fetch the password from the request context. At this point, `process_request` has succeeded, but we still don't know if the body was in the correct format. We're expecting something like: `{'password': 'my_password'}`.

So we proceed with caution. We get the value for the `'_body'` key and, if that is not present, we return an empty dict. We get the value for `'password'` from that. We use `get` instead of direct access to avoid `KeyError` issues.

If the password is `None`, we simply return a 400 error (bad request). Otherwise, we validate it and calculate its score, and then set the result as the body of our response.

You can see how easy it is to validate and calculate the score of the password in the `parse_password` method, by using our helpers.

We return a dict with three pieces of information: `password`, `valid`, and `score`. The password information is technically redundant because whoever made the request would know the password but, in this case, I think it's a good way of providing enough information for things such as logging, so I added it.

What happens if the JSON-decoded body is not a dict? I will leave it up to you to fix the code, adding some logic to cater for that edge case.

Coding the password generator handler

The generator handler has to handle a GET request with one query parameter: the desired password length.

```python
class PasswordGeneratorHandler(HeaderMixin):

    def on_get(self, req, resp):
        self.process_request(req, resp)
        length = req.context.get('_length', 16)
        resp.body = json.dumps(
            PasswordGenerator.generate(length))

    def process_request(self, req, resp):
        self.set_access_control_allow_origin(resp)
        length = req.get_param('length')
        if length is None:
            return
        try:
            length = int(length)
            assert length > 0
            req.context['_length'] = length
        except (ValueError, TypeError, AssertionError):
            raise falcon.HTTPBadRequest('Wrong query parameter',
                '`length` must be a positive integer.')
```

We have a similar `process_request` method. It does a sanity check on the request, even though a bit differently from the previous handler. This time, we need to make sure that if the length is provided on the query string (which means, for example, `http://our-api-url/?length=23`), it's in the correct format. This means that `length` needs to be a positive integer.

So, to validate that, we do an `int` conversion (`req.get_param('length')` returns a string), then we assert that `length` is greater than zero and, finally, we put it in `context` under the `'_length'` key.

Doing the `int` conversion of a string which is not a suitable representation for an integer raises `ValueError`, while a conversion from a type that is not a string raises `TypeError`, therefore we catch those two in the `except` clause.

We also catch `AssertionError`, which is raised by the `assert length > 0` line when `length` is not a positive integer. We can then safely guarantee that the length is as desired with one single `try/except` block.

> Note that, when coding a `try/except` block, you should usually try and be as specific as possible, separating instructions that would raise different exceptions if a problem arose. This would allow you more control over the issue, and easier debugging. In this case though, since this is a simple API, it's fine to have code which only reacts to a request for which `length` is not in the right format.

The code for the `on_get` method is quite straightforward. It starts by processing the request, then the length is fetched, falling back to 16 (the default value) when it's not passed, and then a password is generated and dumped to JSON, and then set to be the body of the response.

Running the API

In order to run this application, you need to remember that we set the base URL in the interface to `http://127.0.0.1:5555`. Therefore, we need the following command to start the API:

```
$ gunicorn -b 127.0.0.1:5555 main:app
```

Running that will start the app defined in the main module, binding the server instance to port `5555` on `localhost`. For more information about Gunicorn, please refer to either *Chapter 10, Web Development Done Right* or directly to the project's home page (`http://gunicorn.org/`).

The code for the API is now complete so if you have both the interface and the API running, you can try them out together. See if everything works as expected.

Testing the API

In this section, let's take a look at the tests I wrote for the helpers and for the handlers. Tests for the helpers are heavily based on the `nose_parameterized` library, as my favorite testing style is interface testing, with as little patching as possible. Using `nose_parameterized` allows me to write tests that are easier to read because the test cases are very visible.

On the other hand, tests for the handlers have to follow the testing conventions for the Falcon library, so they will be a bit different. This is, of course, ideal since it allows me to show you even more.

Due to the limited amount of pages I have left, I'll show you only a part of the tests, so make sure you check them out in full in the source code.

Testing the helpers

Let's see the tests for the `PasswordGenerator` class:

tests/test_core/test_passwords.py

```python
class PasswordGeneratorTestCase(TestCase):

    def test__generate_password_length(self):
        for length in range(300):
            assert_equal(
                length,
                len(PasswordGenerator._generate_password(length))
            )

    def test__generate_password_validity(self):
        for length in range(1, 300):
            password = PasswordGenerator._generate_password(
                length)
            assert_true(PasswordValidator(password).is_valid())

    def test__generate_candidate(self):
        score, password = (
            PasswordGenerator._generate_candidate(42))
        expected_score = PasswordValidator(password).score()
        assert_equal(expected_score['total'], score)
```

```
@patch.object(PasswordGenerator, '_generate_candidate')
def test__generate(self, _generate_candidate_mock):
    # checks `generate` returns the highest score candidate
    _generate_candidate_mock.side_effect = [
        (16, '&a69Ly+0H4jZ'),
        (17, 'UXaF4stRfdlh'),
        (21, 'aB4Ge_KdTgwR'),    # the winner
        (12, 'IRLT*XEfcglm'),
        (16, '$P92-WZ5+DnG'),
        (18, 'Xi#36jcKA_qQ'),
        (19, '?p9avQzRMIK0'),
        (17, '4@sY&bQ9*H!+'),
        (12, 'Cx-QAYXG_Ejq'),
        (18, 'C)RAV(HP7j9n'),
    ]
    assert_equal(
        (21, 'aB4Ge_KdTgwR'), PasswordGenerator.generate(12))
```

Within `test__generate_password_length` we make sure the `_generate_password` method handles the length parameter correctly. We generate a password for each length in the range [0, 300), and verify that it has the correct length.

In the `test__generate_password_validity` test, we do something similar but, this time, we make sure that whatever length we ask for, the generated password is valid. We use the `PasswordValidator` class to check for validity.

Finally, we need to test the `generate` method. The password generation is random, therefore, in order to test this function, we need to mock `_generate_candidate`, thus controlling its output. We set the `side_effect` argument on its mock to be a list of 10 candidates, from which we expect the `generate` method to choose the one with the highest score. Setting `side_effect` on a mock to a list causes that mock to return the elements of that list, one at a time, each time it's called. To avoid ambiguity, the highest score is 21, and only one candidate has scored that high. We call the method and make sure that that particular one is the candidate which is returned.

> If you are wondering why I used those double underscores in the test names, it's very simple: the first one is a separator and the second one is the leading underscore that is part of the name of the method under test.

Testing the `PasswordValidator` class requires many more lines of code, so I'll show only a portion of these tests:

pwdapi/tests/test_core/test_passwords.py

```
from unittest import TestCase
from unittest.mock import patch
from nose_parameterized import parameterized, param
from nose.tools import (
    assert_equal, assert_dict_equal, assert_true)
from core.passwords import PasswordValidator, PasswordGenerator

class PasswordValidatorTestCase(TestCase):

    @parameterized.expand([
        (False, ''),
        (False, '   '),
        (True, 'abcdefghijklmnopqrstuvwxyz'),
        (True, 'ABCDEFGHIJKLMNOPQRSTUVWXYZ'),
        (True, '0123456789'),
        (True, '!#$%&()*+-?@_|'),
    ])
    def test_is_valid(self, valid, password):
        validator = PasswordValidator(password)
        assert_equal(valid, validator.is_valid())
```

We start by testing the `is_valid` method. We test whether or not it returns `False` when it's fed an empty string, as well as a string made up of only spaces, which makes sure we're testing whether we're calling `.strip()` when we assign the password.

Then, we use all the characters that we want to be accepted to make sure the function accepts them.

I understand the syntax behind the `parameterize.expand` decorator can be challenging at first but really, all there is to it is that each tuple consists of an independent test case which, in turn, means that the `test_is_valid` test is run individually for each tuple, and that the two tuple elements are passed to the method as arguments: `valid` and `password`.

We then test for invalid characters. We expect them all to fail so we use `param.explicit`, which runs the test for each of the characters in that weird string.

```
@parameterized.expand(
    param.explicit(char) for char in '>]{<`\\;,[^/"\'~:}=.'
)
def test_is_valid_invalid_chars(self, password):
    validator = PasswordValidator(password)
    assert_equal(False, validator.is_valid())
```

They all evaluate to `False`, so we're good.

```
@parameterized.expand([
    (0, ''),   # 0-3: score 0
    (0, 'a'),   # 0-3: score 0
    (0, 'aa'),   # 0-3: score 0
    (0, 'aaa'),   # 0-3: score 0
    (1, 'aaab'),   # 4-7: score 1
    ...
    (5, 'aaabbbbccccddd'),   # 12-15: score 5
    (5, 'aaabbbbccccdddd'),   # 12-15: score 5
])
def test__score_length(self, score, password):
    validator = PasswordValidator(password)
    assert_equal(score, validator._score_length())
```

To test the `_score_length` method, I created 16 test cases for the lengths from 0 to 15. The body of the test simply makes sure that the score is assigned appropriately.

```
def test__score_length_sixteen_plus(self):
    # all password whose length is 16+ score 7 points
    password = 'x' * 255
    for length in range(16, len(password)):
        validator = PasswordValidator(password[:length])
        assert_equal(7, validator._score_length())
```

The preceding test is for lengths from 16 to 254. We only need to make sure that any length after 15 gets 7 as a score.

I will skip over the tests for the other internal methods and jump directly to the one for the score method. In order to test it, I want to control exactly what is returned by each of the `_score_*` methods so I mock them out and in the test, I set a return value for each of them. Note that to mock methods of a class, we use a variant of `patch`: `patch.object`. When you set return values on mocks, it's never good to have repetitions because you may not be sure which method returned what, and the test wouldn't fail in the case of a swap. So, always return different values. In my case, I am using the first few prime numbers to be sure there is no possibility of confusion.

```
@patch.object(PasswordValidator, '_score_length')
@patch.object(PasswordValidator, '_score_case')
@patch.object(PasswordValidator, '_score_numbers')
@patch.object(PasswordValidator, '_score_special')
@patch.object(PasswordValidator, '_score_ratio')
def test_score(
        self,
        _score_ratio_mock,
        _score_special_mock,
        _score_numbers_mock,
        _score_case_mock,
        _score_length_mock):

    _score_ratio_mock.return_value = 2
    _score_special_mock.return_value = 3
    _score_numbers_mock.return_value = 5
    _score_case_mock.return_value = 7
    _score_length_mock.return_value = 11

    expected_result = {
        'length': 11,
        'case': 7,
        'numbers': 5,
        'special': 3,
        'ratio': 2,
        'total': 28,
    }

    validator = PasswordValidator('')
    assert_dict_equal(expected_result, validator.score())
```

I want to point out explicitly that the _score_* methods are mocked, so I set up my validator instance by passing an empty string to the class constructor. This makes it even more evident to the reader that the internals of the class have been mocked out. Then, I just check if the result is the same as what I was expecting.

This last test is the only one in this class in which I used mocks. All the other tests for the _score_* methods are in an interface style, which reads better and usually produces better results.

Testing the handlers

Let's briefly see one example of a test for a handler:

pwdapi/tests/test_core/test_handlers.py

```
import json
from unittest.mock import patch
from nose.tools import assert_dict_equal, assert_equal
import falcon
import falcon.testing as testing
from core.handlers import (
    PasswordValidatorHandler, PasswordGeneratorHandler)

class PGHTest(PasswordGeneratorHandler):
    def process_request(self, req, resp):
        self.req, self.resp = req, resp
        return super(PGHTest, self).process_request(req, resp)

class PVHTest(PasswordValidatorHandler):
    def process_request(self, req, resp):
        self.req, self.resp = req, resp
        return super(PVHTest, self).process_request(req, resp)
```

Because of the tools Falcon gives you to test your handlers, I created a child for each of the classes I wanted to test. The only thing I changed (by overriding a method) is that in the process_request method, which is called by both classes, before processing the request I make sure I set the req and resp arguments on the instance. The normal behavior of the process_request method is thus not altered in any other way. By doing this, whatever happens over the course of the test, I'll be able to check against those objects.

It's quite common to use tricks like this when testing. We never change the code to adapt for a test, it would be bad practice. We find a way of adapting our tests to suit our needs.

```
class TestPasswordValidatorHandler(testing.TestBase):

    def before(self):
        self.resource = PVHTest()
        self.api.add_route('/password/validate/', self.resource)
```

The `before` method is called by the Falcon `TestBase` logic, and it allows us to set up the resource we want to test (the handler) and a route for it (which is not necessarily the same as the one we use in production).

```
def test_post(self):
    self.simulate_request(
        '/password/validate/',
        body=json.dumps({'password': 'abcABC0123#&'}),
        method='POST')
    resp = self.resource.resp

    assert_equal('200 OK', resp.status)
    assert_dict_equal(
        {'password': 'abcABC0123#&',
         'score': {'case': 3, 'length': 5, 'numbers': 2,
             'special': 4, 'ratio': 2, 'total': 16},
         'valid': True},
        json.loads(resp.body))
```

This is the test for the happy path. All it does is simulate a POST request with a JSON payload as body. Then, we inspect the response object. In particular, we inspect its status and its body. We make sure that the handler has correctly called the validator and returned its results.

We also test the generator handler:

```
class TestPasswordGeneratorHandler(testing.TestBase):

    def before(self):
        self.resource = PGHTest()
        self.api.add_route('/password/generate/', self.resource)

    @patch('core.handlers.PasswordGenerator')
    def test_get(self, PasswordGenerator):
        PasswordGenerator.generate.return_value = (7, 'abc123')
        self.simulate_request(
            '/password/generate/',
            query_string='length=7',
            method='GET')
        resp = self.resource.resp

        assert_equal('200 OK', resp.status)
        assert_equal([7, 'abc123'], json.loads(resp.body))
```

For this one as well, I will only show you the test for the happy path. We mock out the `PasswordGenerator` class because we need to control which password it will generate and, unless we mock, we won't be able to do it, as it is a random process.

Once we have correctly set up its return value, we can simulate the request again. In this case, it's a GET request, with a desired length of 7. We use a technique similar to the one we used for the other handler, and check the response status and body.

These are not the only tests you could write against the API, and the style could be different as well. Some people mock often, I tend to mock only when I really have to. Just try to see if you can make some sense out of them. I know they're not really easy but they'll be good training for you. Tests are extremely important so give it your best shot.

Where do you go from here?

If you liked this project and you feel like expanding it, here are a few suggestions:

- Implement the encryption in the mechanism of a custom Django field.
- Amend the template for the record list so that you can search for a particular record.
- Amend the JavaScript to use JSONP with a callback to overcome the CORS issue.
- Amend the JavaScript to fire the validation call when the password field changes.
- Write a Django command that allows you to encrypt and decrypt the database file. When you do it from the command line, incorporate that behavior into the website, possibly on the home page, so that you don't have access to the records unless you are authenticated. This is definitely a hard challenge as it requires either another database with an authentication password stored properly with a one way hash, or some serious reworking of the data structure used to hold the record model data. Even if you don't have the means to do it now, try and think about how you would solve this problem.
- Set up PostgreSQL on your machine and switch to using it instead of the SQLite file that is the default.
- Add the ability to attach a file to a record.
- Play with the application, try to find out which features you want to add or change, and then do it.

Summary

In this chapter, we've worked on a final project that involves an interface and an API. We have used two different frameworks to accomplish our goal: Django and Falcon. They are very different and have allowed us to explore different concepts and techniques to craft our software and make this fun application come alive.

We have seen an example of symmetric encryption and explored code that was written in a more functional style, as opposed to a more classic control flow-oriented approach. We have reused and extended the Django class-based views, reducing to a minimum the amount of code we had to write.

When coding the API, we decoupled handling requests from password management. This way it's much easier to see which part of the code depends on the Falcon framework and which is independent from it.

Finally, we saw a few tests for the helpers and handlers of the API. We have briefly touched on a technique that I use to expand classes under test in order to be able to test against those parts of the code which would not normally be available.

My aim in this chapter was to provide you with an interesting example that could be expanded and improved in different ways. I also wanted to give you a few examples of different coding styles and techniques, which is why I chose to spread things apart and use different frameworks.

A word of farewell

I hope that you are still thirsty and that this book will be just the first of many steps you take towards Python. It's a truly wonderful language, well worth learning deeply.

I hope that you enjoyed this journey with me, I did my best to make it interesting for you. It sure was for me, I had such a great time writing these pages.

Python is open source, so please keep sharing it and consider supporting the wonderful community around it.

Till next time, my friend, farewell!

Index

S

T

Thank you for buying
Learning Python

About Packt Publishing

Packt, pronounced 'packed', published its first book, *Mastering phpMyAdmin for Effective MySQL Management*, in April 2004, and subsequently continued to specialize in publishing highly focused books on specific technologies and solutions.

Our books and publications share the experiences of your fellow IT professionals in adapting and customizing today's systems, applications, and frameworks. Our solution-based books give you the knowledge and power to customize the software and technologies you're using to get the job done. Packt books are more specific and less general than the IT books you have seen in the past. Our unique business model allows us to bring you more focused information, giving you more of what you need to know, and less of what you don't.

Packt is a modern yet unique publishing company that focuses on producing quality, cutting-edge books for communities of developers, administrators, and newbies alike. For more information, please visit our website at www.packtpub.com.

About Packt Open Source

In 2010, Packt launched two new brands, Packt Open Source and Packt Enterprise, in order to continue its focus on specialization. This book is part of the Packt Open Source brand, home to books published on software built around open source licenses, and offering information to anybody from advanced developers to budding web designers. The Open Source brand also runs Packt's Open Source Royalty Scheme, by which Packt gives a royalty to each open source project about whose software a book is sold.

Writing for Packt

We welcome all inquiries from people who are interested in authoring. Book proposals should be sent to author@packtpub.com. If your book idea is still at an early stage and you would like to discuss it first before writing a formal book proposal, then please contact us; one of our commissioning editors will get in touch with you.

We're not just looking for published authors; if you have strong technical skills but no writing experience, our experienced editors can help you develop a writing career, or simply get some additional reward for your expertise.

Python Essentials

ISBN: 978-1-78439-034-1   Paperback: 298 pages

Modernize existing Python code and plan code
migrations to Python using this definitive guide

1. Learn the essentials of Python programming
    to get you up and coding effectively.

2. Get up-to-speed with the most important
    built-in data structures in Python, using
    sequences, sets, and mappings.

3. Explore typical use cases for various features
    in Python through this compact guide.

**Python Geospatial Analysis
Essentials**

ISBN: 978-1-78217-451-6   Paperback: 200 pages

Process, analyze, and display geospatial data using
Python libraries and related tools

1. Learn to build a complete geospatial
    application from scratch using Python.

2. Create good-looking maps based on the results
    of your analysis.

3. This is a fast-paced guide to help you explore
    the key concepts of geospatial to obtain high
    quality spatial data.

Please check **www.PacktPub.com** for information on our titles

Python Requests Essentials

ISBN: 978-1-78439-541-4   Paperback: 134 pages

Learn how to integrate your applications seamlessly with web services using Python Requests

1. A fast-paced guide that demonstrates the use of Python Requests with the help of examples.

2. Learn web scraping with Beautiful Soup and Python Requests libraries.

3. Interact with social networking sites such as Facebook, Twitter, and Reddit to retrieve data from them.

Mastering pandas

ISBN: 978-1-78398-196-0   Paperback: 364 pages

Master the features and capabilities of pandas, a data analysis toolkit for Python

1. Master and optimally utilize the capabilities of pandas for data analysis using IPython a rich interactive environment for Python.

2. Understand data visualization by plotting data with matplotlib.

3. Learn predictive analytics and machine learning using pandas and scikit-learn in a pragmatic manner.